THE FIRST TUNG CHEE-HWA ADMINISTRATION

Related Titles from The Chinese University Press

Out of the Shadow of 1997?
The 2000 Legislative Council Election in the
Hong Kong Special Administrative Region
Edited by Kuan Hsin-chi, Lau Siu-kai and Timothy Ka-ying Wong

Power Transfer and Electoral Politics
The First Legislative Election in the
Hong Kong Special Administrative Region
Edited by Kuan Hsin-chi, Lau Siu-kai, Louie Kin-sheun and
Timothy Ka-ying Wong

Social Development and Political Change in Hong Kong
Edited by Lau Siu-kai

Public Sector Reform in Hong Kong: Into the 21st Century
Edited by Anthony B. L. Cheung and Jane C. Y. Lee

Hong Kong's Journey to Reunification
Memoirs of Sze-yuen Chung
Sze-yuen Chung

Hong Kong SAR: In Pursuit of Domestic and International Order
Edited by Beatrice Leung and Joseph Cheng

Political Order and Power Transition in Hong Kong
Edited by Li Pang-kwong

76903671-91	197282	9789629960155	BOOK	The First Tung Chee-Hwa Administration the First Five Years of the Hong Kong Special Administrative Siu-Kai Lau **8vo. Original pictorial card covers (softback) (near Fine). Pp. xxxiv + 430, illus with figures and tables (previous owner's red ink inscription on front inside cover).**	$23.95	Sep, 10 2026

76903671-91

alibris

ROTHWELL & DUNWORTH LTD
2 BRIDGE STREET
DULVERTON
TA22 9HJ
UNITED KINGDOM

To: ALIBRIS CONSOLIDATION FT
DEAN CQL UNIT 1 COWLEY MILL IND. EST.
LONGBRIDGE WAY
UXBRIDGE
UB8 2YG
UNITED KINGDOM

Shipping Instructions for RDUNWORT

Print this Packing Slip and enclose inside the front cover of the book.

Please ship this item no later than Tue Sep 22, 2026.

Ship to:

ALIBRIS CONSOLIDATION FT
DEAN CQL UNIT 1 COWLEY MILL IND. EST.
LONGBRIDGE WAY
UXBRIDGE
UB8 2YG
UNITED KINGDOM

The First Tung Chee-hwa Administration

The First Five Years of the Hong Kong Special Administrative Region

Edited by

Lau Siu-kai

The Chinese University Press

The First Tung Chee-hwa Administration: The First Five Years of the Hong Kong Special Administrative Region
Edited by Lau Siu-kai

ISBN 962–996–015–X

THE CHINESE UNIVERSITY PRESS
The Chinese University of Hong Kong
SHA TIN, N.T., HONG KONG
Fax: +852 2603 6692
+852 2603 7355
E-mail: cup@cuhk.edu.hk
Web-site: www.chineseupress.com

Printed in Hong Kong

Contents

Preface

Lau Siu-kai

The first five years of the Hong Kong Special Administrative Region (HKSAR) are arguably an unprecedentedly tumultuous period in Hong Kong's post-war history. Indisputably it is also a period of paradoxes. Between the time of Hong Kong's return to China (1 July 1997) and mid-2002, the place appears to have transformed beyond recognition. The social, political and economic landscape has fundamentally and in all likelihood irreversibly changed. Popular support for the basic institutional structure of Hong Kong, mostly built during colonial rule, has weakened. Hongkongers are unable to agree on the future direction or prospect of the territory. After having gone through the "crisis of confidence" produced by Hong Kong's scheduled return to China, Hongkongers are today in the throes of a second "crisis of confidence" brought about by an uncertain economic future, ineffective governance, a divided society, nasty interpersonal relationship and pervasive malaise. If before 1997 Hongkongers were arrogant, supercilious and optimistic, today they are stricken with defeatism, pessimism, self-doubt and a tendency to self-deprecate.

No one dares to underestimate the difficulties associated with Hong Kong's transition from a British colony to a special administrative region of China. Though allowing Hong Kong to retain its original capitalist system and way of life after 1997, Beijing barely understands and hardly appreciates the way the capitalist enclave operates and the ethos of its people. Hongkongers' mistrust of Beijing and their anti-communist mentality mean that the relationship between Hong Kong and the mainland is bound to be uneasy for a long time to come. The tussle between Beijing and London over Hong Kong before the handover has severely divided both the Hong Kong people and the political elites and contributed to weak political authority and widespread political alienation. The meticulousness of Beijing in keeping its promises of "a high degree of autonomy" and "Hong Kong people ruling Hong Kong" after the handover has substantially alleviated public anxieties about Beijing's political intentions. Nevertheless, post-colonial Hong Kong still has a long way to go to establish a popularly accepted, competent and coherent governmental structure.

The difficulties of the political transition are very much complicated by the untimely onslaught of the Asian financial turmoil a few months after the handover. The economic crisis is unprecedented in its severity, duration and the scope of its impact. The burst of the property "bubble," the bulwark of Hong Kong's pre-handover economic prosperity, has exposed for everyone to see the fragility and narrow base of Hong Kong's economy. It also impresses upon the psychologically ill-prepared Hongkongers the fact that Hong Kong has to undergo a very painful process of economic restructuring before it can aspire to future prosperity. The social and political repercussions of the economic crisis are equally widespread, serious and intractable. The deepening conflict between social classes, the increasing public demands for governmental intervention and assistance in a time of economic hardship, the conflicts stemming from fiscal austerity and public sector reforms, and the inexperience of the new administration in coping with crises are among the major scourges in post-handover Hong Kong.

Tung Chee-hwa, the first Chief Executive of the HKSAR, found himself immersed in a crisis shortly after having been sworn in. When he was considered by Beijing as the first head of the HKSAR government, both Beijing and Tung himself saw the primary duty of the job-holder to be to secure the implementation of the "one country, two systems" arrangement for Hong Kong. Both Beijing and Tung believed back then that with the departure of the British colonists and Beijing's faithful respect for Hong Kong's political autonomy, Hong Kong's economic vibrancy, Hongkongers' political pragmatism and the competence and loyalty of the civil service would enable Hong Kong to remain stable and governable after the handover. The adverse effects of Hongkongers' mistrust of Beijing and the anti-communist elements in Hong Kong could be largely and safely contained. These beliefs have proven to be unsustainable as events unfolded since Tung assumed office.

The way Tung approaches his job in many senses has made things more complicated and difficult. His apolitical or even anti-political proclivity makes him unfit to master an increasingly turbulent and chaotic political situation. His reluctance to build a governing coalition with a broad base of social support has made strong governance impossible in a period of economic crisis and social division. At the same time, Tung is a person of strong commitment to Hong Kong and a person determined to leave his mark in history. Always proud of his vision for Hong Kong, Tung very much disdains the shortsightedness of his fellow Hongkongers. As a chief executive not popularly elected by the Hongkongers, Tung has an urgent desire to establish his political legitimacy through superb administrative performance. In a way the post-handover crisis of Hong Kong provide a godsend for Tung to prove his worth. He tries to rise to the challenge by launching in rapid succession a large number of bold initiatives on various fronts with the purpose of "reinventing" Hong Kong in a short period of time. The initiatives are mostly top-down directives with minimal popular support. However, in a time of economic hardship there are not sufficient public resources to carry out the government's decisions. Most important, Tung does not have the political infrastructure to either handle the conflicts generated by the new initiatives of the government or mobilize societal resources to supplement the shortfalls in public capability. Consequently, Tung's grand policy agenda has achieved little whilst leaving a lot of political resentment in its wake. By the end of Tung's first term, the HKSAR government apparently has lost much public trust and ability to mold the public agenda. Tung's administration is presiding over a crumbling socio-political order. Tung can only find solace in the fact that all political actors in Hong Kong, including his political foes, have lost public support.

Without any doubt, the first term of office of Tung Chee-hwa as HKSAR's first Chief Executive represents a watershed in Hong Kong's history. However, even though it is quite unlikely that Hong Kong would return to its pre-1997 conditions, what Hong Kong will become in the future is still murky. Nonetheless, the way Hong Kong is governed by Tung in his first term has enormous impact on what Hong Kong will become in the future. For better or for worse Tung has laid sort of a foundation for Hong Kong's future development. This foundation is something that Tung has to come to term with in his second term of office even if he intends to a chart a new course of action for his government.

The authors the chapters in this book on the first Tung Chee-hwa administration analyze different aspects of Hong Kong during Tung's first term of office. They bring to their work different perspectives and naturally diverse values. It is hoped that together the various chapters will give the readers a broad and balanced portrayal of Hong Kong under Tung Chee-hwa. Even though it may be too early to come to a reasonable assessment of Tung as a historical figure, some authors still have attempted to evaluate the achievements and failures of Tung as the first Chief Executive of the HKSAR.

Finally, I would like to thank Dr. Steven Luk, Director of the Chinese University Press, for initiating this book project. The hard work of Steven and his staff has made this book possible.

Chronology

1996

December

On the **11th**, the first Chief Executive of the HKSAR was elected by the 400-member Selection Committee, which was formed by the Preparatory Committee of the HKSAR on 2 November. Mr. Tung Chee-hwa, a shipping tycoon, won the election with 320 votes against 49 cast for former Chief Justice Yang Ti-liang and 36 for businessman Peter Woo Kwong-ching. On the **18th**, Mr. Tung Chee-hwa was appointed the Chief Executive of HKSAR by Chinese Premier Li Peng.

A 60-member Provisional Legislature was elected by the Selection Committee in Shenzhen on the **21st**. Of the 34 members of the current legislature who contested the election, 33 were elected. The Democratic Party refused to participate in the election and therefore all of its 19 legislators were not represented in the Council.

On the **28th**, Chief Secretary for Administration Anson Chan Fang On-sang accepted Mr. Tung Chee-hwa's invitation to serve the first SAR government after a two hour meeting.

1997

January

The Legal Panel of the Preparatory Committee proposed on the **19th** that two ordinances — the Public Order Ordinance and the Societies Ordinance — be reinstated to their original status before they were amended in accordance with the Bill of Rights Ordinance in 1991. The proposal was severely criticized by legal experts and pro-democracy groups. Bar Association chairwoman, Audrey Eu Yuet-mee, told the Legislative Council on the **24th** that the Legal Panel's recommendation would deal a serious blow to the rule of law in Hong Kong.

On the **25th**, former Executive Councilor and legislator Rita Fan Hsu Lai-tai was elected President of the Provisional Legislature. The election took place by secret ballot at the first meeting of the Provisional Legislative Council in Shenzhen. Mrs. Fan beat Legislative Council President Andrew Wong Wang-fat 33 votes to 27.

February

At the opening of his new office in the Asia Pacific Finance Tower on the **13th**, Chief Executive designate Tung Chee-hwa accused Democratic Party leader, Martin Lee Chu-ming, of "bad mouthing" Hong Kong and "blackening its reputation" by giving the impression that Hong Kong was collapsing. Martin Lee responded on the next day and said that he would send his apologies if he had done something offending Mr. Tung but insisted to "continue to raise international concern over Hong Kong's future."

April

On the **9th**, a consultation paper on amendment to the Societies Ordinance and Public Order Ordinance was released by the Office of the Chief Executive designate Tung Chee-hwa. The public was given only three weeks to comment.

June

The Provisional Legislative Council in Shenzhen passed on the **7th** three bills re-introducing appointed seats to the post-handover municipal councils and District Boards. With the additional 25 per cent of appointed seats, each District Board would consist of a maximum of 40 members and the two municipal council of up to 50. The Provisional Legislative Council also tabled the Immigration (Amendment) (No. 5) Bill 1997 to clarify the right of abode in the HKSAR.

The amended Societies and Public Order Ordinances were passed by the Provisional Legislative Council on the **14th**. Under the new laws, demonstrators were required to apply for a notice of no objection for planned rallies and the police are empowered to ban protests on grounds of national security.

July

A spectacular ceremony, which was presided over by Chinese President Jiang Zemin and British Prince Charles, marked the resumption of sovereignty over Hong Kong by the People's Republic of China at the Hong Kong Convention and Exhibition Centre on the night of June 30 and the early hours of **1 July**.

Also arrived for the historic occasion were Chinese Prime Minister Li Peng and his British counterpart, Tony Blair. The People's Liberation Army garrison, comprising 4,000 troops, marched across the SAR border under pouring rain early in the morning. On the balcony of the Legislative Council building, the ousted legislators, mainly Democratic Party members, delivered a manifesto vowing to return.

On the **3rd**, about 500 people, including 200 children illegal immigrants, demonstrated at the Immigration Department headquarters in Wan Chai, seeking their right of abode under the Basic Law. After a meeting with the Society for Community Organization director Ho Hei-wah, Assistant Immigration Director Mak Kwai-yan allowed the children illegal immigrants to "go home on recognizance."

The Provisional Legislative Council passed on the **9th** the Immigration (Amendment) (No. 5) Bill 1997, which provided that children who claimed the right of abode in Hong Kong under the Basic Law must produce proof of their rights by way of a Certificate of Entitlement or other acceptable proof of identity. The Bill had retrospective effect dating from 1 July.

On the **16th**, the Provisional Legislative Council passed a bill to suspend three labour laws which empowered trade unions to bargain collectively, use funds for political purposes and prohibit anti-trade union discrimination. These laws — all introduced as private members' bills by ousted legislators — were passed in the last sitting of the pre-handover Legislative Council.

August

The Provisional Legislative Council passed a motion on the **20th** to scrap the port of first asylum policy in Hong Kong and to repatriate immediately all Vietnamese boat people.

September

Hong Kong played host for the first time to the annual meetings of the International Monetary Fund and World Bank from the **23rd** to the **25th**. Chinese Vice-Premier Zhu Rongji pledged at the meetings to refrain from interference in the territory's economic policy.

October

In his first policy address delivered on the **8th**, Chief Executive Tung Chee-hwa announced his controversial housing policy of producing 85,000 flats a year. He also promised to increase home ownership to 70 per cent by 2007.

Following the Asian financial crisis started in July, there were massive and concerted speculative attacks against Hong Kong dollars and the stock market. On the **23rd**, the Hang Seng Index dropped 10.4 per cent to 10426. It recovered some, then took its biggest-ever plunge of 1,438 points to close at 9,059 on the **28th**.

December

The Housing Authority announced on the **8th** details of the sale of public housing under the Tenant Purchase Scheme.

The deadly H5N1 virus or the so-called avian flu aroused fears of an epidemic among the public when the Cheung Sha Wan Temporary Wholesale Poultry Market was closed on the **15th** for three days for a full cleanup because of the suspected discovery of H5N1 virus-infected chickens. Hundreds of people, who feared they were infected, flooded into hospitals and clinics. Up to the **22nd**, 19 people were proved to be infected by the virus, of whom three had died. On the **23rd**, following the death of the fourth victim, the exportation of live chickens from the mainland was suspended by the government to allow for appropriate controls to be introduced. The Situation grew even worse on **28th** when a section of Cheung Sha Wan Poultry Market was closed after people found a large number of chickens died suddenly, and a farm in Yuen Long was also declared infected. The government therefore decided that all the estimated 1.3 million chickens in Hong Kong must be slaughtered in an attempt to rid the territory of the virus. The killing started the following day. However, the progress of the slaughter was much slower than the government had anticipated and it was not until mid-January 1998 that the job was completely finished.

1998

January

The lack of cooperation and efficiency among Departments involving in the slaughter of chickens had aroused much public concern. Acting Chief Secretary for Administration Michael Suen Ming-yeung was ordered by Chief Executive Tung Chee-hwa to coordinate follow-up action on the avian flu crisis on the **6th**. To prevent the return of the virus, the government decided to undertake a series of measures. These included only allowing licensed and monitored chickens from mainland farms to enter Hong Kong, ensuring imported chickens carried health certificate, and a pledge that whole batches of chickens would be killed if any was found to be infected.

Also on this date, the Executive Council decided to abolish the port of first asylum policy which was imposed by the British government on Hong Kong in 1979.

Peregrine Investments Holdings, one of Asia's largest independent investment banks, declared its liquidation on the **12th** as a result of the crushing impact of the Asian financial crisis, particularly the currency crisis of Indonesia. Peregrine was understood to have debts of between US$ 500 million and US$ 600 million, with US$ 400 million in debt tied to Indonesian firms, many of which had already gone bankrupt.

Seven days after the Peregrine collapse, CA Pacific Finance was put into liquidation on the **19th**. Hundreds of investors from all walks of life hurried to the company's offices to settle accounts and claim their shares. After months of demonstrations and petitions, individual claimants were eventually awarded a $53 million compensation package by the government, covering about 70 per cent of each person's claims. But the case had revealed the weaknesses of the government supervision system on financial firms.

The Secretary for Justice Elsie Leung Oi-sie decided to sue the Oriental Press Group on the **25th** for contempt of court after the Company's newspaper, *Oriental Daily News*, had launched a 24-hour surveillance on Justice Godfrey of the Court of Appeal. Editor of the newspaper, Thomas Wong Yeung-ng, was sentenced on June 30 to four months' jail for contempt of court.

The Court of First Instance ruled on the **26th** that the amended Immigration Ordinance passed by the Provisional Legislative Council on July 1997 violated the Basic Law. The amended law denied the right of abode to mainland children born before their parents became permanent Hong Kong residents.

February

To relieve economic burden of Hong Kong people under the Asian financial turmoil, Financial Secretary Donald Tsang Yam-kuen put forward an economic stimulus plan in his budget speech on the **18th**. The measures included a $1.8 billion cut in personal and corporate taxes for the coming fiscal year and $12.9 billion over four years. He also announced a $30 billion, five-year infrastructure development programme.

The Provisional Legislative Council passed unanimously the Provident Fund Schemes Legislation (Amendment) Bill on the **25th**. The Bill cleared the way for a retirement scheme for some two million workers in Hong Kong.

March

On the **4th**, the Provisional Legislative Council passed a bill to scrap the port of first asylum policy.

The Independent Commission Against Corruption (ICAC) charged on the **17th** three current and former senior executives of an English newspaper, the *Hong Kong Standard*, over circulation fraud. Controversy quickly erupted after people knew that the owner of the newspaper, Sally Aw Sian, was spared from prosecution, despite having being named as a co-conspirator by the ICAC. The public became more angry when Secretary for Justice Elsie Leung Oi-sie only sited "public interest" as the reason behind the decision and refused to elaborate more on the case. As public demand for explanation grew, Miss Elsie Leung was forced to attend a special meeting of the Provisional Legislature to explain the government's prosecution policy on the **23rd**. Since Miss Sally Aw was a member of the Chinese People's Political Consultative Conference and also an old friend of Chief Executive Tung Chee-hwa, Miss Elsie Leung's decision raised fears that well-connected people would be above the law.

April

On the **2nd**, the Court of Appeal upheld the legality of the Certificate of Entitlement Scheme and ruled that mainland children born by Hong Kong permanent residents would have the right of abode if they arrived before the handover.

The Provisional Legislative Council passed on the **7th** the Adaptation Law (Interpretative Provision) Bill under which "Crown privileges" would be replaced by "State privileges." The most disputable section of the Bill was that it exempted the Xinhua News Agency and the other mainland organizations from some Hong Kong laws. Legalists warned that the guarantee of autonomy would be undermined by this law.

May

On the **20th**, the Court of Appeal overturned a Court of First Instance decision and ruled that a parent must be a permanent resident at the time of a child's birth if the child was to qualify for the right of abode.

The first post-handover Legislative Council elections held on the **24th** generated a record voter turnout rate of 53.3 per cent for the geographical constituencies, despite torrential rain.

June

Chief Executive Tung Chee-hwa announced a four-part package on the **22nd** to relieve economic hardship. The package mainly focused on reviving the property market, including $890 million in loans for home-buyers, a $500 million tax rebate for property owners and a freeze on sales of government land until March 31, 1999.

July

The new Hong Kong International Airport at Chek Lap Kok was officially opened on the **2nd** by Chinese President Jiang Zemin, who was in Hong Kong with Vice-Premier Qian Qichen for celebrations to mark the first anniversary of the HKSAR. Following the opening to air traffic on the **6th**, the new airport was plagued by various technical problems. Liquid crystal display screens failed to give updated flight information and passengers complained of losing luggage. Hundreds of passengers had to spend the night on the floor of the airport because of flight delay. But it was the air-cargo terminal problems that caused the most headaches. The air-cargo computer system of the Hong Kong Air Cargo Terminals Limited kept crashing, forcing the company to process the cargo at the old Kai Tak airport until the end of August. On the **21st**, Chief Executive Tung Chee-hwa appointed Justice Woo Kwok-hing to organize a commission to investigate the chaos. The Legislative Council also stepped in to explore the issue.

August

The Court of First Instance sentenced legislator Maverick Chim Pui-chung to three years in prison on the **3rd**. Mr. Chim was found guilty of conspiracy to forge 199 transfer documents to help the sale of shares in one of his companies. The Legislative Council deprived him of his councillorship on 8 September.

As Hong Kong sank into recession amid the Asian financial crisis, its U.S. dollar-linked currency came under heavy pressure. The battle to defend the Hong Kong dollar finally broke out in the first week of August, when speculators began heavy selling of the local currency and of local stocks. On the **7th**, the Hang Seng Index closed at 7,018, the lowest point in three and a half years. Share prices continued to drop in the following days and the stock index plunged to a five-year low of 6,660 on the **14th**. In an unprecedented move, the Hong Kong government began to intervene in the stock market by buying large amount of shares. Battles between the government and speculators continued for about two weeks. On the **28th**, turnover on the

Hong Kong Stock Exchange reached a record of $79 billion. Although the government finally won the battle, brokers began to complain about the excessive intervention in the financial sector. Economists also warned of an end to Hong Kong's traditional non-interventionist economic policy.

September

The government announced a 30-point package on the **7th** to tighten procedures in the securities and future market. The package included drastic measures making mal-practices such as illegal short-selling of shares a crime punishable by jail. On the future markets, the threshold for the higher rate of margin or cost of investing in futures would be enforced at the new lower level of 5,000 contracts. The Hong Kong Future Exchange would also have to establish an early warning system for whenever the market exceeded a predetermined level of the cash market.

October

On the **22nd**, former Chief Justice Yang Ti-liang was appointed by Financial Secretary Donald Tsang Yam-kuen head of an 11-member board of the Exchange Fund Investment Limited. The company would manage shares bought by the government in August. On the **26th**, the company revealed that the government had spent $118 billion on shares in August, spread across the 33 firms listed in the Hang Seng Index.

November

Fear of losing judicial autonomy was aroused in Hong Kong when "Big Spender" Cheung Tze-keung was sentenced to death by the Guangzhou Intermediate People's Court on the **12th**. Mr. Cheung had confessed to a long list of major crimes, including armed robberies and two kidnappings in Hong Kong. The kidnap victims were Victor Li Tzar-kuoi, son of business tycoon Li Ka-shing and Walter Kwok Ping-sheung, chairman of property giant Sun Hung Kai. Cheung's defence lawyer in Hong Kong had requested to transfer his client's trial to Hong Kong because many of the crimes were committed in Hong Kong. But Guangzhou court officials said Cheung and his gang had been sued for smuggling arms and explosives and other offences committed on the mainland, so the question of Hong Kong jurisdiction did not arise. Hong Kong officials added that the kidnappings had not been reported and there was insufficient evidence for charges to be laid in Hong Kong. Cheung's case had led to fears among Hong Kong people about the possibility of having to stand trial on the mainland for infringing laws in the SAR.

1999

January

The Commission of Inquiry on the New Airport chaired by Justice Woo Kwok-hing released a report on the **22nd** and blamed the managing staff of the Airport Authority for the chaos at the airport opening. The report said responsibility for the passenger terminal problems was laid squarely on the shoulders of Dr. Hank Townsend, former chief executive officer of the Airport Authority, and other key personnel. It also accused Dr. Townsend of "misleading" the Airport Development Steering Committee (Adscom), chaired by Chief Secretary for Administration Anson Chan Fang On-sang, on the readiness of the opening of the airport by July 1998. Although Mrs. Chan escaped criticism from Justice Woo's report, she was not so lucky again when the Legislative Council Selective Committee delivered its own report on the **27th**. The Legislative Council's report concluded that Mrs. Chan was "responsible for the failure of Adscom to assess readiness of the airport." The report commented that while Mrs. Chan and Adscom were vigilant enough to postpone the initial April 1998 opening date for three months, they "let down their guard" in the final few months of the run-up to the opening day. Chief Executive Tung Chee-hwa made a public apology for the airport chaos the next day.

On the **29th**, the Court of Final Appeal ruled that children born in the mainland of a Hong Kong permanent resident, whether legitimate or not, had the right of abode in Hong Kong, irrespective of the parent's length of residence in the territory. It also ruled that such children did not need a Certificate of Entitlement affixed to their one-way permit when they sought to enter Hong Kong. In a second ruling, the court declared that the creation of the Provisional Legislative Council in late 1996 had not violated the Basic Law.

February

Legislators severely criticized Secretary of Justice Elsie Leung Oi-sie after she had disclosed on the meeting of the Legislative Council Justice and Legal Administrative Affairs Panel on the **4th** that Sing Tao Holdings boss, Sally Aw Sian, was not prosecuted in a *Hong Kong Standard* circulation fraud case because it might lead to the collapse of the newspaper and the loss of jobs. Miss Leung also told the Panel that another main reason for not prosecuting was lack of evidence. Commenting on Miss Leung's explanation, Chief Executive Tung Chee-hwa said the reasons she gave were "not contradictory."

March

The Cyberport project was made known to the public in the budget speech of Financial Secretary on the **3rd**. The government awarded the development rights of Cyberport to the Pacific Century Group headed by Richard Li Tzar-kai, son of business tycoon Li Ka-shing. Of the $13 billion budget of this 26-hectare modern complex in Pok Fu Lam, $7 billion would come from the Pacific Century Group. The government contributed land and built essential infrastructure such as roads and sewage system. However, the failure to award the contract through an open public tender, and later concerns that the project was little more than a dressed-up real estate deal, drew criticism from rival property developers and the public.

After five hours of heated debate, the no-confidence motion against Secretary of Justice Elsie Leung Oi-sie was turned down in the Legislative Council by a 29 to 21 vote on the **11th**. Liberal Party vice-chairman Ronald Arculli walked out of the Legislative Council in tears after delivering his speech. He said the only loser in the motion was Hong Kong.

On the **23rd**, Chief Secretary for Administration Anson Chan agreed to extend her term of office beyond her planned retirement date of January 2000 to June 2002. The move was widely interpreted as a sign that the government feared losing one of its few popular policy secretaries.

April

The government warned on the **28th** that according to a government survey, at least 1.67 million immigrants would flood into Hong Kong over the next 10 to 13 years if the 29 January ruling of the Court of Final Appeal was implemented. The government estimation immediately brought about widespread fears among the public. However, scholars and human right activists attacked the government for greatly exaggerating the number of eligible immigrants.

May

More than 1,300 Housing Department staffs took the afternoon off and rallied outside the Housing Department headquarters in Ho Man Tin on the **5th** to demonstrate against the privatization plan. They pledged to escalate their action if the authority refused to abandon the step-by-step proposal to privatize the Department. According to the government proposal, some 9,000 housing staffs would be phased out in stages and services would be transferred to private companies.

On the **18th**, Chief Executive Tung Chee-hwa announced that he would ask the Standing Committee of the National People's Congress, through the State Council, to interpret Article 22(4) and 24 (2)(3) of the Basic Law in accordance with the true legislative intent of the provisions that concern right of abode in Hong Kong. On the following day, the Legislative Council passed a bill approving the Chief Executive's action. The vote was taken after 19 councilors walked out of the chamber to show their discontent.

More than 10,000 civil servants marched on the **23rd** to condemn the government's proposed civil service reform package, including the introduction of contract system and the privatization of various departments. It was the largest demonstration by any labour organization since the handover. The Federation of Civil Service Unions, which organized the protest, said the reform package was just a pretence and the real intention of the government was to suppress wage.

June

On the **11th**, the Court of Appeal ordered to quash removal order against 17 overstaying mainlanders on the ground that the Director of Immigration had failed to set up a scheme to verify their claims for right of abode. The Court's decision affected about 2,000 other overstayers in Hong Kong.

On the **15th**, the Chief Executive appointed Mr. Leung Chun-ying as the Convenor of the Executive Council for a two-year term, succeeding Chung Sze-yuen.

The Standing Committee of the National People's Congress issued on the **26th** its interpretation of Basic Law concerning right of abode in Hong Kong. It overturned the 29 January ruling of the Court of Final Appeal and declared that the Court had been wrong for not seeking an interpretation from the National People's Congress before making its decision. Under its interpretation, only about 170,000 mainlanders, whose parents were already Hong Kong permanent residents when they were born, were eligible for the right of abode in Hong Kong. For entry into the SAR, those with the right must obtain a Certificate of Entitlement specified by the Hong Kong government and an exit permit from local mainland authorities. The committee's interpretation was fiercely criticized by the pro-democracy camp and the legalists as ruining the rule of law in Hong Kong. To protest the interpretation, more than 600 lawyers dressed in black marched from the High Court to the Court of Final Appeal in a silent walk on the **30th**.

July

Taipei's chief representative in Hong Kong, Cheng An-kuo, spoke on a radio programme broadcast by the Radio Television Hong Kong on the **17th**, defending the assertion a week earlier by Taiwan President Lee Teng-hui that relations between the mainland and Taiwan should be conducted on a "special state-to-state" basis. That drew criticism from both Hong Kong and Beijing officials, who claimed that Mr. Cheng should refrain from advocating such positions while stationed in Hong Kong. Local human rights groups and pro-democracy organizations warned of a curtailment of freedom of speech.

August

On the **22nd**, three people were killed and 213 injured when a China Airlines jet overturned and burst into flames following a crash landing at Chap Lap Kok airport during a typhoon. It was the first major accident at the new airport since it opened in July 1998.

October

On the **11th**, the government launched the public sale of the government shareholdings acquired in a stock market incursion in August 1998. The fund, called the Tracker Fund of Hong Kong, was oversubscribed by almost five times. The initial offering of $10 billion worth of shares was increased to $33 billion to meet demand. The listing and trading of the fund started on 12 November.

November

After 15 months of negotiation, Chief Executive Tung Chee-hwa announced on the **2nd** that a deal with Walt Disney Company to build a Disney theme park on a 126-hectare site at Penny's Bay on Lantau Island was made. The park is planned to open in 2005.

On the **20th**, the government announced Hong Kong would bid for the 2006 Asian Games to boost the SAR's position in the international community.

December

By a vote of 31 in favour and 27 against, the Legislative Council passed on the **2nd** the Provision of Municipal Services (Reorganization) Bill, which provided legal foundation for the government to dissolve the Provisional Urban Council and the Provisional Regional Council. Legislator Ambrose Cheung Wing-sum, who represented the Provisional Urban Council in the legislature, decided to resign from the Legislative Council after the vote. With the abolition of the two municipal councils, a new framework was outlined for the delivery of municipal services from 1 January 2000. A new Environment and Food Bureau would be created, overseeing the work of a new Food and Environmental Hygiene Department, the renamed Agriculture, Fisheries and Conservation Department and the Environmental Protection Department.

In a ruling on the right of abode on the **3rd**, the Court of Final Appeal reversed the judgment it made on January. It declared that the National People's Congress Standing Committee had unrestricted power to interpret the Basic Law and Hong Kong courts were duty-bound to follow those interpretations. The court also overturned the ruling of the Court of Appeal that the Director of Immigration had no right to expel 17 overstaying mainlanders who claimed to have the right of abode. Angered by the decision of the court, about 1,000 mainlanders demonstrated at the SAR government headquarters in Central immediately after the ruling. Some of the radical protestors even clashed with the police. They threw stones and potted plants at the police while the police used pepper spray to strike back. The clash lasted for nearly five hours, left 18 people injured, including six police officers.

2000

January

The Housing Authority announced on the **8th** that the construction of two high-rise housing blocks in Yuen Chau Kok in Shatin would be stopped after piling rods were found to be shallow. Eight people, including three housing staffs, were arrested later. Tony Miller, Director of Housing, told the Legislative Council Special Housing Services Panel on the **21st** that the two buildings might have to be demolished because of serious construction flaws. On the **27th**, Housing Authority chairwoman Rosanna Wong Yick-ming announced that a three-member independent inquiry panel would be set up to determine why the defects were not checked. This scandle, together with other construction flaws found in Tung Chung, Tin Shui Wai and Yau Tong in 1999, brought great pressure on the Housing Authority to reform.

February

On the **18th**, speculative fever erupted at the start of the public offering by a internet company, tom.com, owned by tycoon Li Ka-shing. As people believed the price of shares would rise for sure, thousands of investors scrambled to obtain application forms at the 10 branches of Hong Kong Bank where it was available. Within two hours, all 500,000 copies of forms were snapped up. The situation became more chaotic on the **23rd** when around 280,000 people queued outside the 10 branches to hand in their application forms. Shops near the banks had to close as roads outside branches in Kwun Tong and Mongkok were sealed by the police. The company was listed on 1 March.

On the **29th**, in what was believed to be the biggest deal of its kind in Southeast Asia, Richard Li Tzar-kai's Pacific Century CyberWorks won the battle against Singapore Telecom for Cable & Wireless HKT with a bid of $296 billion.

March

The government announced on the **3rd** the establishment of a committee, chaired by the Chief Secretary for Administration Anson Chan, to bid to hold the 2006 Asian Games in Hong Kong.

In order to regain public confidence, Housing Authority chairwoman Rosanna Wong Yick-ming declared on the **16th** that the Housing Authority would extend structural maintenance guarantees from ten years to 20 years to buyers of all Home Ownership Scheme flats in Tin Shui Wai. On the same day, the findings of an independent panel commissioned to investigate the defective piling incidents occurring in different housing projects were also released. According to the panel, the foundation settlement in Block 2 and Block 11 of Tin Fu Court in Tin Shui Wai was significantly sub-standard.

May

On the **25th**, the independent inquiry panel appointed by the Housing Authority to investigate the piling scandal in Shatin delivered its report. The panel blamed nine housing staffs for the faulty piling work and recommended for strict disciplinary action. It also accused the contractor of the building site of failing to supervise the sub-contractor properly. Chief Executive Tung Chee-hwa promised to take action against civil servants involved in the case after the report was made public. He also announced the government would ban Zen Pacific Civil Contractors Ltd., the contractor involved, from all public works projects.

June

On the **10th**, more than 6,000 teachers marched from Chater Garden to the Government Headquarters in Central to protest at government plans for a benchmark test for English and Putonghua teachers.

Housing Authority chairwoman Rosanna Wong Yick-ming decided to resign on the **24th**. She admitted that the public no longer supported her nor trusted her reforms of the public housing sector. Despite of her resignation, the

Legislative Council passed on the **28th** an overwhelming no-confidence vote — 39 to 9, with 6 abstentions — in her and Director of Housing, Tony Miller. Even though Chief Executive Tung Chee-hwa allowed Mr. Miller to remain in his post, pressure for greater accountability from civil servants grew.

On the **30th**, the Court of First Instance ruled that the mainlanders seeking right of abode in Hong Kong could not be exempted from the National People's Congress Standing Committee's interpretation of the Basic Law a year ago. Judge Frank Stock said the applicants could not rely on the two landmark Court of Final Appeal judgments precedent because of the reinterpretation. The ruling would affect some 5,000 mainlanders seeking right of abode.

Also on the **30th**, Chief Executive Tung Chee-hwa revealed on a television programme that the 1997 target of building 85,000 flats a year had already been abandoned in the midst of the Asian financial crisis in 1998 due to falling housing prices.

July

On the **7th**, pollster Dr. Robert Chung Ting-yiu of the University of Hong Kong alleged in a *South China Morning Post* article that Chief Executive Tung Chee-hwa had more than once give him a clear message via a "special channel" that his surveys on Mr. Tung's popularity and government credibility were not welcome. Rumours erupted after Dr. Chung repeatedly refused to identify the "special channel." Executive Councilor Henry Tang Ying-yen and Information Coordinator Stephen Lam Sui-lung put pressure on Dr. Chung to reveal who was involved. One week later, Dr. Chung broke his silence to reveal that University of Hong Kong vice-chancellor Cheng Yiu-chung was the "third party" who sent pro-vice-chancellor Wong Siu-lun to ask him to stop the polls. Returning from holiday in London, Professor Cheng conceded on the **21st** that Andrew Lo Cheung-on, the Chief Executive's Senior Special Assistant, had met him in January 1999 and raised questions about Dr. Chung and his surveys. But he denied putting pressure on Dr. Chung. On the **25th**, Yang Ti-liang, chairman of the University Council, announced that a three-member commission of inquiry, headed by Justice Noel Power, would be set up to investigate the incident.

August

On the **2nd**, a total of 46 persons, including 23 staff members of the Immigration Department, were injured in a fire caused by right-of-abode seekers at the Immigration Tower in Wan Chai. A senior immigration officer, Leung Kam-kwong died from severe burns nine days later. His death came 11 hours after that of Lam Siu-sing, one of the right-of-abode claimants. The funeral of Mr. Leung was held on the **20th** with the highest honours. His coffin was draped with the national flag. Police classified the case as homicide and arson and subsequently laid charge against 22 persons.

The *Apply Daily* reported successively from the **23rd** to the **25th** that legislator Gary Cheng Kai-nam had failed to disclose to the legislature his interest in his public relations consultancy firm which offered services to company controlled by tycoon Li Ka-shing, and that he had given a confidential government document to a business contact. After initial denial, Mr. Cheng admitted that he had "make a mistake, but not done a bad thing." He confessed that he had passed on to his clients a confidential government document. On the **25th**, he declared to resign as vice-chairman of the Democratic Alliance for Betterment of Hong Kong and to close his public relations firm. He was also forced to admit that he had an extra-martial affair for two years. His scandal aroused much public concern and he was accused by the media of having abused his power to serve his personal interests.

September

On the **1st**, the commission of inquiry on the Chung Ting-yiu incident released its report after an11-day open hearings. The commission claimed that vice-chancellor Cheng Yiu-chung and his deputy, Professor Wong Siu-lun, had tried to stop polls carried out by Dr. Chung Ting-yiu on the popularity of Chief Executive Tung Chee-hwa and his government. Andrew Lo Cheung-on, Senior Special Assistant to the Chief Executive, was described as "a poor and untruthful witness" by the commission. Although Professor Cheng and Professor Wong repudiated the report, they both resigned on the **6th** before the University Council meeting in the midst of a campus-wide signature campaign demanding their resignation.

The second Legislative Council elections were held on the **10th**. About 1.33 million people, or 43.5 per cent of the electorate, cast votes in the geographical constituencies. On the next day, the Democratic Party vowed to start afresh after seeing its vote slip from 42.6 per cent in 1998 to 34.7 per cent in the elections. In comparison, the Democratic Alliance for Betterment of Hong Kong increased its share to 29.7 per cent from 25.2 per cent two years earlier.

Although Gary Cheng Kai-nam won his seat in the Legislative Council elections, the Democratic Alliance for Betterment of Hong Kong decided to strip him of all party positions except membership on the **16th**. Mr. Cheng then gave up his seat in the Legislative Council and quitted all public office on the **19th**.

October

Chinese President Jiang Zemin lost his temper with Hong Kong journalists on the **27th** after he was repeatedly asked if it was "an imperial order" from Beijing for Tung Chee-hwa to serve a second term. He branded the local media's question as "too simple, sometimes naive" and said Hong Kong journalists need to improve their standards. Before President Jiang had met the media, Premier Zhu Rongji and Vice-Premier Qian Qichen had already expressed their support for a second term for Mr. Tung.

November

After a year-long campaign, Hong Kong lost its bid to host the 2006 Asian Games following a vote by the Olympic Council of Asia at Pusan in Korea on the **12th**. Doha, the capital of Qatar, was chosen as the venue.

December

The Mandatory Provident Fund was launched on the **1st**. Under the plan, all employees and employers would each have to contribute 5 per cent of monthly salary, up to a maximum of $1,000 a month, into the employees provident fund account.

On the **18th**, a case against a High Court judge's son, Godfrey Nguyen Gia-huy, who was caught with two ecstasy pills at a disco, was dropped. The prosecutor said it was "not in the public interest" to blight his future with a conviction. The prosecution policy of the government was doubted by the public again in this case.

The Court of Final Appeal ruled on the **22nd** that the system used to elect village representatives breached the Bill of Rights and Sex Discrimination Ordinance. Therefore it was unreasonable to deny non-indigenous villagers the right to vote or stand as a candidate. The ruling was a victory for non-indigenous villagers, Chan Wah and Tse Kwan-sang, who began the legal challenge in 1999.

2001

January

On the **11th**, former legislator Gary Cheng Kai-nam was arrested by the Independent Commission Against Corruption. He was released on bail after being questioned.

Chief Secretary for Administration Anson Chan Fang On-sang announced her resignation from her post for "personal reasons" in a press conference with Chief Executive Tung Chee-hwa on the **12th**. Mrs. Chan said she had no intention to contest the election for Chief Executive but wanted to spend more time with her family after resignation. During the question-and-answer session held after Mr. Tung had left, she mentioned the problem of the "stirrers" when describing her work relation with Mr. Tung. She said sometimes some people outside had stirred things up between Mr. Tung and her but she refused to name the "stirrers." After serving the government for more than 38 years, Mrs. Chan would leave her post at the end of April, a year and two months ahead of the schedule. Many people believed that her departure had been foreshadowed in last September when she met Vice-Premier Qian Qichen in Beijing. In a close-door meeting, Vice-Premier Qian told her to "better support the work of the Chief Executive, to continue to contribute to the prosperity and stability of Hong Kong under the leadership of Tung Chee-hwa." The statement followed months of criticism of Mrs. Chan by pro-Beijing figures, with some accusing her of being the person behind a series of so called "dump-Tung" moves. But Mrs. Chan denied that she had been scolded and said the visit to Beijing was only a routine briefing.

February

In a question-and-answer session in the Legislative Council on the **8th**, Chief Executive Tung Chee-hwa branded the Falun Gong as "more or less an evil cult in nature" and pledged to closely monitor the sect's activities. He said the government had no plan to speed up the introduction of an anti-subversion law but vowed he would not allow anyone to abuse Hong Kong's freedoms to affect public order.

After over a month of speculation and uncertainty, Chief Executive Tung Chee-hwa announced on the **15th** the most far-reaching reshuffle at the top level of government since the handover. Donald Tsang Yam-kuen was appointed the Chief Secretary for Administration. His current position as Financial Secretary would be taken by banker Antony Leung Kam-chung. Both of them would assume duties on 1 May.

Li Shaomin, Associate Professor in the Department of Marketing at the City University of Hong Kong, was detained on the mainland on the **25th** after crossing the border to visit a friend. He was later charged by the Chinese government of spying for Taiwan.

May

Avian flu similar to the one that killed 6 people and forced the slaughter of more than one million chickens in 1997 had resurfaced in May. On the **11th**, influenza expert at the University of Hong Kong detected the H5N1 virus in samples collected from chickens at three markets. From the **15th** to the **16th**, 797 chickens were infected and died. To prevent the spread of avian flu, the government ordered the killing of more than 6,000 chickens and closed 37 stalls at markets in Tsuen Wan, Western and Mongkok on the **16th**. Although the government claimed that the newly discovered goose-type H5N1 virus were different from those of the 1997 and the new virus would not affect man, she decided on the **17th** to slaughter all 1.2 million chickens, geese, ducks and pigeons within two weeks after the virus was found in chickens in another 7 markets. Importation of live poultry from the mainland was also banned on the same day.

On the **31st**, the Independent Commission Against Corruption laid five charges against Gary Cheng Kai-nam, including accepting an advantage as a public servant and misconduct in public office.

June

On the **11th**, Secretary for the Environment and Food Lily Yam Kwan Pui-ying announced that Poultry Wholesale Market would be re-opened on the **15th**. Supply of live poultry from the mainland and sale of chickens from local farms would also be resumed. Live chickens would be available for sale in markets on the **16th**.

In a Legislative Council question-and-answer session on the **14th**, Chief Executive Tung Chee-hwa stated clearly for the first time that Falun Gong was "undoubtedly an evil cult" but it was not yet time to enact an anti-cult law. He also said the sect was well-organized, with plentiful resources and an organization that had political motives. His criticism of the sect raised doubts among local religious groups about Hong Kong's determination to protect freedoms of religion and assembly.

The government launched a consultation paper on the legalization of soccer gambling on the **22nd**. Although the government stressed that she maintained a neutral stance on this issue, it was commonly believed that the government favour legalization. However, the chance of legislation being approved was small, as the two major parties in the legislature, the Democratic Party and the Democratic Alliance for Betterment of Hong Kong, opposed to the plan.

Also on the **22nd**, the Court of First Instance ruled that the Secondary School

Places Allocation system unlawfully discriminated against school girls in favour of boys. The Court dismissed claims by the Education Department that it was attempting to be fair to all and that overturning the present system would cause indirect discrimination against boys who were "late bloomers."

The government declared on the **30th** to award the SAR's highest honour, the Grand Bauhinia Medal, to Yeung Kwong, who was the director of the Anti-British Struggle Committee during the 1967 riots, which left 51 people died and thousands injured. The government said Mr. Yeung was awarded the honour for his "outstanding contribution to the labour movement and labour welfare in Hong Kong and for his dedicated community service." The decision drew criticism from the public. People believed that the reason of Tung Chee-hwa to grant the medal to Mr. Yeung was to consolidate support of the leftists to secure his second term. Mr. Yeung finally received the medal at Government House on 13 October.

July

After ten hours of heated debate, the Legislative Council endorsed on the **11th** the Chief Executive Election Bill, including the controversial provision which gave Beijing the right to remove the Chief Executive at will. Seventeen legislators walked out of the chamber in protest when the bill was passed. The bill was condemned by the democrats as a great blow to the autonomy of the SAR.

The Beijing First Intermediate Court on the **14th** convicted Li Shaomin of spying for Taiwan and ordered him deported. Although human rights activists accused the Hong Kong government of failing to do anything to help Professor Li while he was detained on the mainland, they acknowledged that the government did uphold the "one country, two system" principle when Professor Li was allowed to re-enter Hong Kong on the **30th**. Professor Li later resumed work at the City University of Hong Kong.

In two separate landmark judgments dealing with children's right of abode issues, the Court of Final Appeal ruled on the **20th** that SAR-born children of mainlanders qualified for abode while the adopted children of Hong Kong permanent resident did not. Although Agnes Tam Nga-yin, a 14-year-old adopted mainland girl, lost her right of abode by this ruling, she won public sympathy from all walks of life. Legislators and the media urged the Immigration Department to allow her to stay on humanitarian grounds. Teachers and classmates at her school launched a signature campaign, calling on the government to grant her the right of abode. Eventually, Agnes Tam was granted on 25 October a one-way permit by the Chinese government which qualified her to reside in Hong Kong.

September

On the **3rd**, Chief Secretary for Adminsitration Donald Tsang Yam-kuen announced an immediate ten-month freeze on the sale of Home Ownership Scheme (HOS) flats. After the moratorium, the sales of HOS flat would be kept to just 9,000 units a year until 2005–06, a huge reduction from the existing target of 20,000 a year. To compensate for the decrease in housing supply, the government would increase the quota of Home Purchase Loan Scheme from 4,500 to 16,500 for the first-time buyers. Mr. Tsang's announcement was made two weeks after tycoon Li Ka-shing urged the government to drastically reduce the sale of HOS flats to restore confidence in the property market.

While Premier Zhu Rongji was visiting Ireland on the **4th**, he commented on Hong Kong and said "we cannot always discuss without decision, make decisions without execution. Once decision is made, everyone should make full efforts and move forwards." Information Coordinator Stephen Lam Sui-lung claimed that Premier Zhu had just only wanted to urge people to unite and face challenges positively. However, the media believed it showed the discontent of some Beijing officials about the capability and authority of the SAR government. Some even said it targeted Chief Executive Tung Chee-hwa.

December

Joseph Zen Ze-kiun, coadjutor bishop of the Catholic Diocese of Hong Kong, sent letters on the **7th** to heads of all 300 Catholic schools, asking them to provide school places for mainland children who were waiting for the outcome of their applications for right of abode in Hong Kong. His move was criticized by the government, claiming that it might be illegal to admit the children without approval of the Education and Immigration Departments. On the **9th**, Secretary for Justice Elsie Leung Oi-sie commented that it was impractical to offer formal education to children holding two-way permits, overstayers or illegal immigrants. She said admitting those children to schools was just like providing education for children traveling in Hong Kong. But bishop Zen vowed to protect the children's rights for education even if he had to resort to civil disobedience. Government objection drew immediate fire from human rights activists and pro-democracy legislators, who criticized the government for depriving children of their rights by using twisted arguments. Notwithstanding government disapproval, more than 50 children were admitted by the Catholic schools by the end of December.

On the **13th**, Chief Executive Tung Chee-hwa formally declared to contest for a second term in a function hall at the Hong Kong Convention and Exhibition Centre, where was crowded with about 1,000 supporters, comprising largely of business elites and pro-Beijing figures. In his speech, Mr. Tung admitted that some of his policies had been introduced without thorough assessment and mis-prioritized. He pledged to set up a "ministerial" and accountability system if he was re-elected.

Gary Cheng Kai-nam was sentenced to 18 months in prison on the **21st**. He was found guilty of misconduct in public office, accepting an advantage as a public servant, theft and false accounting.

2002

January

Legal debate on the right of abode of the mainlanders finally ended on the **10th** when the Court of Final Appeal ruled that right of abode applied only to mainlanders arriving before January 29, 1999 with parent who was permanent Hong Kong resident. After the ruling, Chief Executive Tung Chee-hwa promised that the overstayers would not be repatriated until the end of March.

February

Sze kwan-lung was jailed for life on the **4th** after being found guilty of murder in the Immigration Tower arson attack which caused the death of a senior immigration officer, Leung Kam-kwong. His six accomplices were also sentenced to 12 to 13 years in prison for homicide and arson.

Tung Chee-hwa handed in the nomination form that bore the signatures of 706 Election Committee members to the Registration and Electoral Office on the **19th**. Of the 46 sub-sectors represented by the 794 eligible Election Committee members, 30 had unanimously signed up for him. However, only about 60 per cent of committee members from the legal and social welfare sectors nominated him. Since candidates must get the signatures of not less than 100 committee members to support for their candidacy and committee members could only nominate one candidate, the chance for another candidate to join the race was ruled out. Up to the **28th**, Mr. Tung secured 714 valid nominations and he was declared by the returning officer the winner of the election after the close of the two-week nomination period.

March

Financial Secretary Leung Kam-chung announced in his maiden budget speech on the **6th** that civil servants might face a 4.75 per cent pay cut in October as part of the effort to balance the books in five years. Although Mr. Leung emphasized that the 4.75 per cent pay cut was only an assumption, not a decision, nor a proposal, civil service unions believed a reduction was almost certain.

April

On the **9th**, the Executive Council endorsed the blueprint for Chief Executive Tung Chee-hwa's accountability system, paving the way for him to form his cabinet, which would be the core of the policy-making machinery in the next five years. Mr. Tung formally unveiled the framework of the new system to the legislators on the **17th**. Under the new system, 3 Secretaries of Department and 11 Directors of Bureau would become politically appointed ministers. They would be appointed for five-year terms and the Chief Executive had the authority to nominate them and terminate their contracts when necessary. The existing 16 Bureaus would be combined into 11. All ministers would join the Executive Council. The Information Coordinator would be re-titled Director of the Chief Executive Office to oversee the work of the Executive Council Secretariat. While the new system came as little surprise to the public, it nonetheless drew strong criticism from democrats who said it concentrated more power in Mr. Tung's hands while failing to give the public a role in choosing government leaders.

May

On the **10th**, the police arrested Leung Kwok-hung of the April 5th Action Group and Christopher Fung Ka-keung, council chairman of the Hong Kong Federation of Students, at their homes early in the morning. They were immediately charged with organizing an unauthorized public assembly. Another student activist, Chris Lo Wai-ming, surrendered to the police later and was charged with the same offence as Fung. Legalists criticized the police, saying the unusual move was unnecessary as to arouse suspicions that it was politically motivated. Political and student activists even condemned the arrest as "an abuse of power and selective prosecution."

According to the government statistics released on the **21st**, the unemployment rate during the period of February 2002 to April 2002 reached its highest level on record to 7.1 per cent. A total of 245,000 people were out of work.

On the **22nd**, the Executive Council endorsed an unprecedented pay cut, ranging from 1.58 to 4.42 per cent, for Hong Kong's 180,000 civil servants from October 2002. The pay cut would save the government $3.1 billion a year and was in line with the findings of pay trend survey in the private sector.

1

Tung Chee-hwa's Governing Strategy: The Shortfall in Politics

Lau Siu-kai*

Associate Director, Hong Kong Institute of Asia-Pacific Studies
The Chinese University of Hong Kong

Tung Chee-hwa's Governing Strategy: The Shortfall in Politics

On 11 December 1996, shipping tycoon Tung Chee-hwa, with the blessing of Beijing, was elected the first Chief Executive of the Hong Kong Special Administrative Region (SAR) of the People's Republic of China. The SAR, which was set up on 1 July 1997, spells the end of one-and-a-half centuries of British colonial rule. Though Tung was not popularly elected, but instead was "elected" by a 400-strong Selection Committee dominated by Hong Kong's social and economic elites, Hongkongers still heaved a sigh of relief at the electoral outcome. To a people who had suffered enormously from Sino-British strife and internal divisions for more than a decade before the handover, Tung's political ascendancy to the top office

* Some of the survey research findings reported in this paper come from a research project entitled "Learning, Electoral Behaviour, and Democratization in Hong Kong." The project is jointly conducted by Kuan Hsin-chi and the author. The project is generously funded by the Research Grants Council of the Universities Grants Committee (CUHK4359/00H) and is under the auspices of the Hong Kong Institute of Asia-Pacific Studies at the Chinese University of Hong Kong. The author is grateful to Ms Wan Po-san, Research Officer of the Institute, for rendering assistance to the project in many respects. Special thanks are due to Mr Yip Tin-sang and Mr Yiu Chuen-lai, research assistants, for their help in administering the questionnaire survey and in data preparation.

of the SAR represented a form of political redemption. After all, in the mind of Hongkongers, Tung projected the image of a decent, benevolent and honest gentleman who had not been contaminated by a personal history of political conspiracies and who accepted the office only reluctantly, out of a sense of commitment to the place and a duty to the country. Such a man, reckoned Hongkongers, was not about to suppress political freedom or restrict human rights in the SAR. And, in a time of economic vibrancy, political freedom and human rights were the predominant concerns of a people whose fear of the Chinese communists was legendary.

At the end of Tung's first five-year term, the popularity of Tung is at it's nadir. Hongkongers lack confidence in Tung's leadership. Public goodwill towards Tung has by and large dissipated. Fairly or not, Tung is blamed for almost everything that has gone wrong in Hong Kong.

Indisputably, the reversal of Tung's political fortune within his first term has a lot to do with the unexpected economic trauma Hong Kong has suffered since the handover. Hong Kong's economic plight was brought about by an external event — the Asian financial crisis, which in turn pricked the property "bubble" and brought to an abrupt end Hong Kong's economic prosperity which had lasted for more than two decades. The dearth of political experience of Tung as a political novice is certainly another factor that explains his unsatisfactory political performance. And so is the fact Tung comes to the job as a loner who governs Hong Kong without the support of a powerful political coalition. Nevertheless, in my opinion, it is the governing strategy that Tung has crafted right after his election and that he stubbornly adheres to thereafter despite its blatant limitation that accounts for the enormous difficulties encountered by his administration. This governing strategy, I argue, would create insuperable problems for Tung even in the best of circumstances. It is bound to become a recipe for ineffective governance when Hongkongers cry out for political leadership during a time of crisis. In fact, Hong Kong found itself in an unprecedented crisis immediately after the departure of the British. If his governing strategy is not fundamentally revamped, Tung as the second Chief Executive of the SAR will find himself running an increasingly ungovernable place. A Hong Kong which is not able to pull itself together to confront intensifying global competition will no longer be the shining Pearl of the East, but will instead become the liability of China and signify the inoperativeness of Beijing's policy of "one country, two systems."

Tung's Initial Project of Depoliticization

The governing strategy crafted by Tung Chee-hwa faithfully reflected his political beliefs, his style of leadership, his perception of the political and economic situation of Hong Kong, and his assessment of the opportunities and constraints faced by himself and the new regime. Needless to say, it also partly showed the political constraints imposed by Beijing on his behaviour. The term "governing strategy" is used here in a loose sense to describe the actions taken and beliefs evinced by Tung, bearing in mind that his actions and beliefs do not coalesce sufficiently to form a coherent strategy. All the same, it is possible to identify some basic principles underlying the way he handles the tasks of governance. Obviously the overriding objective of Tung is to steer Hong Kong's economic development in a new direction in a context of social stability characterized by drastic depoliticization. Tung's manifest "project of depoliticization" has as its principal objective drastic reduction in the amount of political conflict in Hong Kong, especially conflict between the government and the people on the issues of democratic reform. As a believer in traditional Chinese values, Tung's disgust at the proliferation of political conflicts engendered by the incremental democratic reforms introduced by the departing colonial regime before the handover is obvious. This traditionalistic political proclivity of Tung is clearly reflected in what he said when he was still a candidate for the post of the Chief Executive.

> Hong Kong's socio-political realities are undergoing changes; new sets of rules and relations are in the making. Will internal friction, parochial interests and policy decisions based on short-term political expediency distort our sense of direction and our aspirations, and damage our commitment and our confidence for the future?[1]

> Is our civil service too bogged down in the politics of our legislative processes? Should they be devoting more time and energy to the formulation and efficient implementation of policies?[2]

> As we move forward, there is a need for us to renew our commitment to the values we hold dear. These values have been with us for thousands of years and are as relevant today as they ever have been: Trust, love and respect for our family and our elders; integrity, honesty and loyalty towards all; commitment to education and a strong desire to strive to improve and advance oneself; a belief in order and stability; an emphasis on obligations to the community rather than rights of the individual; a preference for consultation rather than open confrontation. These are some of the shared values which make our society

more cohesive. Together with a strong identity, they will provide us with clarity of direction and unity of purpose.[3]

Similar views were expressed on the day Tung assumed office as the Chief Executive of the SAR:

> We will continue to encourage diversity in our society, but we must also reaffirm and respect the fine traditional Chinese values, including filial piety, love for the family, modesty and integrity, and the desire for continuous improvement. We value plurality, but discourage open confrontation; we strive for liberty, but not at the expense of the rule of law; we respect minority views, but are mindful of wider interests; we protect individual rights, but also shoulder collective responsibilities. I hope these values will provide the foundation for unity in our society.[4]

Tung might have some ideas about the difficulties involved in any attempt to depoliticize Hong Kong after the handover. They include *inter alia* the fact that he can never annul the democratic gains and political freedoms which have been promised Hongkongers by the Basic Law (the SAR's mini-constitution), the impossibility of suppressing opposition forces by coercive means,[5] and the lack of means on the part of the government to exercise ideological control over the people. But they however do not deter Tung from trying. In fact, Tung was determined to blaze a new political trail by re-setting the public agenda, placing his administration on a new political support base, and reshaping the relationship between government and people.

In its last years, the colonial regime resorted to democratic and occasionally even demagogic appeals to seek public support in an environment of declining governmental authority and rising political disaffection. Under the five-year rule of Chris Patten, the departing regime even deliberately but subtly manipulated the anti-Communist sentiments of the Hongkongers to advance its own political interests. Public nostalgia for colonial rule, though diminishing over the years, still remained discernible on the eve of the handover. The British were particularly remembered for their democratic reforms and human rights legislation, all of which took place only after, not before, the 1984 Sino-British Joint Declaration on the return of Hong Kong to China. Given Tung's political conservatism and the objection of Beijing, his administration would not seek to depoliticize society by incorporating the newly emergent political and social forces into the political system through further democratization. Instead an alternative governing strategy has to be crafted. Central to the strategy is a deliberate effort to mobilize political support for the Chief Executive and the new regime. Tung believes that a government supported by a substantial proportion of Hongkongers is in a strong position to set the public agenda, command public deference and resolve political conflicts.[6]

Immediately after Tung's electoral victory in December 1996, the new regime adopted a four-pronged approach in its quest of public support, drawing upon its strengths and the opportunities that beckoned. The principal strategy was to convince Hongkongers that the new regime was given four-square support by Beijing. A relationship of mutual trust between Beijing and the SAR government was depicted as not only capable of averting Chinese interference in local affairs, but also as crucial in procuring China's support in resolving Hong Kong's problems. Since Beijing has played a critical role in Tung's ascendance to the top post of the SAR, he has the unswerving support of China. Beijing's trust in Tung guarantees that he can bank on the reliable support of the pro-Beijing forces in Hong Kong, the more important among which are the Democratic Alliance for the Betterment of Hong Kong (DAB), the Hong Kong Federation of Trade Unions, the Chinese General Chamber of Commerce, an extensive network of community organizations and a substantial portion of the economic elites who are on good terms with the Beijing. More important, Beijing's support would have deterrent effects on Tung's political opponents. It is widely understood in Hong Kong that Beijing equates Tung's challengers with Beijing's foes. In view of the fact that Hong Kong increasingly depends on the mainland for business and professional opportunities, the unfriendly attitude of Beijing towards Tung's opponents does discourage open clash between Tung and the Hongkongers.[7]

Another tactic of Tung to gain public trust was to appeal strenuously to Chinese virtues. Tung's ideal government is a Confucian one practising paternalistic, benign, and active rule. Unlike the colonial regime, Tung, while extolling the free market, is no blind believer in laissez-faire. In Tung's mind, the government has a constructive role to play in promoting economic development. Furthermore, Tung's ideal society is one devoid of serious conflicts, particularly those political in nature. In that society, people are respectful and deferential to authorities, especially political authorities. To all appearances, Tung's governing philosophy should be anachronistic and at odds with a highly modernized society. This however is not the case. Past studies have repeatedly indicated that traditional beliefs remain strong in the ethos of the Hong Kong Chinese.[8]

My 1997 survey[9] also shows that on the eve of the handover, Tung's way of thinking had broad public appeal. In the survey, a large majority of respondents (70 per cent) agreed with the view that "a good government should treat the people as though they are its own children." Most (68 per cent) respondents were of the view that the government should enact laws to punish people who did not take care of their parents. Moreover, many more (76 per cent) respondents agreed than disagreed (12 per cent) with the view that a good government was one that taught the people how to conduct themselves. To the respondents, traditional Chinese values were preferable to Western values. A plurality (32 per cent) of respondents considered traditional Chinese values such as loyalty, filial piety, benevolence, and righteousness suited Hong Kong better than Western values of freedom, democracy and human rights. In addition, a majority of respondents (59 per cent) placed social order above individual freedom. And a plurality (45 per cent) also said that public interest took priority over human rights. Overall, as the majority of Hong Kong people shared Tung's political beliefs, his initial success in winning a decent level of public endorsement is not at all surprising.[10]

The third aspect of Tung's governing strategy was to draw upon his own favourable personal image as perceived by the people. As a political newcomer, Tung was unknown to Hongkongers until immediately before his electoral victory. In contrast with other aspirants to the top job, Tung had the benefit of not having his reputation tarnished and compromised by the political infighting during the transitional period before the handover, which had destroyed the career of many a promising politician. While as a politician Tung was definitely dwarfed by the "populist" and astute Chris Patten, the last colonial governor of Hong Kong, Tung's personal image of sincerity, integrity, modesty, fairness, open-mindedness, amiability, compassion for the common folk, magnanimity and diligence has, in no small measure, allayed public fears of an arbitrary and repressive SAR government. His personal image furthermore went a long way towards convincing the Hongkongers that he would run a benevolent government at a time when Tung still had no tangible policy achievements.

The last prong of Tung's governing strategy was his unequivocal promise of government performance in the economic, social, and livelihood spheres. Many long-standing economic, social, and livelihood problems, which had not been seriously dealt with under colonial rule and were getting even worse during the pre-handover transition,[11] furnished the Tung administration with an opportunity to win public support. As a

Chinese-style politician, Tung envisaged a government more economically and socially interventionist than its colonial predecessor, though he was prudent enough to pay homage to the free market. In his inaugural speech on 1 July 1997, Tung declared that the foremost task of his government was "to enhance Hong Kong's economic vitality and sustain its economic growth."[12] Implicit in this message was Tung's desire to transform Hong Kong's economy from one overly dependent on finance and real estate to a knowledge-based economy. He vowed to improve Hong Kong's education, with particular emphasis on the elementary and secondary levels. He promised to resolve the housing problem by increasing the overall housing supply at a target of not less than 85,000 flats a year, with the aim of achieving a home ownership rate of 70 per cent within ten years. The problem of the elderly was also a major focus of the new government. Tung pledged to "develop a comprehensive policy to take care of the various needs of the territory's senior citizens and provide them with a sense of security, a sense of belonging and a sense of worthiness."[13] All of Tung's promises were undoubtedly credible at the time they were made, for the economy was still vibrant and the SAR government had inherited from the colonial regime an enormous amount of fiscal reserves and no external debt. Further to Tung's political benefit is the fact that his emphasis on economic and social issues was basically in accord with public preferences.

Without any doubt, the Tung administration had an auspicious start. The steadfast support of Beijing was crucial to the buildup of its authority. Tung's personal image initially endeared him to a people who had very limited knowledge of the ability and history of their new chief. The political beliefs championed by Tung struck a responsive chord in society, and his policy agenda was in general accord with that of the Hongkongers. In a nutshell, political paternalism as advocated by Tung was well received by a society that until very recently was reeling from years of political turmoil and was in desperate need of a respite from political upheavals. The initial success of Tung's governing strategy was reflected not only in his rising popularity in the early months of his rule, but also in the generally tranquil political ambience in the SAR. All of a sudden, the inception of the SAR coincided with the eclipse of politics in Hong Kong.[14]

Fundamental Problems in Tung's Approach to Governance

The governing strategy of Tung Chee-hwa represents in essence a project of depoliticization in which coercion plays almost no role. Admittedly, the partial character of Hong Kong's democracy where the head of government monopolizes decision-making powers but is popularly elected by the people contributes significantly to depoliticization by excluding popular interests from the polity. The political culture of the Hongkongers, with its obsession with stability and aversion to chaos, also plays an important role in moderating political conflicts. And public fear of Beijing weighs in as another factor dampening political conflict. Nonetheless, credit still has to be given to Tung's attempt at restoring political calm to Hong Kong in the early months of the SAR.

By deliberatly focusing on social, economic, and livelihood issues, Tung sought to draw people's attention away from political issues such as democratization and towards practical bread-and-butter concerns. By putting forward a public agenda drastically different from that of his predecessor and shadow competitor, Chris Patten, Tung in effect attempted to place his government on a political base at variance with that of the colonial regime. According to the findings of my 1997 survey, Patten's supporters and Tung's supporters differed sharply in political values. People who were Westernized and democratically oriented were more inclined to support Patten. Tung, in contrast, drew support largely from people who embraced traditional values and held strong nationalistic sentiments. There were also marked differences in the socio-demographic characteristics of the two groups. Generally speaking, Tung's supporters were older in age, less educated, and lower in income. These people were more susceptible to the traditionalistic appeals of Tung. They were also more patriotic and nationalistic. Needless to say, they also harboured great expectations that Tung would cater to their material needs and normative aspirations.[15] On the contrary, middle-class Hongkongers are alienated from Tung's administration right from the very beginning. Tung's publicly perceived pro-Beijing stance, his paternalistic style and his traditionalistic proclivity are the traits that turn him off from the middle class of the SAR. Still, if Tung can maintain simultaneously the backing of the lower-class Hongkongers, the business community and Beijing's supporters in the SAR, he can still have a relatively strong social support base on which to rest his administration and to gain a decent degree of popularity and legitimacy.

Nevertheless, it is one thing for Tung to enjoy the goodwill of a substantial proportion of the Hongkongers in the early months of the SAR, to organize a reasonably broad social support base and to maintain it over a long period of time for the sake of effective governance are another thing. The initial favourable reception of those Hongkongers to Tung owes in no small measure to their belief that they would be the major beneficiaries of Tung's rule. The business elites believed that the new administration headed by a prominent member from their ranks, as compared with the already pro-business colonial regime, would be even more willing to serve the interests of the business community. They expected to forge a closer bond between money and politics. Always apprehensive about the surge of political populism in Hong Kong, some outspoken business elites initially even harboured hope that Tung would roll back some of the democratic reforms introduced by the colonial regime before the handover as a means to achieve exit with glory and bolster public support for the departing government. The pro-Beijing elements, on the other hand, had a different set of political considerations and expectations. They were duty-bound to support a regime that was charged by Beijing to implement China's Hong Kong policy of "one country, two systems."[16] More important, as the victims of colonial oppression for about half a century, they expected and in fact demanded measures to compensate for their past sufferings and to be given pride of place in the new regime. The initial support given to Tung by the common people had a lot to do with their confidence in his determination and ability to keep his paternalistic promises. Many lower-class Hongkongers were impressed by the father-like image deliberately projected by Tung and expected his government to be a caring government attentive to their needs.

It is obvious from the very beginning that Tung's social base of support is made up of incompatible elements. Since the late 1970s, the gap between the upper and lower income groups in Hong Kong has been widening unabated and made conflict between social classes increasingly visible.[17] It is well-nigh impossible to build a durable political coalition between the business community and the men in the street. The ultra-conservatism and political intransigence of Hong Kong's businesspeople would be enough to render it unlikely. Furthermore, since the pro-Beijing elements, with their distinctive political subculture and their alienation from the mainstream society, have been treated as political pariahs in Hong Kong for a long time, there is a pervasive fear among Hongkongers that they would serve as Beijing's agents and therefore subvert the principle of "Hong Kong people running Hong Kong." Any attempt by Tung to incorporate them into his administration would meet with stiff resistance. In view of the inherent contradictions in his base of social support, it is obvious that only rapid and sustained economic growth would provide the necessary public resources for Tung to satisfy his key constituencies (the business community and the grassroots people) simultaneously and thereby to ward off challenge from the liberal forces in Hong Kong. Even so, the demands of the pro-Beijing forces for political inclusion would be hard to satisfy without incurring grave political risks.

Apparently Tung has not paid sufficient attention to the question of how to transform the goodwill of his variegated supporters into an organized, durable and stable base of support for the new regime. His apolitical or, more appropriately, anti-political personality also prevent him from doing so. Tung's paternalistic political personality would counsel against building an organized social base of support for that would entail a lot of power sharing and political concessions. In Tung's opinion, the bulk of political conflicts in Hong Kong have economic origins and hence they can be resolved by a growing economy. Tung also sincerely believes that, except for the minority of political do-gooders and political careerists, the majority of Hongkongers are believers in political harmony just like him and hence their support for him is going to be sturdy and sustained even if it does not take on an organizational form. In view of the fact that the Chief Executive is endowed with vast decision-making powers, Tung reckons that he can simply rely on the constitutional powers at his disposal to govern Hong Kong in accordance with his plans without the service of an organized support base. Moreover, in Tung's calculation, though the government does not enjoy stable and organized majority support in the legislature, the labyrinthine electoral arrangements for that political body would still guarantee that most of the legislators would be members of the social and economic elites and will thus share his political position. In addition, under these electoral rules, the legislature would remain fragmented for many years after the handover.[18] Consequently, the legislature would only play an innocuous watchdog role, leaving the government free to run the SAR with only minimal legislative constraints.

Apart from Tung's personal inclination, there are in fact a number of objective factors that make it difficult if not impossible for Tung to build a fairly broad social base of support. In the first place, the fact that Tung has limited political experience before his political ascendancy means that he cannot bank on a preexisting network of political allies to assist him in organizing such a support network. Undeniably, he comes to the top post of the SAR as a political loner instead of as the head of a political coalition. As a result, he can only rely on a few trusted business friends and personal aids for support and advice. Second, in view of Beijing's suspicion of the political intentions of the Hongkongers, it is not unreasonable to argue that Tung is favoured by Beijing as the Chief Executive of the SAR primarily because of his lack of a local power base. Beijing thus would look askance at a Chief Executive actively cultivating a more or less autonomous social base of support. Besides, in all likelihood, Beijing would not countenance a broad base of support that would include those political forces that are unfriendly or even hostile to it. Third, the civil servants, the mainstay of the new regime, are wary of losing power to other social sectors, be they business elites, pro-Beijing elements or the ordinary people. Their perennial suspicion of Communism naturally makes them mistrustful of a Chief Executive who has to declare loyalty to Beijing. Last but not least, the amorphous nature of Hong Kong society and the low degree of social participation of Hongkongers, the unfortunate consequences of a long period of stable colonial rule, do not provide the ingredients to the new regime even if it seriously wants to go about organizing its supporters. As a result, civil servants, particularly senior officials, are determined to hold on to the decision-making prerogatives that they took for granted in the colonial period.

All these factors together have resulted in a situation where Tung can only depend on the shallow political support given to his administration by a hodgepodge of supporters whose goodwill towards the new regime is contingent upon its ability to deliver to them separately the coveted benefits. These supporters are not bound together into a durable political alliance wherein their interests have been effectively aggregated. To be sure, they have vested interests in the new regime, but their relationship with the Tung administration is primarily utilitarian rather than infused with common political ideals. Such a social base of support apparently is unstable and fragile. It is also vulnerable to disintegration if the ability of Tung to hold them together weakens.

Sitting on top of this shallow and disunited base of support is a narrow and factious governing coalition. It can be argued that, notwithstanding the non-existence of a broad and organized social support base, Tung's administration can still be in good shape and his project of depoliticization fairly well executed if he can form a powerful governing coalition made up of a broad alliance of the social and economic elites of the SAR. As long as Beijing respects Hong Kong's high degree of autonomy, the economy remains vibrant and the coalition members enjoy a decent degree of public trust, a cohesive governing coalition, by and large representative of the elites, is very likely to serve Tung reasonably well. Nevertheless, it is quite clear that Tung has not been able to build a fairly broadly based governing coalition. On the contrary, Tung's governing coalition is a narrowly based political alliance. Moreover, it is a collection of incongruent political elements that not only cannot operate cohesively, but also becomes a scourge of effective administration. Most of the members of the coalition serve Tung as individual advisers instead of as representatives of specific interests and quite a number of them are not figures respected by the public. It goes without saying that the governing coalition organized by Tung has failed even to command strong support from the elites.[19]

Occupying a central place in Tung's governing coalition is the civil service that is taken over from the colonial regime. Apart from a few exceptions, the principal officials of Chris Patten are also Tung's principal officials. Most noteworthy is that fact that Anson Chan Fang On-san, who was Patten's Chief Secretary, was appointed by Tung as his Chief Secretary for Administration,[20] and it is widely known that Chan has her own ambitions for the top job of the SAR. The retention of the former colonial officials in the new regime is a move to maintain public confidence in Hong Kong's future because colonial officials, with their track record of administrative performance, are more trusted by the people than the politicians, particularly those who are Beijing's sympathizers. The move is also taken to reassure the jittery civil servants, whose service is indispensable to the new regime, that they are highly valued and that there will be no political reprisal against them after the handover. Tung's relationship with his principal officials is at best an uneasy one. Unlike the process of decolonization in other former British colonies, where the colonial government played an influential role in grooming future political leaders, the colonial government in Hong Kong — reacting to its fights with China — had to transform senior civil servants into politicians in the hope that they would dominate the post-1997 regime. In fact, the most prominent of them were deliberately groomed to fill top administrative posts in the last moment of colonial rule by Chris Patten.[21] Tung's political values and policy agenda are not heartily shared by his principal officials, who are still immersed in laissez-faire thinking, anti-Communism, and a parochial "Hong Kong first" mind-set. Tung is not highly regarded by his principal officials. The differences between Tung and the civil servants have been vividly reflected in the open disagreements between Tung and Anson Chan on a variety of issues and topics bearing on the SAR's relationship with Beijing, human rights and political freedoms, as well as the electoral system for the Legislative Council. At the same time, the principal officials are haunted by the perennial fear that sooner or later Tung would replace them with more loyal political allies. In any case, the lack of stalwart support from the administrative officials has been plaguing the Tung regime since its very beginning. What is even more troublesome is that the civil servants, with their mastery of critical information and the instruments of policy implementation, have gradually marginalized Tung's other political allies, leaving him increasingly dependent on them as a source of support.

The other components in Tung's governing coalition represent a loose collection of political friends and other political elements whose loyalty to Tung is tenuous. His Executive Council (Exco), presumably his "inner cabinet," is basically a form of political compromise or balancing act. He "chooses" his Executive Councilors from different political backgrounds, who can hardly form a cohesive team. Apparently some of the Exco members have gained entry into the body through the support of other political patrons and do not owe Tung any political favour. A few of them even manifestly pursue their own political agenda. What is worse is that most of the Exco members have strong connections with big business. They share with Tung the same disdain for politics, and are by and large detached from the people. Most of them serve Tung on a part-time basis, and their own business and professional interests are a constant source of conflict-of-interest allegations. Politically, Exco members are not in the combative mood. They are not willing to take on the legislature or the public in defense of Tung's policy. In addition, they do not have the political ability or networks to win popular support for Tung. In any case, the political reputation of the Exco is low throughout Tung's first term of office.

The relationship between Exco and the civil service is uneasy and occasionally combative. Unlike under colonial rule, in which civil servants exercised strong influence on who would become Exco members, most of the Exco members appointed by Tung hold different political views and policy ideas from those of the civil servants. Moreover, a number of Exco members, especially those with pro-Beijing bias or business background, hold the principal officials in contempt, which is fully and bitterly reciprocated. The pro-Beijing figures in the Exco are the major targets of mistrust by the principal officials. Bickering among Exco members and the principal officials is occasionally reported in the press as some of them deliberately use information leakage as a means to embarrass or harass their political rivals. Originally Tung intended to have the Exco members lead and oversee the principal officials by giving some of them a prominent role in policy making and political leadership. This, however, led to the eruption of both latent and open friction between them. Eventually, the Exco members prove unable to perform the function expected of them by Tung, who has perforce to depend more on his principal officials. Still, the relationship between the two groups is difficult at best.

Much to the chagrin of the pro-Beijing elements, their demand for substantial participation in the new regime has been politely rebuffed by Tung. Their presence in the governing coalition is minimal to say the least. Tung's reluctance to admit them into the inner circle of his administration is based on the realistic assessment of the negative reaction of the civil servants and the Hongkongers. It is obvious that Beijing also concurs in the exclusion of its longtime followers in Hong Kong. Nevertheless, the pro-Beijing forces, the more powerful of which are the workers, are expected by Beijing to give full support to the SAR government even though it follows a basically pro-business policy agenda. Out of patriotism and deference to Beijing, these forces dutifully side with Tung. Inevitably, however, feelings of resentment and frustration have been smouldering within the pro-Beijing camp since the establishment of the SAR. It can thus be argued that the support given to Tung by the pro-Beijing elements is at best half-hearted. And they chafe at the fact that Tung and his officials tend to blithely take their support for granted.

On the whole, despite his enormous powers to make political appointments and formulate public policies, Tung has not been able to convert them into a political alliance in support of his administration. Moreover, as Tung's conservative and paternalistic political beliefs are not widely shared by Hong Kong's modernized and Westernized elites, his efforts to attract political allies would definitely encounter difficulties. Consequently, the kinds of political appointments Tung has made fail to draw a large enough pool of politically and socially prestigious figures into his fold.

Obviously, for a number of reasons, the disunited and narrow-based governing coalition crafted by Tung and the unavailability of a strong social base of support make it difficult for him to effectively implement his project of depoliticization even under the best of circumstances. First and foremost, they do not furnish the new regime with the necessary cohesive and politically trusted leadership for effective administrative performance even under normal circumstances. The splits within the government have severely marred the functioning of the new regime since the establishment of the SAR. The government suffers particularly from the lack of organizational means to aggregate the huge amount of demands directed at it and to reconcile the various interests behind them. Since the onset of the economic crisis, the SAR government has been bombarded with numerous raw demands, creating serious problems of political and administrative overload. The inability of the government to aggregate these demands into workable policy programmes and to galvanize the public behind them has fueled political discontent in society. Moreover, a slew of glaring examples of administrative failures — notably the clumsy handling of the avian flu, the confusion connected with the opening of the new multi-billion dollar airport, the erratic policy in the linguistic medium of instruction in secondary schools and the chaotic housing policy — show that there is a lack of clear policy direction or competent implementation of policies. Policy making and policy implementation are erratic and chaotic. The fact that the officials responsible for the administrative failures are civil servants endowed with job security means that Tung is deprived of the means to punish them. As a result, public anger is directed at Tung himself, further undermining his popularity. Moreover, the Tung administration is deprived of the means to mobilize societal resources to complement governmental means in the process of problem solving. As a non-democratically elected government, the Tung regime desperately needs excellent performance to sustain its political legitimacy. The lackadaisical performance of the new administration is a major reason for the decline of public support for it.[22]

Second, unlike the colonial regime, which abstains from intervening in economic and social affairs, Tung has a grandiose agenda for his new government. He envisages a Hong Kong as a knowledge-based society run by the economic elites. Public deference and obedience to the visionary government is expected if not demanded. As a successful businessman Tung is troubled by the conservatism, inefficiency and the costliness of the public sector. As a result, since assuming office Tung has spelled out a long list of reforms — in areas such as the civil service and the public sector, the financial sector, education, municipal administration, health and hygiene, and land and housing supply — which he intends to undertake in his first term of office. In addition, he wants to promote high technology and high value-added industries by government action. A notable example along this line is the government's joint effort with Richard Li, son of tycoon Li Ka-shing, to build the Cyberport in Hong Kong. Nevertheless, successful implementation of these reforms and endeavours demands not only an administratively competent and politically skillful governmental machinery, they also require the building of public consensus, the mobilization and deployment of societal resources, and the delicate reconciliation of interests and resolution of conflicts. At the same time, these reforms and endeavours are also forces of politicization because they are bound to create public dissension and resistance to government initiatives. It can thus be argued that Tung's activistic style ironically runs counter to his original plan of depoliticization of the SAR and renders it impossible. The incoherence and weak social base of the new regime fuels further politicization, particularly conflicts between the government and the people, because it does not have the necessary political means to handle an increasingly politicized society.

Third, true to the essence of the Tung administration as a paternalistic regime, the decision-making style of the new government is characterized by a top-down policy making format and limited public consultation. No structured system of consultation and deliberation is built to support the decision-making process. As compared with its predecessor, the Tung administration is less sensitive to public opinion and sentiments as well as the variety of interests in society. In the 2000 survey, more respondents agreed (41 per cent) than disagreed (17 per cent) that there was less transparency in public policy making under Tung than under Patten. Likewise, more respondents (42 per cent) agreed than disagreed (16 per cent) that in the running of Hong Kong the SAR government paid less attention to public opinion than the Patten administration. Since the early 1980s Hongkongers have become increasingly accustomed to an open and fairly responsive though not democratic government. It is no wonder that they are offended by the aloofness and arbitrariness of the Tung regime. In view of the peculiar combination of political freedoms and authoritarianism in the political system of Hong Kong, Hongkongers can take various protest actions to apply pressure on and vent their displeasure with the government. An increasingly strained government–people relationship is bound to undermine effective governance.

Fourth, the pro-business nature of the Tung administration severely limits his ability to nurture political popularity. Though business elites occupied a prominent place in society throughout Hong Kong's colonial history, particularly in view of the fact that as a society of migrants Hong Kong society had failed to attract the scholar-literati — the Confucian elites who dominated China — to come to the British colony. The prominent place of the business elites however has not enabled them to command respect and trust from the Hongkongers who, under the influence of traditional Chinese values, refuse to hold the business elites in high regard. As the colonial government did not owe its right to rule to local business elites, it could play a relatively autonomous and effective role in reconciling the differences between business and the people. Since the business elites have enormous influence in choosing the Chief Executive, they not surprisingly enjoy privileged access to the Tung administration. The cozy relationship between the government and business has irked a lot of Hongkongers, especially those belonging to the middle class who treasure equal opportunity and fair play and abhor nepotism and cronyism. The 2000 survey has found that almost half of the respondents (48 per cent) believed that the SAR government, as compared with the Patten administration, practiced favouritism, with only 11 per cent thinking otherwise.

Fifth, Tung's depoliticization project is oblivious to the already highly politicized Hong Kong society. The process of politicization, which was palpable as early as the early 1970s, was driven by Hong Kong's modernization, the rise of the middle class and the growing dependence of society on the government for problem-solving and service delivery.[23] The process has accelerated since the early 1980s with the emergence of the prospect of Hong Kong returning to China, the anxieties and fears it has generated, the gradual opening up of the political system, the rise of political groups, the strife between Beijing and London and their competition for Hongkongers' support. By the time of the handover, a vibrant mass political arena had matured and it co-existed uneasily with the longstanding elite political arena. Notwithstanding the absence of popular election of the government, the "masses" of Hong Kong are still capable of bringing pressure on or resisting the dictates of the governing elites by a variety of political means both conventional and unconventional.[24] Among the newly emergent political actors, the liberals — advocating democratic reform, a Hong Kong-first agenda and a defiant stance towards Beijing — have largely galvanized popular support. The post-handover political system of the SAR however only gives the liberals and other popular forces a marginal presence. Tung's attitudes towards the liberals and other popular forces are basically unfriendly, and the latter reciprocate by dogged opposition to the new regime. Instead of skillfully manipulating, pacifying, dividing or co-opting these forces, Tung chooses to ignore them if possible and confront them when necessary. The fact that these forces are also classified by Beijing as its adversaries also limits Tung's options in dealing with them. In any case, the failure of Tung to come to terms with the most popular political forces in the SAR becomes a perennial source of trouble for the new government.

Sixth, in all likelihood, both Beijing and Tung have underestimated the contradictions between the government and the Legislative Council. It is true that the electoral system for the legislature ensures that a majority of its members share with Tung similar socioeconomic backgrounds and ideas. On the surface at least, the executive-led political system of the SAR has operated in accordance to design as close to 100 per cent of the bills introduced into the legislature by the executive have been dutifully passed. Increasingly, however, cracks in the executive–legislative relationship appear. Intrinsic institutional jealousies between the executive and the legislature explain part of the strains and stresses in their relationship. Tung's unskillful treatment of the legislators, including those who are his political supporters, exacerbates friction between the two bodies. Even Tung's supporters in the legislature such as the DAB, the Liberal Party and the Hong Kong Progressive Alliance are by and large deprived of a meaningful role in the making of public policy. Feeling slighted by the government, the legislators have become increasingly antagonistic, critical and obstructionist. Tung and his officials have to devote arduous efforts to organize ad hoc majorities in the legislature in order to have governmental bills passed. More fundamentally, contradictions between the government and the legislature stem from two irreconcilable differences between them. The different electoral methods for the Chief Executive and the legislature are such that the government has to be partly responsible to Beijing whereas the legislators owe their positions solely to the Hongkongers. As long as mistrust between Beijing and the Hongkongers persists, a harmonious relationship between the government and the legislature is impossible. Moreover, these different electoral methods also spur the legislators, whatever their socioeconomic background, to pay more heed to the voices of the people than the Chief Executive who has to do the bidding of the economic elites. The strains in the executive–legislative relationship are made more serious by the non-existence of a stable and reliable legislative majority in support of the government. The inability of Tung to cultivate such a legislative majority through power sharing with the legislators and their parties is part and parcel of his inability to develop a strong governing coalition and a broad social base of support.[25]

The absence of a strong governing coalition and a broad social base of support would definitely hamper the functioning of any regime. Nevertheless, through the exertion of effective personal leadership some of the adverse effects arising from them can be partially overcome. If Tung can make full use of the powers at his disposal and exploit to the maximum the bully pulpit for political appeal and public education, he might still be able to galvanize the Hongkongers by forging emotional and personal ties between himself and the people. He can for example use the mass media for the purposes of political mobilization and rally public opinion against his political foes inside and outside the government. In any case, the strategy of depoliticization by non-coercive means would demand an active political strategy skillfully devised and executed by the political authorities, especially by Tung himself. It involves setting the public agenda in such a manner that divisive political issues be safely expurgated or marginalized. It entails political techniques to sideline those political forces with political demands that are hard to accommodate. It also calls for a deliberate attempt to unite a majority of Hongkongers on the basis of issues that transcend social classes and underscore the common interests between Beijing and the SAR. It in effect requires firm, astute, powerful and charismatic leadership from Tung himself. However, instead of adopting a shrewd and active political strategy targeted at depoliticization, Tung instead seeks to depoliticize by passively avoiding politics. The low and passive political profile adopted by Tung after assuming office is undoubtedly a reflection of his anti-political bent, his deep-seated aversion to politicking, his aversion to demagogy, his uneasiness with the press and his lack of populist skills. In contrast with the Patten government, Tung's is very reluctant to reach out to the people. This passive, or more appropriately escapist, political strategy wobbles along throughout Tung's first term of office and wreaks havoc with his administration.

The Unraveling of Tung's Governing Strategy

Given its fundamental problems, Tung's governing strategy with the explicit objective of depoliticization is bound to falter sooner or later. In fact, the level of politicization has not gone down. On the contrary, except for four months of political tranquillity at the beginning of the SAR, there is an inexorable trajectory of escalating politicization in post-handover Hong Kong. The end of Tung's first term of office coincides with an explosion of political conflict that renders his governing strategy untenable.

Many political conservatives and economic elites in Hong Kong are adamant that but for the onslaught of the Asian financial crisis and the collapse of the property bubble in late 1997, Tung's governing strategy would still be able to achieve its goals of depoliticization whilst maintaining political stability. They argue that since Beijing has largely kept its promise of not interfering in the SAR's affairs, there has been increasing public confidence in its pledge of "one country, two systems" to the Hongkongers. Frictions stemming from mistrust between Beijing and the Hongkongers will no longer be a source of politicization in the SAR. In addition, the withdrawal of the British from SAR politics removes another source of political division. Therefore, if economic prosperity is maintained, there is reason to believe that Hong Kong's political tranquillity in the first four months of the SAR would go on. It is indeed true that the success of Tung's governing strategy hinges upon a prosperous economy which provides the material resources to reward and hold together his key constituencies — the business community and the grassroots people — and to ward off challenges from the liberal forces in Hong Kong. He will then be able to offer a favourable investment environment to business but at the same time take care of the welfare needs of his grassroots supporters. The early success of Tung's governing strategy owes in no small measure to public confidence in his determination and ability to keep his paternalistic promises. The congenial economic environment in the first months of the SAR had boosted public confidence.

The economic crisis starting in late October 1997 has upset the apple cart. Being unprepared psychologically for the sudden change of the territory's economic fortunes, it is inevitable that the people would blame Tung and his government for their plight, even though they are fully convinced of the external origin of the crisis and also believe that the former colonial government is partly to blame. Consequently the Tung administration suffers immensely from the crisis in terms of popularity, because it is widely perceived as neither competent nor caring. Public officials are criticized as aloof from the people, arrogant and incapable of coping with crises.

Admittedly, given the international origin of the economic crisis, which is beyond Hong Kong's control, it is impossible for the SAR government to come up with effective remedies to cure Hong Kong's economic woes. However, if Tung's governing strategy is sound, he could at least minimize the damage suffered by his government and even turn the crisis into an opportunity to bolster his personal popularity, assert moral leadership and boost the prestige of his government. In other words, if Tung could convince the jittery people that the SAR government is capable of minimizing the adverse impact of the crisis, make them believe that his government is caring and benevolent, inspire them with hope and enthusiasm and bring them together to chart a better future of Hong Kong, it is possible that public support for him would not decline so significantly.

Nevertheless, it is doubtful that Tung would succeed in his way of governance even with a booming economy. The reason is simple: the political context of Hong Kong had changed so much in the one-and-a-half decades before the handover that, contrary to the beliefs of Tung's sympathizers, his project of depoliticization is by all means a non-starter. Even if Tung does not harbour grandiose plans to reform Hong Kong's institutions and policies or to reconstruct its economy, the political tasks confronting the new regime will still be herculean and tax severely his political capabilities. The major political challenges which Tung has to meet upon his accession to the top post of the SAR include, *inter alia*, institution-building and re-setting of the political rules of the game in the wake of Hong Kong's transformation from a British colony to a Special Administration Region of China, re-building the social contract in the SAR in a context of de-industrialization, diminishing economic security and declining public confidence in the untrammelled capitalist system, re-positioning the relationship between Hong Kong and the mainland after the end of the colonial rule in accordance with the principle of "one country two systems," restoring public respect for and trust in political and social authorities which have been in secular decline,[26] enhancing public confidence in the government amidst rising public skepticism of the political abilities of the civil servants, mastering a political system where multiple institutional and political actors coexist and vie for influence and coping with a political situation where mass politics has raised its head.

More importantly, there are two even longer-term political projects that demand Tung's attention. The first one is the mobilization and organization of the conservative forces in the SAR to cope with the irreversible process of democratization that has been enshrined in the Basic Law. Up to the present moment, Hong Kong's vested interests, primarily the business interests, depend on Beijing and the SAR government for political protection. Eventually, as popular politics becomes increasingly prominent with the gradual opening up of the political system, the amorphous conservative forces will find themselves more and more vulnerable to the challenge of the liberals and grassroots politicians. The first ten years of the SAR are still a time of conservative dominance and Hong Kong's social and economic elites need to form their own political organizations, groom conservative political leaders and strengthen their ideological and political influence in society. The Tung administration, with the massive public resources and appointive powers at its disposal, should and has to play an instrumental role in politically preparing the elites for an increasingly democratic game.

The second long-term project entails the making of a new social contract in Hong Kong. Under the existing social contract, an authoritarian regime is granted political legitimacy by the people in return for ensuring widespread economic opportunity and security for all. Hongkongers can expect to achieve a middle-class status in return for commitment to hard work, fair competition and an unfettered capitalist economy. Economic globalization, Hong Kong's de-industrialization, the rapid expansion of the service sector and growing economic inequality have together rendered the existing social contract increasingly obsolete. The erosion of that social contract is accompanied by intensifying conflicts between social classes and growing disagreements on the role of the government in society and the economy. A new social contract will redefine the relationship between the various social classes on one hand, and the relationship between them and the government on the other. Work on that project has been delayed before 1997 by the need to address the more immediate issues connected with Hong Kong's political future and the lack of farsightedness of the colonial rulers. In view of the economic crisis of the SAR, the unrelenting transformation of Hong Kong's economic structure, and rising unemployment (particularly middle-class job losses), devising a new social contract has become even more urgent today as a new contract is need to restore social, economic and political order in the SAR. Social and economic changes elsewhere have already inaugurated changes in the social contract, and in this area Hong Kong is lagging behind.[27] Even before the onset of the Asian financial crisis, Hongkongers were increasingly skeptical of the fairness of the capitalist society and concerned about the widening gap between the rich and the poor. They progressively perceived collusion between the government and big business. The post-handover economic crisis has generated greater public demand for narrowing economic inequalities and a greater welfare role for the government. The decline of the middle class and its transformation into a discontented and insecure social stratum portend a new and powerful political threat to the Tung regime. In view of the shortage of alternative leaders in the SAR, the responsibility to produce a new social contract inescapably falls on the new regime. Tung's inability to provide political leadership in this area not only makes effective governance difficult, but also brings about further social disintegration and erosion of public consensus on the socioeconomic order of the SAR.[28]

Without any doubt, Tung faces daunting political tasks. These tasks would not disappear just because Tung turns his back on them but instead will persist in haunting his administration. More unfortunately, Tung has not observed seriously and carefully some basic principles of political leadership, so much so that his original favourable political image is so damaged that by the end of his first term he suffers from an image problem. This comes about because of three reasons. One is that Tung has not been active in cultivating his political image. Another reason is that Hongkongers have come to change their impression of Tung after seeing him in action. Yet another reason is that since the onset of the economic crisis they have developed different expectations for Tung and his government.

Tung has not been sufficiently focused on guarding his public prestige. Apparently he has taken his initial positive image too much for granted. It is evidently also the case that he does not place a high value on popularity as a significant political resource. In any case it is difficult to expect a person who intends to depoliticize Hong Kong to be concerned about his public image and to employ political gimmicks to burnish that image. Nevertheless, public prestige is of enormous importance to a Chief Executive who does not have the popular electoral mandate, who has no track record of performance, who cannot draw on the support of a powerful governing coalition and who does not have a broad, organized base of social support. Inattention to image building will simply weaken his power to lead. In his first term, glaringly absent is a deliberate strategy to guard and promote Tung's public reputation as the paramount leader of the SAR. No carefully crafted plans are visible to boost his prestige among the Hongkongers. Even actions taken to control damage to his image are scanty and ineffective.[29]

Most unfortunately, Tung's political image undergoes a fatal transformation as his popularity falls. Generally speaking, people's perceptions of the leader will change if they find themselves in an uncertain situation or if they develop new expectations for the leader. As observed by Neustadt, "[i]mpressions of the person will form early and last long, but the values men assign to what they see can alter rather quickly. 'Decisiveness' may turn into irascibility; 'cleverness' may come to seem deceitfulness; 'openmindedness' to seem softheadness; 'courage' to seem rashness."[30] Tung's image has suffered from a reversal not only because of changed public expectations of the Chief Executive but also because of the way he conducts himself as the SAR's top leader.

Hongkongers' initial expectations of Tung are pragmatic and minimal. Their mistrust of Beijing does not allow them to greet with enthusiasm a Chief Executive many of them believe handpicked by the central government. Confident that Hong Kong's economy after the handover will remain prosperous, Hongkongers primarily expect Tung to respect the institutions and rules of the game inherited from colonial rule. They also want him to protect all the basic freedoms that Hongkongers have enjoyed for quite some time. As long as Tung can preserve Hong Kong's stability and prosperity, he would be treated as a successful Chief Executive. In short, the status-quo orientation of the majority of Hongkongers, their anxieties about their freedoms and their mistrust of Beijing leave Tung only a caretaker role as head of government. As a matter of fact, in its effort to allay fears in the SAR, Beijing not least also envisages a minimal role for the Chief Executive of the SAR.

Public expectations of the Chief Executive and the SAR government have undergone sea changes since the onset of a series of crises and unexpected events in the SAR not long after the handover. In essence, faced with an uncertain future, Hongkongers demand political leadership from Tung. They in particular demand skills in crisis management, proactive governance, visionary thinking and political capability in fostering social solidarity and conflict resolution. They look to Tung for reassurance, "a feeling that things will be all right, that [he] will take care of his people."[31] In short, they become dependent on the government for remedies and direction. At the same time, in times of distress, people are reluctant to face the harsh realities, ambivalent about change, resistant to painful solutions and look to authority for protection. Instead of exercising leadership from a position of authority in adaptive situations which challenges the people to face problems for which there are no simple, painless solutions — problems that require people to learn new ways,[32] Tung reinforces public dependency on his government by telling Hongkongers that he has the answers. Furthermore, he has largely failed to "teach reality" to the people through rhetoric.[33] Therefore, he cannot prevent unrealistic public expectations of the government from eventually turning into perilous public disappointment. At the end, when Hongkongers discover that the government has failed, they naturally scapegoat Tung not just for the government's failures, but also their own failures. Thus, after all the bold decisions and reform initiatives have failed to restore economic prosperity to Hong Kong, and the people's suffering persists unabated, Tung's political image is damaged.

Tung's political image has also been dented by a series of events that serve to change Hongkongers' perception of Tung as a leader. They include the government's failure to succour the victims of Hong Kong's economic crisis, the all-out support Tung has given to malfeasant officials, and Tung's many rash reform initiatives. A series of governmental actions have spawned suspicions in society that the government does not respect the rule of law and institutional rationality. Even Tung's forte, his honesty, has been questioned after he announced casually to a shocked people that he had eschewed the policy of building 85,000 flats a year — the most important policy commitment of his administration — two years before telling the people about it. The incident brought about by Robert Chung Ting-yiu — a public opinion pollster at the University of Hong Kong — accusing Tung of trying to stop his polling on his popularity has led many people to believe that Tung is disrespectful of academic freedom. In addition, people increasingly see Tung as indecisive and losing touch with public sentiments. Admittedly, Tung is still seen by the people as an extremely hardworking and humble man as well as a man strongly dedicated to Hong Kong, but these characteristics are no longer sufficient to sustain a positive public image.

The persistence of Hong Kong's economic crisis, the proliferation of social and economic problems, the mushrooming of social and political conflicts, the rise in political alienation and public hostility towards the government, Tung's worsening political image, the strained relationship between the executive and the legislature, the overloading of the government with public demands, the increasing fiscal difficulties and the fraying of the social fabric have brought about a situation where effective government is extremely difficult. Instead of an increasingly depoliticized society as envisaged by Tung, the SAR is seriously embroiled in political turmoil. The inability of Tung to handle the rising political conflicts has in turn intensified the unrelenting process of politicization. Without any doubt, Tung's governing strategy has in effect broken down. It has not achieved depoliticization, but has become a potent source of politicization.

Two good indicators of the failure of Tung's governing strategy and his project of depoliticization are the erosion of his social support base and the fracturing of the governing coalition. The two major constituencies of the Tung administration — the grassroots Hongkongers and the business community — are no longer reliable supporters of the government. The lower-class people have been hit hard by rising unemployment, declining standard of living and growing incidence of poverty. Naturally, they are disappointed by Tung's failure to deliver on his promise of a benevolent government true to the Confucian tradition. The SAR government's decision to roll back social welfare in a time of economic hardship and its inability to jump-start the economy have produced widespread social grievances. At the same time, there is a conspicuous rise in class consciousness and class conflict as economic inequality worsens. Hongkongers are more and more intolerant of the privileged status granted to business by the Tung administration. In a 1999 questionnaire survey of mine,[34] a large plurality (46 per cent) of the respondents was of the view that the SAR government primarily took care of the interests of the rich. Only 16 per cent saw the government as placing emphasis on the interests of the ordinary people whilst 25 per cent thought that it took care of the interests of both the rich and the common people. Public discontent with Tung and the SAR government is amply reflected in the escalating conflicts between the authorities and the people, plummeting public trust and confidence in the new regime and surging societal resistance to government action. By the end of Tung's first term, it is inordinately difficult for the government to obtain public consent to new governmental initiatives, not least those that demand pain and sacrifice from the people.

The business community, on the other hand, is also increasingly alienated from the Tung administration. Despite the pro-business character of the Tung regime, businesspeople however tend to see Tung as too accommodative to populist demands. In addition, they are frustrated by Tung's indecisiveness, inconsistent economic policies and disorderly economic interventionism. Small and medium-sized enterprises, which suffer particularly hard from the economic downturn, harbour great grudges against the government for turning its back on their plight. In the eyes of these enterprises, Tung is only solicitous about the interests of big business. Big business however has its own share of grudges against Tung. Many big businesspeople are of the view that Tung gives preferential treatment to a few corporations owned by his business friends who have played an influential role in Beijing's decision to support Tung for the top job of the SAR. All in all, business displeasure with the Tung administration is apparent. Fortunately for Tung, Hong Kong's businesspeople still appreciate the basic business-friendly nature of the SAR government. Their fear of the liberals and mass politics still lead them to see Tung as the defender of their interests. Moreover, as long as Beijing is behind Tung, the businesspeople see no reason to offend the central government by openly opposing Tung. But they would not give wholehearted support to Tung either. Therefore, except for a few stalwart business supporters who have benefited from his rule, Tung cannot bank on solid support from Hong Kong's business community.

Hong Kong's middle class has never been a major constituency of the Tung administration. However, as the middle class is a principal beneficiary of Hong Kong's postwar economic prosperity, before the handover it was basically a complacent and stable social stratum. The post-handover economic crisis has fundamentally changed the conditions of the middle class. For the first time they feel the heat as they are increasingly threatened by unemployment, job insecurity, falling standard of living, diminishing economic opportunities for themselves and their progeny and indebtedness and bankruptcies. The middle class has become an aggrieved and volatile social stratum. Their discontent with the Tung administration has risen dramatically. Moreover, middle-class people strongly believe that their needs are deliberately ignored by the government in its single-minded focus on seeking support from the lower and upper-stratum. They see Hong Kong as gradually losing its level playing field under the new regime. It is quite likely that sooner or later middle-class anger and frustration would turn into middle-class political actions against the government, the lower class and the privileged stratum of Hong Kong.

The pro-Beijing forces, the bulk of which is made up of lower-class people, are also increasingly alienated from the SAR government, though they still have to give it support because of Beijing's support of Tung. Fissures within the pro-Beijing camp however are discernible. They reflect the divisions between business and labour on the one hand, and Tung's supporters and detractors on the other. The strained relationship between the DAB and the Hong Kong Federation of Trade Unions is indicative of an increasingly divided pro-Beijing camp. Also reflective of an increasingly fragmented pro-Beijing camp is the heterogeneity of views of its members on public policies at a time of economic crisis and widespread uncertainties about Hong Kong's economic future. Nevertheless, as public trust in Tung falls, the pro-Beijing forces have to increasingly come forth to his aid especially when controversial or unpopular issues are involved.

Since the pro-Beijing forces want to narrow its gap with the mainstream society and remove its "pariah" label, its support for Tung cannot be unswerving in a time of growing public opposition to the new regime.

In general, as the Tung administration's social base of support weakens, its governing coalition is bound to fragment for the simple reason that more and more elites are unwilling to affiliate with a government suffering from declining popularity. The conflict between the senior civil servants and Tung has come to a head with the increasingly open clash between Tung and his deputy, Anson Chan. The final resolution of their differences comes with Chan's "voluntary" resignation in early 2001,[35] but she leaves behind an insecure civil service which is uncertain of its role in the political system and its relationship with Beijing, the Chief Executive and the "political appointees" inserted by Tung into the government. In any case, the prestige of the civil service has dropped appreciably since the handover. In the 1999 survey, only 30 per cent of the respondents had confidence in the civil servants and 31 per cent trusted them. Senior officials fare even worse as they were trusted by only 23 per cent of the respondents in the 2000 survey. Obviously the unsatisfactory performance of the SAR government is the major reason behind public disillusionment with the civil service. Another important reason most probably is that people increasingly see the SAR officials as reluctant to assume political responsibility for policy failures and unwilling to show solidarity with the people in a time of unprecedented difficulty. In any case, senior civil servants, because of their personalities and the lack of prior training, cannot become political leaders overnight and rise to the political challenge. On the contrary, they are overwhelmed by the political pressure churned up by the economic and political crises. Senior officials have gradually lost their flamboyance and self-confidence and thus cannot serve as a strong pillar of support for the Tung administration. The political passivity of the senior officials leaves the new regime defenseless against public attack and reinforces public disenchantment with the government.

The last couple of years of the first Tung administration also witness the diminution of Tung's political allies, leaving Tung increasingly politically exposed and isolated. The non-official Exco members, supposedly Tung's close allies, are conspicuous by their low political profile and political irrelevance. Not only do they not come forth to Tung's defense when he is under siege, but they also seem to be excluded from major decision-making.[36] As Tung's popularity goes down, it is inevitable that political figures closely associated with him will also suffer.

In addition to its diminishing clout, the governing coalition also suffers from growing disunity. The two political parties — the DAB and the Liberal Party — which used to support the Tung administration in the legislature have become increasingly assertive and unreliable. The behaviour of the Liberal Party — an elitist party representing chiefly business interests but also harbouring hope of becoming a popular conservative party — is increasingly unpredictable. The DAB, on the other hand, continues to provide the Tung administration with stable support as a result of Beijing's demand. It however has to pay a hefty political price in the sense of increasing middle-class disaffection with the party and growing rank-and-file complaint. Both the Liberal Party and the DAB are progressively frustrated by the unequal political exchange with the government and the skimpy political rewards meted out by Tung. The leaders of the two parties even openly aired their displeasure and advocated power sharing with the government.

By the end of Tung's first term, the ranks of Tung's political allies have substantially thinned. Most of those still associated with Tung have found their prestige lowered to such an extent that they no longer are valuable political assets to the new regime. Generally speaking, the members of the Executive Council — theoretically the highest decision-making body of the SAR — should be given the chairs of the most important advisory and statutory bodies in charge of public policies. The purposes are to ensure better coordination of governmental actions and ensure a greater degree of coherence to the governance of the SAR. Yet most of the chairs are instead awarded to Tung's friends who are mostly successful businesspeople. Many of these people however do not visualize a political role for themselves despite the importance of their functions.

The new regime's eroded social base of support and its fragmenting governing coalition have severely weakened its ability to exercise effective governance. The last couple of years of Tung's first term of office are plagued by a long list of political woes. They include a proliferation of public demands on the government, the inability of the government to aggregate these demands into a viable public agenda, public disagreements on practically all major policy issues, chaotic and erratic public policies, policy failures and botched reforms, unremitting defiance of governmental authority, escalating political protests, incessant bickering among political actors, an increasingly antagonistic executive–legislative relationship, intensifying clashes between the political authorities and various interested parties, widespread social conflicts, the rise of political populism and political disaffection, cynicism, mistrust and alienation. The new regime apparently has lost the ability to command the political situation or to set the public agenda. It does not have the political or moral clout to bring about social solidarity or solidarity between itself and the people. Even though it has the power to resist public demands, it has lost the capability to pursue those bold initiatives whose success depends on public consent. Under these circumstances, it is almost impossible for the government to raise tax or other sources of public revenue to meet its fiscal needs other than by dipping into its still substantial reserves. An enfeebled government has left behind a leadership vacuum which however has yet to be filled by other political forces. Hong Kong is fast becoming a society devoid of political leadership. Hongkongers are gripped by a sense of malaise. They and their society are adrift. The SAR is shrouded in an atmosphere of pessimism, fear, discontent and self-doubt. Fairly or not, it is not surprising that Tung is widely scapegoated for the plight of Hong Kong.

Conclusion

The political system laid down by the Basic Law is widely understood as an executive-led system wherein the powers to make public policies are practically speaking controlled exclusively by the Chief Executive and his government. Nevertheless, as in other polities, constitutional designs are not equivalent to political reality. In the case of Hong Kong, the government is checked and balanced by a legislature which is weak in decision-making powers but nonetheless endowed with the real power to veto the initiatives coming from the Chief Executive. The complicated electoral system to a certain extent has made it difficult for the legislators to unite to confront the government with the powerful weapon of the veto, but it however does not guarantee the executive reliable and stable majority support in the legislature. More important, the partially democratic political system of the SAR coexists with widespread political freedoms for the governed. Moreover, the government is also denied the use of coercion as a means to obtain political compliance. The SAR government has practically no power or means to organize and control society. It has extremely limited ability in ideological control and thus has to compete with others for political influence. Therefore, the executive-led government of Hong Kong exists solely in the constitutional sense. It becomes a political reality only after it has obtained political and ideological preeminence in society. Therefore, the executive-led system of Hong Kong is a highly messy and unwieldy system. It can only function well with a politically astute and skillful Chief Executive at the helm. The first order of business for the Chief Executive is by necessity political in nature. He has to develop broad-based political support for his government through careful crafting of a politically representative governing coalition.

For a political newcomer such as Tung Chee-hwa, the need to obtain political allies and build political organizations is imperative even in the best of circumstances. In order to govern effectively, the primordial project that should be undertaken by Tung is a political project. It is no exaggeration to say that the fundamental job of the Chief Executive as the job of political leadership. The immediate goal of such a project is to enhance his ability to govern in a politically divided society. The long-term objective of the project is to bring about a smoother process of democratization in the SAR by preparing and coaxing the conservative forces of Hong Kong for participation in popular politics.

Nevertheless, right from the very beginning Tung defines his priorities in the opposite direction. By focusing on socioeconomic issues he wants to shift public attention away from politics. He fails to realize that to succeed in reorienting public preferences and satisfying the longstanding socioeconomic needs of the Hongkongers requires a viable political framework under his command. Central to this framework is a strong governing coalition and a broad social support base. Only through such a framework can Tung put together a coherent and efficient administration, assemble a pro-government legislative majority, control the public agenda, meet the challenge from other political actors and mobilize societal resources to support his bold initiatives. And that framework has to be put together by meticulous and skillful political work in view of the serious political divisions inherited from the last years of colonial rule. The absence such a political framework has proven to be an obstacle to effective governance even before the attack of the Asian financial turmoil. The sudden intrusion of the economic crisis and the social and political unrest its has produced have evidently exposed the flaws of Tung's governing strategy which evidently leaves no place for political organization. These problems are further revealed in the failures of Tung's ambitious institutional and policy reforms that are undertaken as a result of Tung's genuine attempt to bolster the popularity of his government through performance in the socioeconomic realms. The lack of a political foundation to sustain Tung's governance eventually pushes Hong Kong's politicization to an unprecedented level.

By the end of his first term, Tung seemed to have conducted a self-reflection on the factors behind the increasing ungovernability of the SAR. Based on his accumulated experience as the Chief Executive of the SAR, Tung apparently has a better grasp of the major issues of governance in Hong Kong. He is aware of the need to change his governing strategy and restore politics to its proper place in a new approach to governance. He is more cognizant of the need for building a more coherent and popular governing coalition and broadening his administration's social base of support.

In a speech announcing his decision to seek a second term of office in December 2001, Tung openly admitted the inadequacies in the way he governed Hong Kong in his first term: "Much work has been done since the handover. During this period, I have constantly reflected on how we could have done better, for there are undoubtedly deficiencies. In particular, I believe implementation of some policy initiatives could have been better managed; the interests of different sectors could have been better balanced; the reform initiatives could have been better managed; the interests of different sectors could have been better balanced; the reform initiatives could have been better prioritised; and the response and reaction of the community could have been better assessed. For these deficiencies and other shortcomings, I will ensure that they are properly addressed."[37] He pledged to improve the strategy of governance in the future to ensure that policy planning, development and implementation are in step with the times. More specifically, he promised to place more emphasis on public opinion, political accountability, a broader social base of support for the government and fairness to all interests. Tung's speech was well received by the community, though many people still took his promises with a pinch of salt. As a result, Tung's popularity rating had increased palpably.

In his second term, Tung will change the status of a number of principal officials from career civil servant to political appointee and build a leadership team with a shared vision and camaraderie, and, needless to say, loyalty to Tung. Apparently, this scheme of "Hongkong-style ministers" has received Beijing's blessing, indicating that the central government is apprehensive about the political situation of the SAR.[38] In addition, Tung and his senior officials have become less averse to conducting political "shows" for the sake of improving the popularity of the SAR government. Eventually it is very likely that these "Hongkong-style ministers" will become the core of a more broad-based governing coalition that in turn commands a wider social base of support.

Even if Tung is determined to reshape his governing strategy, he still needs to obtain the blessing of Beijing and the support of the business sector. He has to convince Beijing that some form of power sharing with political actors whose relationship with Beijing is far from cordial is unavoidable. He also needs to get Beijing's blessing in cultivating an autonomous base of social support in Hong Kong. The support of business is also necessary because Tung's new governing strategy would require the SAR government to change its overly favourable policy towards the business community and instead to be fairer to everyone. It would also entail further opening up of the political system to meet the rising public aspiration for political participation. At the present moment, both Beijing and the business community still do not have a compelling sense of political crisis. Both Beijing and the business elites still believe that economic recovery in the future will dissolve many of the SAR government's political difficulties. Some business leaders even advocate the use of strong-arm tactics to deal with Tung's challengers and rolling back Hong Kong's past democratic gains.

It can be anticipated that in his second term Tung would try very hard to develop himself into a political leader and exercise political leadership in a very difficult period in Hong Kong's history. After neglecting politics for five years, apparently Tung is prepared to give prominence of place to the crafting of a governing strategy geared to the effective management of politics.

Notes

1. Tung Chee-hwa, *Building a 21st Century Hong Kong Together* (Hong Kong: 22 October 1996), p. 5.
2. Ibid., p. 5.
3. Ibid., p. 10.
4. Tung Chee-hwa, *A Future of Excellence and Prosperity for All* (Speech by the Chief Executive the Honourable Tung Chee-hwa at the Ceremony to celebrate the Establishment of the Hong Kong Special Administrative Region of the People's Republic of China, 1 July 1997), p. 18.
5. Though the use of coercion to eradicate political opposition is theoretically possible, in practice it is unthinkable. Not only will it destroy public confidence in Hong Kong's future and generate a mass exodus of Hongkongers from the SAR, it will also spell the total failure of Beijing's policy of "one country, two systems." Strong and adverse reactions from Western countries are almost inevitable. Given Hong Kong's dependence on

the goodwill of the advanced countries and the international community for its economic prosperity and its ability to serve as a linkage between China and the rest of the world, the Western governments in effect play the role of the guardian of Hongkongers' human rights and freedoms.

6. Lau Siu-kai, "Government and Political Change in the Hong Kong Special Administrative Region," in James C. Hsiung (ed.), *Hong Kong the Super Paradox: Life After Return to China* (New York: St. Martin's Press, 2000), pp. 35–57.
7. Admittedly, given public mistrust of the Chinese Communists, Tung's close association with Beijing is also a political liability. However, since Beijing has behaved "correctly" since the handover by not tampering with the SAR's affairs, the negative aspects of Tung's Beijing connections has so far been overshadowed by their positive aspects.
8. Lau Siu-kai and Kuan Hsin-chi, *The Ethos of the Hong Kong Chinese* (Hong Kong: Chinese University Press, 1988).
9. The sampling method used in the questionnaire survey is the same as that used in 2000. Fieldwork was conducted mostly from 7 May to 30 June 1997. At the end of the survey, 701 interviews were successfully completed, yielding a response rate of 50 per cent.
10. Lau Siu-kai, "The Rise and Decline of Political Support for the Hong Kong Special Administrative Region," *Government and Opposition*, Vol. 34, No. 3 (Summer 1999), pp. 352–71.
11. Lau Siu-kai, "The Fraying of the Socio-economic Fabric of Hong Kong," *The Pacific Review*, Vol. 10, No. 3 (1997), pp. 426–41.
12. Tung, *A Future of Excellence and Prosperity for All*, p. 13.
13. Ibid., p. 16.
14. Lau Siu-kai, "The Eclipse of Politics in the Hong Kong Special Administrative Region," *Asian Affairs*, Vol. 25, No. 1 (Spring 1998), pp. 38–46; and idem, "The Hong Kong Special Administrative Region Government in the New Political Environment," in Lee Pui-tak (ed.), *Hong Kong Reintegrating with China: Political, Culture and Social Dimensions* (Hong Kong: Hong Kong University Press, 2001), pp. 59–77.
15. Lau, "The Rise and Decline of Political Support."
16. Lau Siu-kai, "The Hong Kong Policy of the People's Republic of China 1949–1997," *Journal of Contemporary China*, Vol. 9, No. 23 (March 2000), pp. 77–93.
17. Lau Siu-kai and Wan Po-san, "Social Conflicts: 1987–1995," in Lau Siu-kai (ed.), *Social Development and Political Change in Hong Kong* (Hong Kong: The Chinese University Press, 2000), pp. 115–70; Lau Siu-kai, "Confidence in the Capitalist Society," in Lau Siu-kai et al. (eds.), *Indicators of Social Development: Hong Kong 1999* (Hong Kong: Hong Kong Institute of Asia-Pacific Studies, The Chinese University of Hong Kong, 2001), pp. 93–114.

18. Lau Siu-kai, "The Making of the Electoral System," in Kuan Hsin-chi, Lau Siu-kai, Louie Kin-sheun and Timothy Ka-ying Wong (eds.), *Power Transfer and Electoral Politics: The First Legislative Election in the Hong Kong Special Administrative Region* (Hong Kong: The Chinese University Press, 1999), pp. 3–35.
19. Lau Siu-kai, "From Elite Unity to Disunity: Political Elite in Post-1997 Hong Kong," in Wang Gungwu and John Wong (eds.), *Hong Kong in China: The Challenges of Transition* (Singapore: Times Academic Press, 1999), pp. 47–74.
20. According to the English version of the Basic Law, the title of the post is "Administrative Secretary." The title "Chief Secretary for Administration" in fact contradicts the Basic Law. The fact that it is still used reflects the political clout of Anson Chan who insists on projecting a more powerful image for the post.
21. Lau Siu-kai, "Decolonization à la Hong Kong: Britain's Search for Governability and Exit with Glory in Hong Kong," *The Journal of Commonwealth & Comparative Politics*, Vol. 35, No. 2 (July 1997), pp. 28–54.
22. Chung Sze-yuen — a veteran politician and former Convenor of Tung's Executive Council — has long been aware of the problems of governance associated with Hong Kong's executive-led political system. He acknowledges the impossibility of effective governance in such a system if the Chief Executive is not supported by a cohesive leadership team and a strong political party even though he possesses enormous constitutional powers. "Hong Kong, in accordance with its Basic Law, is committed to an executive-led government with a democratically elected legislature acting as its checks and balances. But for such a system to work, and work effectively, the Chief Executive has to have his senior officials who are able, share his vision, trust each other, act in solidarity as well as come and go together as a team. The Chief Executive also needs a political party, which nominates him, assists him in the election, stands by him, and helps him shape, explain, advocate, defend and implement policies both inside and out of the Legislative Council. Ideally he should be able to recruit from his party loyal and competent colleagues to serve as his senior officials (ministers). This support was woefully lacking when the Government botched many responsibilities through the SAR's teething period during which no party rallied to the Administration or to the innocent Chief Executive who was taking the blame for his subordinates' bungles." (Chung, *Hong Kong's Journey to Reunification: Memoirs of Sze-yuen Chung* [Hong Kong: The Chinese University Press, 2001], p. 303 and p. 305.) Chung's explanation of Tung's predicament of course is only partial for he fails to mention the part played by Tung's political personality and policy orientations. Nonetheless, Chung recognizes the essentiality of a strong governing coalition and a broad social support base to the Chief Executive in the SAR's executive-led political system.

23. Lau Siu-kai, *Society and Politics in Hong Kong* (Hong Kong: The Chinese University Press, 1982); and idem, "Social Change, Bureaucratic Rule, and Emergent Political Issues in Hong Kong," *World Politics*, Vol. 35, No. 4 (July 1983), pp. 544–62.
24. Lau Siu-kai, "Political Order and Democratisation in Hong Kong: The Separation of Elite and Mass Politics," in Wang Gungwu and Wong Siu-lun (eds.), *Towards a New Millenium: Building on Hong Kong's Strengths* (Hong Kong: Centre of Asian Studies, The University of Hong Kong, 1999), pp. 62–79.
25. Lau Siu-kai, "Hong Kong's Partial Democracy under Stress." (Unpublished manuscript, 2000).
26. Lau Siu-kai, "Decline of Governmental Authority, Political Cynicism and Political Inefficacy in Hong Kong," *Journal of Northeast Asian Studies*, Vol. 11, No. 2 (Summer 1992), pp. 3–20; idem, "Democratization and Decline of Trust in Public Institutions in Hong Kong," *Democratization*, Vol. 3, No. 2 (Summer 1996), pp. 158–80; and idem, "Attitude towards Political and Social Authorities," in Lau Siu-kai et al. (eds.), *Indicators of Social Development: Hong Kong 1999* (Hong Kong: Hong Kong Institute of Asia-Pacific Studies, The Chinese University of Hong Kong, 2001), pp. 55–91.
27. The remaking of the social contract takes different forms in different societies. In Western societies, it means the rollback of the welfare state and cutback in labour protection. In the United States, for example, in the late 1990s, the social compact within the corporations or in the nation was under attack. The old social contract between a company and its employees consists of four elements: "*permanence* in the employer-employee relationship, producing long-term job security and mutual commitment; *entitlement*, not only to a job but also to steady pay advancement and generous benefits, for all employees who performed adequately and didn't violate company policies; *paternalism*, in the form of a shared view of employees as part of a company "family"; and *hierarchy*, such that lines of authority and levels of status were clearly defined within the firm and carried over into the outside world." (Marina v.N. Whitman, *New World, New Rules: The Changing Role of the American Corporation* [Boston: Harvard Business School Press, 1999], p. 45.) This social contract is no longer the bond that ties many corporations and their employees. At the national level, according to Frances Fox Piven and Richard A. Cloward, "the unions are on the ropes, their membership decimated; welfare state programs are being rolled back; and income and wealth inequalities have widened to historic extremes." (*The Breaking of the American Social Compact* [New York: The Free Press, 1997], p. 4.) European countries are desperately trying to hold on to their old social contract, but changes are still on the way. In the words of Richard C. Longworth, "[o]nce the social contract expressed a deal between the wealthy and the poor, between

businesses and their employees. Economic change has always brought both gain and pain. But in the short run, the wealthy were more likely to get the gain, and the poor more likely to feel the pain.... This social contract has been broken. Footloose global corporations have stopped paying the taxes that financed it. The slack has been taken up, at least partly, by higher taxes on workers. In other words, workers are financing their own social contract." "This linkage between higher productivity, more jobs, and higher wages is one of many that have been broken in the age of globalization." (*Global Squeeze: The Coming Crisis for First-World Nations* [Chicago: Contemporary Books, 1998], p. 61 and p. 83.) See also Evelyne Huber and John D. Stephens, *Development and Crisis of the Welfare State: Parties and Policies in Global Markets* (Chicago: University of Chicago Press, 2001) and Edward S. Cohen, *The Politics of Globalization in the United States* (Washington, D.C.: Georgetown University Press, 2001).

In East Asia, according to Stephan Haggard, the financial crisis of 1997–98 demonstrates the weakness of the growth-with-equity model. This model relies on economic growth and informal mechanisms to provide social insurance. It leaves a minimal government role in providing a social safety net. The government is thus badly equipped to respond to large-scale social distress. The limits of the model are brought about by an aging population, decline in opportunities for upward social mobility, rising inequality of income and wealth, the detrimental consequences of globalization and increasing political contentiousness. In East Asia, accordingly, a new social contract requires more governmental commitment to social insurance. Political debate is likely to revolve around five central policy areas: the provision of social insurance, the reform of industrial relations and labour market issues, education, decentralization, and how to address persistent or structural poverty. See his *The Political Economy of the Asian Financial Crisis* (Washington, D.C.: Institute for International Economics, 2000).

28. Lau Siu-kai, "Confidence in Hong Kong's Capitalist Society in the Aftermath of the Asian Financial Turmoil," *Journal of Contemporary China* (forthcoming).
29. Tung did announce the creation of the post of information coordinator in December 1998. Among the duties of the information coordinator are: public relations and media strategy, acting as spokesman for the Chief Executive's Office at press sessions and monitoring and analysing opinion polls. Judging from subsequent developments, the appointment of the information coordinator has not been effective in arresting the decline in Tung's popularity.
30. Richard E. Neustadt, *Presidential Power and the Modern Presidents: The Politics of Leadership from Roosevelt to Reagan* (New York: The Free Press, 1990), p. 80.

31. James D. Barber, *The Presidential Character: Predicting Performance in the White House* (New Jersey: Prentice-Hall, 1992), p. 6.
32. For details about leadership in adaptive situations, see Ronald A. Heifetz, in *Leadership Without Easy Answers* (Cambridge, Mass.: The Belknap Press of Harvard University Press, 1994). According to Heifetz, adaptive situations "tend to demand a more participative mode of operating to shift responsibility to the primary stakeholders. Because the problem lies largely in their attitudes, values, habits, or current relationships, the problem-solving has to take place in their hearts and minds." (p. 121) He outlines five steps in the exercise of "adaptive" leadership: (1) identify the adaptive challenge, (2) keep the level of distress within a tolerable range for doing adaptive work, (3) focus attention on ripening issues and not on stress-reducing distractions, (4) give the work back to people, but at a rate they can stand, and (5) protect voices of leadership without authority (pp. 128–29).
33. "Teaching reality" involves the explanation of contemporary problems and issues but, at its best, must invoke and interpret the perennial ideals of Hongkongers' collective experience as expressed in the past and present, and as guides for the future. It naturally relies on the politician's faculty of discernment in the effort to articulate plausible remedies for emerging policy problems that will win general political support. See Erwin C. Hargrove, *The President as Leader: Appealing to the Better Angels of Our Nature* (Lawrence: University Press of Kansas, 1998), pp. vii–viii and p. 43.
34. The sampling method used in the questionnaire survey is the same as that used in 2000. Fieldwork was conducted mostly from May to July 1999. At the end of the survey, 839 interviews were successfully completed, yielding a response rate of 50 per cent.
35. Chan announced her resignation from the post of Chief Secretary for Administration on 12 January 2001. Major differences between Chan and Tung include the place of functional constituencies elections in Hong Kong's political system, the pace of democratic reform, the dismissal of Tung's trusted aide and confidant, Andrew Lo Cheung-on, and the handling of the Falun Gong. Beijing is increasingly displeased with Chan's "disloyalty" and apprehensive about her political intentions. During a visit to Beijing, Qian Qichen, a vice-premier in charge of Hong Kong affairs, even publicly told Anson Chan Fang On-sang and the civil service to give "better support" to Tung Chee-hwa. Xinhua quoted Mr. Qian as telling Mrs. Chan that he hoped she, "together with the whole civil service, can better support the work of the Chief Executive, to continue to contribute to the prosperity and stability of Hong Kong under the leadership of Mr. Tung Chee-hwa." (*South China Morning Post*, 27 September 2000, p. 1.) The decision to dismiss Chan is apparently made with Beijing's tacit approval.
36. Many Exco members apparently were kept in the dark before a number of

major decisions were announced by Tung or the SAR government: the decision of the government to intervene in the stock market to repel the international speculators in 1998, the announcement by Tung in 2000 that he had scrapped a key housing policy two years ago without informing the public, and the government's decision to stop selling home ownership flats in 2001.

37. Tung Chee-hwa, "Governance in Step with the Times and Strengthening Competitive Advantage," *South China Morning Post*, 14 December 2001, p. 4.

38. Tung broached the idea of politically appointed principal officials in his fourth policy address to the Legislative Council. He promised that he would "examine how, under the leadership of the Chief Executive, the accountability of principal officials for their respective policy portfolios can be enhanced.... We should need to consider devising a compatible system of appointment for these principal officials, setting out their powers and responsibilities and at the same time defining clearly their role in formulating and implementing government policies under the new system." (Tung Chee-hwa, *Serving the Community, Sharing Common Goals* [Hong Kong: Printing Department, 11 October 2000], p. 41.) The scheme of "Hongkong-style ministers" was further elaborated in Tung's last address to the Legislative Council in his first term. His idea is to introduce a new system of appointing principal officials, applicable to the top three Secretaries and most Directors of Bureaux. The Chief Executive would nominate and the Central Government would appoint suitable candidates for all these positions from within or outside the civil service. These officials would be appointed on terms different to those in the civil service. The appointment contract would clearly state their rights and obligations. Their term of office would not exceed that of the Chief Executive who nominated them. These officials would each be responsible for policy areas designated by the Chief Executive and would lead the departments within their particular portfolios. In addition, the principal officials under the new accountability system would be appointed to the Executive Council. As a result, the Executive Council would be changed from an advisory body to the Chief Executive to an executive cabinet. (Tung Chee-hwa, *Building on our Strengths, Investing in our Future* [Hong Kong: Printing Department, 10 October 2001], pp. 35–37.)

2

The Changing Political System: Executive-led Government or "Disabled" Governance?

Anthony B. L. Cheung

Professor, Department of Public and Social Administration
City University of Hong Kong

Introduction

When the Basic Law drafters designed the Hong Kong Special Administrative Region (SAR)'s political system in the late 1980s, their primary concern, reflecting also the preference of the Chinese government which appointed them, was to preserve the pre-existing institutions as far as possible and to maintain the so-called "executive-led" principle which underpinned the then colonial system of governance. This approach was welcomed by both the British government and the Hong Kong civil service bureaucracy which saw it as a vindication of the superiority of the Hong Kong model. Public debate then focused mostly on the method of electing the Chief Executive and the Legislative Council (Legco). Scant attention went to equally pertinent constitutional issues such as the executive–legislative relationship, the role of the civil service and how the newly emerging political groups (later to become full-fledged parties) should be accommodated within the SAR polity.[1]

Since the promulgation of the Basic Law in April 1990, there have been significant changes in Hong Kong's political scene, which render the original constitutional design no longer workable or compatible with the new political realities. First, the prospect of self-rule by Hong Kong residents under the "one country, two systems" framework had triggered political activism and the rise of political parties and elected politicians during the transitional period leading to the reversion of Hong Kong to China's sovereignty on 1 July 1997. Second, with the introduction of partial direct election to the Legco since September 1991, the legislature has become rapidly "politicized," giving rise to a new *modus operandi* in executive–legislative relations as well as the role of top government officials who became further politicized and "ministerialized" under Chris Pattern's governorship from 1992 to 1997.[2]

After the 1997 handover, executive–legislative relations have experienced new tensions and occasional political deadlocks. Political parties and legislators have increasingly acted as an "opposition" towards the new SAR government headed by Chief Executive Tung Chee-hwa. At the same time, intra-executive tensions also emerged within the government between Tung and his close advisers on the one hand and the civil service headed by former Chief Secretary for Administration Anson Chan on the other. In his 2000 Policy Address, Tung announced his intention to introduce a new system of accountability for principal officials. This is read as a prelude to a political "ministerial" system.

This chapter identifies the features and inherent defects and limitations of the SAR's political system, discusses the various resulting problems and crises faced by it, and finally examines those forces that are currently driving change, despite the previous preference for minimum disruption of the inherited colonial institutions. Although Tung has so far refrained from undertaking a major review of the political system — mainly pertaining to the method of election of the Chief Executive and Legco — promised by the Basic Law to take place before 2007 (Annexes I and II of the Basic Law), it is argued that there are increasing signs that the system is undergoing a major, though quiet, overhaul. Such overhaul, interestingly, is mainly motivated by intra-elite political dynamics rather than popular demand per se, least of all demands from the pro-democracy opposition in the SAR. Instead of being the main forces to keep Hong Kong's pre-existing political institutions intact as anticipated by the Basic Law designers, the government elite has turned out to be their chief challengers.

The Institutional Setting — Sticking to the Logic of the Previous Administrative State

The Political Debate on Methods of Election

The story has to begin with the Basic Law debate during the late 1980s. At that time there were both forces in favour of democratic change and those advocating preserving the status quo.[3] The former, usually portrayed loosely as the pro-democracy camp, demanded the direct election on universal franchise of both the Chief Executive (as head of the executive branch) and the Legislative Council. At the same time they wanted the executive to be accountable to the legislature, in line with the relevant provision (Annex 1 clause 50) of the 1984 Sino-British Joint Declaration which set the overall framework for Hong Kong's political future upon the territory's return to China, and akin to a Westminster model of government with which people in Hong Kong were more familiar. The fight for direct elections eventually became the hallmark of the pro-democracy political campaign, so much so that those taking part in the big debate ignored other issues of the political system, such as executive–legislative relationship and the role of the civil service.

For those more conservative forces, chiefly represented by the Group of Business and Professional Members of the Basic Law Consultative Committee, direct election meant the rise of grassroots power, that would result in "free-lunch" welfare policies and an erosion of Hong Kong's capitalist foundation. Apart from keeping the functional constituencies which the British administration introduced in 1985 in the aftermath of the Sino-British Joint Declaration, as part of its decolonization plan to develop "representative government" (Hong Kong Government 1984) but in effect to legitimize the reservation of Legco seats for the major business and professional sectors from which previous appointed members came, the conservatives urged the capping of directly elected seats to one-quarter of the Legco, with the rest of the seats to be returned by an electoral college elected along functional constituency lines. They further advocated the election of the Chief Executive through this electoral college.

As far as the Chinese government was concerned, it favoured a system in which the executive would continue to be predominant — Deng Xiaoping when addressing Basic Law drafters in March 1987 ruled out the adoption of either the British parliamentary system or the US congress system, or of the principle of "separation of powers" for the SAR constitutional design (Deng 1993: 220). Chinese leaders clearly preferred that Hong Kong remains bureaucratically controlled and governed in much the same way as it had been during the more typical British colonial days. Such a preference somehow converged with that of the local civil service bureaucracy which saw 1997 as an opportunity for them to strengthen their hold on government administration. For them, the post-1997 SAR polity should be executive-led by career mandarins politically loyal to the new sovereign.

The final blueprint accepted by the Chinese government and prescribed by the Basic Law promulgated in April 1990 provided for the indirect election of the Chief Executive by an Election Committee (EC), which would also elect initially 10 of the 60 seats of the Legislative Council of the SAR, with 30 seats returned by functional constituencies and 20 by direct election in geographical constituencies. The EC seats would disappear by the third team (to begin in 2004) so that the legislature would be equally split between functional and geographical seats. Although the Basic Law (Annexes I and II, read together with Articles 45 and 68) allows the Chief Executive and the whole of the Legislative Council to be directly elected on universal franchise after 2007,[4] any transition towards that ultimate target has to receive the consent of a sitting Chief Executive and a two-thirds majority of all members of the legislature, and to be reported to the Standing Committee of the National People's Congress of China (Annex I of Basic Law).

The Executive-led Tradition of Government

Apart from these constitutional elements of the political structure, other features of the Hong Kong SAR's system of government remain essentially the same as the colonial one under British rule. Even though the executive is in theory to be accountable to the legislature, the latter is not backed up by a corresponding distribution of powers between the two branches of government.[5] The executive continues to control the introduction of laws and the budget. The power of legislators to introduce bills is restricted — Article 74 of the Basic Law provides that they can only introduce bills "which do not relate to public expenditure or political structure or the operation of the government" and that "[t]he written consent of the Chief Executive shall be required before bills relating to government policies are introduced." Such restrictions are even harsher than those imposed on the colonial legislature, in which legislators could move private member's bills that would not impose any charging effect on public revenue.

Although it is not explicitly spelt out in the Basic Law, both the Drafting Committee and Chinese government officials have alluded to the executive-led principle, which is supposed to have underpinned colonial rule. In the past, as a colony in which political participation was greatly restricted and electoral and party politics were absent,[6] Hong Kong was a kind of "administrative state" (Harris 1978: 53–61) governed by the local bureaucracy subject only to the control of the governor sent by London, who, until 1992 when Chris Patten assumed office, was similarly of a mandarin background either from the colonial or diplomatic service. The executive-led tradition during the era of colonial governance was exemplified in the following terms:

- There were no checks and balances as such among the key institutions of government. Constitutionally speaking, the governor had supreme authority. As in a typical British crown colony set-up, the two major councils — the Executive and Legislative Councils — were there to advise him on the making of important policy decisions and on legislation. Unofficial members of these two councils (known as "UMELCO") operated to supplement the administration, rather than to balance or challenge its power. Officials and non-officials therefore were engaged in a collaborative instead of adversarial relationship.
- The Legislative Council, though having all the wrappings of parliamentary procedure borrowed from the House of Commons in London, did not function as an independent political institution on a par with the administration. Indeed until 1991, the governor doubled as the president of Legco; he continued to appoint members to it until 1995.
- All public policies, public legislation and public finances were at the disposal of the executive authorities.
- While a network of consultative and advisory bodies existed, giving the sense of what some observers described as "government by discussion" (Endacott 1964: 229), its importance laid more with enabling the colonial rulers to "[co-opt] the political forces, often represented by elite groups, into an administrative decision-making body, thus achieving some level of elite integration" (King 1981: 130). Those absorbed into boards and committees came predominantly from the trade, business, finance and industry sectors, with the participation of the professions on steady increase during the 1980s and 1990s, while the labour sector had all along been under-represented (Cheung and Wong 2000). Through the process of "administrative absorption of politics" (King 1981), the colonial bureaucracy as ruler was able not only to direct the affairs of

government, but also to integrate strategic elite interests similar to what mainstream political parties do in competitive politics.

Government by Civil Servants

The Basic Law drafters had no intention to alter the *modus operandi* of the government into the SAR era. The civil service was expected to continue its institutional role and functions including the assumption of ministerial responsibilities. Although not explicitly prescribed, all "principal official" positions in the government below the Chief Executive — including Secretaries — come under the section dealing with "Public servants" in the Basic Law (Chapter IV, Section 6), thus implying that these would be filled essentially by career civil servants as before.

This was in line with the Chinese leaders' preference for bureaucratic governance, as "[w]hat China seeks is a governing agent, and the civil service that had done its job so efficiently and loyally under the British political masters is considered most suitable for the new but similar role under the Chinese sovereign" (Cheung 1997: 732). If not for the disruption by Chris Patten of China's plan for Hong Kong's transition, Beijing would have worked with London in grooming a former or serving top civil servant of Chinese ethnicity as the future Chief Executive by first appointing the person to a new office of vice-governor to understudy the job (ibid.: 732; see also Chung 2001: 176–77).

Marginalization of Party Politics

The original colonial regime had not tolerated political activities, formal (i.e. electoral) or informal. Indeed, from the 1950s until just before the 1997 handover, the law in Hong Kong forbade the discussion of politics in schools. Since the 1970s, local civil society groups began to emerge and become active in putting pressure on the government on various social policies, but these were closely monitored by the government as hostile "pressure groups" (Miners 1991: 191–92 and 194 [note 10]). The wide-spread public debate on the future of Hong Kong in the 1980s, particularly after the signing of the Sino-British Joint Declaration in 1984, saw the burgeoning of political commentary groups and some local politicians who took part in the district board elections introduced in 1981 (Cheung 1991). The Hong Kong "administrative state" had therefore been essentially a party-less state.

The rise of political parties was only a recent phenomenon, coming along with the introduction of direct elections to the Legislative Council in 1991. There are now seven parties or proto-parties represented on the legislature, namely: Democratic Party (DP), Democratic Alliance for the Betterment of Hong Kong (DAB),[7] Liberal Party (LP), Hong Kong Progressive Alliance (HKPA), The Frontier, The Association for Democracy and People's Livelihood (ADPL), and the New Century Forum. Since the withdrawal of official members and appointed members in 1995, the Legislative Council has comprised only of elected members. The government does not form into a "government party"; neither does it possess any votes on the Legislative Council. It now relies largely on the pro-Beijing parties such as DAB and HKPA and the pro-business LP for political support in Legco.

However, this does not mean that parties are able to dominate politics. On the contrary, in an extension of the previous executive-led logic and in line with colonial tradition, it was presumed by the central government in Beijing and the SAR Preparatory Committee it appointed, that the executive should be clear of partisan politics — hence the rules made by the Preparatory Committee for the selection of the first Chief Executive in 1996 explicitly required candidates for the post to have no party affiliation (Article 4 of *The Procedure for Selecting the Candidates for the First Chief Executive of the Hong Kong Special Administrative Region of the People's Republic of China*, passed by the Preparatory Committee on 5 October 1996. See *Ta Kung Pao*, 6 October 1996). The Chief Executive Election Ordinance introduced by the SAR government and passed by the Legislative Council in July 2001 still requires that any person with party affiliation who contests for the Chief Executive election has to give up such affiliation upon election to the office. Tung Chee-hwa's Executive Council is also dominated by personalities not connected to any parties. Out of its ten non-official members, only three are party-affiliated — to the DAB, LP and HKPA respectively. Such sidelining of parties has made it difficult for smoother executive–legislative interactions.

Changes during the Late Transitional Period and Regression Following the Change of Sovereignty

Last-minute Constitutional Reforms

In the final years of the transition, the British administration in Hong Kong made some significant changes to the system of government, beginning with "representative government" during the 1980s by the phased introduction of various elected elements — direct election on universal franchise to newly created district boards and reorganized municipal councils, and indirect and functional constituency elections to Legco. In 1991, direct election to 18 of 60 seats of Legco was introduced. Then, after Chris Patten's arrival as governor in 1992, he made further political reforms and an open government his main platform of governorship. All appointed elements were removed from the three tiers of representative institutions in 1994 and 1995. The overlap or fusion of part of the membership between the Executive and Legislative Councils, dating from the UMELCO model of the appointed membership era, was abolished soon after he assumed office. Increasingly Legco acted as a countervailing force to the administration. Patten set the example of accountability by introducing the Governor's Question Time in Legco, modeled on the Prime Minister's Question Time in the British parliament. Under him, senior civil servants, particularly policy secretaries, had to actively explain government policies and address matters of public concern in open meetings of the Legco panels.

Being a former Conservative Party chairman in Britain, Patten gave due recognition to party politics and treated the pre-handover legislature as a mini-parliament in which major parties were to play a steering role. His relative leniency towards parties caused some departure to take place within the senior civil service from the previous anti-politics culture of the colonial regime. But still, the old scepticism remained deep in the minds of many top officials — for example, then Chief Secretary Anson Chan, who has subsequently gained international applause as the conscience of Hong Kong, slammed elected legislators in 1994 for "using every available public opportunity to criticize and belittle" civil servants (*Eastern Express*, 27 October 1994).

Post-handover Regression

Operating under a conspiracy mindset and in order to respond to Beijing's longstanding suspicions that Patten had "corrupted" Hong Kong's system of government, the new SAR government under Tung Chee-hwa tried hard to roll back Patten's political reforms. Under the excuse that the "through-train" arrangements for the political system could not be honoured because of the Patten disruptions,[8] all previously existing representative institutions were abolished at the time of handover on 1 July 1997. A Provisional Legislative Council was selected by a Selection Committee of the Preparatory Committee to replace the elected legislature of 1995. Similarly, provisional district boards and provisional urban and regional councils were appointed, largely comprising former elected members of such bodies but also including newly appointed members up to about one-third of the total membership.

The First Legislative Council of the SAR was elected in May 1998 — following the relevant provisions of the Basic Law. The Election Committee that elected 10 of the 60 seats was constituted on the basis of sub-sector representatives returned by narrowly based constituencies. As for the district boards and the two municipal councils, a government proposal to reorganize district organizations (Constitutional Affairs Bureau 1998) was passed into legislation in 1999. As a result, the municipal councils were abolished. The district boards were renamed "district councils," but with basically no change to their purely advisory functions on district matters. In addition, appointed members were reintroduced to the district assemblies.

This constitutional change to municipal and district administration was regressive in terms of reducing the room for political participation (municipal councils were regional representative bodies with executive powers on hygiene, leisure and recreation services) and of diluting the influence of elected district councillors by adding appointed elements. It also served to break the previous political ladder whereby parties groomed their activists by first fielding them for district elections, to be "promoted" to the municipal and then finally the legislative level. The loss of municipal seats — totaling a hundred — means that there are now much fewer opportunities for career politicians, further restricting the growth of party politics.

A more subtle change to the political system related to the method of direct election to the Legislative Council. Under British rule, Hong Kong adopted the British "first-past-the-post" voting method to return legislators (double-seat constituencies in 1991 and single-member constituencies in 1995). Such method gave the pro-democracy parties, who enjoyed a relatively higher level of popular support, a sweep of most of the seats contested. After the handover, the new government changed the rules by introducing proportional representation — in effect ensuring that pro-Beijing and politically conservative groups are able to secure a decent number of directly elected seats, hence balancing the force of the pro-democracy camp.

Tung Chee-hwa, in contrast to Patten, hates popular politics and has little enthusiasm for the legislature. He does his minimum round of Question Time but otherwise tries to distance himself from legislators. As the attitude of the boss has changed, government officials down the line gradually revert to the old colonial culture of administrative arrogance. According to a study of the post-1997 Administrative Officer culture, the SAR government has seen "a reinforced paternalism, more 'Confucian' but also 'more colonial again'; less accountability downwards ('just as dedicated to our jobs, but forgetting what they are for'); more caution and conformity upwards" (Vickers 2001: 951). Senior officials do not treat legislators as political equals and increasingly detest their politics of criticism and blame. On the other hand, being left with little room for a constructive policymaking and lawmaking role, legislators have turned more and more towards "oppositionist" rhetoric.

Institutional Inclinations to Depoliticize the System of Government

The attempt of the central government in Beijing to "de-Pattenize" Hong Kong's politics and to revert the territory from a political city to an economic city seems obvious enough, given its preference for political stability and for the business and bureaucratic interests which resist democratization as a threat to the status quo. The Basic Law design, as analyzed in the foregoing paragraphs, reflects such political conservatism. Not only that, contrary to calls for democratic reforms and political accountability, the Basic Law institutional framework has in fact made the government more susceptible to elite pressures for intervention to promote functional interests in some form of corporatist governance (Cheung 2000: 302–3).

During the period of the transition, Beijing had worked hard to lure and incorporate local business, financial, industrial and professional interests into the new "takeover" elites, in addition to the traditional pro-Beijing camp, in order to counter-balance the British colonial establishment — a process described by King (1986) as the "political absorption of economics." The institutionalization of these elite-interests has been facilitated by their appointment into various China-centred bodies — the Basic Law Drafting Committee, Basic Law Consultative Committee, SAR Preparatory Committee and Selection Committee (which selected Tung as Chief Executive) — and after 1997 the Election Committee. Beijing's preference for elite-corporatist representation in the governance of Hong

Kong means that various functional interests have been able to enjoy direct and favourable access to sovereign officials in Beijing and to influence them in their policies towards the SAR, as well as to secure seats on the legislature and various statutory boards and advisory bodies.

It is therefore logical that Tung and his administration would come under greater institutional pressure than previous British governors for "small-circle" political rent-seeking and for maintaining a political system that continues to preserve the interests of the institutionalized elites. While the administrative state tries to depoliticize in terms of party politics and popular democratic elections, it is ironically being further politicized in terms of appointment politics, political patronage and closet decision-making. The civil service bureaucracy also attempts to take advantage of the post-1997 conservative backlash to regain its supremacy under the executive-led paradigm, which was challenged by elected legislators in the final days of British rule. What is unexpected is that in doing so, senior mandarins find themselves increasingly clashing with the Chief Executive and his close advisers (Cheung 1997: 735–37).

Crisis and Problems Encountered after 1997

The intentions of the Chinese government, the Basic Law drafters and those elite forces in favour of preserving the administrative state logic of governance, were fully reflected in the institutional design of the SAR's political system. However, intentions have failed to lead to results as expected. Contrary to achieving a stable and strong administration, Tung Chee-hwa's government has since the early days of the takeover encountered one crisis after another. His popularity rating has suffered an alarming decline. According to the polls conducted by the Hong Kong Policy Research Institute, the confidence index in the Chief Executive has plummeted from the base of 100 in January 1998 to 97.0 in July 1999, and to 83.3 in July 2001 (Hong Kong Policy Research Institute, www.hkpri.org.hk). Despite openly expressing words of support to him over the past year, and urging both business leaders and civil servants to give him fuller backing, central government leaders are obviously getting nervous about Tung's leadership. On 3 September 2001, Premier Zhu Rongji commented that Hong Kong was always "discussing without deciding, and deciding without acting" (*South China Morning Post*, 4 September 2001). The media and most local commentators considered that a remark targeted at Tung for his lackluster performance. The government's crises are many and relate to various aspects of governance, ranging from more mundane problems of efficiency to those of government capacity and overall effectiveness.

Crises of Efficiency, Probity and Efficacy

Problems immediately faced by the new SAR government after the handover have to do with efficiency and effectiveness. Although the Asian financial crisis breaking out in late 1997 was an external stress which impacted on the Hong Kong economy and helped to expose the latter's vulnerability built up through years of economic bubble sustained only by the much inflated property boom, the crisis did test the capability of Tung Chee-hwa as a government leader in terms of how he dealt with its impact, as well as the capacity of the SAR institutions to cope with the economic setback and the social anxieties and unrest which followed. The outcome was that Tung's administration was much criticized for its incompetence in turning the economy around and combating rising unemployment.

The mess created by the government in coping with the outbreak of "bird flu" in December 1997 and the unpleasant chaos during the early days of the opening of the new and hugely expensive international airport at Chek Lap Kok in July 1998 did much damage both to Tung and to the civil service bureaucracy which until then was regarded as almost invincible as a highly efficient and effective administrative force. However, the government did not seem to be aware of the severity of these problems and had failed to take swift steps to regain political legitimacy and strengthen its capacity to face crises. In the case of the new airport chaos, for example, despite the public outcry and three concurrent inquires (a commission of inquiry appointed by the Chief Executive, the Legco special inquiry and the investigation by the Ombudsman), the government had waited until February 1999 before the Chief Secretary for Administration Anson Chan finally apologized for the fiasco in a Legco debate.

Apart from those problems exposed in crisis management, the SAR government has also been greatly troubled and weakened by the various cases of probity and misuse of public resources exposed by a series of audit reports,[9] probity scandals involving senior officials and the public housing "short piling" scandal that led to a vote of no-confidence by Legco in July 2000 in the chairperson of the Housing Authority and the Director of Housing. Eventually the Housing Authority chief resigned prior to the vote, setting the first ever precedent in local administrative history for someone to take responsibility for policy blunder and misadministration. The widening gap between civil service pay and private sector wage rates has served to point further to the lack of competence and value-for-money of the government.[10]

Crisis of Coordination

The crisis of coordination was two-fold. First, there was increasing sign that the SAR government was not as coherent in policy and administration as it should be. At the most senior level, the question of who should lead the government under the so-called "executive-led" system has become an open one, with two competing paradigms — the mandarins favouring a bureaucrat-dominated system and Tung's supporters probably preferring a more presidential style of executive government. Increasing cracks were seen between the Chief Executive and his Executive Council on the one hand and the civil service bureaucracy headed by the Chief Secretary on the other. While top civil servants complained in private that they were not listened to by the amateur Executive Councillors who assisted Tung in making policy, the latter too felt aggrieved that they were not well respected by the bureaucrats and were not given any proper policy role to play. As a result, Executive Councillors seldom came out to defend government policies. Not only that, there were examples of them saying one thing and the administration saying another. The most notorious case involved the Chief Executive himself stating before television camera on 29 June 2000 that the 85,000-unit annual housing target, which he introduced in his first Policy Address in October 1997, was no longer in existence, while his housing policy chief was still defending it a few days before (*South China Morning Post*, 30 June 2000).

Within the administration, there is a deficiency in overall government policy coherence among policy bureaus. The "bird flu" saga and the messy way in which 1.2 million live chickens were slaughtered in December 1997 exposed an alarming lack of communication and coordination among government departments (Agriculture and Fisheries, Urban Services, Regional Services and Health). Institutional rivalries for policy influence have also been observed in the housing and education arenas, not only between the policy bureau and the principal advisory or statutory body (namely the Housing Authority and Education Commission), but also between the policy bureau mandarins and those senior administrative and departmental officers at the departments.

Second, the relationship between the two main branches of government — the legislature and the executive — has simply worsened to the extent that government officials feel that legislators are not being constructive and, irrespective of their party affiliation, have all behaved as if an opposition that only excels in criticizing and ridiculing the administration. On the other hand, the legislators and political parties feel that they are not being respected and that they lack any genuine policy role to play. Under the provisions of the Basic Law, as mentioned before, legislators face more restriction than in the colonial legislature when trying to move private member's bills.

Tung is not good in cultivating goodwill and trust with legislators, even with those in the pro-Beijing camp who should naturally be his political allies. Indeed, the DAB has openly complained that the government only takes its votes in the legislature for granted without heeding to its policy demands or giving its core members some role to perform in government advisory committees and statutory authorities. Unlike his predecessor Chris Patten, Tung dislikes legislative politics and keeps his meetings with legislators and his opportunity to attend Legco for questions to the bare minimum. As a result of such executive–legislative deadlock, policy-making is often made more time-consuming and conflict-ridden. In times of a major crisis, as during the present economic recession, when the need for unified political efforts at crisis management is most pertinent, what is in place on the ground is a system much in disarray, incapable of facilitating and strengthening political consensus.

Crisis of Accountability

Given the continuing distrust of Beijing and the concern about the communist central government's propensity to intervene in local affairs after the 1997 handover, the SAR government has to all the more demonstrate its political accountability and responsiveness to domestic sentiments and demands. Also, it has to be seen as standing firm in guarding the Hong Kong system's integrity and autonomy from the mainland system, even though the population is happy to see expanding economic cooperation and interaction between Hong Kong and the mainland. There have been several cases of perceived failure of political accountability — in the SAR government's active solicitation of the National People's Congress Standing Committee's reinterpretation of the Basic Law provisions in June 1999 so as to overrule the SAR Court of Final Appeal's earlier decision to grant the right of abode in Hong Kong to those children born in the mainland of parents with Hong Kong permanent resident status; in the handling of the Falun Gong followers in Hong Kong, by calling them an evil cult even though they have so far not committed any act either infringing the law or causing harm to others in society; and in the passage of a Chief Executive Election Bill in July 2001 which explicitly empowers the central government to dismiss an elected Chief Executive "under any other circumstances" than those stated in the Basic Law. In the last case, even though the central government can be argued to have such power of dismissal if it already enjoys the power to appoint the Chief Executive, to legislate such power of dismissal in Hong Kong without being coerced to do so by Beijing is seen in many quarters as a unilateral surrender of Hong Kong's local autonomy.

Problems of political accountability are also observed in the implementation of domestic reforms. The new SAR government seems keen to initiate various policy reforms. This on the surface is good and normal for any incoming administration. However, the rhetoric behind reform is often couched in a mindset which suspects the former British administration as laying too many policy mines before its departure or that it had failed to do what it should in the last years of the transition for selfish reasons. Such a mindset has unnecessarily portrayed new reforms as a matter of political correctness, which is seldom subject to more extensive debates in society. In the end, reforms which should have been popular with the public, such as in the civil service and in education, have been pursued very much in a top-down bureaucratic manner. There is insufficient involvement of political actors such as legislators and political parties, who thus feel no sense of ownership in these reforms. The SAR government reformers have also failed in cultivating support and involvement of relevant policy stakeholders. As a result, too many reforms launched on various fronts, but without a clear political mandate and social consensus that could only be obtained through an inclusive style of governance, have only served to alienate too many in society, creating incessant and sometimes unnecessary opposition, and discontent among most stakeholders. The lesson is that effective reform implementation relies as much on good intentions and sound concepts, as on a strong and coordinated government capacity for action premised on bottom-up social support and endorsement.

A System of "Disabled" Governance

Deficiency in State Capacity and Leadership

While facing so many problems, some being un-encountered in the past (such as the economic crisis), and with so many reforms to implement, the government should have taken great care in nurturing an adequate state capacity to carry out its multifarious tasks. Instead, still living within the outdated pre-1997 logic of executive supremacy and top-down administrative coercion, the SAR government has failed to articulate state capacity by bringing together and coordinating the efforts of industry and society in economic adaptation and restructuring and in public policy reforms. As Linda Weiss argues when reviewing the East Asian experience,

> [I]n this new era of international, innovation-driven competition, East Asia's advantage resides in institutions that have enabled and encouraged a coordinated and cooperative approach to economic change …
>
> … East Asian capacity for coordinating change rests not on greater coercive power (i.e. the capacity of A to impose her or his own wishes over B regardless of B's desires); it rests above all on greater infrastructural, or *negotiated*, powers (the capacity of A to *cooperate* with B *from a position of organizational autonomy* and to coordinate responses to achieve outcomes) (Weiss 1998: 80, 81, original emphasis).

If we substitute "Hong Kong" for "East Asia," her arguments still hold true for the post-1997 era.

Ian Scott, a long-time observer of Hong Kong politics, sums up the SAR's crisis well by depicting it as "the disarticulation of Hong Kong's post-handover political system" (Scott 2000), with the following features:

> [T]he relationships between the executive, the legislature and the bureaucracy today are uncoordinated, poorly developed, fractious and sometimes dysfunctional.... [W]ith a system which is neither parliamentary fish nor presidential fowl, the executive, the bureaucracy and the legislature (which is divided within itself) each pursue their own agendas, punctuated by occasional skirmishes on the boundaries of their domains and by subterranean campaigns to extend their jurisdictions. (ibid., p. 29)

As a result, the formal power arrangements as configured in the Basic Law have displayed increasing incompatibility with the actual interplay of powers and sanctions among various political players and institutions —

the political executive, the senior civil service, the legislature, political parties, big business, pressure groups and so on. Instead of having a government with unchallenged executive power, as exemplified in the heydays of the British colonial administration in the name of an executive-led system, the present SAR government is constrained in power in terms of getting things done and policies made.

What is worse is that under the existing arrangements, none of the major institutional actors feels that it is performing. The government laments at being obstructed by the legislative opposition; supporters of the Chief Executive complain about the top bureaucrats not serving their political master well and making their own different interpretations of policies. Senior civil servants, on the other hand, privately complain about the lack of leadership from the Chief Executive and the lack of responsibility by his Executive Councillors in defending and promoting government policies. Legislators and parties feel aggrieved by an administration which largely ignores their demands and proposals, giving rise to a paradox of "having votes but no power," while the latter finds the former unconstructive and blocking the way of government initiatives with their votes. Each of these complaints and misgivings may have some ground, and what the final picture constitutes in real terms is a political system which is essentially "*disabled*"— one where there is no winner and everybody is a loser.

A "No-winner" Political Straitjacket

This brings us to perhaps the most fundamental political problem the government is facing and the most basic defect of the SAR's political system — the lack of incentives and the absence of facilitating factors to bring about and sustain a change in governance logic (or "paradigm") that is essential to reforming the governing institutions and their total configuration in order to cope with problems and crises more effectively and to take the SAR out of the current political stalemate and administrative quagmire.

Instead of facilitating institutional development and renovation, the Basic Law has become a straitjacket on Hong Kong's necessary constitutional evolution. Instead of enabling people to look forward and make due changes to the Hong Kong system so as to cope with new challenges and solve emerging institutional problems, such as the "disabling" or "dis-articulated" features of the existing constitutional design, the Basic Law has underpinned a mindset that prompts looking backwards — to ensure that the SAR does not deviate from the former logic of colonial governance that, to say the least, has already outlived its usefulness and relevance to the post-1997 environment. The executive-led principle, for example, can no longer work as effectively as before because society and its major stakeholders have changed to such an extent that they do not take any administrative fiat as given. Within the executive, there is now a distinction between political executives (i.e. the Chief Executive, being the most prominent of them, and his political appointees to official portfolios and the Executive Council) and the career bureaucrats (who in the colonial past, though subservient to the British governor, were very much at the centre of governmental power as his most trusted allies and co-ruled with him over the "subject" society).

Hong Kong's formal political scene has also seen much transformation since the introduction of popular elections, no matter how limited its impact has been on major representative institutions, and the rise of parties and elected politicians. These new political players, unlike the appointed non-officials of the colonial type, are not willing to succumb to administrative dominance. They have increasingly demanded more say in policy-making and a share of governmental power, which both the Chief Executive and the bureaucracy have refused to grant them so far. Those constitutional reforms introduced by the British administration in the final days of colonial rule, particularly under Patten, have helped unleash new public sentiments keen on transparency and political accountability on the part of the government. The mass media have been driven into a more vigorous role of a political watchdog. The Audit Commission and newly created agencies, such as the Ombudsman, the Privacy Commissioner and the Equal Opportunities Commission, have exerted new pressures and demands on the administration for change. In the words of a local journalist, Tung has inherited "pent-up populism but not the political apparatus to manage it" (Pritchard 2001).

Need for Institutional Reforms

The old system and its underlying logic of executive-led administration is simply unsustainable amidst the new institutional and political realities. However, Tung Chee-hwa is still reluctant to accept that changes have occurred and that Hong Kong needs desperately to revisit its constitutional framework as embedded in a Basic Law which was drawn up over ten years ago in a political, economic and social environment that was vastly different from what is obtained today. For him and probably those officials in charge of Hong Kong affairs in Beijing, the Basic Law is almost sacrosanct and not amendable, for fear of upsetting a difficult political settlement which it represents.

Institutional reforms are needed to help strengthen the legitimacy and accountability of the government in broad terms. These involve:

- Direct election of the Chief Executive and all seats of the Legislative Council on the basis of universal franchise;
- Introduction of a full political "ministerial" system to enable a proper political executive to emerge and the civil service to settle into a meritocratic and politically neutral institution;
- Instituting proper checks and balances between the executive and legislature by relaxing the restrictions over the moving of bills by legislators; and
- Enabling political parties to form an active intermediary role within the political process through participation in both the legislative as well as executive branches of government, so that there will be incentives for parties to engage in more constructive policy-making activities and for people with political calibre to join parties.

Instead of the present political malaise, reforms should facilitate a more engaging kind of executive–legislative, politician–bureaucrat and government–parties interactions, which can then enhance the overall capacity of the state.

Despite the calls from many quarters for an early review of the political system so as to allow ample time for social consensus building, Tung has persistently refused to entertain such calls. In his final policy address in the present term, he intimated that the post-2007 political structure would only be considered after reviewing the operational experience gained from various elections including the 2004 Legislative Council election (Tung 2001: para. 150). In other words, even if a review then comes to any breakthrough in constitutional reforms, such reforms are unlikely to be implemented in time for the 2007 Chief Executive election.

In the meanwhile, Hong Kong's political system will continue to suffer those structural defects that have been highlighted in the above discussion. The more the formal arrangements are held onto, the more imperative it is for some temporary solutions to be found through informal means. However, Tung is not known for his skills of political communication and dialogue with other political actors. On the contrary, he has managed to alienate too many stakeholders in the few years of his term. Those that feel aggrieved by him include not only the pro-democracy opposition and civil society groups, but also many of his previous political supporters in the business, professional and traditional leftist sectors, the middle classes as well as the grassroots. While all the time stressing the executive-led principle, he has failed to realize that a strong government in the modern society can only come about through the exercise of power through society — by securing a broad consensus and alliance among major stakeholders — rather than of power over society.

Move towards Political "Ministerial" Appointments — A Political Revolution by Default

Although Tung Chee-hwa has so far refrained from undertaking a major review of the political system, there are signs that the system is up for some important changes, largely motivated by intra-elite political dynamics instead of popular demand or pressures from the legislature. These changes have mainly to do with the appointment of the principal officials of the government.

The Recruitment of "Outsiders" to Ministerial Portfolios

Until most recently, "principal official" posts (i.e. secretary posts and heads of some important government departments such as Police, Immigration, Customs and Excise) are assumed to be career posts of the public service to be filled by the internal promotion of civil servants, mainly from the Administrative Class. After the handover, the only exception to this "rule" of appointment was Elsie Leung, a former private solicitor and Hong Kong delegate to the National People's Congress, who was appointed as Secretary for Justice to fill the vacancy left behind by the former Attorney General, Jeremy Matthews, who could not serve beyond 30 June 1997 because of his British nationality.[11] All other incumbents of principal official posts were retained in the same portfolios of the new SAR government and they were all civil servants.

In August 1999, when the former Secretary for Health and Welfare Katherine Fok retired from the civil service, her replacement was E. K. Yeoh, the former chief executive of the Hospital Authority. Though Yeoh's appointment could be regarded as an example of bringing in an outsider, it was a borderline case because he used to be a civil servant working as a government medical consultant before he joined the newly created Hospital Authority in 1990. Apart from Elsie Leung who had no previous connection with the civil service before, the recent appointment of private banker and Executive Councillor Antony Leung as Financial Secretary in May 2001 to succeed Donald Tsang, who took over from Anson Chan as Chief Secretary for Administration, is the only other case of an outsider-appointment. However, both Elsie Leung and Antony Leung are appointed on civil service fixed-term contract as Hong Kong's present political system still defines all the top officials, with the exception of the Chief Executive, as civil servants in the same way as in the British colonial administration.

In his October 2000 policy address, when confronting the question of governance, Tung identified executive accountability as a major issue of public concern. He referred to those principal officials who play "an important role in the formulation and implementation of policies pivotal to the effectiveness of the administration" (Tung 2000: para. 109) (namely the 20-odd Secretaries from the Chief Secretary for Administration downwards) and proposed that their appointment might need to be reconsidered in order to enhance their policy accountability. The rationale for change was put as follows:

> ... At present, most of the principal officials' posts are held by pensionable civil servants. The advantages of having civil servants appointed as civil servants are that they focus on objective analysis, establish internal consensus, maintain the continuity of our policies and ensure a high degree of administrative efficiency. The civil service places special emphasis on discipline, follows very strict codes of conduct and disciplinary procedures, and has maintained a very high standard of integrity ... I have noted that the previous Legislative Council and the community have expressed the view that as senior officials are involved in policy making and playing a leading role in public affairs, they should be held accountable for the outcome of their policies. (Tung 2000: para. 110–1).

He proposed to make a distinction between these policy chiefs and the rest of the civil service (ibid.: 112–13), so that the former's accountability for their respective policy portfolios should be enhanced, together with a compatible system of appointment setting out their powers and responsibilities and at the same time defining clearly their role in formulating and implementing government policies under the new system. What these considerations amount to is the introduction of non-civil service terms for those principal officials, who may likely see their appointment turned into a political rather than career one.

In his 2001 policy address he provided further details of his plan:

> Our idea is to introduce a new system of appointing principal officials, applicable to the top three Secretaries (the Chief Secretary for Administration, the Financial Secretary and the Secretary for Justice) and most Directors of Bureaux.... The Chief Executive could nominate suitable candidates for all these positions from within or outside the civil service. These officials would be appointed on terms different to [sic] those in the civil service, including remuneration and conditions of service. The appointment contract would clearly state their rights and obligations. Their term of office would not exceed that of the Chief Executive who nominated them.... [Their] responsibilities would include formulating and explaining policies, defending policies, *canvassing support from the Legislative Council and the public, and be answerable to the Chief Executive for the success or failure of their policies....* (Tung 2001: paras. 133–35. Emphasis ours).

Under such an arrangement, top civil servants will become "permanent secretaries" of bureaus like those in the British system. Although Tung has partly justified his review of executive accountability by referring to the Legco's and the public's demand for greater policy accountability on the part of policy secretaries, as most vividly exemplified by the legislature's vote of no-confidence over the public housing "short piling" scandal, it was mainly the incessant tensions and policy conflicts between his Executive Councillors and supporters and the top civil servants over the post-handover years that have finally driven him (and Beijing) into accepting the prospect of introducing a political "ministerial" system that was thought undesirable at the time when the Basic Law was drafted.

During the few years since the handover, many of Tung's close advisers and those in the pro-Beijing camp have blamed the lack of cooperation from senior civil servants, particularly the obstruction of former Chief Secretary for Administration Anson Chan who was head of the civil service, for the many policy failures that Tung has suffered. The president of the pro-Beijing Federation of Trade Unions, Cheng Yiu-tong, for example, has defended Tung's lacklustre performance by saying that he has brought into the government only three personal staff and been at the mercy of the bureaucracy (*Mingpao Daily*, 7 October 2001).

Towards the "Presidentialization" of the Chief Executive

One of the key advocates of ministerial system is Chung Sze-yuen, a former Senior Member of Executive Council in the 1980s, who was invited by Tung to be the convenor of his Executive Council until June 1999. Chung has on the record proposed party-nomination of the Chief Executive who should enjoy his party coalition's full support in Legco. He also advocated turning principal officials into non-civil service political appointees, with them constituting the Chief Executive's cabinet in the form of a new-style Executive Council, while retaining only a few full-time non-officials as "cabinet minister without portfolio" (Chung 2001: 196–200, 224–31). In that case the Executive Council will become a full-fledged cabinet with both power and responsibility while the civil service will be returned to a politically neutral institution. As such, the meaning of an executive-led government will become clear — a presidential style of government dominated by the Chief Executive and his cabinet.

So far public response to such ideas of "ministerialization" has not been particularly enthusiastic. Many legislators, though keen on enhancing policy accountability, see that political appointment of Secretaries to be effective only if the Legco has a role to play both in their appointment and dismissal — such as through appointment hearings and non-confidence votes as in some Western parliaments. Pro-democracy groups are particularly worried that instead of making policy chiefs more accountable to the legislature, it will render them totally loyal to the Chief Executive personally. In the absence of a democratically elected Chief Executive, they would rather prefer some internal checks on Tung's authority by meritocratic bureaucrats who do not serve merely at his pleasure but are protected in their jobs by the civil service system.

Possible Rise of a New Political Cadre Class and a Governing Coalition

The reaction of senior civil servants is probably mixed, with some quite willing to accept a backseat role of a politically neutral mandarin. Some members of the administrative elite are keen to retain their policy formulation powers. Realizing that the status quo is difficult to sustain, they are resigned to some form of political appointment. Instead of giving up the top portfolios to outsiders, these politically ambitious mandarins are prepared to retire from the civil service and to join Tung's future cabinet as political appointees. In any case, the top layer of the administration will become politicized and separated from the career civil service, hence paving the way for the formation of a new political class as opposed to the administrative elite which has dominated the government for so long.

Pro-Beijing and pro-business parties, and even some non-affiliated legislators, will likely welcome the change, which may open up opportunities of political advancement to their leaders beyond seats on the Legco. If appointed by Tung to his cabinet and to head some policy bureaus, these parties will become more willing to form into a formal governing coalition with him, which, if in majority control of Legco, can help ensure legislative support to government bills and policies. Executive–legislative relations will then change. Hong Kong will move from a bureaucratic polity into a political system more similar to the US presidential form of government which Deng Xiaoping had expressly disapproved of in the 1980s. The political parties on the side of the government will find new room for expansion and the opportunity to achieve governmental experience through cabinet appointments. In the long-run, it is not inconceivable for some form of party-based government to emerge in the SAR. This will well go against the original intention of the Basic Law drafters, who decided not to craft a political system that depends on the operation of party politics.

Concluding Remarks

The whole logic of Hong Kong's political transition into an SAR under China's sovereignty has assumed minimum change and maximum continuity of the previous system of governance under an executive-led administration. As Beijing's handpicked first Chief Executive of the SAR, and always careful to stay close to the central government's line towards Hong Kong, Tung Chee-hwa is the least likely person to democratize the political system or to disrupt the inherently conservative ethos of government. However, partly because of increasing policy failures and political setbacks, triggering incessant crises of governance, and partly due to intra-elites competition for policy influence within the government, Tung is driven to reforming the system of appointing principal officials.

If a political "ministerial system" is indeed fully implemented, this will likely see some drastic changes to the role of the civil service, the role of pro-government parties, and even executive–legislative relations. These changes, when carried to their logical conclusions, may result in a political system much beyond the recognition of the Basic Law drafters — one that may open up a proper political career in government alongside the bureaucratic one, a bigger institutional role for parties, and perhaps a legislature that relates to the Chief Executive more like other parliaments in which there is a government party. The impact of Tung's enhanced executive accountability reform should therefore in no way be underestimated. It may yet prove to be a silent political revolution in disguise, unleashed by default if not by design. But whether or not the reform will enable the government to deal effectively with the various crises enumerated in this chapter without going through more fundamental constitutional changes, has yet to be seen.

Notes

1. In the 1980s, Chinese government officials expressly rejected the notion of any "ministerial system," preferring career civil servants to remain in all the top government posts. Both Li Hou and Lu Ping, then Secretary-General and Deputy Secretary-General of the Hong Kong and Macao Affairs Office of China's State Council, also openly spoke against the formation of political parties in Hong Kong (according to Xu Jiatun, former Director of the New China News Agency Hong Kong Branch and China's de facto representative in Hong Kong — see Xu 1993:189).
2. Under Patten, senior civil servants were required to be more responsive to both Legco and public opinion. The policy secretaries had to act as if full-fledged ministers in other governments. Their ministerial control over executive departments and non-departmental public bodies and public corporations was strengthened by further rounds of public sector reform, which gave them resource allocation powers in addition to policy management responsibilities (Huque, Lee and Cheung 1998: 148–49).
3. There were three main political camps in Hong Kong during the drafting process of the Basic Law — the pro-democracy camp, the business and professional camp, and the "middle" camp. The pro-democracy camp articulated their demands for direct election on universal franchise of both the Chief Executive and Legco in the so-called "Proposal of 190," a constitutional proposal signed by 190 groups and individuals. The business and professional camp referred to 89 members of the Basic Law Consultative Committee coming from the business and professional sectors, who signed the "Proposal of 89," advocating the establishment of a grand electoral college dominated by business and professional members, to elect the Chief Executive and part of the Legco. The "middle camp," comprising mostly Basic Law Consultative Committee members coming from pro-Beijing traditional leftists, tried to steer a middle way between the first two camps.
4. Even so, under Article 45, the nomination of candidates for the Chief Executive post will still be controlled by a Nomination Committee constituted in the same way as the Election Committee.

5. Article 64 of the Basic Law, in dealing with the government's accountability to the legislature, sees such accountability as achieved through the former implementing laws passed by Legco, presenting regular policy addresses, answering questions raised by legislators and obtaining the approval of Legco for taxation and public expenditure.
6. Though there existed bitter rivalries between the Communists and Nationalists (*Kuomintang*) for the political loyalty of Hong Kong Chinese during the 1950s to 1970s, these groups otherwise refrained from taking part in local political institutions such as the Urban Council which contained a limited elected membership returned by a restricted franchise.
7. The formation of DAB in 1992 as a flagship party to unite most pro-Bejing leftist forces signaled a shift of attitude of Beijing towards party politics in Hong Kong. That change came after pro-Beijing candidates, posing as independents in the first-ever direct election to Legco in September 1991, suffered a damaging setback vis-à-vis pro-democracy candidates fielded by party groups including the United Democrats of Hong Kong (UDHK) formed in 1990. The pro-Beijing camp then realized that party politics were no longer avoidable in legislative elections. UDHK subsequently merged with Meeting Point, another pro-democracy group, to form the Democratic Party in October 1994.
8. As a result of Sino-British understanding, and in order to reduce uncertainties to the minimum at the time of the 1997 handover, the Basic Law originally provided for the members of the last colonial legislature elected in 1995 to constitute the first SAR Legislative Council, on condition that the composition of the former was in conformity with the relevant provisions of the Basic Law and that such "transiting" members would pledge allegiance to the SAR and be confirmed by the Preparatory Committee (para. 6 of the *Decision of the National People's Congress on the Method for the Formation of the First Government and the First Legislative Council of the Hong Kong Special Administrative Region*, adopted at the 3rd Session of the 7th National People's Congress, 4 April 1990, Beijing). This is the so-called "through-train" arrangement.
9. Since November 1998, the Director of Audit has published repeated value-for-money audit reports accusing outdoor staff of several departments (such as Housing, Water Supplies, Urban Services and Regional Services) of over-reporting their working hours and being poorly supervised. There reports generated a public uproar about sleazy civil servants, whose better pay and conditions vis-à-vis private sector employees suffering from lay-off and wage cuts following the Asian financial crisis have not helped to find them sympathy.
10. Though starting salaries for new civil servants have been cut in late 1999, civil service pay is otherwise significantly above the corresponding market level

because of the failure to conduct any comprehensive pay level reviews for various grades since 1989–90.

11. The Basic Law (Article 101) requires that all holders of principal official posts must be permanent residents of Hong Kong Chinese nationality.

References

Cheung, A. (1991) "Democracy and the Democratic Movement in Hong Kong: Origin and Prospects," Discussion Paper 10, July, Centre for Public Choice Studies, School of Economic and Social Studies, University of East Anglia, Norwich, UK.

Cheung, A. B. L. (1997). "Rebureaucratization of Politics in Hong Kong: Prospects after 1997," *Asian Survey*, Vol. 36, No. 8 (August), pp. 720–37.

Cheung, A. B. L. (2000). "New Interventionism in the Making: Interpreting State Interventions in Hong Kong after the Change of Sovereignty," *Journal of Contemporary China*, Vol. 9, No. 24 (July), pp. 291–308.

Cheung, A. B. L., and Wong, P. C. W. (2000). *Who Advised the Government? — A Study of Absorption Politics in Hong Kong from the Mid-1970s to 1997*, research report, August, Department of Public and Social Administration, City University of Hong Kong, Hong Kong.

Chung, S. Y. (2001). *Hong Kong's Journey to Reunification — Memoirs of Sze-yuen Chung*, (Hong Kong: The Chinese University Press) [in Chinese].

Constitutional Affair Bureau (1998). *Review of District Organizations*, June (Hong Kong: Printing Department).

Deng, Xiaoping (1993). *Selected Writings of Deng Xiaoping — Volume 3* (Beijing: People's Press) [in Chinese].

Eastern Express (1994). 27 October, Hong Kong.

Endacott, G. B. (1964). *Government and People in Hong Kong, 1841–1962: A Constitutional History* (Hong Kong: Hong Kong University Press).

Harris, P. (1978). *Hong Kong: A Study in Bureaucratic Politics* (Hong Kong: Heinemann Asia).

Hong Kong Government (1984). *White Paper: The Further Development of Representative Government in Hong Kong*, November, Hong Kong: Government Printer.

Hong Kong Policy Research Institute, http://www.hkpri.org.hk.

Huque, A. S., Lee, G. O. M., and Cheung, A. B. L. (1998). *The Civil Service in Hong Kong: Continuity and Change* (Hong Kong: Hong Kong University Press).

King, A. Y. C. (1981). "Administrative Absorption of Politics in Hong Kong: Emphasis on the Grass Roots Level," in A. Y. C. King and R. P. L. Lee (eds), *Social Life and Development in Hong Kong* (Hong Kong: The Chinese University Press), pp. 127–46.

King, A. Y. C. (1986). "The Hong Kong Talks and Hong Kong Politics," *Issues and Studies*, Vol. 22, No. 6 (June), pp. 52–75.

Miners, N. (1991). *The Government and Politics of Hong Kong*, 5th ed. (Hong Kong: Oxford University Press).

Mingpao Daily (2001). 7 October, Hong Kong [in Chinese].

National People's Congress, China (1990). *Decision of the National People's Congress on the Method for the Formation of the First Government and the First Legislative Council of the Hong Kong Special Administrative Region,* 4 April, Beijing.

Pritchard, S. (2001) "Avoid disastrous recipes for property," *South China Morning Post*, 10 October, p. 14, Hong Kong.

Scott, I. (2000). "The Disarticulation of Hong Kong's Post-Handover Political System," *The China Journal*, No. 43 (January), pp. 29–53.

South China Morning Post (2000). 30 June, Hong Kong.

South China Morning Post (2001). 4 September, Hong Kong.

Ta Kung Pao (1996). 6 October, Hong Kong [in Chinese].

The Basic Law of the Hong Kong Special Administrative Region of The People's Republic of China (1990), adopted by the Seventh National People's Congress of the People's Republic of China at its Third Session, 4 April, reproduced by the Government Printer, Hong Kong, June 1996.

The Sino-British Joint Declaration on the Question of Hong Kong (1984) [Joint Declaration of the Government of the United Kingdom of Great Britain and Northern Ireland and the Government of the People's Republic of China on the Question of Hong Kong], September (Hong Kong: Government Printer).

Tung, C. H. (2000). *Serving the Community, Sharing Common Goals*, Address by the Chief Executive at the Legislative Council meeting, 11 October (Hong Kong: Printing Department).

Tung, C. H. (2001). *Building on Our Strengths, Investing in Our Future*, Address by the Chief Executive at the Legislative Council meeting, 10 October (Hong Kong: Printing Department).

Vickers, S. (2001.) " 'More Colonial Again?' — The Post-1997 Culture of Hong Kong's Governing Elite," *International Journal of Public Administration*, Vol. 24, No. 9, pp. 951–76.

Weiss, L. (1998). *The Myth of the Powerless State: Governing the Economy in a Global Era* (Cambridge: Polity Press).

Xu, Jiatun (1993). *Xu Jiatun's Hong Kong Memoirs* (Hong Kong: United Daily Press) [in Chinese].

3

The Constitution and the Rule of Law

Albert H. Y. Chen
Professor, Department of Law
The University of Hong Kong

Introduction

When Hong Kong was a British colony, the Rule of Law, which was transplanted from Britain to Hong Kong in the course of colonization, was considered to be one of the pillars of Hong Kong's economic and social success. When Hong Kong's fate of re-integration into China was decided, one of the primary concerns was about the possible deterioration of the Rule of Law after the handover. To alleviate this concern, the Sino-British Joint Declaration made numerous provisions regarding the preservation of the existing legal system in Hong Kong after Hong Kong became a Special Administrative Region (SAR) of the People's Republic of China. These provisions were reproduced in the Basic Law of the Hong Kong SAR, which serves as Hong Kong's constitutional foundation after its transition to Chinese rule. In addition to guaranteeing the maintenance of the existing institutions of the Rule of Law, the Basic Law also confers on Hong Kong a "high degree of autonomy" consonant with the concept of "one country, two systems."[1]

More than four years have now elapsed since the handover. To what extent has the pre-1997 legal system of Hong Kong been preserved? To what extent does the Rule of Law still thrive in Hong Kong? Have the constitutional principles regarding Hong Kong's autonomy enshrined in the Basic Law been upheld in practice? How do we interpret the constitutional controversies that occurred in the last few years in which a conflict between the operating principles of the two systems was manifested? It is the purpose of this chapter to answer these questions.

This chapter will be divided into two main sections, apart from this introduction and the conclusion. The first section discusses the legal aspects of "one country, two systems" as provided for in the Basic Law. It also reflects on the nature of the constitutional arrangement and its strengths and weaknesses. The second section reviews briefly the major constitutional controversies that Hong Kong has experienced in the last few years. The concluding section provides an overall assessment of how well Hong Kong has fared in terms of the Rule of Law after the handover.

Reflections on the Constitutional and Legal Aspects of "One Country, Two Systems"

Federalism is the most well-known constitutional mechanism for enabling a sub-unit of a sovereign nation-state to enjoy autonomy over a wide range of local affairs.[2] However, the People's Republic of China has always insisted that it is a unitary rather than a federal state, and the federal concept was adopted by neither the Sino-British Joint Declaration nor the Basic Law.[3] What the Basic Law does is to delegate power, which originally vests centrally in the National People's Congress, to the government of the Hong Kong SAR.[4] The word "government" here is used in a broad sense to include the executive, legislative as well as judicial branches of government. Each of these branches of the SAR government has been conferred power of a specified scope by the Basic Law.

The Basic Law's delegation of power to the SAR is a generous one as befits the grandeur of the phrase "one country, two systems." From the legal point of view, "two systems" has at least two meanings. First, the Hong Kong system is an autonomous system whose operation should not be tempered with by the central government. Secondly, the Hong Kong system is one very different from the system on the Chinese mainland, and the principles and norms of the mainland system should not be forced upon Hong Kong.

Let us consider some examples of each of these two meanings of "two systems." An example of the first meaning, autonomy, relates to legislative affairs. The SAR is "vested with legislative power,"[5] and laws enacted by the Hong Kong Legislative Council cannot be invalidated by the National People's Congress Standing Committee (NPCSC) except where the law is considered by the NPCSC to be inconsistent with Basic Law provisions "regarding affairs within the responsibility of the Central Authorities or regarding the relationship between the Central Authorities and the Region."[6] As regards judicial matters, the SAR is "vested with independent judicial power, including that of final adjudication"; its courts basically "have jurisdiction over all cases in the Region."[7] This is judicial autonomy, although it is subject to the Court of Final Appeal's obligation to refer certain matters to the NPCSC, and to the NPCSC's overriding power to interpret the Basic Law, as we can see later.

The second meaning of "two systems" relates to the huge differences that are allowed to exist between the systems in force in Hong Kong and on the mainland respectively. As far as the legal system is concerned, this meaning of "two systems" is manifested in those provisions of the Basic Law which serve to preserve the existing institutions and principles of Hong Kong's legal system even though they are very different from those practised on the mainland. For example, the common law and other laws previously in force in Hong Kong shall continue to be valid.[8] Mainland laws are not to be in force in Hong Kong except for a narrow category of mainland laws listed in Annex III to the Basic Law.[9] And the principles and institutions for the protection of human rights and fundamental freedoms, a matter dear to the hearts of the people of Hong Kong and concerned members of the international community, are enshrined in the Basic Law.[10]

The two meanings of "two systems" discussed above are complementary to one another. In a sense, the second meaning is more fundamental, because it provides that the point for departure in Hong Kong's post-1997 journey is Hong Kong's existing system at that time, and that there is no need to change the system even though it is so different from that on the mainland. The first meaning of "two systems," that of autonomy, then comes into play, to ensure that as Hong Kong moves along its post-1997 journey, it can decide for itself how to develop its existing system, and how that system needs to be adapted to changing circumstances.

The main strength of the constitutional arrangement for "one country, two systems" established by the Basic Law lies in the very high degree of autonomy that the SAR is able to enjoy. The scope of the Hong Kong SAR's autonomous powers far exceeds that enjoyed by member states of the USA or Australia, or the provinces of Canada. For example, the mainland's criminal and civil laws are not applicable to Hong Kong; Hong Kong does not need to pay any tax to the mainland government; Hong

Kong has its own currency, administers its own system of entry and exit controls on persons, is a separate customs territory, and can sign international agreements relating to non-sovereign business. These powers and capacities are unimaginable for the constituent units of federal states like the USA, Canada and Australia.

The "one country, two systems" model of autonomy enshrined in the Basic Law is, however, not a perfect arrangement for autonomy. Apart from the limited degree of democratization in the SAR political system, which is a political rather than a legal matter and therefore largely outside the scope of this chapter, the major legal limitation or weakness of the Hong Kong model of autonomy lies in the lack of judicial safeguards for Hong Kong's autonomy in situations where disputes between the central government and the SAR regarding the respective scope of their jurisdiction arise. In federal countries such as the USA, Canada and Australia, where the Rule of Law is already highly institutionalized, the federal supreme court can be trusted to resolve such disputes in a fair and impartial manner in accordance with the text and the spirit of the federal constitution which stipulates the division of power between the federal government and the member states. The problem in the case of "one country, two systems" for mainland China and Hong Kong is that the mainland system has not yet evolved a judicial institution of similar stature as the US Supreme Court, the Canadian Supreme Court or the High Court of Australia. Under the Basic Law and the Constitution of the People's Republic of China, the constitutional function of safeguarding "one country, two systems" in case of dispute that is equivalent to the function performed by these supreme courts in federal systems is vested, not in judges, but in the NPCSC as advised by a Basic Law Committee. Even at the time of the drafting of the Basic Law, the legal community in Hong Kong understood that this arrangement did not portend well for the future. As we now know, the NPCSC's role within the constitutional arrangement of "one country, two systems" ultimately proved to be the major source of controversy in Hong Kong's legal history as an SAR.

A Brief Constitutional History of the SAR

We now begin our review of the most important events that are of constitutional significance in Hong Kong's legal history as an SAR. Due to space limitations, the events or cases discussed will be highly selective. Those selected are what I believe to be of the greatest significance from the point of view of the constitutional arrangement under the Basic Law and the Rule of Law in Hong Kong.

The first major constitutional case litigated after the handover in July 1997 was *HKSAR v Ma Wai Kwan*,[11] decided by the Court of Appeal on 29 July 1997. This was a criminal case, and the main issue was whether the common law had survived the handover. Since one of the arguments for the common law's survival was that the Provisional Legislative Council (PLC) had enacted an ordinance[12] which provided for the common law's survival, the question arose as to whether the PLC had been lawfully established as a legislature having law-making authority under the Basic Law. Since the Basic Law was enacted in 1990 on the assumption that there would be a "through train" so that the pre-1997 legislature could become the first legislature of the SAR, there was no provision for the establishment of the PLC, which was a contingency measure to deal with the "derailing" of the through train as a result of Governor Patten's political reforms.

The Court of Appeal affirmed the legality of the PLC, pointing out that its establishment was consistent with the text and the purpose of the Basic Law. But another reason given by the court in support of its ruling proved to be controversial, and paved the way for the subsequent constitutional crisis of February 1999. What the court said was that as a local or regional court, it had no power to review or overturn an act of a sovereign authority such as the NPC or the NPCSC. The exact relationship between the authority of the Hong Kong courts and that of the NPC and NPCSC has proved to be the most controversial and difficult issue in the legal history of the SAR, as will be demonstrated below.

In 1998, the cases arousing the greatest controversies were those of Aw Sian (Sally Aw), Cheung Tze-keung and Li Yuhui. Aw Sian, chairman of the Sing Tao newspaper group which published the *Hong Kong Standard*, is a prominent member of the Hong Kong community with close ties to the Chief Executive and Beijing. In March 1998, several members of *Hong Kong Standard*'s senior management were prosecuted for conspiracy with Ms Aw to defraud advertisers in the newspaper. There was immediate public outcry as to why Ms Aw herself was not prosecuted. Ms Elsie Leung, the Secretary for Justice, refused to comment on the details of the case on the ground that the trial was pending. The trial was concluded in January 1999, when the three defendants were convicted. Public pressure mounted for Ms Leung to explain the non-prosecution of Ms Aw. The explanation she gave at the Legislative Council on 4 February 1999 proved to be counter-productive. One of the reasons she mentioned for the non-prosecution was the public interest consideration that if Ms Aw were prosecuted, the Sing Tao group of newspapers, which was having financial difficulties at the time, would collapse, and this would not be in the community's interest. To many people, this was not a legitimate consideration. The public criticism was so severe that a motion of no confidence in the Secretary for Justice was introduced in the Legislative Council, although it was defeated when put to the vote. The Aw Sian incident did much damage to public and international perception of the Rule of Law in Hong Kong.

Cheung Tze-keung, nicknamed the "Big Spender," was the head of a criminal syndicate in Hong Kong the operations of which extended to Macau and the mainland and the members of which included both Hong Kong and mainland residents. His crimes included the kidnap in Hong Kong of a Hong Kong tycoon and the son of another (thus obtaining ransom money in the order of hundreds of millions of dollars), as well as smuggling and illegal trading of huge quantities of firearms and explosives from the mainland. When he was arrested on the mainland, there was public debate in Hong Kong as to whether he should be returned to Hong Kong for trial. The case raised the issue of whether the mainland courts have the criminal jurisdiction to try Hong Kong permanent residents accused of having committed a crime in Hong Kong. Cheung was ultimately tried in Guangzhou in October 1998, found guilty and executed in December 1998. The mainland court asserted jurisdiction on the ground that he had committed crimes on the mainland as well as in Hong Kong, and some of the crimes had cross-border elements. The question remains unresolved as to whether the mainland court would have jurisdiction if a Hong Kong resident arrested on the mainland is suspected only of having committed an offence in Hong Kong, and the offence has no cross-border element.

The case of Li Yuhui is in a sense the converse of Cheung's case. Li Yuhui was a mainlander (from Shantou), but he murdered five Hong Kong residents at the Telford Garden estate in Hong Kong. When he was arrested in Shantou, the question arose as to whether he should be sent back to Hong Kong for trial. The general principle governing criminal jurisdiction is that a person who is suspected of having committed a crime in a particular country or jurisdiction should normally be tried in that country or jurisdiction, and if he has escaped to another country and is arrested there, he should be extradited to the country or jurisdiction where he is suspected of having committed the crime. Another factor in this case is that the Chinese Criminal Code does not apparently apply to Hong Kong,[13] and this would make it difficult for a mainland court to apply the Chinese Criminal Code to Li's acts in Hong Kong. However, these legal niceties seemed to have been passed over by the Shantou court when Li was tried and sentenced to death in March 1999. In any event, the court could still justify its assertion of jurisdiction on the basis that the preparatory acts (e.g. the purchase of the poison) for the murder in this case were perpetrated on the mainland.

The cases of Cheung and Li underscore the need for the Hong Kong and mainland sides to delineate the respective scope of the criminal jurisdiction of their courts, and to enter into a rendition agreement whereby fugitive offenders who have committed crimes on one side and absconded to the other side can be returned for trial. The negotiation of such a rendition agreement has however proved to be difficult. It is believed that the major difficulties surround the question of the extent to which the safeguards normally applicable to extradition in the international context (such as the rule of double criminality (requiring the crime for which extradition is sought to be a crime under the laws of both the requesting and requested states), the rule against extradition for political offences, and the rule against the application of the death penalty) should be applicable to rendition as between the "two systems" of "one country." There is also the concern that Hong Kong residents extradited to the mainland might not receive a fair trial, given the perception that the Rule of Law is not yet as highly developed on the mainland as in Hong Kong.

We now come to 1999, the most eventful year of the legal history of the Hong Kong SAR so far. On 29 January 1999, the Court of Final Appeal (CFA) rendered its judgments in the cases of *Ng Ka Ling v Director of Immigration*[14] and *Chan Kam Nga v Director of Immigration.*[15] In these decisions, the CFA attempted to assert its supreme judicial authority as the constitutional guardian of the Basic Law, of Hong Kong's autonomy and of the rights of the people of Hong Kong. Unfortunately, the decisions backfired and ultimately led to Beijing's intervention.

Both *Ng Ka Ling* and *Chan Kam Nga* were appeals to the final appellate court from lower courts by seekers of the right of abode in Hong Kong. The applicants were children of Hong Kong permanent residents, but they were born on the mainland. Some were born before their parents became Hong Kong permanent residents; some were born after their parents became such residents (e.g. the children were born on the mainland to women whose husbands were Hong Kong permanent residents living in Hong Kong); some were illegitimate children. The children claimed the right of abode in Hong Kong under the Basic Law,[16] and argued that the immigration legislation (passed by the Provisional Legislative Council)[17] that restricted such a right was invalid because it contravened the Basic Law. The task of the CFA, therefore, was to give a final and authoritative interpretation of the relevant Basic Law provisions.

In *Ng Ka Ling*, the CFA, like the Court of Appeal below it in *Ma Wai Kwan*, had to deal with the question of the legality of the PLC, because it was argued that the immigration legislation passed by the PLC was invalid as the PLC itself was not lawfully established. While the CFA reached the same conclusion as the Court of Appeal regarding the legality of the PLC, it attempted in its judgment to overrule the Court of Appeal's ruling that Hong Kong courts had no jurisdiction to overturn acts of the NPC or NPCSC. The CFA stated in *Ng Ka Ling* that the Hong Kong courts had the constitutional jurisdiction, not only to review whether ordinances passed by the local legislature were consistent with the Basic Law, but also to review whether the legislative acts of the NPC or NPCSC were consistent with the Basic Law, and to declare them as invalid if found to be inconsistent.

This sweeping statement regarding the authority of the Hong Kong courts with regard to the NPC and NPCSC proved to be totally unacceptable to Beijing.[18] From the point of view of Chinese constitutional law, the NPC and the NPCSC are the supreme organs of state power, and if whether they can assert their authority in relation to Hong Kong matters is ultimately a question to be determined by a Hong Kong court, then Hong Kong will be close to an independent entity. This view is not unreasonable, when we take into account the fact that in federal systems, it is the federal supreme court, and not the provincial or state court, that has the ultimate authority to adjudicate on whether a federal legislative act affecting the province or state is valid or is an unconstitutional infringement of the latter's constitutionally guaranteed autonomy.

After considering Beijing's views, the Hong Kong government on 26 February 1999 took the unusual and unprecedented step of applying to the CFA for a "clarification" of the relevant part of its judgment in *Ng Ka Ling*. The CFA acceded to this request and clarified that the judgment in *Ng Ka Ling* was not intended to question the authority of the NPC and the NPCSC "to do any act which is in accordance with the provisions of the Basic Law and the procedure therein," and that any interpretation of the Basic Law made by the NPCSC under Article 158 of the Basic Law would be binding on the Hong Kong courts.[19]

The significance of the "clarification" is that the Hong Kong courts' power to interpret the Basic Law and to determine whether an act of any authority is consistent with the Basic Law, albeit a real and important power, is nevertheless not an absolute one. It is not absolute because it is subject to the overriding power of the NPCSC. In the absence of an interpretation by the NPCSC, the Hong Kong courts have full authority to interpret the Basic Law on their own and to decide cases in accordance with their own interpretation. But once the NPCSC has spoken, the Hong Kong courts must comply. But when can the NPCSC speak? Can it only speak when the CFA asks for its interpretation in accordance with Article 158(3) of the Basic Law?[20] Or can it speak even when not asked by the CFA? This question was soon to be answered.

The impact of the CFA's decisions in *Ng Ka Ling* and *Chan Kam Nga* at the practical rather than the theoretical level concerned the migrant population pressure generated by the decisions. The immigration legislation that the decisions invalidated (on the ground that it was inconsistent with the Basic Law) had attempted to restrict the migration of mainland-born children of Hong Kong permanent residents by requiring them to apply for the exit permit issued by the mainland exit control authority (for which they would have to queue up and wait for years). The CFA in *Ng Ka Ling* held (on the basis of its interpretation of Article 22(4) of the Basic Law) that the Hong Kong immigration authorities could not legitimately require the migrant children to hold such an exit permit before they were allowed entry to Hong Kong. The immigration legislation had also defined the category of children eligible for the right of abode in such a way as to exclude children born on the mainland at a time when neither of their parents had acquired Hong Kong permanent resident status. The CFA in *Chan Kam Nga* held that this definition was inconsistent with Article 24(2)(3) of the Basic Law, which, according to the CFA's interpretation, conferred the right of abode on mainland-born children of Hong Kong permanent residents irrespective of whether the parents had already acquired permanent resident status at the time of the children's birth.

After the CFA decided these cases at the end of January 1999, the Hong Kong government conducted sample surveys and statistical studies for the purpose of estimating the number of people eligible to migrate to Hong Kong as a result of the decisions. It announced on 28 April 1999 that 1.67 million people would be so eligible in the coming decade if the CFA's decisions were to be implemented. It was then pointed out that the CFA's interpretation of the relevant provisions in the Basic Law was probably inconsistent with the original intent behind the Basic Law, of which the NPCSC would be the most appropriate interpreter. Under the Chinese Constitution[21] and Article 158 of the Basic Law, the NPCSC has the power to interpret the Basic Law. On 21 May 1999, the SAR government requested the State Council to refer the relevant Basic Law provisions to the NPCSC for interpretation. The interpretation was issued on 26 June 1999.[22] According to the NPCSC's interpretation of Articles 22(4) and 24(2)(3) of the Basic Law, the provisions of the immigration legislation mentioned above which the CFA had determined to be inconsistent with the Basic Law were not in fact so inconsistent.

The reference to the NPCSC for interpretation was extremely controversial because there is nothing in the Basic Law which suggests that the executive branch of the SAR government can request the NPCSC to interpret the Basic Law. Furthermore, the reference to the NPCSC was criticized as a self-inflicted blow to Hong Kong's autonomy, judicial authority, Rule of Law and system for protecting individuals' rights. The SAR government probably recognized that these were indeed the negative implications of the reference to Beijing, but decided nevertheless that this price was worth paying as the alternative scenario of absorbing the huge number of migrants from the mainland was even less palatable.

The government encountered vehement opposition to its proposal to refer the matter to the NPCSC from the legal community of Hong Kong, particularly the Bar Association and most leaders of opinion in the legal community, as well as from a significant section of the political elite in Hong Kong, particularly the Democratic Party and its allies in the legislature, which comprised most of the directly elected members of the Legislative Council. The public had mixed feelings about the reference: on the one hand, people recognized that the reference would strike a severe blow to the courts of Hong Kong, its autonomy and its system for the protection of human rights; on the other hand, there was widespread concern about the negative economic and social impact of a massive influx of migrants from the mainland. The government was ultimately able to secure a majority vote in the Legislative Council in support of the proposed reference to the NPCSC, although the majority of the directly elected legislators opposed the reference.

In December 1999, the CFA had the opportunity to pronounce upon the effect of the NPCSC's interpretation on the Hong Kong legal system in the case of *Lau Kong Yung*.[23] The CFA held that the interpretation made by the NPCSC in June was binding on the Hong Kong courts. It pointed out that the NPCSC's power to interpret the Basic Law under Article 158(1) of the Basic Law is a "free-standing" one,[24] in the sense that it can be exercised at any time, even in the absence of a reference by the CFA in accordance with Article 158(3) of the Basic Law. Any interpretation issued by the NPCSC, whether on its own initiative or upon a reference by the CFA, is binding on the Hong Kong courts.

The acknowledgement by the CFA in *Lau Kong Yung* of the binding authority of the NPCSC's interpretations of the Basic Law, even where the interpretation is not made pursuant to a reference by the CFA to the NPCSC under Article 158(3) of the Basic Law, further clarifies the position it adopted in the "clarification" of February 1999. The full implications of Article 158 of the Basic Law now become apparent. What it means is that although the CFA has the power of final adjudication of cases, and the NPCSC has no power to try and decide any case litigated in the Hong Kong courts, the NPCSC, at least in theory, may issue an interpretation of the Basic Law at any time, and thereupon the Hong Kong courts must follow such interpretation when they decide cases. If the NPCSC were to exercise this overriding power frequently, the autonomy and authority of the Hong Kong courts in deciding cases on their own (at least in cases that touch upon an interpretation of the Basic Law) would be severely hampered. Such an erosion of the common law system in Hong Kong would undermine local and international confidence in the Rule of Law in Hong Kong.

However, I do not think that such a pessimistic inference from Article 158 and *Lau Kong Yung* is justified if we take into account not only the formal legal position, but the reality of the situation. It is well established that in constitutional law, the reality is determined not only by formal legal provisions, but also by the constitutional conventions that evolve gradually to supplement the formal provisions. Constitutional conventions are built upon practices, habits, customs and legitimate expectations. They deal with matters that are not expressly covered by the written text of the constitution and the laws. They are, as it were, the flesh of the body of constitutional law, in which the written text constitutes the bones.

On the basis of the actual practice of the parties concerned in the last five years, it seems that the following constitutional conventions are evolving regarding the NPCSC's exercise of its power to interpret the Basic Law. First, it will not interpret the Basic Law on its own initiative, even if a major case is being litigated in the Hong Kong courts which raises important questions of the interpretation of the Basic Law. Secondly, the NPCSC will, if the Hong Kong SAR government so requests, interpret the Basic Law. (It will also do so when requested by the CFA, but this is governed by the express provision of Article 158(3) rather than by a constitutional convention.) Thirdly, the SAR government will only make such a request in the most exceptional circumstances, and then only with the support of the Legislative Council and a significant section of public opinion. In deciding whether to make the request, the SAR government will take into account the cost of doing so, particularly the damage to the Rule of Law it necessarily entails.

We now turn to another major constitutional case decided by the CFA in December 1999. This is the case of *HKSAR v Ng Kung Siu*.[25] The issue in this case was whether the criminalization of acts of desecration of the Chinese national flag and the SAR regional flag in Hong Kong's laws[26] was an unconstitutional restriction of the freedom of expression guaranteed by the Basic Law, the Hong Kong Bill of Rights and the International Covenant on Civil and Political Rights. The case was a difficult one, not only because the court had to engage in a balancing exercise — weighing the individual's freedom of expression against the public and national interest in the protection of the national flag as a symbol of national unity and of Hong Kong's reunification with China — but also because the law on the criminalization of the desecration of the national flag was enacted by the Hong Kong legislature for the purpose of implementing a national law which the NPCSC had decided to apply to Hong Kong.[27] If the CFA were to uphold the decision of the Court of Appeal below it (which declared the flag desecration laws to be unconstitutional), this would bring the Hong Kong courts into direct conflict with the NPCSC.

In *Ng Kung Siu*, the CFA managed to avoid this conflict, but not by holding that laws that the NPCSC applies to Hong Kong are unquestionable. Instead, the CFA held that even though the flag desecration laws impose restrictions on the freedom of expression, the restrictions are legitimate, reasonable and proportionate restrictions justified by public interest and public order considerations. The CFA emphasized that in the early period of Hong Kong's history as an SAR of China, the flag is particularly important in serving as a symbol that Hong Kong is now part of China. This evaluative judgment which the CFA made is, I believe, correct. The CFA's decision in *Ng Kung Siu* is a sound one: on the one hand, it demonstrated respect for the legitimate desire of the People's Republic of China to assert its sovereignty in the Hong Kong SAR symbolically; on the other hand, it upheld the power of the Hong Kong courts to review local laws for the purpose of checking whether they are consistent with the human rights guarantees enshrined in the Basic Law, the Hong Kong Bill of Rights and the International Covenant on Civil and Political Rights, and to declare the laws as invalid if determined to be so inconsistent.

The year 2000 was a relatively quiet year as far as constitutional issues were concerned. After the legal drama of the preceding year, the situation seemed to calm down for a while. One of the more notable events from the perspective of legal history in 2000 was the controversy generated by the arrest of a few university students who were suspected of having violated the Public Order Ordinance[28] when they demonstrated against the government on 20 April 2000 (regarding university tuition fee policy) and on 26 June 2000 (the anniversary of the NPCSC's interpretation of the Basic Law). There was much sympathy in the community for the students, although it was recognized that they had not complied with the relevant application procedures before the demonstrations. The public discussion focused on whether such procedures were too strict, and whether the controls on assemblies and demonstrations in the Public Order Ordinance should be relaxed. As a result of the public pressure, the government ultimately decided not to prosecute the students. At the same time, it resisted the calls for the review of the Public Order Ordinance. The public debate on the matter ended when the Legislative Council decided by a majority vote on 20 December 2000 in favour of the retention of the Ordinance in its existing form.

It is appropriate that our review of the post-1997 legal history of Hong Kong should end with the CFA's decision in *Director of Immigration v Chong Fung Yuen*,[29] for this case marked the restoration of the self-confidence of the Hong Kong courts after the "trauma" of 1999, and the aftermath of this case demonstrated the spirit of accommodation and tolerance of the difference between the "two systems" on the part of the mainland authorities. In *Chong Fung Yuen*, the issue was whether, as a matter of interpretation of Article 24(2)(1) of the Basic Law, the right of abode in Hong Kong vests in children born in Hong Kong to parents who are not Hong Kong residents but who are mainlanders visiting Hong Kong temporarily or illegally staying in Hong Kong. On a literal interpretation of Article 24(2)(1), such children are Hong Kong permanent residents and have the right of abode. However, the SAR Preparatory Committee in 1996 had suggested otherwise when it issued an opinion on the implementation of Article 24. In the NPCSC's interpretation of June 1999, it stated that the Preparatory Committee's opinion reflected the legislative intent behind Article 24 of the Basic Law. The question for the CFA in *Chong Fung Yuen* was whether it should follow the views of the Preparatory Committee in this regard.

The CFA's judgment in this case was an emphatic statement that when Hong Kong courts interpret the Basic Law, they should adopt the common law approach to interpretation, and do not need to resort to or otherwise take into account any principle or norm of the mainland legal system. Applying the common law approach to interpretation in this case, the CFA held that there was only one possible answer to the legal question raised: the child concerned was entitled to the right of abode in Hong Kong. As regards the Preparatory Committee's opinion, since it was issued years after the enactment of the Basic Law, it could hardly be regarded (from the common law perspective) as evidence of the legislative intent behind the Basic Law. The CFA also did not attach any weight to the passage in the June 1999 interpretation by the NPCSC suggesting that the Preparatory Committee's opinion reflected the legislative intent behind Article 24 of the Basic Law. The CFA stressed that the June 1999 interpretation was an interpretation only of Articles 22(4) and 24(2)(3) of the Basic Law. It was not an interpretation of Article 24(2)(1) of the Basic Law, which was the provision being interpreted in the *Chong Fung Yuen* case. In the absence of any binding interpretation by the NPCSC of Article 24(2)(1), the CFA was free to interpret it on its own, applying the common law approach to interpretation.

In *Chong Fung Yuen*, the CFA also rejected the government's argument that the interpretation of Article 24(2)(1) should be referred to the NPCSC because the "implementation" of the provision would have a "substantive effect" on the relationship between the Hong Kong SAR and the Central Authorities or on affairs which are the responsibility of the central government. The CFA held that in determining whether a reference to the NPCSC should be made, the court should look at the character of the provision rather than the factual determination of the effect of its implementation. On this basis, the court held that Article 24(2)(1) need not be referred to the NPCSC.

The CFA's decision in *Chong Fung Yuen* was generally applauded by the legal community of Hong Kong, although there was some public concern about pregnant women from the mainland being induced to come to Hong Kong to give birth to their babies. In a very unusual manner not seen since the constitutional crisis of February 1999, Beijing reacted publicly to the decision as well. On 21 July 2001, the morning immediately following the date of the CFA's decision, a spokesman of the Legislative Affairs Commission of the NPCSC in a widely reported statement pointed out that the CFA's decision in *Chong Fung Yuen* was "not consistent" with the NPCSC's interpretation, and "expressed concern" about the matter. However, apart from this terse statement, no further action on the matter was taken by the Beijing side subsequently.

The statement of 21 July 2001 is an indication that the NPCSC would like to distance itself from the CFA's interpretation of Article 24(2)(1), and suggests that if the NPCSC itself were to interpret the provision, it would probably have interpreted it differently. The statement can also be understood as an expression of Beijing's displeasure about the CFA's lack of respect for the text of the NPCSC's interpretation of June 1999, which, after all, did say that the Preparatory Committee's opinion reflected the legislative intent behind the whole of Article 24(2). Given these considerations, Beijing's reaction to the *Chong Fung Yuen* decision must be considered a very muted one. Utmost self-restraint has been adhered to in order not to undermine the authority of the Hong Kong courts and public confidence in the Rule of Law in Hong Kong.[30]

Conclusion

We now return to the questions posed at the beginning of this chapter. *To what extent has the pre-1997 legal system of Hong Kong been preserved?* The answer is that it has been preserved to an extremely large extent, in the sense that more than 99 percent of the pre-existing laws are still in force, lawyers and judges continue to practise their callings in exactly the same manner as before, the common law approach is still used in deciding cases, and the pre-existing institutions of the legal system have all been maintained, with the exception of the abolition of appeals to the Privy Council and the establishment of a new Court of Final Appeal. Furthermore, it seems that there has been no change in Hong Kong's British-style legal culture. If there has been any change, it is in the direction of more public vigilance with regard to issues of the Rule of Law, human rights and judicial independence.

To what extent does the Rule of Law still thrive in Hong Kong? This is more a matter of personal opinion, but I would suggest that despite isolated instances such as the *Aw Sian* case, there is no evidence to suggest any significant or general deterioration of the Rule of Law in Hong Kong. The Rule of Law is an ideal which all legal systems should aspire to but which is seldom perfectly realized. Even before the handover, the Rule of Law in Hong Kong was not perfect, and was subject to a gradual process of evolution and improvement. For example, corruption was rampant before the establishment of the ICAC in the 1970s. Legal fees were high and there were problems in terms of access to legal services and to justice. Legal guarantees of internationally recognised human rights were only emphasized after the enactment of the Hong Kong Bill of Rights Ordinance in 1991. After the handover, Hong Kong has continued its journey towards the ideal of the Rule of Law. What is important is that the ideal is still upheld and cherished.

The paradigm used by most observers and commentators in assessing the legal system and the Rule of Law in post-1997 Hong Kong focuses the inquiry on whether the pre-1997 laws and legal system have been *preserved* and whether there has been any *deterioration* in the Rule of Law and in human rights in the territory. However, it is doubtful whether this paradigm will remain useful in future. Ever since the Sino-British Joint Declaration of 1984, Hong Kong's legal community has been striving to ensure that the Rule of Law could continue beyond 1997. Now that we are at a point almost five years after the handover, and given that the previous fear about Hong Kong's death or collapse in 1997 has not materialized, a paradigm shift in our thinking about Hong Kong's legal system is perhaps called for. The new paradigm should recognize that the legal system and laws that the Hong Kong SAR inherited from Hong Kong's colonial past were far from perfect, and it is inadequate to aim merely at the preservation of that system and the prevention of its deterioration. We should strive to improve it, and to adapt it to the rapidly changing world of the 21st century. On the other hand, it should not be taken for granted that the cherished values, principles and beliefs of English common law which were transplanted to Hong Kong during its colonial era have taken root in Hong Kong and will automatically continue to flourish in future. If the community do not understand them, accept them, treasure them and stand up when necessary to defend them, they may erode away.

Have the constitutional principles regarding Hong Kong's autonomy enshrined in the Basic Law been upheld in practice? I would give an emphatic "yes" in answer to this question. The Beijing side has practised utmost self-restraint in exercising its powers under the Basic Law. For example, no Hong Kong law has been invalidated even though the NPCSC has the power to review and invalidate Hong Kong laws under Article 17 of the Basic Law. After 1 July 1997, only one national law has been applied to Hong Kong (under Article 18 of the Basic Law), and it is a law relating to the law of the sea.[31] The NPCSC has made one interpretation of the Basic Law, and, as discussed above, this occurred only because the SAR government actively sought the interpretation when faced with a social crisis that it believed it could not resolve itself.

How do we interpret the constitutional controversies that occurred in the last few years in which a conflict between the operating principles of the two systems was manifested? In the preceding discussion, I have already offered some comments on the relevant events. From episodes such as the "right of abode" controversy, it may have been seen that there is indeed a clear divergence between the values, principles and even basic assumptions of the two systems. There are some fundamental features of the Hong Kong legal system that are alien to the mainland Chinese legal system, and vice versa; here lies the seed of possible misunderstanding, distrust or conflict. For example, the degree of the sanctity of the law (as distinguished from policy) in the two systems is different. The scope of judicial power in the two systems is different. There are also differences in people's attitudes, mentalities and values regarding matters such as procedural safeguards, the rights of the accused, human rights or criminal punishment.

However, I think it is important to have a sense of proportion and perspective, and not to exaggerate the "conflict" between the two systems. The constitutional and legal design of "one country, two systems" is such that the points of contact and interface between the two systems are few, and in the overwhelming majority of cases and circumstances, the two systems operate autonomously without any interaction with one another. In my opinion, the "conflict" between the two systems is negligible, not because the operating principles and fundamental premises of the two systems are not radically different (they are indeed radically different), but because the interface and interaction of the two systems is minimal. This is not to say that this is a good thing; it is simply an objective condition which renders practically meaningless the talk about the "integration" of the two systems (e.g. the Hong Kong system gradually changing and adapting itself to accommodate the mainland system).

The looseness of the connection between the two systems (at least from the legal point of view) is exemplified by the fact that despite the long negotiations between the SAR government and Beijing on a possible rendition agreement on fugitive offenders, no agreement has yet been reached, and neither side sees the matter as a pressing one. Another example is that in the five years since the handover, the SAR government has not taken legislative steps in pursuance of Article 23 of the Basic Law to deal with questions like "subversion" or "seccession." In the meantime, the annual vigils and marches to commemorate the Tiananmen events of 1989 continue in Hong Kong; the Falun Gong practitioners carry on their activities and demonstrations in Hong Kong; Dr. Li Shaomin, professor at City University of Hong Kong, was permitted to come back to Hong Kong again after being "expelled from the territory" of China upon his conviction for espionage by a mainland court.

The experiment of "one country, two systems" is a bold one from the constitutional and legal point of view, given that the Rule of Law had not developed to a sophisticated level in China when the experiment began. It is noteworthy that in successful federal systems of autonomy like the USA, Canada and Australia, the constitutional and judicial arrangements supporting federalism and autonomy were built upon already well-established traditions of the Rule of Law. When Hong Kong began its constitutional journey as an SAR of the People's Republic of China, it did not have the benefit of a mature and modernized system of the Rule of Law in China. Given this inherent genetic deficiency, the record of the actual constitutional and legal practice of "one country, two systems" in the last few years is, I believe, one that we can consider satisfactory. But there is no reason for complacency. Many challenges lie ahead; many tasks await to be done.

Notes

1. See generally Yash Ghai, *Hong Kong's New Constitutional Order* (Hong Kong: Hong Kong University Press, 2nd ed. 1999).
2. See generally Albert H. Y. Chen, "The Relationship Between the Central Government and the SAR," in Peter Wesley-Smith and Albert Chen (eds.), *The Basic Law and Hong Kong's Future* (Singapore: Butterworths, 1988), pp. 107–40.
3. See generally Wang Shuwen (ed.), *Introduction to the Basic Law of the Hong Kong Special Administrative Region* (Beijing: Law Press, 2000), pp. 57–88.
4. See the Basic Law, Articles 1–2, 12.
5. Basic Law, Articles 2 and 17.
6. Basic Law, Article 17.
7. Basic Law, Article 19. See also Articles 80–85 of the Basic Law.

8. Basic Law, Articles 8, 18, 84.
9. Basic Law, Article 18.
10. Basic Law, Article 4 and Chapter III ("Fundamental Rights and Duties of the Residents"). See also the Hong Kong Bill of Rights Ordinance (Chapter 383 of the Laws of Hong Kong).
11. [1997] *Hong Kong Law Reports and Digest* 761.
12. The Hong Kong Reunification Ordinance 1997.
13. Article 18 of the Basic Law provides that mainland Chinese laws are not applicable in Hong Kong except for those listed in Annex III to the Basic Law. The Chinese Criminal Code is not in Annex III. See also Articles 6 and 7 of the Chinese Criminal Code 1997.
14. [1999] 1 *Hong Kong Law Reports and Digest* 315.
15. [1999] 1 *Hong Kong Law Reports and Digest* 304.
16. Basic Law, Article 24(2)(3).
17. The Immigration (Amendment) (No. 2) Ordinance 1997 and the Immigration (Amendment) (No. 3) Ordinance 1997.
18. See generally Albert H. Y. Chen, "The Court of Final Appeal's Ruling in the 'Illegal Migrant' Children Case: Congressional Supremacy and Judicial Review," in J. M. M. Chan, H. L. Fu and Y. Ghai (eds.), *Hong Kong's Constitutional Debate: Conflict over Interpretation* (Hong Kong: Hong Kong University Press, 2000), pp. 73–96.
19. For the text of the "clarification," see [1999] 1 *Hong Kong Law Reports and Digest* 577.
20. Article 158(3) requires the CFA to seek an interpretation of the Basic Law from the NPCSC if the CFA in the course of adjudicating a case needs to interpret a Basic Law provision "concerning affairs which are the responsibility of the Central People's Government, or concerning the relationship between the Central Authorities and the Region."
21. The 1982 Constitution, Article 67(4).
22. For the text of the interpretation, see *The Government of the Hong Kong Special Administrative Region Gazette Extraordinary, Legal Supplement, No. 2* (28 June 1999), p. 1577 (L.N. 167 of 1999).
23. [1999] 3 *Hong Kong Law Reports and Digest* 778.
24. Ibid., at p. 820.
25. [1999] 1 *Hong Kong Law Reports and Digest* 783 (Court of Appeal), [1999] 3 *Hong Kong Law Reports and Digest* 907 (Court of Final Appeal).
26. National Flag and National Emblem Ordinance, section 7; Regional Flag and Regional Emblem Ordinance, section 7.
27. The Law of the National Flag of the People's Republic of China, which is one of the laws added to the list of applicable national laws in Annex III to the Basic Law in July 1997. See "Promulgation of National Laws (No. 2) 1997," *The Government of the Hong Kong Special Administrative*

Region Gazette, No. 1/1997, Legal Supplement No. 2, p. B119 (L.N. 386 of 1997).

28. The Public Order Ordinance was amended by the Provisional Legislative Council in 1997 in pursuance of the NPCSC's Decision on 23 February 1997 on the Treatment of the Laws Previously in Force in Hong Kong. See generally Albert H. Y. Chen, "Continuity and Change in the Legal System," in L. C. H. Chow and Y. K. Fan (eds.), *The Other Hong Kong Report 1998* (Hong Kong: Chinese University Press, 1999), pp. 31–34.
29. [2001] 2 *Hong Kong Law Reports and Digest* 533.
30. See generally Albert H. Y. Chen, "Another Case of Conflict Between the CFA and the NPC Standing Committee?" [2001] 31 *Hong Kong Law Journal* 179.
31. This is the Law on the Exclusive Economic Zone and the Continental Shelf. See "Promulgation of National Law 1998," *The Government of the Hong Kong Special Administrative Region Gazette*, No. 52/1998, Legal Supplement No. 2, 24 December 1998, L.N. 393 of 1998.

4

Civil Liberties, Rule of Law and Human Rights: The Hong Kong Special Administrative Region in Its First Four Years

Johannes Chan*

Head, Department of Law

The University of Hong Kong

Historically, more than half of the population in Hong Kong came from the mainland China. Many of them came to Hong Kong after the Second World War to avoid the civil wars. Between the late fifties and the mid seventies, many came to Hong Kong to escape from the lawlessness during the Cultural Revolution or to flee from the communist power. Since the late seventies, Hong Kong has witnessed the rise of the middle class and the rise to power of a new and locally bred generation who is better educated and who has greater expectation and demand for liberalism and democracy. Thus, when the "one country, two systems" model was proposed in the early eighties, a major concern was whether human rights would be adequately protected after the changeover. The concern was natural, as the transfer of sovereignty over Hong Kong involved also an unprecedented transfer by peaceful means of a population of over six million to a political power from whom half of the population originally fled. Thus, the Sino-British Joint Declaration provides that "rights and freedoms, including those of the person, of speech, of the press, of

* This chapter is based on an earlier version of a conference paper presented in March 2001 at the University of Kobe, to which the author is grateful for permitting him to reproduce a substantial part of that paper.

assembly, of association, of travel, of movement, of correspondence, of strike, of choice of occupation, of academic research and of religious belief will be ensured by law in the Hong Kong Special Administrative Region."[1] It further provides that "the provisions of the International Covenant on Civil and Political Rights and the International Covenant on Economic, Social and Cultural Rights as applied to Hong Kong shall remain in force."[2] A full chapter in the Basic Law is devoted to the protection of fundamental rights and freedoms.

The guarantee on paper does not allay the worries of the people of Hong Kong, as witnessed by the brain drain in the late eighties and the earlier nineties. At the same time, China has undergone great changes and is moving towards a more liberal regime. It also shows great determination to uphold the principle of "one country, two systems." However, the worries remain — not so much about direct suppression of freedom, by military force or otherwise, which seems unlikely, but whether the cherish for individual freedom in Hong Kong can withstand the strong but subtle political influence or intervention from the north which has a dominant belief in collective rights and cultural relativism and a great sensitivity to anything remotely related to sovereignty.

It is expected that human rights will be respected, or at least be tolerated, at the time of the changeover when the whole world was watching with great interest on Hong Kong. However, as time passes, the tolerance level of the Central Government may drop, especially if the relative economic importance of Hong Kong is diminished in view of the rapidly developing economy in the mainland. This chapter will review the protection of human rights in the Hong Kong Special Administrative Region (HKSAR) in the four years after the changeover.

The International Labour Conventions and the International Covenants on Human Rights

An important guarantee for human rights which features prominently in the Joint Declaration and the Basic Law is the continued application of the International Covenant on Civil and Political Rights (ICCPR), the International Covenant on Economic, Social and Cultural Rights (ICESCR) and the International Labour Conventions. These international conventions were extended to Hong Kong before 1 July 1997 by the United Kingdom, albeit subject to reservations. Agreements were reached between the United Kingdom and the People's Republic of China (PRC) on the continued application of these treaties in the HKSAR after the changeover.

Over 50 Conventions of the International Labour Organization (ILO) were extended to Hong Kong prior to the changeover by the United Kingdom on the basis that Hong Kong was a non-metropolitan territory of the United Kingdom pursuant to Article 35 of the ILO Constitution. Although HKSAR is not a non-metropolitan territory, the PRC agreed that the various ILO Conventions could continue to apply to Hong Kong under the same principle by way of analogy in view of the autonomous status of the HKSAR in relation to its labour legislation and the administration of labour affairs.[3] The complaint procedure under the ILO Constitution has been invoked by workers' unions in Hong Kong against the United Kingdom,[4] as well as by workers' organizations against the PRC.[5] While most of the rights in these various ILO Conventions have been implemented in Hong Kong, a significant omission is the right to collective bargain guaranteed by Convention No 98. Although the Convention has been extended to the HKSAR, various implementing legislation that were introduced shortly before the changeover to implement the right to collective bargaining and to strengthen various labour rights were first suspended and subsequently repealed by the Provisional Legislative Council in 1997.[6] Upon a complaint by the Hong Kong Federation of Trade Union, the ILO Committee found the repealing legislation a violation of the ILO Conventions No 87 and 98.[7] It rejected the government's argument that collective bargaining would change "the present harmonious labour relations into confrontational, and thus deal a direct blow to Hong Kong's economy and its attractiveness to foreign investment, thereby reducing the employment opportunities" and hence has an "adverse impact on the prosperity and stability of Hong Kong." The committee held that such an approach was in direct contradiction with the obligation incumbent upon the government under Article 4 of the Convention No 98.

The ILO Conventions posed less a problem of treaty succession for Hong Kong because both the UK and the PRC are parties to the ILO Constitution. The succession of the ICCPR and the ICESCR is more problematic because the PRC is not yet a party to these covenants.[8] However, whatever be the legal position, the *de facto* position is that the PRC has submitted the 5th periodic report on Hong Kong pursuant to the ICCPR, and the 2nd comprehensive report on Hong Kong pursuant to the ICESCR since 1 July 1997.

The ICCPR is implemented in Hong Kong by the Hong Kong Bill of Rights Ordinance. Part II of the ordinance, which is titled the Bill of Rights, reproduces verbatim the substantive rights provisions of the

ICCPR. The Hong Kong Bill of Rights Ordinance came into force on 8 June 1991. Although some of the operational provisions were not adopted by the Standing Committee of the National People's Congress of the PRC (NPCSC) as the laws of the HKSAR pursuant to Article 160 of the Basic Law, this has not in any way affected the operation of the Bill of Rights in the HKSAR.[9] However, the importance of the Bill of Rights is diminished in the sense that Article 39 of the Basic Law has entrenched the ICCPR, thereby rendering it unnecessary to refer to the Bill of Rights. Article 39 provides:

> "The provisions of the ICCPR ... as applied to Hong Kong shall remain in force and shall be implemented through the laws of the HKSAR.
>
> The rights and freedoms enjoyed by Hong Kong residents shall not be restricted unless as prescribed by law. Such restrictions shall not contravene the provisions of the preceding paragraph of this Article."

Since the provisions of the ICCPR as applied to Hong Kong have been implemented in the domestic legal system of the HKSAR through the Bill of Rights, the Hong Kong courts have accepted that any restriction which is inconsistent with the ICCPR as applied to Hong Kong will be in violation of Article 39 of the Basic Law and will therefore either not be adopted as the law of the HKSAR pursuant to Article 18 of the Basic Law (if the restriction is embodied in the law previously in force in Hong Kong) or is null and void pursuant to Article 11 of the Basic Law (if the restriction is contained in legislation passed by the legislature of the HKSAR).[10] As encroachment of fundamental rights in modern society is frequently done through legislation, sometimes due to an over-zealous legislature, the power of constitutional review of legislation for its conformity with the human rights provisions in the ICCPR (and it follows in other provisions of the Basic Law) is an important guarantee for the protection of human rights in the HKSAR.

This power of constitutional review which exists in many common law jurisdictions (including Hong Kong which has a written constitution before the changeover) has been regarded as uncontroversial until challenged recently by Mr. Shiu Sin-por, the executive director of the One Country, Two Systems Research Institute, which is commonly perceived to be the think tank of the HKSAR government.[11] Mr. Siu attacked the Hong Kong courts for engaging in judicial activism in relying on the ICCPR as a yardstick to measure local legislation. As the ICCPR is an international treaty, it does not automatically apply to Hong Kong without implementing legislation under the common law. Mr. Siu asserted that it has never been the intention of the PRC that the ICCPR could be directly invoked in domestic law. The Bill of Rights, which implements the ICCPR, is, so Mr. Siu contended, the result of the irresponsible act of the former colonial government; the court, in invoking the ICCPR as the yardstick, is in fact engaged in a legislative exercise and this has rendered the court a centre of controversy. He urged the NPCSC to clarify the meaning of Article 39.

The article provoked strong reaction in the community.[12] Mr. Siu's argument might have more force if the Bill of Rights is not adopted by the NPCSC as the law of the HKSAR. The NPCSC decided only not to adopt three provisions in Part 1 of the Bill of Rights Ordinance, leaving intact the Bill of Rights properly so-called, which is Part 2 of the Bill of Rights Ordinance. By choosing to adopt the Bill of Rights as the law of the HKSAR, the NPCSC must effectively be affirming the implementation of the ICCPR through the Bill of Rights. Therefore, the central argument of Mr. Siu that the implementation of the ICCPR is the irresponsible act of the colonial government is simply inaccurate.

Mr. Siu's argument also assumes that there is only one mode of implementing the ICCPR, and that this mode of implementation of international treaties shall be entrenched and cannot be changed from 1984 onward. This cannot be right. Any person familiar with English constitutional law will know that it is always possible to incorporate an international treaty directly into domestic law or in domestic constitution.[13] He has also overlooked that the ICCPR imposes on State Parties a duty to implement the provisions of the ICCPR into domestic law. It is generally for the State Parties to choose their methods of implementation in their territories, and these methods include implementation in constitutional and legislative enactments.[14] If the intention of the Joint Declaration is that the UK should exercise self-constraint and confine the implementation of the ICCPR to one single method, this could easily have been clearly expressed in the Joint Declaration. This is not what the Joint Declaration said, and there is no evidence of such an agreement of self-restraint. It is not open to a State to plead ignorance of international law and claim to be misled by another State in concluding an international treaty. Such argument is also inconsistent with the subsequent adoption of the Bill of Rights Ordinance by the NPCSC as the law of the HKSAR. Whatever be the position in 1984, the PRC must have known the implications of implementing the ICCPR by the Bill of Rights when it adopted the Bill of Rights as the law of the

HKSAR in 1997. The Bill of Rights Ordinance as adopted is no different from any other domestic legislation implementing an international treaty, such as the Crimes (Torture) Ordinance.

Attack Against the Judiciary

A more worrying message in the argument of Mr. Siu is that the judiciary should be blamed for its eagerness to protect human rights. In the common law system, protection of human rights has always been a fundamental role of the judiciary. To put a brake at this judicial activism in protecting human rights in the way as Mr. Siu argued will effectively destroy a fundamental pillar of one of the two systems in the "one country, two systems" model.

This is not the first time the judiciary is attacked since the changeover. It is most disappointing that the attack is made on racial or nationalist ground. In February 1999, in criticizing the controversial judgment of the Court of Final Appeal in *Ng Ka Ling v Director of Immigration*,[15] some critics had tried to attribute the blame to the presence of expatriate judges. In mid 1999, when the Court of Appeal (comprising three expatriate judges) held that the offence of desecration of national flag was inconsistent with the protection of freedom of expression, the expatriate judges were again made the target of attack for making such misguided decision which insulted national feelings. In November 2000, after the Court of Final Appeal delivered its important judgment in the defamation case in *Albert Cheng v Tse Wai Chun Paul*,[16] Mr. Ma Lik, a delegate to the NPC, criticized the presence in the Court of Final Appeal of overseas judges, whom he described as "parachute judges." This time the Secretary for Justice has to defend the judiciary:

> ... the fact that judges from other common law jurisdictions can sit on the Court of Final Appeal has received widespread support, both locally and overseas. Moreover, the judges appointed to the Court from such jurisdictions are of the highest international standing. Their appointments have played an important part in establishing the excellent reputation of the Court. They also reflect the confidence placed in Hong Kong's judicial system by other major common law jurisdictions. These have been important factors in preserving confidence in the independence of the judiciary in Hong Kong and in the integrity and wisdom of our judges.[17]

Independence of the Judiciary

The independence of the judiciary suffers a setback when the Court of

Final Appeal decided to make a clarification of its judgment in *Ng Ka Ling v Director of Immigration* after it had rendered its final judgment in that case.[18] In holding unconstitutional certain aspects of the certificate of entitlement scheme under the Immigration Ordinance, which was introduced after 1 July 1997 to deny the claim of the children of Hong Kong Permanent Residents born in the mainland for a right of abode in Hong Kong, the Court of Final Appeal also held that it had power to review the compatibility of a decision of the National People's Congress with the Basic Law. This provoked strong criticisms from the mainland. Upon strong political pressure, the Court of Final Appeal decided to make a clarification of its judgment in order to pacify the concern of the mainland. Although the clarification did not really clarify any issue or change its original judgment, the decision of the Court of Final Appeal to get itself involved in resolving a political crisis has attracted criticisms of its independence. Its independence suffered a further blow when the HKSAR government eventually decided to seek an interpretation from the Standing Committee of the National People's Congress (NPCSC) on the proper interpretation of the relevant provision of the Basic Law. The interpretation of the NPCSC effectively overruled the judgment of the Court of Final Appeal. The binding authority of the NPCSC's interpretation was acknowledged by the Court of Final Appeal in subsequent cases,[19] though there were various attempts by the courts to confine the scope of application of the interpretation.[20]

In the last few years, an increasing number of cases of a highly political nature has been brought before the Hong Kong courts. Apart from the series of cases on the right of abode, the courts have decided on the constitutionality of the Provisional Legislative Council,[21] the dissolution of the two municipal councils,[22] the offence of desecrating national flag,[23] and the recognition of a judgment from the court of Taiwan.[24] On the whole, it is fair to conclude that the court has retained its impartiality and independence in all these cases, and even in the highly controversial right of abode case, the Court of Final Appeal held that, subject to the constraints on the court under the Basic Law, it should approach the interpretation of the Basic Law in accordance with the common law principles.[25]

Equality before the Law

A fundamental principle of the rule of law is the principle of equality before the law. This principle is entrenched by Article 25 of the Basic Law and Article 26 of the ICCPR. A number of prosecution decisions have, however, cast doubt on the government's commitment to this fundamental principle.

On 17 March 1998, three members of the senior management of Hong Kong Standard, one of the two English language newspapers in Hong Kong, were charged with the common law offence of conspiracy to defraud advertisers in the newspaper by fraudulently inflating the circulation record of the newspaper. Ms Sally Aw, the chairman of Sing Tao Group which owned the newspaper, used to have close tie with the family of the Chief Executive of the HKSAR. She was also a member of the National Committee of the Chinese People's Political Consultative Conference. She was expressly named in the indictment as a party to the conspiracy. However, she was not prosecuted. The decision created an uproar in the community.

As a result of mounting public pressure, the Secretary for Justice appeared on 4 February 2000 before a Legislative Council's Panel to justify her decision. The Secretary for Justice explained that her decision was in accordance with settled prosecution policy. There was no reasonable prospect to secure a conviction against Ms Aw. It was also not in the public interest to bring the prosecution. On the first ground, the Secretary referred to various items of the evidence to show that they were insufficient to satisfy the criminal standard of proof. It was also pointed out that the evidence of a co-accused could not be used against Ms Aw if she were to be charged. While reasonable persons may differ on the assessment of the strength of evidence, the Secretary has failed to provide a satisfactory explanation in at least two respects. First, as Ms Aw was named as a conspirator with the defendants, the prosecution has to prove this fact beyond reasonable doubt. If there is a reasonable prospect of proving this against the three defendants, why is there no reasonable prospect of proving this against Ms Aw? Secondly, the three defendants were subordinates to Ms Aw, who would be the person that would stand to gain by the conspiracy. It is true that the evidence of a co-accused cannot be used against other co-accused, but has any consideration been given to turn one of the co-accused into a prosecution witness whose evidence would then be admissible against Ms Aw?

Despite these unanswered queries, the most controversial aspect of the explanation lies in the Secretary of Justice's interpretation of public interest. She said:

> As a result, from the public interest point of view, I considered it not to be right to prosecute Ms Aw. At that time, the Sing Tao Group was facing financial difficulties and was negotiating restructuring with banks. If Ms Aw was prosecuted, it would be a serious obstacle to that restructuring. If the Group should collapse, its newspapers (which include one of the only two English newspapers in Hong Kong) would, in all likelihood, be compelled to cease operation. I wish to add that several other newspapers had folded in late 1996, 1997 and 1998. Apart from the staff losing employment, the failure of a well-established and important media group at that time could have sent a very bad message to the international community. At a time when unemployment was on the rise, the prospect of a prosecution occasioning yet further widespread redundancies filled me with foreboding. It was my duty, in those circumstances, firstly, to consider the potential effects of a prosecution upon other people. Then, secondly, it was necessary to ask myself whether the possible consequences of the prosecution were proportionate to the seriousness of the alleged offence. I decided they were not. The failure of an important media group at that time could have sent all the wrong signals to the international community, quite apart from the damage it would have done to local morale. Thus it was that I also decided that it was not in the public interest to initiate a prosecution of Ms Aw.

Whether the prosecution would ruin the restructuring of the company or result in unemployment is highly speculative and can hardly be a relevant factor of public interest. The explanation is tantamount to admitting that the rich and the influential enjoys a privilege not to be subject to criminal prosecution. The argument that the failure of an important media group could have sent the wrong signals to the international community is unconvincing either, as it depends on the reason of the failure. A newspaper sustained by fraudulent and corrupt practice is likely to send a worse signal to the international community. Indeed, the Bar Council published a public statement describing the Secretary of Justice's interpretation of public interest as "totally indefensible." An unprecedented motion of no confidence was put forward at the Legislative Council. It was defeated by a narrow margin after intensive lobbying done by the government.[26]

In January 2001, the Secretary for Justice made another two controversial decisions not to prosecute Godfrey Nguyen and Poon Kai-tak. Godfrey Nguyen was the son of a judge of the Court of First Instance. He was found to be in possession of a small quantity of soft drug. He was 23 years of age with a clear record. The prosecution decided not of offer evidence against him upon his agreeing to be bound over. Mr. Poon

Kai-tak was the Deputy Director of Housing. He was found to have stolen certain items from a supermarket. Again the prosecution decided not to offer evidence against him upon his agreeing to be bound over.

These decisions aroused widespread public concern. On the one hand, the government has repeatedly stated that it was not going to tolerate soft drug, a social problem which has been getting worse in recent years. On the other hand, no prosecution was laid against Mr. Nguyen when there are many similar cases involving a small amount of soft drug and the defendants in those cases, some of whom are no doubt young offenders with clear record, are routinely prosecuted. Similarly, the public, particular the adolescents, are repeatedly reminded that shoplifting is a serious criminal offence. Was Mr. Poon allowed to walk free because of his status?

The decision not to prosecute in these two cases may be right. However, if this represents government's prosecution policy, the principle of equality of the law would demand a similar exercise of discretion in similar cases. The Director of Public Prosecutions maintained that there was no change in prosecution policy over cases involving soft drug and young first offenders. Yet from the material provided by government to the Legislative Council, the treatment accorded to Mr. Nguyen and Mr. Poon was certainly rare. It is difficult to see how these two cases differ from many other cases which are prosecuted routinely in magistrates' courts. Indeed, a magistrate was so frustrated by the inconsistent prosecution policy that he gave an absolute discharge in a number of cases involving similar facts when the prosecution refused to offer no evidence.[27]

Article 63 of the Basic Law provides that the Department of Justice shall control criminal prosecutions free from any interference. It must be right that criminal prosecution should not be used for political purposes or be used in a discriminatory manner. Compliance with this principle was challenged when some university students were singled out for prosecution. In April 2000, some university students held a public demonstration to oppose the government's proposal to introduce differential composite fees for different disciplines of studies in the universities. The demonstration was peaceful. Under the Public Order Ordinance, seven days' advance notice of any proposed demonstration of more than 30 persons or of any proposed assembly of more than 50 persons has to be given to the police, failing to comply with which constitutes an offence which carries a maximum of five years' imprisonment. The seven days' advance notice requirement has been regarded as a nuisance and, according to the police, over 1,000 demonstrations since 1 July 1997 have failed to comply with this requirement. The students did not give seven days' notice as a matter of protest against the Public Order Ordinance. They were arrested in August 2000 for this demonstration and for another demonstration in June 2000 against the interpretation of the Basic Law by the NPCSC (the latter demonstration resulted in confrontation and the police were accused of using excessive force). Many commentators expressed the concern of selective enforcement of the law. As the Bar Association stated, "notwithstanding many public meetings and public demonstrations which were held in the past without complying with the current law, some university students were apparently singled out for intended prosecution."[28] The government denied that the students were singled out,[29] and the Secretary for Security kept emphasizing that the students did not have a licence to transgress the law.[30] Subsequently, the Secretary for Justice decided not to prosecute them, though the Secretary for Security emphasized that the decision not to prosecute them did not preclude the possibility of future prosecutions in similar circumstances.

Freedom of Peaceful Assembly

Public assemblies and demonstrations are governed by the Public Order Ordinance, the current version of which was first enacted during the riots in 1967.[31] The Ordinance has since undergone a number of major amendments. Prior to 1980, any public assembly of three or more persons without the prior permission of the Commissioner of Police constituted a criminal offence. "Public assembly" was widely defined to include any meeting of three or more persons in public during which any public affairs were discussed. Thus, a family gathering on Sunday in a public restaurant when some members began to discuss public affairs would turn the social gathering into a "public assembly," and all members participating in the gathering would commit a criminal offence because no prior permission from the police has been obtained. The absurdity of the law was highlighted in *Chow Shui v The Queen*.[32] In that case, some boat people living in wrecked boats at Yaumati Typhoon Shelter decided to petition the government for their early resettlement in public housing. Two coaches taking the boat people, some social workers and a few activists helping the boat people were stopped by the police at the Hong Kong Island exit of the Cross Harbour Tunnel on their way to the government House. When the boat people refused to disperse, a number of them were charged with and subsequently convicted of the offence of holding an unauthorized public assembly. While the Court of Appeal accepted the absurdity of the law, it felt bound to hold that the activities in the form of a procession in a coach constituted an "unlawful assembly." The community was outraged. As a result, the Public Order Ordinance was amended in 1980 to introduce a licence requirement for a public meeting (which was more liberally defined) and a notification system for public demonstrations.[33]

Throughout the eighties, the restrictions in the Public Order Ordinance on the holding of public assemblies and demonstrations remained a constant source of conflict. The law was also heavily criticized by the United Nations Human Rights Committee in the hearing of the 2nd periodic report on Hong Kong in 1988.[34] The law was further amended and liberalised in 1995 in order to bring it in line with the Bill of Rights. The 1995 amendments were perceived by the Chinese government as an attempt to undermine the ability of the HKSAR government to maintain public order and social stability. As a result, the 1995 amendments were declared, in February 1997, by the NPCSC pursuant to art 160 of the Basic Law to be inconsistent with the Basic Law and they were therefore not adopted as the law of the HKSAR. Non-adoption of these amendments did not automatically revive the previous law repealed by these amendments. Some members of the Provisional Legislative Council therefore proposed the restoration of the former law. This had attracted strong opposition from the community. The Public Order (Amendment) Ordinance 1997 represented a compromised position.[35]

The Public Order (Amendment) Ordinance 1997 re-introduced a disguised licensing system for holding any public demonstration. Under the new system, it is necessary to notify the Commissioner of Police seven days in advance for holding any public demonstration of more than 30 persons, and no demonstration shall be permitted until the Commissioner of Police has granted a certificate of no objection, although there is a deeming provision of no objection if the certificate of no objection is not issued before certain time limit. The government insisted that this was a notification system, and not a licensing system. This appears to be a matter of semantics.

The Amendment Ordinance also introduced "national security" as a new ground justifying a prohibition of public demonstrations. It is well established in international human rights law that "national security" as a ground of justifying restrictions of fundamental rights has to be construed narrowly and is confined to those situations where "the existence of a nation or its territorial integrity or political independence is endangered by force or threat of force."[36] It refers to forces or threats of forces endangering the security of the entire nation, and not certain region of the nation. Seen in this light, it is difficult to see how any public demonstration in Hong Kong could threaten national security of the PRC. Unfortunately, the vague and undefined notion of national security means that its interpretation is largely left to the police in their day-to-day enforcement of the Public Order Ordinance (at least until the decision of the police is challenged in court). In an internal guideline, the Commissioner of Police stated that he "will take into consideration, among other things, whether or not the declared purpose of the notified public meeting or procession is to advocate separation from the People's Republic of China including advocacy of the independence of Taiwan or Tibet."[37] Mere expression which is lawful before the changeover (and which is still lawful after the changeover in the sense that there is as yet no law restricting such expression) is now made a ground to ban public assemblies and demonstrations.

Indeed, the police had tightened up its control over public assemblies and demonstrations after the changeover.[38] What is of concern is that the control is not on the ground of public disorder but is increasing directed at the content of the message. On a number of occasions when non-governmental organizations wished to stage a demonstration during the visit of senior leaders from Beijing, not only did the police designate a place for public demonstrations which was far away from the leaders, but that the demonstrators were surrounded by walls of policemen so that the demonstrators could hardly be seen. On one occasion, the police even put on Beethoven's Fifth Symphony to drown the slogans chanted by the demonstrators to ensure that the senior leaders could not hear the protest. The police explained that classical music was put on so that policemen on duties could feel relaxed; this explanation was rightly rejected by the Independent Police Complaints Council as ludicrous![39] On another occasion, a van was stopped miles away from the venue where an important international conference was held, and the demonstrators on board the van were subsequently charged with the offence of obstructing the police.[40] When the prosecution failed, the demonstrators were then charged with various traffic offences!

The attempted prosecution of the university students in the summer of 2000 provoked another round of public demonstrations against the Public Order Ordinance. Led by many community leaders and politicians, a number of these demonstrations deliberately defied the seven-days' advance notice requirements in the Public Order Ordinance in the name of civil disobedience. This is probably the first time when there is a public challenge to the authority of law. The community generally accepted that some form of advance notice to the police should be given, but there was a sharp division on the length of the advance notice and the power of the police to prohibit public assemblies and demonstrations upon notification. Many union activists pointed out that it was often unrealistic to expect them to give seven days' advance notice when an employer closed down his business and fled from jurisdiction. Critics also pointed out that in many international cities the length of notification was much shorter. The police response was that Hong Kong was a highly congested city, that seven days were required to conduct negotiation with the organizers of the demonstration, and that there was a discretion to receive shorter notice.

A more fundamental challenge was directed at the negative veto power of the police, which was regarded as effectively a licensing system and turned the right to peaceful assembly into a privilege which could only be enjoyed at the mercy of police discretion.[41] It was pointed out that the police already enjoyed wide powers in controlling and dispersing any public assemblies and demonstrations if there was a breach of the peace. They should not enjoy a further power to prohibit a public assembly or demonstration in advance, which power can be exercised on political grounds. The purpose of the advance notice system should be to enable the police to facilitate the holding of public assemblies and demonstrations, not to control them. The fact that over 1,000 peaceful public meetings and assemblies have taken place without complying with the advance notice requirements amply showed that such power of advance control was unnecessary. It has been suggested that if the police wish to oppose the holding of any public assemblies or demonstrations, they should apply for an order of prohibition from an independent tribunal or even from the court, as it is the case in New South Wales or England. The government rejected these suggestions and insisted on the need to have sufficient power to control in advance any public demonstrations and assemblies. On 20 December 2000, the government pushed through a motion debate in the Legislative Council to re-affirm the existing ordinance. The motion was passed by 36 votes to 21.

Freedom of Association

The Societies (Amendment) Ordinance 1997 follows a similar historical path. Originally introduced to curb communist activities in Hong Kong, the Societies Ordinance set up a repressive regime under which the government enjoyed enormous powers to monitor and control all lawful societies. The law was liberalised in 1992 to bring it in line with the Bill of Rights. Like the Public Order (Amendment) Ordinance 1995, the Societies (Amendment) Ordinance 1992 was not adopted as the law of the HKSAR by the NPCSC. The Provisional Legislative Council then enacted the Societies (Amendment) Ordinance 1997, which was even more controversial. It re-introduces the requirement of registration of all lawful societies; failing to do so constitutes a criminal offence on the part of the office bearers. "Societies" is widely defined to include "any club, company, partnership or association of persons, whatever the nature or objects."[42] The Societies Officer may refuse to register a society on the ground of "national security." It is generally believed that the purpose of this power is to outlaw those organizations which support democratic movement in China. Indeed, the Hong Kong Bar Association forcefully argued that if a society is engaged in illegal activities, its responsible members could be prosecuted; but if a society engages in perfectly lawful activities, there is no reason why its office bearers should be guilty of a criminal offence for failing to register, an offence which may be committed out of inadvertence or ignorance of law.[43] The law will catch the innocent and the lawful societies, whereas triad societies will not register itself under the ordinance. Apart from control, it is difficult to see what public interest a registration system of lawful and non-trading societies would serve.[44]

Another controversial aspect of the amendment is that it prohibits any connection with a foreign political organization or a political organization of Taiwan. "Connection" is widely defined to cover any financial support or affiliation or control of the decision-making process. "Foreign political organization" covers an agent of a foreign government or a political party in a foreign country. The Consultation Document stated explicitly that the concern was not so much foreign political influences in Hong Kong domestic affairs, but their influences on China:[45]

> Hong Kong is an international cosmopolitan city. Coupled with freedom of movement both in and out, Hong Kong is open to influences and opinions from different directions. Indeed, we attach importance to developing an international outlook among the people of Hong Kong, and in building social, economic and cultural ties with other countries. This is essential to our economic growth. On the other hand, we must also take steps to prevent Hong Kong

> from being used for political activities against China. This has been a long-standing policy of the Hong Kong government. This policy should be maintained after the establishment of the HKSAR.

Interestingly, there is no prohibition of any connection with a political organization, including the Communist Party, in the mainland. It is perhaps ironic that when the Societies Ordinance was first enacted in 1949, the repressive regime contained in the ordinance was targeted at communist activities in Hong Kong. Almost half a century later, a similarly repressive regime was re-introduced for exactly the opposite reason — to curb any attempt to affect party leadership in the mainland.

Despite strong opposition from the community, the Public Order (Amendment) Ordinance 1997 and the Societies (Amendment) Ordinance 1997 were passed and came into effect on 1 July 1997. The amendments were destined, as they were motivated by the worries of the SAR government that the HKSAR could be used as a base for anti-communist activities by either pro-democratic activists or Taiwanese political fractions. Such activities would shake the stability of the HKSAR, something which the first SAR government could not afford.

As it turns out, it is neither the pro-democratic activists nor the Taiwanese political fractions but Falun Gong that puts the Societies Ordinance to test. As a result of launching a protest involving over 100,000 members of Falun Gong in Beijing, this religious sect was soon labelled as a cult and was outlawed in the mainland. Since January 2001, members of Falun Gong have adopted a rather high profile in Hong Kong, such as staging practice sessions outside the Ministry of Foreign Affairs of the PRC in Hong Kong, organizing public conferences and exhibitions showing how members of Falun Gong were tortured by the security forces in the mainland, and putting up large billboards in urban areas advertising the teachings of Falun Gong. These high profile activities have presented considerable embarrassment to the HKSAR government. Some Hong Kong deputies of the NPC and the National Committee of the Peoples' Political Consultative Conference of the PRC urged the HKSAR government to prohibit the activities of Falun Gong.[46] There is, however, no legal basis for so doing so long as the activities of Falun Gong are lawful in Hong Kong. The Chief Executive tried to exercise some self-restraint, though obviously not totally successful, to abate the issue by adopting mild language and emphasizing the rule of law when it was raised at the Legislative Council. Yet the pressure against Falun Gong has been mounting up. The Secretary for Security castigated the sect as preaching "heretical thinking" and "leading people into superstition." She pointed out that the sect is highly organized with plenty of resources. Therefore it should be placed under "close watch." Her speech provoked strong rebuke from many religious organizations, pointing out that they could easily be placed in the same league and be subject to "close watch" for the same reasons. In the course of debates, it has been suggested that Falun Gong should be de-registered as a society either on the ground of national security or in view of its close connection with unidentified foreign political organizations. Once de-registered, it will become an unlawful society and its activities can be prohibited.

Falun Gong will provide a litmus test to the high degree of autonomy of Hong Kong and the determination of the HKSAR government and the Central Government to uphold two different systems. Unlike the mainland, Hong Kong is a pluralistic society governed by the rule of law. As long as the activities of Falun Gong is lawful, any attempt to prevent it from expressing its views, albeit political views, should be resisted. Freedom will have an illusive meaning if it can only mean freedom to express views that are politically acceptable and to express them in a manner that is acceptable to the government.

Freedom of Religion

The Falun Gong issue also raises the important question of freedom of religion. While religious freedom is largely enjoyed in Hong Kong, there are a few disturbing incidents which suggest that the boundary of such freedom is not as wide as one would have expected. The Roman Catholic Church is one of the largest denominations in Hong Kong. In August 1999, it was reported that the Pope of the Roman Catholic Church was not permitted to visit Hong Kong, presumably because of the Vatican's continuing relationship with Taiwan and its critical comments on the mainland's religious policies against the Roman Catholic Church.[47] The previous Pope has visited Hong Kong in 1970. As a world religious leader, the visit of the Pope certainly carries symbolic importance to the followers. The ban, if true, shows how interference with religious freedom can easily be disguised as issues of immigration policy and foreign affairs.

On 1 October 2000, the Roman Catholic Church decided to canonize in Vatican 120 Christian martyrs who had been killed in China in the 17th to 20th centuries. The Central Government was not pleased with the canonization and refuted the suggestions that these were Christian martyrs. The canonization was perceived to be an unfriendly act of provocation. In early October, coadjutor Bishop Joseph Zen Ze-kiun of the Roman Catholic Church in Hong Kong revealed that the Church had been asked by the Liaison Office of the Central People's Government to ensure that their celebration of the canonization was to be done in a low-key manner. The Bishop expressed publicly his disappointment over the message from the Liaison Office, which explained subsequently that it was only a "friendly advice." On 29 October 2000, the canonization was celebrated in a large-scale mass in Hong Kong. Although the attempt to interfere with the canonization was unsuccessful, the fact that it was attempted is itself a worrying sign.

Freedom of Expression

The extent of press freedom is probably one of the best indicators of the degree of freedom enjoyed in any society. Hong Kong has a vibrant media industry and a healthy number of daily newspapers and periodicals which represent a wide cross-section of views and political stances. Many significant political issues are freely discussed and debated in the media. While a number of newspapers closed down in recent years, this is largely a result of keen market competition. Press freedom is highly prized and jealously guarded. While the press remains relatively free,[48] there is no ground for complacency.

On 12 April 2000, Mr. Wang Fengchao, Deputy Director of the Liaison Office, warned that the Hong Kong media should not disseminate views advocating the independence of Taiwan. Such view should not be treated in the same way as ordinary news. The warning came shortly after Cable Television interviewed Ms Annette Lu Hsiu-lien, the new Taiwan Vice-President who expressed the view that Taiwan should enjoy independent sovereignty.[49] The warning was alarming, as it suggested that the Central Government was prepared to draw the limits of freedom of the press for the HKSAR. The Hong Kong Journalists Association issued a strong press statement re-affirming the independence of the press and editorial freedom. The Acting Chief Executive of the HKSAR also reaffirmed that the Hong Kong media was free to report and comment on all matters of current interest.[50] Nonetheless, the extent of coverage on views advocating the independence of Taiwan has obviously been reduced following the warning of the Chinese government official.

Self-censorship is also seen in handling views critical of the Central Government. This is a difficult issue as evidence of self-censorship is hard to come by.[51] There is an incident of particular concern. In November 2000, Mr. Willy Lam, a senior and experienced journalist, was replaced as China Editor of the *South China Morning Post*. It was widely believed that the replacement was due to his critical views on the Chinese government and his refusal to tone down or de-politicize his coverage of Chinese affairs. Indeed, in a rather exceptional manner, the owner of the *Post* made a public criticism of Mr. Lam's political view by writing an open letter to the *Post*. The newspaper denied such allegation, stating that this was a purely editorial management decision. Interestingly, the China Editor replacing Mr. Lam was a former editor of *China Daily*, a Beijing official newspaper.[52] Mr. Lam subsequently resigned from the newspaper and joined CNN.

Another thorny issue is the role of the Radio and Television of Hong Kong (RTHK). RTHK is wholly government-funded, yet it enjoys virtually complete editorial independence. Over the years, it has produced many internationally acclaimed and award-winning programmes which are also well received in Hong Kong. Among its current affairs programmes are various satirical programmes which are very critical of the HKSAR government, and this has led to dissatisfaction in certain quarters of the community. They queried the proper role of the RTHK. It was argued that public funds should not be spent on a station which keeps producing satirical programmes and making sarcastic remarks about the government. Mr. Xu Simin, a long-time veteran supporter of the Beijing government and an influential figure in Hong Kong, even voiced his dissatisfaction at the RTHK at a meeting of the National Committee of the Chinese Peoples' Political Consultative Conference. Both the Chairman of the Conference and the President of the PRC reminded him that this was not a matter for the Central Government but something which should be resolved in Hong Kong. Despite such clear message, RTHK remains a constant subject of attacks. It was heavily criticized again after it broadcast an interview with Mr. Cheng An-kuo, the Taiwan representative in Hong Kong who explained the view of Mr. Lee Teng-hui, the former Taiwan President, on his 2-state theory.[53] Ms Cheung Man Yee, the director of RTHK who is regarded as a staunch defender of editorial freedom of RTHK, admitted that there had been political pressure during her 13 years as head of RTHK.[54] Her transfer to Tokyo as the Hong Kong Economic and Trade Representative in September 1999 only added to the suspicion of submission of the HKSAR government to external political pressure.

Another worrying trend affecting press freedom is the significant increase in defamation suit against the media. Because of the nature of its activities, the media is particularly susceptible to defamation suit. Although this is only a civil claim which would not result in the deprivation of personal liberty, the chilling effect of a civil claim on freedom of the press, especially against a small publisher, should not be undermined. As Thompson CJ put it in the leading case of *City of Chicago v Tribune Co*, "while in the early history of the struggle for freedom of speech the restrictions were enforced by criminal prosecutions, it is clear that a civil action is as great, if not a greater, restriction than a criminal prosecution. If the right to criticize the government is a privilege which, with the exceptions above enumerated, cannot be restricted, then all civil as well as criminal actions are forbidden. A despotic or corrupt government can more easily stifle opposition by a series of civil actions than by criminal prosecutions."[55]

Ironically, many of the defamation suits were brought by the media against one another. Traditionally freedom of expression is a struggle by the media against government intervention.[56] The number of defamation suits in the last few years suggests that the greatest threat for freedom of the press now comes from within the media itself when the media organizations are engaged in the business of civil suits against one another. How did it all start?

An important case is *Cheung Ng Sheong v Eastweek Publisher Ltd*.[57] The plaintiff was a leading professor of economics at the University of Hong Kong. He brought an action for libel against Eastweek magazine for publishing an article in which he said he was defamed. The case was heard before a jury. Professor Cheung succeeded in his action, and was awarded an unprecedented amount of damages by the jury in the sum of $2.4 million. The damages were subsequently set aside by the Court of Appeal on the ground that such unprecedented jury award was well above the general level of awards made by judges and that an award of such size was likely to have a serious effect on freedom of expression and could not be justified by the need to protect the reputation of the plaintiff. The case was remitted to the Court of First Instance for re-assessment for damages, and it was subsequently settled privately between the parties. Nonetheless, the success of this case at first instance has had a profound impact on subsequent libel suits. In the first place, it becomes increasingly common to elect for jury trial in defamation suit, which has not been the case for over 80 years in Hong Kong before the *Cheung* case. Secondly, it is somehow expected that this case may mark the beginning of more generous awards of damages in defamation case, as the level of awards in the past has always been criticized as unrealistically low which make defamation suit impractical. Indeed, the high level of award for damages has even attracted Beijing Television to bring defamation proceedings in Hong Kong.[58]

A quick glance at the law reports in the last few years reveals that Oriental Press Group and its associated publications are active suitors in defamation proceedings against other media organizations.[59] The most well known suit is *Eastern Express Publisher v Mo Man Ching Claudia.*[60] The defendants were a television presenter and the Director of Broadcasting of RTHK. They were sued for defamation in relation to two statements made by the first defendant in a television programme which focused on the activities of the news media. The words complained of indicated a reference to a trend of the media of treading on each other by legal process (the first statement), and the imputation was that the second plaintiff was prone to threaten legal proceedings "every time; it was mentioned, even incidentally," that it appeared "to want to frighten people into keeping their mouths shut" (the second statement). At first instance, the trial judge held that the first statement was not defamatory, and the second statement, while defamatory of the second plaintiff, constituted in substance fair comment on a matter of public interest, and the plaintiffs' claims were dismissed. On appeal, the Court of Appeal reversed the judge's decision in relation to the second statement. The defendants were only able to point to one occasion when the plaintiff had acted in the over sensitive and bullying way as suggested in the statement. It held that one incident alone could not be "regarded as evidence of a persistent attitude describable by the words 'every time'" as used by the first defendant in the programme. On further appeal, the Court of Final Appeal allowed the appeal and held that the defence of fair comment had been made out. The main difference between the Court of Appeal and the Court of Final Appeal lies in their different approach to interpreting the words "every time." The Court of Final Appeal held that the Court of Appeal had taken the words "every time" too literally. The statement was in a sense rhetorical and should be taken as a figure of speech. Litton PJ stated:

> It is a defence to an action for libel that the words complained of, though derogatory of the plaintiff, are fair comment on a matter of public interest. It is

> a matter of balance. There is a public interest in the airing of views honestly held on matters of general concern even if those views be prejudiced or exaggerated. On the other hand, one cannot go too far and a defendant actuated by malice cannot rely on the defence….
>
> The question as to whether the pleaded comment was fair is not reached simply by numbers. The weight and substance of the underlying facts on which the comment was based had to be weighed….
>
> As to the ultimate question: was the comment "fair," the judge said that it was "cynical and even possibly prejudiced against the plaintiff, but it was a comment which an honest person could have made." She therefore found in favour of the defendants on their defence of fair comment. In my judgment, Yuen J was entitled to reach this conclusion upon the evidence. The grounds upon which the Court of Appeal reversed her were unwarranted….
>
> This is the type of case where the actionable harm done to the plaintiffs, if there be any, turned on what has been called an "impressionistic view" formed in the mind of the average viewer of the television programme. Finely chewing over the words used, matching them against the pleadings, tend more to distort the issue than to elucidate it.[61]

The approach of the Court of Final Appeal is to be welcome. The question whether a comment is fair turns on the relationship between the facts and the comment made upon them. The law does not require a comment to be "warranted." It only requires the comment to be such that a fair-minded man might honestly make it, provided that there is a substructure of fact to justify the comment. In resolving the issues, an impressionistic approach should be adopted. The general public is not to dissect a newspaper article or a fleeting glance of a television programme with the relentless surgical knife of the lawyer in a courtroom.

Of course, the war among media is not confined to the Oriental Group, which has also been sued by other media organization.[62] Another well known defamation suit is that between two celebrities, *Tse Wai Chun Paul v Cheng Albert.*[63] The plaintiff was a solicitor and a public figure, and the defendants were the hosts of a very popular radio programme on current affairs. The alleged defamation arose from certain statements made by the respondents in a radio programme in relation to the role of the plaintiff in rescuing a tour guide who was sentenced to life imprisonment in the Philippines for alleged drug trafficking and in advising him on claiming compensation from his ex-employer. The defendants relied, among other things, on the defence of fair comment, and the main issue was whether the defence of fair comment was defeated by malice, and whether the proof of honesty is sufficient to show that there is no malice. At first instance, the trial judge ruled that there was no evidence of malice on the part of the radio station. The jury found in favour of the radio station, but found against the hosts of the programme, thereby implicitly accepting that the plaintiff had succeeded in proving malice in respect of the hosts. The jury awarded damages in the sum of $80,000. The Court of Appeal held that although the defence of qualified privilege and fair comment are not the same, the test of malice for both defences is the same. This test depends on a number of factors, including whether a defendant knows what he says is true, whether he honestly believes in the truth of what he says, whether he has any motive to serve other than expressing an honest opinion, whether that other motive is the dominant motive for saying what he says. If he knows what he says is not true, or that he does not believe in the truth of what he says, that is generally conclusive evidence of malice. While honesty or honest belief is a necessary condition, their presence is not always sufficient to absolve the defendant from liability if it can be shown that he makes his comment about the plaintiff for some other motive and that such motive is the dominant motive behind what he says. In a landmark judgment, the Court of Final Appeal reversed the decision of the Court of Appeal. It held that the right to fair comment was a most important element in freedom of speech. The Court should therefore adopt a broad view on the defence so that the right of fair comment on matters of public interest was maintained in full vigour. The defence of fair comment rested on the basis that everyone was at liberty to conduct social and political campaigns by expressing his own views, subject to the objective safeguards which marked the limits of the defence. Therefore, as those who made public comments in the social and political fields would usually have some objective of their own in mind, the presence of malice was not by itself a reason for excluding the defence.

A final case of interest here is *Oriental Press Group v Commercial Radio*. The plaintiff sued the defendants for defamation in relation to certain words spoken by a caller to a radio phone-in programme. The radio station, but not the programme hosts, was found liable. This case exposes a difficulty for radio and television in broadcasting live programmes. Even after taking precautionary measures, it is not possible to control what a participant is going to say in a live programme. In England, section 1 of the Defamation Act 1996 provides a defence if a person can show that he was not the author, editor or publisher of the statement complained of, that he took reasonable care in relation to its publication, and that he did not know, and had no reason to believe, that what he did caused or contributed to the publication of a defamatory statement. In this context, a person shall not be considered the author, editor or publisher of a statement if he is only involved as the broadcaster of a live programme containing the statement in the circumstances in which he has no effective control over the maker of the statement.[64] There is no doubt a strong case for the introduction of a similar amendment in Hong Kong.

Freedom of speech is one of the fundamental freedoms in our society. That freedom is subject to limits which are necessary to protect, *inter alia*, the rights and reputation of others. As far as the media is concerned, the exercise of freedom of expression carries special duties and responsibilities not to abuse their position. In some of the defamation cases in the last few years, the defamatory statements are clearly unwarranted. In some situations, taking out defamation suits can hardly be justified. A free society should be able to tolerate different kinds of views and opinions, even when those views are shocking or offensive. If the media expects the government to be tolerant of all kinds of criticisms against it, some of which may even be groundless or frivolous, then the media should be expected to show the same kind of tolerance towards comments of other media organizations. The present culture of litigating against one another is hardly conducive to the maintenance of freedom of the press.

The Press Council

In August 1999, the Law Reform Subcommittee on Privacy published a consultation paper on the Regulation of Media Intrusion. It documented numerous incidents of media intrusion to privacy and proposed the introduction of a statutory Press Council for the Protection of Privacy. This was the second time when a press council was proposed, and like the previous occasion, the proposal was met with strong opposition. However, various studies and surveys did point out that the community was not satisfied with the quality of newspaper and the blatant intrusion to privacy.[65] The media felt the pressure and discussed the need to establish a self-regulatory body to address the problem. Eventually, 11 major daily newspapers, the Hong Kong News Executives Association and the Hong Kong Federation of Journalists agreed to establish a Press Council which was a private self-regulating body comprising representatives of the press and public members. Two major newspapers, the *Oriental Daily* and the *Apple Daily*, which have the largest circulation in Hong Kong, as well as the Hong Kong Journalists Association and the Hong Kong Press Photographers Association refused to join the Press Council. The Press Council was incorporated on 23 June 2000 as a company under the Companies Ordinance.

In its first year of operation, the Press Council has received over 40 complaints, over half of which were directed against non-member newspapers. In view of its lack of jurisdiction over non-member newspapers and its concern for legal action against itself or against any newspaper that is willing to publish the comment of the Council, the Press Council decided to incorporate itself, though a private member bill, to become a statutory body, to introduce a statutory complaint mechanism, and to confer qualified privilege on its decisions made pursuant to the complaint mechanism and on any newspaper in reporting such decisions. Under the proposed Press Council Bill, the proposed Press Council had no power to award compensation or fine or even legal cost. All it could do was to make a public censure, and there were detailed provisions governing its membership to ensure that it was an independent self-regulatory body.

The proposed private member bill received strong opposition from the Hong Kong Journalists Association and the Hong Kong Press Photographers Association, both of which took the stance that any press council to regulate the press was an unjustifiable restriction on press freedom and that it was wrong to provide a licence and to confer immunity on a body to attack other press. They proposed that the best way to deal with media intrusion of privacy and to uphold the quality of the press was by way of education and self-restraint. Supporters of the Press Council were not impressed by the resort to education alone, and pointed out that the private member bill merely introduced an independent voice to monitor the quality of the press and the complaint mechanism could contribute to the education purpose. Some political parties took the view that a statutory body would open to manipulation by the government, although the argument, taking to its logical end, would mean that no statutory body could ever be independent. At the time of writing, the fate of the proposed Press Council is still unclear, but it does highlight increasing dissatisfaction with the quality or practice of the press, which does not seem to have done enough to uphold its professional ethics or standards.

A Subservient Culture

In July 2000, Dr Robert Chung, a researcher at the University of Hong Kong, made a public allegation that he was told by the Vice-Chancellor of the University via a Pro-Vice-Chancellor that the Chief Executive of the HKSAR wanted him to stop carrying out opinion polls on his popularity.[66] In view of the serious nature of the allegation, an independent inquiry chaired by Mr. Justice Power, a retired judge of the Court of Appeal, was conducted. The investigation revealed that the message was the result of a conversation between the Vice-Chancellor and Mr. Andrew Lo, the aide of the Chief Executive. The meeting as well as the discussion on the opinion polls were admitted, though the precise content of the conversation was unclear. The Chief Executive denied any knowledge of the visit of the Vice-Chancellor by Mr. Andrew Lo, and announced his complete trust in Mr. Lo even before the commencement of the enquiry. In contrast, the inquiry found Mr. Lo a poor and untruthful witness. He might well be acting on what he thought the Chief Executive wanted, and the Vice-Chancellor in turn acted on what he thought the Chief Executive would like him to do. The Chief Executive himself may not know about what Mr. Lo has done, nor would he have approved of what Mr. Lo did if he knew about it. It is most likely that the Chief Executive himself might have expressed some displeasure about the popular poll; those near him then took the decision to do something which they thought would please the Chief Executive. On a more macro level, such "eager to please" attitude could be found among some senior civil servants and influential public figures, who appear to be regularly second-guessing the wishes of Beijing. As one witness at the inquiry rightly remarked, such subservient culture was going to erode Hong Kong and would present the greatest threat to freedom of expression.[67] The Vice-Chancellor was found guilty of interfering with academic freedom by the Committee of Inquiry. He resigned on 6 September 2000 without admitting that he had done anything improper. The University Council, apparently under heavy lobby, decided to receive without endorsing the report of the inquiry. The Legislative Council tried unsuccessfully to launch an independent investigation on the role of Mr. Lo.

Democratic Development

Prior to the changeover, Hong Kong has a three-tier political system: the

Legislative Council, the Regional and the Urban Council, and the District Boards. As a result of the controversial political reform introduced by the last Governor, all three tiers of political organs comprised directly or indirectly elected members since 1995. The Chinese government refused to accept such political reform, and declared that the electoral provisions concerning the election of these organs were not adopted as the law of the HKSAR. The through-train was derailed, so it was known. As it was not possible to hold election before the changeover, all three tiers of government were replaced by provisional bodies upon the changeover.

A Provisional Regional Council and a Provisional Urban Council were formed on 1 July 1997. The two provisional municipal councils comprised appointed members only. All the former elected members of the two councils were appointed to the provisional municipal councils alongside other appointed members. Their terms of office expired on 31 December 1999.

For many years the two municipal councils provided environmental, hygiene, licensing and artistic and cultural services throughout Hong Kong. They were largely autonomous bodies which had their own sources of revenue and executive arms to implemented policies that they decided upon. In late 1999, the government introduced the Re-Organisation of Municipal Services Ordinance which abolished the municipal councils and transferred their functions to the government. The government argued that it was unnecessary and inefficient to have a three-tier structure in Hong Kong, and that the two municipal councils had not been working efficiently in the past. Members of the two Provisional municipal councils criticized the move as a retrograde step. They argued that the municipal councils were the only tier of political structure where members of the public could meaningfully participate in policy making in the areas of hygiene, arts and culture, and sports development. They proposed to merge rather than to abolish the two councils. The government rejected this proposal and successfully persuaded the Legislative Council to support the Re-organisation Ordinance, partly on the promises that some of the existing functions would be transferred to the newly formed District Councils (which will replace the former District Boards and which will enjoy wider decision making power). The two municipal councils were abolished on 1 January 2000, but the promise to transfer the functions of the two municipal councils to the District Councils was not implemented. A former member of the Regional Council challenged without success the abolition of the two municipal councils as a violation of the right to participate in public affairs.[68] The Human Rights Committee, in its concluding observation made on the 5th periodic report submitted by the HKSAR government, also expressed concern that the abolition of the two municipal councils would "further diminish the opportunity of HKSAR residents to take part in the conduct of public affairs that is guaranteed under article 25 of the ICCPR."[69]

Conclusion

On the whole, the people of the HKSAR still enjoy a relatively high degree of freedom. There is a vibrant press and a strong and independent judiciary. On the other hand, there are worrying signs which may suggest a gradual erosion of human rights. Members of the judiciary have been subject to personal attack on racial grounds. Self-censorship is noticeable. The government has shown a weak commitment to the rule of law. The inconsistent prosecution policy, the readiness to subdue public demonstrations, the lukewarm approach in democratic reform, and the prevalence of a subservient culture, are all signs of concern. Without a strong commitment to human rights and the rule of law, protection of human rights in Hong Kong rests on a precarious foundation, namely the degree of self-restraint and tolerance by the Central Government. The Falun Gong issue and the enactment of treason and sedition law (which is required under Article 23 of the Basic Law) will provide a litmus test on the commitment and determination of the government in upholding human rights and a separate legal system in Hong Kong. Unfortunately, the prevalence of a subservient culture means that the HKSAR government may be too ready to identify itself with the interests of the Central Government and too ready to compromise fundamental rights and the rule of law in light of the slightest competing interests or policies of the Central Government. It is not sufficiently recognized that by defending the rule of law and the protection of human rights, Hong Kong can in fact be making great contribution to the modernization and judicial and political reform in China. The danger of a subservient culture is that it is too easy to go beyond what the lord pleases in pleasing the lord.

To some extent the problem is inherent in the system. "One country, two systems" is a journey without destination. It is unclear whether the ultimate goal is to retain two equally thriving but different systems, or whether it is to assimilate Hong Kong into the mainland politically, legally, culturally and ideologically. As long as there is no clear destination, there will be tensions to maintain a separate liberal tradition on the one hand and to assimilate Hong Kong into the mainland on the other. Protection for human rights in such circumstances will always be precarious.

Notes

1. Joint Declaration, para 5. This guarantee is further elaborated in Annex I, para 14 of the Joint Declaration.
2. Joint Declaration, Annex I, para 14.
3. See Communication from the government of the PRC to the Director-General of the ILO dated 1 September 1989, reproduced in A Byrnes and J Chan (eds), *Public Law and Human Rights: A Hong Kong Source Book* (Butterworths, 1993), p. 525.
4. *Case No 1553 v United Kingdom (Hong Kong)*, 277th Report of the ILO Committee on Freedom of Association, ILO Doc GB 249/8/14 (1991), paras 448–468.
5. *Case No 1550 v China*, 270th Report of the ILO Committee on Freedom of Association, ILO Doc GB 245/5/8 (1990), paras 287–334; *Case No 1652 v China*, 286th Report of the ILO Committee on Freedom of Association, ILO Doc, paras 674–728.
6. They were the Trade Unions (Amendment) (No 2) Ordinance 1997 (Ord No 102 of 1997), Employee's Rights to Representation, Consultation and Collective Bargaining Ordinance 1997 (Ord No 101 of 1997), and Employment (Amendment) (No 4) Ordinance 1997 (Ord No 98 of 1997). See Legislative Provisions (Suspension of Operation) Ordinance 1997 (Ord No 126 of 1997) (18 July 1997) for the suspension and Employment and Labour Relations (Miscellaneous Amendments) Ord 1997 (Ord No 135 of 1997) (29 Oct 1997) for the repeal.
7. *Case No 1942 v HKSAR/PRC*, ILO Doc GB 273/6/1, http://www.ilo.org/public/english/20gb/does/gb273/gb-6-1.htm#Case no 1942.
8. For a more detailed discussion, see J Chan, "State Succession to Human Rights Treaties: Hong Kong and the International Covenant on Civil and Political Rights" (1996) 45 *International and Comparative Law Quarterly* 928–946; R Mushkat, "Hong Kong and Succession of Treaties" (1997) 46 *International and Comparative Law Quarterly* 181–201. The PRC has ratified the ICESCR since then, but not the ICCPR which it has signed.
9. See J. Chan, "The Status of the Bill of Rights in the HKSAR" (1998) 28 *Hong Kong Law Journal* 152–55. The provisions that were not adopted as the law of the HKSAR were section 2(3) (the purposes of the ordinance), section 3 (the effect of the Bill of Rights on pre-existing legislation) and section 4 (the requirement to interpret subsequent legislation in line with the ICCPR as applied to Hong Kong).

10. See *HKSAR v Ng Kung Siu* [2000] 1 HKC 117 at 134. See also *Ng Ka Ling v Director of Immigration* [1999] 1 HKC 291 at 337 where the Court of Final Appeal struck down the provision of the Immigration (Amendment)(No 3) Ordinance which created retrospective criminal offence for being inconsistent with Article 15 of the ICCPR and Article 39 of the Basic Law.
11. Siu Sin-por, "'Judicial Activism' Creates Court Chaos," *South China Morning Post*, 20 Feb 2000; Siu Sin-por, "Abide by Rule of Law — Not Judges" *South China Morning Post*, 2 March 2001.
12. See, for example, Margaret Ng, "Covenant Must Be Honoured," *South China Morning Post*, 27 Feb 2001; Audrey Eu, "Our Judges, Our Law," *South China Morning Post*, 25 Feb 2001; Ronny Tong, "Is the Judiciary a Human Right Activist?" *Hong Kong Financial Daily*, 26 Feb 2001.
13. For example, the Tokyo Convention Act which incorporates into domestic law the Tokyo Convention, and the Crimes (Torture) Ordinance which incorporates the Torture Convention. Decolonization history of the UK since the early 1950s provided plenty of examples of incorporating the European Convention on Human Rights into domestic constitution. The Human Rights Act in the UK is the latest example of incorporating the European Convention on Human Rights into UK domestic law.
14. General Comment 3(13), adopted by the United Nations Human Rights Committee at its 311th meeting on 28 July 1981.
15. [1999] 1 HKLRD 315.
16. [2000] 4 HKC 1, see below.
17. Quoted in Secretary of State for Foreign and Commonwealth Affairs, *Six-monthly Report on Hong Kong: July–December 2000 to the UK Parliament*, Cm 5067, Feb 2001, para 23.
18. [1999] 1 HKLRD 315. This case also raised important issues on the central-local relationship and the degree of autonomy of the HKSAR. For a more detailed discussion, see Chan, Fu and Ghai (eds.), *Hong Kong Constitutional Debates: Conflict over Interpretation* (Hong Kong University Press, 2000).
19. *HKSAR v Ng Kung Siu* [2000] 1 HKC 117; *Lau Kong Yung v Director of Immigration* [1994] 4 HKC 731; *Director of Immigration v Chong Fung Yuen* [2001] 2 HKLRD 533.
20. See, for example, *Chong Fung Yuen v Director of Immigration* [2000] 1 HKC 359 (CFI); *Chan Shu Ying v Chief Executive of the HKSAR* [2001] 2 HKC 342 (when the court rejected the relevance of the report of the Preparatory Committee which was regarded by the NPCSC to embody the legislative intention of Article 24 of the Basic Law).
21. *HKSAR v Ma Wai Kwan David* [1997] 2 HKC 315.
22. *Chan Shu Ying v Chief Executive of the HKSAR* [2001] 2 HKC 342.
23. *HKSAR v Ng Kung Siu* [2000] 1 HKC 117.

24. *Chen Li Hung v Ting Lei Miao* [2000] 1 HKC 461; *CEF New Asia Co Ltd v Wong Kwong Yiu John* [1999] 3 HKC 1.
25. *Director of Immigration v Chong Fung Yuen* [2001] 2 HKLRD 533 at 545–547.
26. The motion was debated at length on 11 March 1999 and was defeated by 30 to 21, with eight abstentions.
27. See 'Magistrate discharged another two theft suspects', *Ming Pao*, 3 March 2001, p. A12.
28. Hong Kong Bar Association, "Rights of Peaceful Assembly or Procession," 25 Nov 2000, http://www.hkba.org/press-release/20001125.htm.
29. The government explained that no action was taken against other demonstrators in the previous occasions because they were only involved in "breaches of a minor or technical nature." HKSAR government, "Responses to Frequently Asked Questions on Public Order Ordinance," 14 Dec 2000, http://www.info.gov.hk/gia/general/200012/14/poo.htm.
30. The Secretary for Security had on various occasions stated that the students were a source of headache. She also lamented over a tragedy where some illegal immigrants pending repatriation as a result of the NPCSC's interpretation of Article 24 of the Basic Law set fire at the Immigration Department resulting in the death of an immigration officer. Support for the illegal immigrants in fighting for their right of abode was seen as an encouragement to the illegal immigrants and a cause to the tragedy.
31. Ord No 64 of 1967, Cap 245. It was also partly a consolidation ordinance which consolidated various provisions dealing with public order in the Public Order Ordinance, the Peace Preservation Ordinance, the Summary Offences Ordinance and the common law. For a useful discussion, see R Mushkat, "Peaceful Assembly," in R. Wacks (ed.), *Human Rights in Hong Kong* (Oxford University Press, 1992), pp. 410–38.
32. [1979] HKLR 275. See also Bernard Downey, 'Public Gatherings' (1979) 9 *Hong Kong Law Journal* 114–115.
33. Public Order (Amendment) Ordinance 1980.
34. See J. Chan and K Lau, "Some Reflections on the Human Rights Committee's Hearing of the United Kingdom Second Report on Dependent Territories, held November 4–5, 1988 in Geneva" (1990) 20 *Hong Kong Law Journal* 150 at 170–173.
35. For a detailed comment on these amendments, see J Chan, "Human Rights: From One Era to Another", in Joseph Cheng (ed), *The Other Hong Kong Report 1997* (Hong Kong: Chinese University Press, 1997), pp. 137–67.
36. See *Siracusa Principles on the Limitation and Derogation Provisions in the ICCPR* (1985) 7 *Human Rights Quarterly* 3–14, and Erica-Irene Daes, *Freedom of the Individual under Law*, Special Rapporteur's Report to the United Nations Sub-Commission on Prevention of Discrimination and

Protection of Minorities, UN Sales No E99.XIV.5 (United Nations, 1990)

37. Reported in Hong Kong Journalists Association, *Annual Report 1998*, p 11.
38. See, for example, *HKSAR v Tam Chun-yin* (1998) Mag, ESC 5206 of 1997 (3 June 1998).
39. See *South China Morning Post,* 5 June 1998.
40. "Police Political Neutrality Compromised," press statement of Human Rights Monitor, 24 September 2001.
41. For a critical analysis of the police power, see Hong Kong Bar Association, "Rights of Peaceful Assembly or Procession," supra. There is also a list of US authorities which held that any licencing system on the exercise of the right to public demonstration or peaceful assembly was unconstitutional: see *Kunz v New York*, 340 US 290 (1951), *Shuttlesworth v Birmingham*, 394 US 147 (1969), *Cox v New Hampshire*, 312 US 569 (1941). See also *Hubbard v Pitt* [1976] QB 142.
42. Section 2, Societies Ordinance (Cap 115). A society which is established *solely* for religious, charitable, social or recreational purposes or as a rural committee can be exempted, but even in such cases exemption has to be sought: section 5A.
43. Hong Kong Bar Association, *Submission on the Consultation Document on Civil Liberties and Social Order*, 23 April 1997.
44. To make things worse, any appeal against the decision of the Societies Officer shall be made to the Chief Executive in Council, and not to an independent tribunal, which is the case when there is an appeal against the decision of the Police Commissioner under the Public Order Ordinance.
45. Chief Executive's Office, *Civil Liberties and Social Order: Consultation Document* (April 1997), para 4.4.
46. See, for example, the editorial of *Ta Kung Pao*, 9 January 2001.
47. Human Rights Monitor, "A Profound Symbolic Loss of Freedom," press statement on 9 August 1999.
48. See the 8th Report of the Hong Kong Journalists Association and Article 19 on freedom of expression in Hong Kong (July 2000).
49. See Hon Sin Mi May, "Mainland Has History of Warnings on News Coverage," *South China Morning Post*, 21 Dec 2000. In December 2000, President Jiang Zemin reminded the press of their social responsibilities and asked the press to play a more positive role in matters bearing on Macau's prosperity and stability and the interest of the state and the people. See Carmen Cheng, "Jiang Calls Media Tune," *HK iMail*, 21 December 2000.
50. Secretary of State for Foreign and Commonwealth Affairs, *Six-monthly Report on Hong Kong: January–June 2000*, Cm 4809, July 2000, para 5. The report also documented another incident in June 2000 when another senior official of the Liaison Office said that Hong Kong businessmen trading with

Taiwanese firms supporting Taiwanese independence were "taking a risk" and should observe the Central Government's policy that "absolutely prohibited" trade with such firms. See para 6, ibid.

51. In April 2000, shortly after the remark made by Mr. Wang Fengchao, an internet service provider apparently deleted an email discussion on independence of Taiwan and blocked such messages. See *Hong Kong Standard*, 30 April 2000.
52. See M. Zee, "Silencing the Lam," *South China Morning Post*, 6 Nov 2000; "Intervention in SAR Criticised," *South China Morning Post*, 1 December 2000.
53. Wu Kay Wen, "Cheng An Kuo Incident," *Ming Pao*, 23 August 1999.
54. A. Li, "Head of RTHK Admits There Was Pressure over Politics," *South China Morning Post*, 25 October 1999. See also R Cullen, "Media Freedom in China Hong Kong" (1998) 11 *Transnational Lawyer* 383 and the annual reports of the Hong Kong Journalist Association between 1997 and 2000.
55. (1923) 139 NE 86 at 90. The passage was endorsed by the Supreme Court of the United States in *New York Times v Sullivan* (1964) 376 US 254 at 277.
56. In *Hong Kong Polytechnic University v Next Magazine* (1997) 7 HKPLR 286, while the Court of Appeal held that the university had a right to sue in defamation, it accepted that the central or local government had no right to sue in defamation.
57. (1995) 5 HKPLR 428.
58. *Beijing Television v Brightec Ltd* [1999] 2 HKC 665.
59. See, for example, *Oriental Press Group v Hong Kong Daily New* [1997] 3 HKC 622, *Oriental Daily Publisher Ltd v Tin Tin Publication Development Ltd* [1998] HKCU 164, *Oriental Press Group Ltd v Next Magazine Publishing Ltd* [1999] HKCU 1382, *Oriental Daily Publisher Ltd v Ming Pao Holdings Ltd* [1999] 4 HKC 354.
60. [1998] 2 HKC 593 (CFI), [1999] 1 HKC 64 (CA), [1999] 4 HKC 425 (CFA).
61. At 431, 433, 434.
62. For example, *Oriental Daily Publisher Ltd v Easy Finder Ltd* [1997] 3 HKC 348 (CFI), [1998] 1 HKC 546 (CA).
63. [1999] 4 HKC 272 (CFI), [2000] 1 HKC 712 (CA). [2000] 4 HKC 1 (CFA).
64. Section 1(1) & (3)(d), Defamation Act 1996, c 31.
65. See, for example, the Subcommittee on Privacy *Consultation Paper on The Regulation of Media Intrusion* (Law Reform Commission, August 1999), ch 2.
66. For a more detailed account, see C Peterson, "Preserving Academic Freedom in Hong Kong: Lessons from the 'Robert Chung' Affair" (2000) 30 *Hong Kong Law Journal* 165–76.
67. In January 2001, the Cultural and Entertainment Bureau reserved an unprecedently large number of tickets for senior government officials for the piano performance of an award winning pianist from the mainland who gave

only one performance in Hong Kong: see *Ming Pao*, 19 January 2001. A minor affair as it may be, it amply demonstrates the prevalence of the subservient culture in Hong Kong.

68. *Chan Shu Ying v Chief Executive in Council* [2001] HKLRD 405.
69. UN Doc CCPR/C/79/ADD.117, para 12.

5

Hong Kong Economy in Crisis

Yun-Wing Sung
Professor, Department of Economics
The Chinese University of Hong Kong

Hong Kong Economy in Crisis

The year of Hong Kong's reversion to the mainland, 1997, has been a watershed for the economy. Hong Kong's economic performance deteriorated sharply in the post 1997 era. Though the Central government has largely honoured its promise to refrain from intervention in Hong Kong affairs and also maintained the pre-1997 economic framework, Hong Kong's economic performance nevertheless fell flat in the post 1997 era.

The sharp deterioration in economic performance since 1997 can easily be seen in major economic indicators. The average annual rate of growth of per capita GDP fell from 4.5 per cent in the pre-reversion era (1983–97) to 1.9 per cent in the post-reversion era (1997–2001). The unemployment rate from 1985 to mid 1997 was very low, ranging from 1.3 per cent to a maximum of 3.5 per cent. In the post-reversion era, the unemployment rate rose sharply, shooting up from 2.1 per cent in mid 1997 to a record of 7.4 per cent in May 2002.

The deterioration is largely not the responsibility of Beijing. It is partly coincidental, as the Asian Financial Crisis that started with the devaluation of the Thai Baht occurred exactly one day after Hong Kong's reversion. Furthermore, Hong Kong's hitherto unchallenged position as the gateway of China also started to erode in the late 1990's. The rapid economic development in China has rapidly narrowed the gap between Hong Kong and the mainland in skills and also in infrastructure. Hong Kong faces a loss of competitiveness.

Many of the seeds of Hong Kong's post-1997 economic malaise were sown in the heady pre-1997 prosperity. In the lengthy period of transition from the signing of the 1984 Sino-British Declaration to the 1997 reversion, the elites of Hong Kong spent their energies on speculation in real estate, or in getting foreign passports as a hedge against the 1997 handover. Few worried about erosion of competitiveness.

The long prosperity before 1997 had generated a huge economic bubble, which was unwittingly exacerbated by a clause in the 1984 Sino-British Declaration restricting the annual lease of land to 50 hectares. The clause was inserted by China to forestall a possible pre-emptive attempt on the part of the British administration to lease excessive amounts of land, leaving too little land for the post-1997 government. The clause was intended to ensure a smooth transition. Ironically, it led to a huge real estate bubble, which proved to be a most destabilizing factor in Hong Kong's reversion.

In itself, the bursting of the bubble would at most led to an economic recession. Hong Kong had serious real estate bubbles before, e.g., in 1981, and the economy managed to recover in 1984. The prolong economic malaise of Hong Kong in the post-reversion era cannot be accounted for entirely by the bursting of the real estate bubble, or by the Asian Financial Crisis, or by the slowdown of the US economy in 2001. Hong Kong faces a loss of competitiveness, and improvement in economic performance would require a fundamental restructuring of the Hong Kong economy.

Unfortunately, the HKSAR government is ill equipped to deal with the economic crisis. The Sino-British dispute over Governor Pattern's reform proposals before the reversion led to "elite fragmentation" as both Britain and China tried to win over Hong Kong's elites (Lau 1999: 51–60). Tung Chee-hwa, the first HKSAR Chief Executive, failed to build a strong coalition as a result of his limited political experience (Lau 1999: 61–70). The HKSAR government was inexperienced and its ability to manage the economic crisis was severely limited. The erratic responses and policies of the Tung Chee-Hwa Administration have compounded the economic malaise.

Loss of Competitiveness

The opening of China in 1979 naturally led to the re-integration of the

Hong Kong economy with its hinterland. There is a huge wage-gap between Hong Kong and the mainland and Hong Kong has relocated its less skill intensive activities to the mainland, first in manufacturing and then in services. Through outsourcing, Hong Kong gains through specializing on the more skill-intensive processes. This leads to productivity gain, as the relocation of low-end services would free Hong Kong's manpower for high-end services such as financial services, order-taking, logistics, and headquarter functions. As Hong Kong is a developed economy, it should concentrate on the knowledge-intensive part of the production chain, following the example of New York and London.

However, productivity gain by outsourcing low-value added activities (whether labour-intensive manufacturing or low-end services) is once-for-all. The process would eventually lead to the outsourcing of all low-value activities that could be relocated, and there would be no more productivity gain through outsourcing. Sustained growth would require improvement in efficiency and technology. Without continuous improvement in technology, Hong Kong would not be able to maintain its lead in skills, and outsourcing would only lead to the hollowing out of the Hong Kong economy.

Unfortunately, empirical study confirmed that there was no improvement in technology or efficiency in the Hong Kong economy from 1984 to 1996 (Kwong 2000). In the prosperity of the pre-1997 era, there was little pressure to improve technology and efficiency as easy money could be obtained through relocation of manufacturing or low-end services. The rapid economic development of China has greatly narrowed the gap in skills and in infrastructure between the mainland and Hong Kong. Though the economies of Hong Kong and the mainland are still complementary in many ways, there is increasing competition between the two. For instance, as a result of the development of ports in Shanghai and in Guangdong, the mainland is no longer so dependent on the port of Hong Kong. The share of China's trade re-exported via Hong Kong fell from a peak of 42 per cent in 1996 to 27 per cent in 2001.

Outsourcing, Adjustment, and Unemployment

Outsourcing of less skill-intensive activities from the metropolis to its hinterland is beneficial for the metropolis as long as it maintains a lead in skills and technology over its hinterland, or over rival hubs that may emerge in the hinterland. Even then, the gain from specialization has a price. Outsourcing involves structural adjustment because unskilled workers in the metropolis lost their jobs while skilled workers have to be trained to support the growing skill-intensive activities. If unskilled workers can easily be retrained into skilled workers, the adjustment process would not be painful. Unfortunately, this is often not the case. Displaced workers in sunset industries are often advanced in age, and the effectiveness of retraining declines with age.

To be sure, New York or London also supports some less skill-intensive jobs because highly skilled people also demand personal services that are less skill-intensive, e.g. haircuts and restaurants. However, the number of such unskilled jobs is limited. Moreover, the hairstylists and restaurants in New York or London have to be of a high quality to satisfy the demand of their cosmopolitan yuppies. By and large, it is still true that the less skilled will have a hard time surviving in London or New York.

In the case of New York, London and the other cities, adjustment has not been too painful as the process of outsourcing is very gradual, taking place naturally as the cities grow. In the case of Hong Kong's reintegration with the mainland, adjustment has been very rapid. A huge wage gap had emerged between Hong Kong and the mainland during the 1949–79 Cold War in which Hong Kong was estranged from its hinterland. The barriers to reintegration were rapidly removed starting 1979 and Hong Kong firms have since relocated to the mainland in droves. Unemployment in Hong Kong reached record-breaking levels in 1999–2001, deepening the sense of economic malaise.

Coping with Unemployment

Besides retraining, there are three other ways to tackle the adjustment problem, namely, migration, public assistance, and protection. Each method has its limitations and adjustment can be very painful for the displaced workers.

As mentioned above, retraining is usually of limited value. Displaced workers can migrate elsewhere to look for work. In Hong Kong, more people are looking for work in the mainland. However, migration is painful as it involves a disruption of the social network of the entire family. Moreover, while migration can help the young and the skilled, it cannot really help the old and the unskilled. Needles to say, public assistance for the unemployed is a palliative rather than a solution.

When all else fails, which is often the case; governments usually turn to protectionism to preserve the jobs of the less skilled. For instance, the US has long restricted imports of textiles and clothing from developing economies to protect the jobs of US clothing workers. In the case of Hong Kong, the congestion of border checkpoints protects Hong Kong retailers as Hong Kong people have swarmed across the border to shop.

Economic textbooks usually argue against protection because it can be shown that, in dollar terms, the costs to consumers due to the higher prices vastly exceeds the gains of the protected workers in the form of wages obtained. While the logic behind the economic argument is quite sound, it can be argued that protection is politically and ethically desirable. Though consumers lose a significant amount, the per capita loss is quite small as the loss is spread over many consumers. Though the gains of protected workers are small relative to the total loss of consumers, the gains are concentrated on those who are in need, namely the displaced workers. While it is possible to think of taxation schemes to help displaced workers, such schemes can be costly in terms of economic efficiency or political opposition.

The textbook case against protection is quite academic and does not capture the worst aspects of protection. The real cost of protection is that it is difficult to dismantle and easily becomes permanent. By protecting an unskilled, sunset industry for a long time, young workers will continue to enter that industry, and the younger generation fails to perceive the importance of upgrading their skills. Protection thus discourages skill accumulation and economic development. Protection sacrifices long-term interests (the welfare of posterity) for short-run gains (the benefit of the present generation of displaced workers).

However, if unemployment reaches a point that is socially explosive, governments may have no choice but resort to protection. In the case of Hong Kong's re-integration with the mainland, the delays over the introduction of 24-hour operation of border checkpoints can be regarded as a form of protection. The wage gap between the mainland and Hong Kong is so large that the process of re-integration has to be managed. Otherwise, the tempo of reintegration may be highly destabilizing.

Two Phases of Outsourcing

After the opening of China in 1979, Hong Kong first relocated its labour-intensive manufacturing to the mainland. Relocation of manufacturing was near completion in the mid 1990s as manufacturing dwindled to negligible proportions in Hong Kong. Relocation of services did not start in earnest till 1992 because foreign investment in services had been severely restricted in the early stage of China's opening. Gradual liberalization only occurred after Deng Xiaoping's 1992 southern tour in support of economic reforms.

It is important to distinguish the two phases of outsourcing. The first phase involves the outsourcing of manufacturing while the second phase involves the outsourcing of services. While outsourcing (whether of manufacturing or of services) increases the competitiveness of the parent firm in Hong Kong, the problem of unemployment is much more severe for outsourcing of services than for outsourcing of manufacturing.

In fact, outsourcing of manufacturing went relatively smoothly in Hong Kong. Though manufacturing employment fell from a record of 919,200 in 1986 to 443,000 in 1997, so many new jobs were created (largely in the service sector) that total employment rose from 2.62 million to 3.16 million in the same period. The unemployment rate was less than 3.5 per cent throughout the period. In contrast, the adjustment problem for outsourcing of services appears to be far more difficult. Though new jobs were also created as the parent firms become more competitive and expand their output, the process of new job creation appears to be quite slow.

There are two reasons for the difference in new job creation between the two phases of outsourcing. First, output expansion is much faster in outsourcing of manufacturing than in services because goods, especially light manufactures, can be easily transported to different parts of the world, while provision of services to different parts of the world is time consuming as it requires establishment of subsidiaries in many locations through foreign investment. In technical terms, the price elasticity of demand for light manufactures is much higher than services. In fact, Hong Kong's manufacturing firms rapidly expanded their output after relocation across the border, and Guangdong rapidly became the world's largest supplier of toys, travel goods, and many kinds of consumer electronics. This rapid expansion of output created many jobs, not only for mainland workers, but also for the parent firms in Hong Kong, which have to manage and support the vast industrial network in Guangdong.

Second, up until the mid-1990s, as a result of the restriction of foreign investment in services in China, China's services were underdeveloped, and Hong Kong has a *temporary monopoly* in South China in port facilities, order-taking, financing, and logistics services. The vast industrial base that Hong Kong had built up in Guangdong depended on Hong Kong for services, creating many jobs in Hong Kong for skilled workers (e.g., logistics management) and also less skilled workers (e.g., container truck drivers). Hong Kong became the service hub of an industrialized Guangdong. As a result of the vast expansion of employment in services, unemployment in Hong Kong was very low.

Outsourcing of manufacturing in phase one was exceedingly benign for Hong Kong. The Hong Kong economy grew rapidly by out-sourcing low-value added manufacturing operations to the mainland, while expanding the higher value-added services in Hong Kong. In the mid 1990's, income generated by China-related services accounted for over 25 per cent of Hong Kong's GDP (Sung and Wong 2000: 225). This led to rapid economic growth in the pre-1997 era.

In the second phase of outsourcing, Hong Kong firms started to relocate backroom services such as accounting, paging services, and data processing to the mainland after its gradual liberalization of foreign investment in services since 1992. Hutchison Whampoa invested in container ports in the mainland, ranging from Yantian near Hong Kong to Shanghai at the mouth of the Yangzi River. These ports started to compete with Hong Kong, and the share of China's trade re-exported via Hong Kong started to decline in 1997.

While the diversion of cargo from Hong Kong to mainland ports has been bad for Hong Kong truck drivers, it has been good for the profits of Hutchison Whampoa and also for the profits of Hong Kong's manufacturing operations in Guangdong as they have access to a less costly port.

There is a misconception that outsourcing of services will lead to the complete hollowing out of the Hong Kong economy. This will not be the case as long as Hong Kong maintains a lead in skills over its hinterland. For instance, New York and London have largely outsourced their less-skilled activities to their hinterland, and they have benefited from specialization in skill-intensive activities.

As mentioned above, outsourcing of low-end services increases the competitiveness of the parent firm, which expands its output and thereby creates more jobs. There are, however, three caveats. The first is that the job creation process is slower than the case in the outsourcing of manufacturing. The second is that the jobs created are largely for the highly skilled. The third is that some of the jobs created may not be in Hong Kong because the parent firm markets its services by establishing subsidiaries elsewhere. This implies that, besides upgrading their skills, Hong Kong workers have to be willing to work outside Hong Kong.

In fact, it is fortunate for Hong Kong that China did not open up both manufacturing and services right from the start. In the first phase of outsourcing of manufacturing, Hong Kong had a temporary monopoly in services because mainland's service sector was not open. The strong demand for Hong Kong services from the vast industrial base in Guangdong fed the growth of Hong Kong's service providers such as Hutchison Whampoa and the Hongkong Bank. These service providers grew big and competitive, and they are well prepared to compete with multinationals as China opens up its services after the entry to WTO.

Knowledge-based Economy

In the long run, Hong Kong has to transform itself into a knowledge-based economy on the model of New York or London, which had relocated most of their less skill-intensive operations to their hinterland. Though they specialize in only a small part of the production chain, that part of the production chain is lucrative as it is knowledge-intensive. For instance, both New York and London are strong in financial services and are prime sites for company headquarters. Needless to say, such activities are very lucrative.

Given the high cost-structure of Hong Kong, there is no alternative but to become a knowledge-based economy. However, the road for Hong Kong will not be easy. Besides the stagnation in technology, Hong Kong also lags behind in skills and in education in comparison with Singapore, Taiwan, and South Korea. Only 18 per cent of the Hong Kong population aged 15 and above has at least post-secondary education, while 48 per cent have an education level of Secondary Three or below (*2001 Policy Address*: p. 11). The goal of the HKSAR government is to double the number of senior secondary school leavers receiving tertiary education from 30 per cent to 60 per cent within the next decade.

According to the report of the World Economic Forum based in Geneva, the Growth Competitiveness Index of Hong Kong slipped from the 2nd place in 1999 to the 7th place in 2000, and slipped again to the 13th place in 2001, ranking way behind Singapore (4th place) and Taiwan (7th place). The Index is determined by three factors: Level of technology, quality of public organizations, and macroeconomic conditions. Technology has a weight of 0.5 while the other two factors each has a weight of 0.25. Hong Kong's poor ranking largely reflects its weak technological base (*Hong Kong Economic Times*, 19 October 2001).

Though Hong Kong is weak in technology and skills, it has many valuable assets that would facilitate its transformation to a knowledge-based economy. Despite the competition from strong rivals such as Singapore and Shanghai, Hong Kong is unique in many ways. As stressed in the 2001 Policy Address of the Chief Executive, Hong Kong is one of the world's freest economies. It has a strong legal system, a level playing field, a stringent and transparent regulatory system, a very liberal foreign exchange regime, the free flow of information, a clean government, a sound financial position, and a simple taxation system (*2001 Policy Address*: p. 3). Moreover, China is the world's fastest growing economy and Hong Kong is its gateway to the world. Hong Kong is well positioned to take advantage of the many business opportunities that will arise from China's entry into the WTO.

Competition with Shanghai

Though Shanghai has grown rapidly in recent years, there are still many obstacles to Shanghai's development as a world-class service hub. The growth of high-end services (e.g., financial services, telecommunications and the media and information industry) requires the rule of law, a fair and efficient regulatory regime, and a clean and transparent administration. Shanghai needs not only economic reforms, but also political reforms, especially reforms of its bureaucracy and government. Political reforms are often time-consuming and risky. It will be very difficult for Shanghai to surpass Hong Kong in rule of law, free flow of information, transparency of regulation and government.

It is well known that Shanghai's development as a financial center has been hampered by the weakness of China's banks and the lack of convertibility of the *Renminbi*. China's banks are burdened by huge bad debts, and cleaning up such debts will take a long time. Unless China's banks are financially sound, opening China's capital account will risk speculative attacks on the *Renminbi*. According to official statements, the *Renminbi* may become fully convertible on the capital account in ten or fifteen years.

In comparison with Hong Kong, Shanghai has the advantage of location as it is situated at the mouth of the Yangzi River, the largest and most prosperous river basin in China. Shanghai is ahead of Hong Kong in industrial technology and it has a diversified industrial base with both light and heavy industries. However, Shanghai does not have a good natural harbour due to the silting of the Yangzi. Shanghai has a plan to build modern container facilities that may rival that of Hong Kong in ten or fifteen years time on Zhejiang's Yangshan islands some 28 kilometers from Shanghai. While the plan is technically feasible, it involves the costly transfer of cargo from big ships to small vessels offshore. Rivalry between Shanghai and Zhejiang, which has the best port, Beilun, in the region, is another problem.

While Shanghai is a serious competitor, there are many areas of complementarity between Shanghai and Hong Kong. For instance, Shanghai is clearly the premier domestic financial center in China, simply because the *Renminbi* does not circulate in Hong Kong. However, Hong Kong has a huge lead over Shanghai as an international financial center. Moreover, the China market is so big that it allows the growth of more than one financial and business center.

Competition with Singapore

Singapore is a tough competitor as its quality of skills, facilities, and infrastructure rival that of Hong Kong. However, Southeast Asian economies, which are the natural hinterland of Singapore, have been severely hit by the Asian Financial Crisis. Indonesia has yet to regain political stability and Malaysia is also in trouble. After the September 11 terrorist attacks on New York, Islamic fundamentalism is a potential source of instability for Singapore. Hong Kong's hinterland is benign, while that of Singapore is hostile.

Singapore has tried to capitalize on its links with China without notable success. Singapore's flagship project, its industrial park in Suzhou, has been a failure. Singapore's dependence on the electronics industry has been a source of official concern due to the worldwide glut in production capacity, especially in chips. In 2001, Singapore's GDP declined by 3.6 per cent while that in Hong Kong still rose by 0.1 per cent. Singapore's response to the 2001 downturn is to diversify out of electronics to high-end services. The competition between Singapore and Hong Kong in high-end services may become more severe.

Singapore has entered into many "new style" Free Trade Agreements (FTAs) that promotes liberalization of services with key economies (e.g., Japan, New Zealand, and Australia). The "new style" FTAs are mainly complements to the multilateral WTO process. Such FTAs proliferated with the stalling of the new round of talks of WTO in Seattle in 1999.

Hong Kong has lagged behind Singapore in cultivating free trade agreements with its major partners for two reasons. First, traditionally, Hong Kong had tried to rely on the multilateral framework of the WTO rather than bilateral or regional agreements. Second, as Hong Kong had been a Colony, its government is very inexperienced in international relations. However, Hong Kong has lately made some headway in negotiating a FTA with New Zealand. More significantly, Hong Kong has started to negotiate a FTA with the mainland.

It should be stressed that Singapore and Hong Kong are in many ways complementary rather than competitive because they serve different regions. Hong Kong and Singapore are separated by a four-hour flight. Singapore is ideally situated to serve Southeast Asia whereas Hong Kong is better located to serve the Chinese mainland, Taiwan, Korea, or even Japan. The size of the Northeast Asian economy is much larger than that in Southeast Asia, and this gives Hong Kong an edge over Singapore as a regional service center.

Impacts of China's WTO Entry on Hong Kong

It is widely recognised that entry into the WTO will pose adjustment problems for some of China's major economic sectors, especially agriculture and heavy industries (steel, chemicals, and automobiles). As long as China can manage the transitional problems, the long run benefits are large, as WTO entry will boost reform and opening in China. China is going through the most difficult phase of her reform process, namely, reform of state-owned enterprises (SOEs), banks, and financial institutions. Entry into the WTO may well provide the decisive boost to China's reform and opening, assuming China can manage the pains of transition.

While Hong Kong is not heavily involved in the mainland's disadvantaged sectors, namely agriculture and heavy industries, she is heavily involved in it's export-oriented light industries, which stand to benefit directly from WTO entry. Hong Kong, as the service hub of China, is also heavily involved in China's services sector. WTO entry will speed up the opening of China's services, providing many opportunities for Hong Kong.

Impacts on Exports

Besides gaining NTR status from the US, China will also gain some protection against anti-dumping duties that are getting more and more prevalent. Moreover, China's textile and clothing exports will expand because the MFA (Multi-Fibre Arrangement) will be phased out in 2005. The greater part of Hong Kong's remaining textile and clothing industries will relocate to the mainland. The gain to Hong Kong will be substantial as Hong Kong has expertise in marketing and organizing production in these industries.

Impacts on Industries Selling to China's Domestic Market

While Hong Kong's outward processing industries will benefit from China's entry to WTO, the impact on Hong Kong's manufacturing companies selling in mainland's domestic market is uncertain. These companies will face a more open market, but there will also be more competition.

Hong Kong has a strong reputation in the production of auto parts, especially micro motors for automobiles. The mainland's automobile industry is quite inefficient, and needs restructuring. To capitalize on the opportunity, Hong Kong has to upgrade the quality of its products and also forge strategic alliances with Chinese and foreign partners (Hong Kong Trade Development Council 2000).

Impacts on Services Trade

China's entry into the WTO will expand both China's imports and exports. Given the efficiency of Hong Kong as a trading centre, the expansion of mainland's trade will imply a greater demand for Hong Kong services.

As Hong Kong has a strong comparative advantage in services, China's entry to WTO will strengthen the position of Hong Kong as the service hub of China. Hong Kong already has a head start in the services sector in the mainland built upon its pioneering investments in outward processing. Hong Kong banks, including the Hong Kong and Shanghai Bank, the Bank of China Group, and the Bank of East Asia have long-established branches in the mainland. Mainland's offshore markets in stocks, bonds, loans and foreign exchange are active in Hong Kong. Besides financial services, Hong Kong should be able to find opportunities in telecommunications, IT, e-commerce, advertising, and freight forwarding.

However, Hong Kong service providers will face keen competition. Mainland's high capital requirements for foreign banks and high sales requirement for foreign retail and wholesale businesses (annual sales over US$2 billion and US$2.5 billion, respectively) imply that smaller Hong Kong businesses cannot enter mainland's market on its own. However, with their knowledge and experience of the China market, Hong Kong firms can form alliances with foreign partners (Hong Kong Trade Development Council, 2000).

The Middleman Role of Hong Kong

The Hong Kong stock market has reacted very positively to the prospect of China's entry to the WTO. However, there are observers that worry Hong Kong will lose its middleman role if China becomes more open because foreign businesses can deal directly with China.

Though the gap in economic development between the mainland and Hong Kong is certainly narrowing, it is not likely that Hong Kong will rapidly lose its comparative advantage as a service hub. There are significant economies of scale and economies of agglomeration in trading and services activities and it is very difficult for other cities such as Taipei, Singapore, and Shanghai to compete with Hong Kong because Hong Kong is the established centre for China's trade and investment (Sung 1991: 28–42). For the same reason, other cities have found it very difficult to challenge the leading positions of New York and London in world finance.

China is entering the third decade of its reform era and many big multinationals have already entered the China market and they are already dealing directly with China. China's entry into the WTO will attract a wave of small and medium-sized enterprises (SMEs) into the China market. Most SMEs will not be big enough to enter the China market directly on its own, and they will seek help from Hong Kong firms and partners. In this age of electronics and the Internet, the average firm size in developed countries are getting smaller, and SMEs are proliferating. Moreover, even though big multinational are dealing with China directly, they still source supporting services from Hong Kong.

Cooperation with the Mainland

Though cooperation with the mainland is crucial to Hong Kong's economy, policy coordination with the mainland had not been smooth due to "elite fragmentation" in Hong Kong. A Hong Kong/Guangdong Co-operation Joint Conference was established in March 1998, headed by

Hong Kong's Chief Secretary and Guangdong's Vice Governor. The Joint Conference was supposed to meet twice a year. However, it had only met thrice in the three years from March 1988. This was a sign that the Hong Kong government has not been very active in pushing for coordination with Guangdong.

After the retirement of Mrs. Anson Chan as Chief Secretary in 2000, the HKSAR government has been more proactive in promoting economic integration with Guangdong and the mainland. In July 2001, the fourth meeting of the Joint Conference agreed to facilitate border crossing, to protect the environment, and to allow more mainland tourists to visit Hong Kong. The two sides also agreed to cooperate on e-commerce, to promote cooperation between the Hong Kong and Zhuhai airports, and to develop logistics and high-tech industries in Nansha, an economic and technological development district in the Pearl River Delta approved in 1993.

Mainland-Hong Kong FTA

In November 2001, China announced that the central government would discuss with Hong Kong about the establishment of a mainland-Hong Kong FTA. While such an FTA has some merits, the difficulties should not be overlooked.

If Hong Kong and the mainland are to form an FTA, they should open their markets to each other beyond their WTO commitments. This should not be difficult for Hong Kong, as its economy is already quite open. However, opening beyond WTO commitments is a problem for the mainland as the present commitments already pose painful adjustments for the mainland.

The FTA is the brainchild of the Hong Kong Chamber of Commerce. The chamber proposed that the mainland should open up to Hong Kong faster than the pace of China's WTO commitments, which schedule opening in various service sectors in three to five years after China's WTO entry. This would allow Hong Kong firms to establish a foothold in mainland's market before the entry of foreign firms. The proposal may also help the mainland to smooth its adjustment to outside competition as competition from Hong Kong businesses is allowed on a selected basis before the full opening to outside competition. The chamber also proposed to allow smaller Hong Kong businesses that do not meet the high threshold requirements to enter the mainland market. This is undoubtedly of tremendous benefit to Hong Kong.

However, opening to Hong Kong in advance of WTO commitments may compromise China's freedom of action. China's commitments are not set in stone. If the adjustment proves too painful, China may want to delay its opening and face possible litigation, which can buy time, as litigation is usually time-consuming. However, if mainland has opened in advance to Hong Kong, China's freedom of manoeuvre will be compromised. Moreover, multinationals can circumvent China's rules by setting up subsidiaries in Hong Kong. To prevent abuses, the identity of Hong Kong business must be carefully defined. This may be difficult as Hong Kong is highly cosmopolitan.

While a mainland-Hong Kong FTA agreement has to clear many hurdles, negotiation of the agreement does signify that economic cooperation between Hong Kong and the mainland has entered a new stage.

Conclusion

Though the Hong Kong economy is in serious trouble, Hong Kong has been known to be very resilient. The Heritage Foundation still ranked Hong Kong number one in the world in economic freedom. While the second structural transformation of the Hong Kong economy may be long and painful, Hong Kong has many assets that would steer her through the storm. Hong Kong is still the world's busiest container port as well as airport for international cargo. According to a survey of over 8,000 multinationals by the Economist Intelligence Unit in 2000, Hong Kong is the best location for the regional headquarters of multinationals in East Asia. Thirty-five per cent of the surveyed companies have their regional headquarters in Hong Kong, versus 30 per cent for Singapore, 9 per cent for Tokyo, 5 per cent for Sydney, 3 per cent for Shanghai, 2.2 per cent for Beijing, and 1.3 per cent for Taipei. The study concludes that Hong Kong's dominance will increase in the next few years due to the expected rapid growth in China (*Hong Kong Economic Times*, 10 January 2001). Despite Hong Kong's economic crisis, the number of regional headquarters and regional offices of overseas companies reached an all time high at the end of June 2001. The total number grew by 20 per cent in 2000 and 8 per cent in 2001, partly as a result of the expectation of China's WTO entry (Hong Kong Census and Statistics Department, 2001).

Above all, Hong Kong is still China's number one world city. As long as Hong Kong maintains its uniqueness in rule of law, freedom of information, transparency of government and regulation, and continues to upgrade its skills, Hong Kong would be able to benefit from, and also contribute to, the dynamic growth of the Chinese economy.

References

Hong Kong Census and Statistics Department (2001). *Report on 2001 Annual Survey of Regional Offices Representing Overseas Companies in Hong Kong*, Hong Kong.

Hong Kong Trade Development Council (2000). *China's WTO Accession and Implications for Hong Kong*, January, Hong Kong.

Kwong, Kai-Sun (2000). "Sectoral Decomposition of TFP Growth: The Case of Hong Kong," paper presented at the East Asian Economic Association Conference, Singapore, 17–18 November 2000.

Lau, Siu-kai (1999). "From Elite Unity to Disunity: Political Elite in Post-1997 Hong Kong," in Wang Gungwu and John Wong (eds.), *Hong Kong in China: The Challenges of Transition* (Singapore: Times Academic Press), pp. 47–74.

Sung, Yun-Wing (1991). *The China-Hong Kong Connection: The Key to China's Open-Door Policy* (Cambridge: Cambridge University Press).

Sung, Yun-Wing, and Wong, Kar-yiu (2000). "Growth of Hong Kong Before and After its Reversion to China: The China Factor," *Pacific Economic Review*, Vol. 5, No. 2, pp. 201–28.

6

The Financial Sector: Crisis and Recovery

Y. C. Jao

Honorary Professor, School of Economics and Finance
The University of Hong Kong

Introduction

On 2 July 1997, just one day after Hong Kong was reunited with China, the Asian Financial Crisis (AFC) broke out in full force, first in Thailand, and then in other countries, notably Indonesia and South Korea. The contagion soon spread to Hong Kong, even though it did not share the gross financial mismanagement and imprudence characteristic of many other countries affected.

Owing to space constraint, this essay is concerned with the impact of the AFC on the financial sector, and the Hong Kong SAR government's handling of the crisis only.

Speculation against the Hong Kong Dollar

During the first three months of the AFC (2 July–20 October 1997), Hong Kong was relatively sheltered from external pressures. Some probing attacks on the Hong Kong dollar were easily repulsed by the Hong Kong Monetary Authority (HKMA) without the need of raising interest rates. From mid-October onwards, however, the situation deteriorated rapidly.

As one currency after another in Southeast and East Asia were devalued after speculative attacks, including those of the stronger economies like Singapore and Taiwan, the Hong Kong dollar had, by 17

October 1997, become the only freely convertible currency in East Asia whose peg to the US dollar remained intact.[1]

In the week beginning 20 October many hedge funds and other assorted speculators mounted a massive onslaught on the Hong Kong dollar by selling it short or forward (typically three to twelve months). Legitimate hedging activities by overseas investors undoubtedly also increased, but the ferocity of the selling clearly indicated that speculations dominated the transactions. Moreover, many commercial and investment banks either funded the speculators, or themselves jumped on the bandwagon. To counter this selling, the HKMA sold a substantial amount of US dollars from its reserves.

Under the Real Time Gross Settlement (RTGS) inaugurated in December 1996, the HKMA automatically debited the clearing account of the banking system with the sale of US dollars. Since no overdraft was allowed, any bank short of Hong Kong dollars would have to either borrow it from the interbank market, or to approach the Liquidity Adjustment Facility (LAF) of the HKMA for assistance.

On 23 and 24 October, as settlements for sales of Hong Kong dollar came due, the banks collectively found themselves caught short in Hong Kong dollars for delivery to the HKMA, as their total credit balance was grossly insufficient for this purpose. A scramble for Hong Kong dollars therefore began, as the spot rate remained intact, and both the Hong Kong government and the HKMA were resolute in their commitment to the linked exchange rate regime. Three other developments further exacerbated the scramble for liquidity. One was that, on the morning of 23 October, the HKMA issued a circular to all licensed banks warning them that the HKMA might impose penal interest rates for repeated borrowers to discourage the use of LAF to fund a short Hong Kong dollar position.[2] The second was that certain major interbank lenders held on their surplus liquidity under the very tense and uncertain market conditions. The third was that there was a rumour that the HKMA would, like the Bank of Thailand about five months ago, charge an exorbitant penal rate of 1000 per cent on LAF borrowing. The combined result of these developments was that the overnight Hong Kong Inter-bank Offered Rate (HIBOR) shot up to 280 per cent around noon time, though it eased to 100–150 per cent in the afternoon. Under the pressure of such a high rate, many speculators were forced to unwind their positions. The exchange rate closed on that day at 7.735, which fell further to 7.725 on the following two days, indicating clearly that the HKMA had won a tactical victory, at least temporarily, over the speculators. On 24 October, both lending and deposit rates were raised by 0.75 per cent across the board by the Hong Kong Association of Banks. The daily closing US dollar exchange rates and trade-weighted exchange rate index for the month of October are given in Table 1. Although the Hong Kong dollar was saved, the abrupt rise in interest rates and the squeeze on liquidity caused a heavy fall on the Hang Seng Index of stock prices by 1,211 points (10.4 per cent) on 23 October with a record turnover of HK$34 billion. The day therefore came to be known as "Black Thursday."

Some critics have claimed that the HKMA "shut down" its LAF on Black Thursday, thus causing an unprecedented debacle. It is true that the

Table 1. Daily Exchange Rates of US Dollar and Trade Weighted Exchange Rate Index, October 1997

	HK$ per US$	Trade-Weighted Exchange Rate Index (November 1983 = 100)
October 3	7.736	130.8
4	7.737	130.5
6	7.736	130.6
7	7.736	130.6
8	7.736	130.6
9	7.736	130.3
11	7.733	130.2
13	7.735	130.3
14	7.736	130.3
15	7.737	130.4
16	7.737	130.3
17	7.740	130.6
18	7.738	130.8
20	7.748	131.0
22	7.750	131.2
23	7.735	131.5
24	7.725	131.6
25	7.725	131.8
27	7.730	131.8
28	7.730	131.9
29	7.725	131.7
30	7.730	131.6
31	7.732	131.5

Source: HKMA *Monthly Statistical Bulletin*.

HKMA did not inject liquidity into the interbank market except when it bought back US dollars, in accordance with the well-known groundrule and discipline of the Currency Board Arrangement (CBA). But the chief culprits were those banks that funded the speculators, or participated in the speculation. Why should the HKMA come to the aid of such banks, which only had themselves to blame for aiding the speculators, and for not managing its Hong Kong dollar liquidity properly?

This said, however, the HKMA did make a technical error when, in its circular of 23 October, it did not define what was meant precisely by "repeated borrowers." Thus while overnight HIBOR soon eased, term HIBOR remained higher than the best lending rates, as shell-shocked banks stubbornly held on to their liquidity. It was not until the HKMA issued another circular on 12 November, clarifying the definition of "repeated borrowers," that term HIBOR began to drift downwards across the board.[3]

Table 1 shows that, even during the critical month of October 1997, the US dollar rate fluctuated within the narrow range of 7.25–7.75, while the trade-weighted exchange rate index, comprising 17 currencies of Hong Kong's most important trading partners, also remained remarkably stable within the range of 130.2–131.9. These figures clearly demonstrated the effectiveness of HKMA's defence of the linked rate at around 7.75.

Nevertheless, despite the apparent stability of the exchange rate, conditions in the forex market and money market remained tense. Interest rate differential between Hong Kong and the United States widened substantially, reflecting not only the "Asian premium," but also doubts about the sustainability of Hong Kong's own currency peg, among international investors. In January 1998, confidence was shaken further by the failure of two securities investment firms, the Peregrine Group and C. A. Pacific, the political and economic turmoil in Indonesia, and the deterioration of the Japanese economy. On 12 January, the best lending rate was raised again by 0.75 per cent to 10.25 per cent, the highest since 1991. It was lowered only marginally by 0.25 per cent on 30 March.

During the spring and summer of 1998, both the domestic economic situation and the external environment continued to deteriorate rapidly. At the end of May, the government announced that real GDP growth in the first quarter had turned negative. For Hong Kong which was used to continuous positive growth even during the severe downturn of 1974–75, this worse than expected news came as a great shock. Externally, Indonesia was engulfed in political strife and economic turmoil, while Japan's recession worsened sharply, with the yen caught in a downward spiral. In mid-June, the yen fell to as low as 145 to US dollar, and only a one-off joint intervention temporarily stopped the free fall.

In fact, beginning from about early 1998, hedge funds had been borrowing and building up Hong Kong dollar funds up to about HK$30 billion through swaps with multilateral institutions such as the World Bank, Asian Development Bank, European Investment Bank, Nordic Investment Bank, European Bank for Reconstruction and Investment, The Council of Europe, etc. At the same time, they had also built up short positions in the securities and futures markets, so that by August, they held some 80,000 short contracts.[4] Thus began the infamous "double market play" by international speculators in July and August of 1998. The *modus operandi* can be roughly described as follows. They aggressively sold short Hong Kong dollar on both the spot and forward markets, coupled by simultaneous shorting of Hong Kong stocks on both the cash and futures markets. Since the selling of the Hong Kong dollar would normally push up HIBOR, the stock market and futures market would fall heavily. If the speculators were not checked, they could reap enormous profits from both the forex and securities markets. The collapse of the asset markets could cause serious difficulties for the banks or even trigger a banking crisis, which in turn would make the currency peg impossible to defend, as had happened in other countries like Thailand etc.

Moreover, in July and August, the speculators and their friends orchestrated a campaign of lies and rumours concerning the *Renminbi* and the Hong Kong dollar, exploiting unscrupulously a series of bad news, such as the floods in China, and the deepening slump in Hong Kong and Japan. In effect, the objective of the vicious "double market play" was to bring down the whole financial system.

Confronted with this threat, the Hong Kong government and the HKMA decided on 14 August to launch a counter-attack against the speculators and manipulators by directly buying in the securities markets. Since this operation concerned the securities markets, we will discuss it in the next section.

As far as the forex market is concerned, the speculators' attempt to topple the linked rate again failed. Table 2 presents daily closing exchange rates of the US dollar, and the trade-weighted exchange rate index during the critical month of August 1998.

As may be seen from the table, from 1–22 August, the US dollar rate was perilously close to 7.75, where the HKMA drew a line for its defence.

Table 2. Daily Exchange Rates of US Dollar and Trade Weighted Exchange Rate Index, August 1998

		HK$ per US$	Trade-Weighted Exchange Rate Index (November 1983 = 100)
August	1	7.748	138.1
	3	7.748	139.1
	4	7.749	139.1
	5	7.749	138.9
	6	7.749	139.2
	7	7.748	139.5
	8	7.748	139.8
	10	7.747	139.9
	11	7.749	140.1
	12	7.748	139.6
	13	7.748	139.8
	14	7.750	139.3
	15	7.750	139.6
	18	7.750	139.8
	19	7.747	139.7
	20	7.748	139.2
	21	7.747	139.2
	22	7.751	139.4
	24	7.749	139.8
	25	7.741	139.8
	26	7.743	139.8
	27	7.743	139.8
	28	7.745	139.8
	29	7.746	139.1
	31	7.743	139.3

Source: HKMA *Monthly Statistical Bulletin*.

Indeed, on 14–18 August, the rate closed at 7.75, and on 22 August, the line was briefly breached to close at 7.751. After that, however, the rate eased again to below 7.75, signifying that the speculators were once again repulsed.

Although the HKMA had successfully beaten back four major waves of speculative attacks against the Hong Kong dollar, the territory's economic and financial situation in the summer of 1998 was extremely grave and precarious. By the end of July, the authorities had realized that, in order to prevent further speculations, it was necessary to strengthen public confidence in the currency. But public confidence could not be strengthened without some tangible commitment of some form of the government itself. Second, the authorities also realized that they could not rely on interest rate alone as the sole weapon of defence, given that interest rate was a double-edged weapon. Specifically, the monetary base, defined until that time as the sum of legal tender currency plus the banking system's clearing balance, was too narrow. Even a moderate amount of selling US dollars by the HKMA in response to speculators' attack would be enough to drive the aggregate balance into negative territory, forcing up HIBOR to an unnecessarily high level. In short, the authorities had to come to grips with the crux of the matter, which its *Report on Financial Market Review* published in April failed to address.

On 5 September, the HKMA unveiled a new strategy known as the "Seven Technical Measures."[5] Space prevents any detailed treatment, suffice it to say that the most important measures were the "convertibility undertaking" by the HKMA to convert on demand the licensed banks' Hong Kong dollar balance in their clearing accounts into US dollars at the fixed rate of HK$7.75 to US$1, the setting up of a formal Discount Window to replace the former Liquidity Adjustment Facility (LAF), and the widening of the monetary base to include Exchange Fund bills and notes which must be fully backed by US dollars. Through these reforms, the HKMA, as it were, put its money where its mouth was, and this had a very positive effect on public confidence. For instance, the most sensitive and reliable indicator of confidence in the linked rate, the premium on the US dollar forward rate, fell steadily from August 1998 onward across the board, as shown in Table 3.

As is clear from the table, the forward premium for all maturities rose to unprecedented highs in August 2000, the most critical point of the Asian crisis. If one takes the 12-month premium for illustration, the monthly average was 5,010 decimal points in August 1998, but since then it had steadily fallen, and by the end of 2000, it had turned negative, implying that the market was expecting appreciation, rather than depreciation, of the Hong Kong dollar in 12 months' time. In 2001, the 12-month premium generally became positive again, partly because of the economic slowdown, partly because of the psychological fallout from the financial crisis in Argentina. However, even the highest monthly average was only 270 decimal points, while the average figure for ten months up to the end of October was only 33.4 decimal points.

Other relevant indicators, such as the term structure of HIBOR, the

Table 3. Premium on US Dollar Forward Exchange Rates (HK$ per US$) (decimal points, period averages)

During		1-week	1-month	3-month	6-month	9-month	12-month
1996		–1	–2	5	37	92	161
1997		19	96	302	608	880	1,153
1998		32	149	543	1,356	2,266	3,264
	Aug	116	438	1,203	2,488	3,703	5,010
	Sep	35	187	765	1,826	3,015	4,235
	Oct	8	41	267	826	1,568	2,394
	Nov	5	28	179	648	1,232	1,896
	Dec	4	8	93	448	951	1,512
1999	Jan	6	44	223	624	1,099	1,650
	Feb	9	47	215	662	1,160	1,776
	Mar	4	26	139	489	947	1,547
	Apr	0	7	62	233	519	931
	May	0	5	58	266	568	915
	Jun	8	29	94	286	593	959
	Jul	11	50	154	378	662	996
	Aug	14	66	205	508	833	1,171
	Sep	5	31	123	351	615	909
	Oct	4	17	73	222	426	691
	Nov	2	9	58	175	343	573
	Dec	–8	–12	11	99	220	396
2000	Jan	–1	–5	–10	38	105	205
	Feb	1	5	10	33	75	130
	Mar	–3	–16	–28	–28	–23	–21
	Apr	7	22	38	45	50	60
	May	–1	0	15	33	53	68
	Jun	–13	–37	–56	–58	–48	–43
	Jul	–16	–57	–113	–176	–193	–200
	Aug	2	–19	–79	–140	–165	–177
	Sep	–5	–25	–73	–122	–135	–137
	Oct	–12	–50	–117	–168	–178	–173
	Nov	–14	–57	–136	–187	–195	–185
	Dec	–8	–37	–100	–155	–174	–167

Source: HKMA *Monthly Statistical Bulletin*.

differential between Exchange Fund notes and US Treasury bonds, etc., also showed declining trends. Due to lack of space, the relevant tables are not presented.

Note that the exchange rate at which the "convertibility undertaking" took effect was initially fixed at 7.75, not the official rate of 7.8. This was because the HKMA had chosen 7.75 as the "intervention rate" when the AFC broke. In time, the market came to regard 7.75 as the de facto official rate. The HKMA's strategy had been severely criticized by some purists as a violation of the automatic adjustment mechanism inherent in the CBA. The HKMA's response was that allowing the exchange rate to rise above 7.75 might well precipitate a *sauve qui peut* due to the public's "herd instinct." It is difficult to either support or reject this claim, because of the impossibility of conducting controlled experiments. But there are two undesirable side-effects which the HKMA implicitly acknowledged: overvaluation of the domestic currency, and excessive interest rate volatility. Accordingly, shortly after the seven "technical measures" were implemented, the HKMA also accepted a recommendation of the Sub-Committee on Currency Board Operations that effective from 1 April 1999, the exchange rate would be raised by HK$0.0001 every day, so that by the end of 500 calendar days, the convertibility undertaking rate would coincide with the official rate in August 2000. This scheme worked very well, without any adverse effect on the forex market, because the adjustments had been preannounced and infinitesimal. Indeed, the actual market rate since 13 August 2000 has tended to be slightly below the daily announced "convertibility undertaking" rate.

Why Has the Linked Rate Survived the AFC?

Why has Hong Kong's linked rate survived the AFC, despite the opinion of a host of pundits, financial analysts and other self-appointed experts, that no fixed exchange rate regime can survive sustained speculative attacks?

The first reason is obviously Hong Kong's strong foreign exchange reserve. Table 4 shows an abbreviated account of Hong Kong's foreign reserve from the end of 1996 to the end of September 2001. As may be seen, the reserve exhibits a rising trend except for 1998, during which the territory had to use part of it to resist the attacks of speculators. At the end of September 2001, Hong Kong's total foreign exchange reserve stood at US$113.4 billion, the third largest in the world. Its foreign reserve per capita at US$16,850 was the second highest in the world, next to only

Table 4. Hong Kong's Foreign Currency Reserve

As at end of	Foreign currency reserve assets (US$ million)	Foreign currency reserve per capita (US$)	Foreign currency reserve assets in terms of months of retained imports of goods (No. of months)	Ratio of foreign currency reserve to currency in circulation
1996	63,840	9,776	10.7	5.7
1997	92,823	14,049	14.6	7.8
1998	89,625	13,399	17.1	7.5
1999	96,256	14,236	19.8	6.0
2000	107,560	15,667	18.3	8.0
2001 (Sept)	113,434	16,850	19.5	7.9

Source: HKMA *Monthly Statistical Bulletin.*

Singapore's. Hong Kong's foreign reserve is equal to 7.9 times its currency in circulation, and 19.5 months of retained imports.

The mere existence of strong reserves, however, is not enough to deter speculators. There must also be the willingness to use such reserves if and when necessary. Thus, Singapore and Taiwan also have enormous reserves. In fact, on a *per capita* basis, Singapore has ranked first in the world for many years. Yet, very early during the AFC, both Singapore and Taiwan had chosen "competitive devaluation" as a way out of their difficulties. There is therefore a crucial difference between the ability and the will to defend the currency. By contrast, Hong Kong has always had both the ability and the will to defend its currency. Quite early on in the AFC, Hong Kong had decided to tough it out and to accept the costs of domestic adjustments.

Second, Hong Kong's linked exchange rate regime is a variant of Currency Board Arrangement (CBA). The working of this regime is too technical and complicated to be treated in this short paper.[6]

Briefly, in words, under the CBA, the monetary base is fully backed by foreign reserves, primarily in terms of the anchor currency. Whenever there is a loss of reserves, due to whatever reasons, such as outflow of capital, speculative attack, balance of payments deficit etc., the monetary base will contract because of the foreign exchange constraint. This contraction of monetary base will cause a contraction of money supply, and drive up interest rates and initiate a series of downward adjustments in prices, costs and wages as required for the fixed exchange rate. Eventually, both the higher interest rates and the improved competitiveness will attract capital inflow and restore the original equilibrium, while keeping the exchange rate stable. This was basically what happened in Hong Kong during 1997–99. The "seven technical measures," explained earlier, have further improved the working and efficacy of the CBA.

By contrast, under the non-CBA fixed exchange rate regime, there is no prior foreign exchange constraint. Even after a substantial loss of foreign reserve, the monetary base will not necessary contract, and there is no automatic adjustment mechanism to restore the original equilibrium. Thus, the Central Bank can still print or create more money in the face of a serious payments deficit. Under such a regime, it is indeed true that the fixed exchange rate cannot withstand prolonged speculative attacks. In current economic parlance, Hong Kong's version of the CBA is a "hard peg," while the non-CBA fixed exchange rate regime is a "soft peg."

Another important reason why the Hong Kong dollar has remained solidly stable is the territory's traditional fiscal discipline and probity. Fiscal deficit is the exception rather than the rule. In the half century before the AFC, there was a surplus of varying size in all but five fiscal years. Hong Kong has little or no sovereign debt, denominated in foreign currencies. The HKMA, it is true, has issued sizeable Exchange Fund bills and notes, but they are designed for monetary policy and debt market development purposes, not for covering fiscal deficit. Such debt, moreover, is adequately covered by the Exchange Fund's assets and operating profits. Other public bodies such as the Mass Transit Railway and the Airport Authority, have issued bonds, mostly in Hong Kong dollars. In short, the default of foreign currency debt, which triggered the AFC, was not a problem for Hong Kong at all.

As a result, the government has accumulated a sizeable fiscal surplus, which stood at HK$458 billion (US$59 billion) as at 31 March 1998. Because of the serious recession in the wake of the AFC, the government has had to use expansionary fiscal policy for stabilization purposes, resulting in a slight decrease of the fiscal reserve which amounted to HK$432 billion as at 31 March 2001.[7] In the fiscal year 2001–2002, due to the rapid economic slowdown, in particular the sharp decrease in government revenue from land sales, fiscal deficit suddenly ballooned, and the government began to talk about "structural deficit." This is a very recent phenomenon which cannot be adequately discussed in this paper, but it does not affect the basic argument that fiscal discipline was one important factor for the stability of the Hong Kong dollar.[8]

Last but not least, China's support is also a key factor for the robustness of the linked exchange rate. This support has taken three forms. First, on the very day of the reunification, 1 July 1997, China transferred the huge Land Fund worth some HK$197 billion (of which US$15.8 billion were in foreign currencies) to the Hong Kong SAR government, punctually in accordance with its pledge.[9] Hong Kong's foreign exchange reserves and fiscal reserves thus grew overnight by 23 per cent and 20 per cent respectively. This boosted not only Hong Kong's financial resources, but also enhanced tremendously public confidence in the currency. Second, ever since the outbreak of the AFC, China's leaders, from President Jiang Zemin downwards, have repeatedly declared China's support for Hong Kong's currency peg, and that it will come to Hong Kong's aid if requested. Although Hong Kong has never requested such aid, China's pledge has nevertheless been an important morale booster. Moreover, China's premier, Zhu Rongji, has also repeatedly pledged that the *Renminbi* will not be devalued in the course of the AFC, a pledge that has been fully honoured. Third, under the Basic Law, China is responsible for Hong Kong's defence. By the same token, China absorbs itself the cost of its garrison in Hong Kong. By contrast, under British rule, Hong Kong had to pay 65 per cent of the foreign exchange cost of the British garrison, under the bilateral "Defence Cost Agreement." In the last three years of British rule, such costs averaged about HK$1 billion annually. Although the sum is not large, it is still a saving for Hong Kong, adding to the territory's fiscal reserves, and can be used to support the economy.

Intervention against "Double Market Play"

As mentioned in the previous section, during the summer of 1998, speculators and manipulators were busily engaged in the "double market play" by short-selling both the Hong Kong dollar and Hong Kong stocks in the stock and futures markets. By 13 August the HSI was down to 6,660, or 60 per cent off from its previous peak reached in August 1997. The speculators aimed to drive the HSI down to 3,000. If they succeeded, not only would the securities markets collapse, but also the banking system and the currency peg would be jeopardized.

The government therefore decided to counter-attack by buying shares in the stock market, and a complicated combination of both buying and selling actions in the futures market to squeeze the speculators.

This intervention lasted until the end of August, and by that time the government had accumulated blue-chip shares worth some HK$118.1

billion. On 8 September, it further unveiled a 30-point package to tighten regulations of both the stock and futures markets, including criminalizing unreported short selling, and sharply increasing penalties for illegal short-selling.[10]

This unprecedented intervention, while generally understood and supported by the population, were severely criticized by sections of the financial community and the mass media, both inside and outside Hong Kong, for violating the territory's traditional non-interventionist policy and principles, and for attempting to prop up stock prices, which was bound to fail. Subsequent developments have proved that both criticisms were false and misplaced.

The government argued that its counter-attack was a one-off intervention designed to frustrate the speculators' "double market play," so that when the markets were stabilized and free of manipulation, the government would withdraw in an orderly manner. In November of the same year, the government announced the formation of an independent company called Exchange Fund Investment Ltd. (EFI), to take over the custody and management of the acquired shares. This company then transformed its portfolio into a unit trust named the Tracker Fund, so called because it would closely track the movement of the HSI.

An initial public offering (IPO) of the Tracker Fund was made in October 1999, which was four times over-subscribed. As a result, the government disposed of shares worth $33.33 billion, representing about 16 per cent of the original portfolio. Subsequently, further orderly sales were made, as long as they did not exert any negative impact on the market. According to the then Financial Secretary, Donald Tsang, by the end of 31 March 2001, the EFI had received a total of $119 billion from sales and dividends, more than the original costs of acquisition of $118 billion. However, the EFI still hold a portfolio of $110 billion as investments at current value.[11]

Thus, the counter-attack has been much more successful than expected: the government has succeeded not only in punishing the speculators and manipulators, and preventing the collapse of the equity market, but also making a huge profit from its investment.

Banking and Finance

One of the characteristics of the AFC is that, for three of the most affected economies, Indonesia, South Korea, and Thailand, there was a mixture of banking, currency, and debt crises. Scores of banks and near-bank financial institutions were ordered by the International Monetary Fund (IMF) to be closed or restructured.

Hong Kong's banking sector was, however, conspicuously robust during the AFC. It had not always been so, of course, in the past, as evidenced by the banking crises of 1965–66, and 1983–86. However, in 1986, the Hong Kong authorities began a sweeping reform by overhauling the supervisory framework, upgrading the management quality of banks, and strengthening banking capital and liquidity requirements and other measures. By the early nineties, Hong Kong had already one of the best supervised and managed banking sector not only in Asia, but in the whole world. For instance, Hong Kong's domestic banks satisfied the Basle Committee's minimum capital ratio of 8 per cent in 1990, two years ahead of the internationally agreed target date.

This programme of banking reform passed its acid test in the form of the AFC. During that crisis, not one single Hong Kong bank failed. To be sure, all banks suffered reduced profitability in the deep recession of 1998, but nearly all banks resumed positive profit growth from 1999 onwards. Hong Kong and Singapore banks had the best Camel ratios in Asia, but on balance Hong Kong banks were slightly ahead of their Singapore counterparts. Moreover, even during the critical years of 1997–2000, the capital adequacy ratio (CAR) of Hong Kong's domestic banks still averaged 18.7 per cent, one of the highest in the world, and far in excess of the Basle ratio of 8 per cent.[12]

Hong Kong is aware that it cannot afford to be complacent in the light of the AFC and the increased competition among international financial centres. The government therefore commissioned in March 1998 a consultant firm, KPMG Barents, to conduct an in-depth review of the banking sector for the next five years. Some of the consultant's recommendations, such as the full deregulation of interest rates, clarification of HKMA's "lender of last resort" role, relaxation of the restrictions on the number of branches of newly licensed foreign banks, have already been accepted. Others, such as simplification of the 3-tier banking structure, and the introduction of deposit insurance, are still in the process of consideration or consultation.[13]

Finally, what is the effect of the AFC on Hong Kong's position as an international financial centre (IFC)? In 1997, on the eve of the handover and the AFC, I published a book on the origins, causes and current status of Hong Kong as an IFC.[14] I estimated in my book that in 1995–96, on the basis of a number of quantitative criteria, Hong Kong was the second largest IFC in the Asian-Pacific region, and between the 6th and 7th largest IFC of the world.

Hong Kong was inevitably hard hit by the Asian crisis as an IFC, but so were Singapore and Tokyo, the two other major IFCs in the Asian-Pacific region. Hong Kong's relative ranking as the second largest IFC in the region was therefore not affected. However, because other IFCs, such as London, New York, Frankfurt, Paris, Zürich etc., were not affected at all by the AFC, Hong Kong's relative ranking has unavoidably suffered. For example, according to the triennial survey by central banks under the auspices of the Bank for International Settlements (BIS), Hong Kong's world ranking in the forex market slipped from No. 5 in 1995 to No. 7 in 1998, while that in the over-the-counter derivatives market slipped from No. 9 to No. 11 during the same period.[15] Hong Kong's stock market capitalization also fell from No. 9 in 1997 to No. 11 in 1998, but recovered to No. 10 in 1999.[16] Hong Kong however remained the 5th largest banking centre in 1999 in terms of foreign assets and liabilities.[17] Full details cannot be discussed here in this short paper, but an educated guess would be that Hong Kong's world ranking as an IFC went down one notch to between the 7th and 8th largest IFC of the world as a result of the Asian crisis.[18]

Conclusions

Considering the severity of the Asian crisis, the record of the Tung Administration must be given its due credit, as far as the financial sector is concerned. Hong Kong was the only economy with a fully convertible currency that did not devalue;[19] it was the only economy which defeated decisively international speculators in their own game. By refusing to join "competitive devaluation," Hong Kong has contributed to exchange rate stabilization in Asia, thereby paving the way for the easing and passing of the AFC. Its banking system remains one of the best managed and supervised in Asia and the world. Hong Kong is still the second largest IFC in the Asian-Pacific region, and still counts among the top eight IFCs of the world.

However, the relative success of the financial sector could not save the economy from a deep recession in 1998 which was the worst in 40 years. Nor could it prevent the economy from sliding into another incipient recession from the third quarter of 2001 onwards.

To be sure, events like the AFC, the collapse of the high-tech craze and the subsequent sharp slowdown of the US economy, which was further aggravated by the 11 September terrorist attacks, were beyond the control of Hong Kong. But public opinion seldom takes cognizance of the external environment when assessing the domestic record of the government. The fact that there were two recessions in four years is sufficient to explain why, despite the soundness of the financial sector, the popularity rating of the Tung Administration has remained so low.

Notes

1. For a much more detailed in-depth analysis of the AFC on Hong Kong's economy and financial sector, see my new book Jao (2001).
2. The full text of the circular is given in Financial Services Bureau (1998: 17–18).
3. See ibid., Annex 3.3. "Repeated borrowers" are defined as those licensed banks which have borrowed through LAF on eight occasions in any period of 25 days, or on four consecutive days in which LAF is open.
4. See Yam (1998b).
5. I was a member of the Exchange Fund Advisory Committee of the government from 1 April 1997 to 31 December 1998, and in that capacity, I took part in all the major decisions for the defence of Hong Kong's monetary and financial system during that time. Moreover, on 1 August, I was appointed a member of the Sub-committee of Currency Board Operations. During the extremely critical month of August 1998, the sub-committee met frequently, and discussed intensively, a new strategy for defending the Hong Kong dollar and strengthening the working of the currency board arrangement called "Seven Technical Measures." For details, see HKMA Research Department (1998).
6. For a more detailed analysis, see Jao (1998), and Jao (2001: Chapter 4). See also Tsang (1998), Tsang, Cheng, and Sin (1998), and Yam (1998c).
7. See *The 2000–02 Budget*, Speech by the Financial Secretary, 7 March 2001, para. 74.
8. The importance of fiscal prudence for financial stability can be illustrated by the case of Argentina. Although Argentina also adopts the CBA, it suffered a severe financial crisis, caused by fiscal deficit, in early 2001, and had to be bailed out by the International Monetary Fund with a massive package of US$39.7 billion.
9. The Land Fund was established in 1986 in accordance with the 1984 Sino-British Joint Declaration, under which one half of land sales prior to 1 July 1997 would be paid into the Land Fund and reserved for the future Hong Kong SAR government. Until 1 July 1997, the Land Fund was under the custody and management of the Central Government of the People's Republic of China.

10. See Jao (2001: Chapter 5) for a more detailed treatment.
11. See "Tsang gets back crisis billions," *South China Morning Post Business*, 13 April 2001.
12. CAMEL is the acronym of the five criteria for evaluating the soundness of banks: capital adequacy, asset quality, management quality, earnings, and liquidity. Pioneered by the Federal Reserve System in the US, it has now been widely adopted elsewhere, including Hong Kong. This section on banking draws heavily on Jao (2001: Chapters 3 and 6). Due to lack of space, relevant tables are not presented.
13. For more details, see Jao (2001: Chapter 6).
14. See Jao (1997).
15. See "Turnover of Foreign Exchange and Derivatives Markets in Hong Kong," *HKMA Quarterly Bulletin*, November 1998, pp. 54–56. Hong Kong's 7th position in the global forex market was maintained in the 2001 Triennial Survey. See "Turnover of Foreign Exchange and Derivatives Market in Hong Kong," *HKMA Quarterly Bulletin*, November 2001, pp. 62–71.
16. Underlying data from International Federation of Stock Exchanges.
17. Underlying data from IMF *International Financial Statistics*, October 1999.
18. For a more detailed treatment of Hong Kong as an IFC, see Jao (1997), *passim*, and Jao (2001: Chapter 6).
19. China's currency, *Renminbi*, also did not depreciate, but *Renminbi* is not fully convertible. China still retains strict foreign exchange control on the capital account.

References

Financial Services Bureau (1998). *Report on Financial Market Review* (Hong Kong: Hong Kong SAR Government Printing Department).

HKMA Research Department (1998). "Strengthening of Currency Board Arrangements in Hong Kong," *HKMA Quarterly Bulletin*, No. 17 (November), pp. 7–11.

Jao, Y. C. (1997). *Hong Kong as an International Financial Centre: Evolution, Prospects and Policies* (Hong Kong: City University of Hong Kong Press).

——— (1998). "The Working of the Currency Board: The Experience of Hong Kong," *Pacific Economic Review*, Vol. 3, No. 3, pp. 219–43.

——— (2001a). *The Asian Financial Crisis and the Ordeal of Hong Kong* (Westport, CT, and London: Quorum Books, Greenwood Publishing Corporation).

——— (2001b). "The Banking Sector and Economic Growth: Hong Kong's Recent Experience," paper presented to the APEC Economic Outlook Symposium, Hong Kong, 28–29 June 2001.

Tsang, Shu-ki (1998). "The Case for Adopting the Convertible Reserves System in Hong Kong," *Pacific Economic Review*, Vol. 3, No. 3, pp. 265–75.

Tsang, Shu-ki, Cheng, Y. S., and Sin, C. Y. (1998). "The Robustness of Hong Kong's Linked Exchange Rate as a Currency Board Arrangement," paper presented to an international conference on exchange rate stability, 28 November 1998, Hong Kong Baptist University.

Yam, J. (1998a). "Why We Intervened," *HKMA Quarterly Bulletin*, No. 17 (November), pp. 1–4.

——— (1998b). "Defending Hong Kong's Monetary Stability," *HKMA Quarterly Bulletin*, No. 17 (November), pp. 75–79.

——— (1998c). *A Modern Day Currency Board System* (Hong Kong: Hong Kong Monetary Authority).

7

Reinventing the Wheel: Educational Reform

Kai-ming Cheng

Professor, Chair of Education
The University of Hong Kong

Preamble

Education has been one of the major areas of reform in the first five years of the SAR. It is an area that has aroused the greatest public concern, and it was one of the major emphases in Tung Chee-hwa's platform. However, education has also been one of the areas of widest and continuous controversies. In a way, education is a very good window that reflects the deep crisis that Hong Kong is facing, and is therefore also a real test for the Tung administration. What is contained in this chapter are observations of the writer as a participant in the process of educational policy-making. Such observations inevitably involve subjective elements of interpretation, but extreme care has been taken such that such interpretations are only based on facts known to the writer. Meanwhile, the writer does not claim comprehensive knowledge in the policy-making process, hence will only limit himself to what he knows.

The Context

An understanding of Hong Kong's education development in the first five years of the SAR is not possible without an understanding of the context in which the education system operated before and at 1997.

Hong Kong's education system was ever a pride for the colony until the 1990s. In 1978, when McLehose announced the introduction of compulsory nine-year basic education, Hong Kong was only second to Japan in launching what was seen as ambitious in those days. However, the universalised education system soon experienced discomfort with the increase of students who were academically less motivated and with teachers who were not prepared for spreading education to the populace. There was no shortage of solutions to such problems. However, the existing machineries are simply unprepared to co-ordinate the segmented government organs and to effectively implement plans of actions.

The Overall Review of Hong Kong's education system in 1980, and the publication of the international panel's report in 1982,[1] were attempts to streamline the divided machinery for education policy-making and to create the infrastructure for self-renewal of the system. The most significant outcome of the review recommendations was establishing in 1984 the Education Commission, which is to "co-ordinate but not direct" the other three policy bodies: the Board of Education,[2] the Vocational Training Council[3] and the University Grants Committee.[4] The Education Commission subsequently issued seven reports in the following decade until 1997. The seven reports addressed critical issues that are crucial to the development of Hong Kong's education. Among others, the most significant outcomes brought about by the Education Commission reports were the establishment of the Hong Kong Institute of Education at the merger of the former teacher training Colleges of Education (Education Commission Report No. 5), the construction of a framework for improving school quality (Education Commission Report No. 7), the tackling of the issue of medium of instruction (Education Commission No. 6), and the introduction of the Direct Subsidy Scheme where public schools are given more autonomy. It is fair to say that most of the problems at stake were addressed, solutions recommended, but few of them have brought about desirable results.

By the end of the colonial era, the seven Education Commission reports made more than 279 recommendations,[5] but few of them could comfortably claim effective implementation. Hence the system was there, rather comprehensive compared with other systems, but the system did not quite deliver. The system and government machinery were more apt for times when developments in quantity and structure were the chief goals. They did not quite evolve into mechanisms that would cope with issues of quality and require co-ordination and value decisions. The system was therefore stagnant.

One of the perceivable reasons for the stagnancy in education development has been the fragmentation of policy-making, as was identified in the 1980 review, which was not solved by the installation of the Education Commission. Each policy sub-sector maintains its own territory, with no commitment and indeed requirement of submitting to a large vision of Hong Kong's education. The other perceived reason for the poor implementation of the policies has been the inefficiency of the government executive arms, which have sometime grown into a huge bureaucracy that is not capable of self-reflection and self-renewal, and where procedural concerns have taken over the real interest in student learning.

In the meantime, tertiary education started expansion in the early 1990s. Although there had been proposals to expand tertiary education as early as 1981, there was a general hesitation on the part of the government towards substantial expansion. Indeed, Hong Kong relies its high-level manpower from local as well as overseas institutions, and felt comfortable for the model where local institutions played a significant role yet only a small part. By the end of 1980s, there was a slow increase in the intake of tertiary education institutions, from two per cent of the age group to around six per cent by the end of the 1980s. More aggressive plan was drawn in 1988, for expansion of the enrolment to 14 per cent. It is believed that the plan was due to the anticipated shortage of high-level manpower in view of the enormous emigration of professionals as part of the 1997-related exodus. The plan was further revised upwards in 1989 to 18 per cent, and with an early target date, at the wake of the political incident in Beijing. The substantial expansion started in 1991, where the annual intake to higher education moved towards 14,500 per year or nominally 18 per cent of the age cohort. All the way, the plans were handed down from the governor. There was no discussion or debate in the policy advisory bodies. The real considerations that had led to such a fundamental revision of higher education policies have never been known.

This was accompanied by the upgrading of the polytechnics to university status, hence prompting the institutions to engage in massive recruitment of world-class academics. There was at once a general mirage that all institutions would become world-class research universities. This was reinforced by the introduction of Research Assessment Exercise (RAE) in 1994, which was almost a total adoption of a British model. The RAE on the one hand has indeed constructed a basic framework which wakened, refreshed and enhanced the research capacity among Hong Kong's tertiary institutions. Academic publications in international journals, as a major symbol, skyrocketed in a matter of a few years. On the other hand, RAE also started a decade of managerialism in tertiary educations policies, again following the British trend, where indicators, appraisals and league-tables have since prevailed as pretended proxies for genuine scholarship.

Hence, it is safe to say that at the political transition at 1997, Hong Kong's education was at the juncture where the quantitative scale had been remarkably achieved, but the system was awaiting refreshed paradigms and mechanisms to move itself out of quality crisis and towards loftier goals.

Preparation for Reform

Reform in education has always been an essential concern in Tung's policies. As early as 1996, when his candidacy for the Chief Executive was just announced, Antony Leung, on behalf of Tung, organised an ad hoc, informal and small group of educators to advise on preferred orientations in education policies. The output of this group was very much reflected in Tung's first policy speech made in 1997.

The deliberation of this informal group was very much reflected in his opening statement on education in the 1997 policy speech, Tung said:

> [E]ducation is the key to the future of Hong Kong. It provides a level playing field for all and the human resources for further economic development. Our education system must be firmly rooted in the needs of Hong Kong; it must enable us to contribute to the development of our country; it must give us an international outlook. It should be diverse, drawing on the strengths of East and West. It must inspire commitment to excellence.

The messages were: he would give education high priority; he regarded education as key to Hong Kong's economic development; there should be national as well as international elements in education; it should honour cultural diversity as well as cultural heritage; and it should aim at excellence.

The detailed policy measures mentioned in Tung's 1997 speech, understandably, did not go very far from the items on the existing agenda. Most of the items had been recommended by the Education Commission, others were largely known to the education community as decisions within the Education and Manpower Bureau (the branch in the old government). Nonetheless, the speech did present determination and commitment. However, a few characteristics were already showing.

First, there was remarkable insensitivity in the way he presented the policy items. The teachers' language benchmarking, which would virtually put all teachers under re-examination, was mentioned without much caution. The issue later led to strong protests from the teachers' union. Apparently there had been no discussion of the issue within the government about the way the benchmarking should be announced and implemented. The issue of medium of instruction, though determined during the colonial years, was taken for granted as non-controversial, but indeed raised territory-wide concern when it was implemented later in 1998. The implementation, which rather drastically forced schools to opt to become English Medium Schools (EMI) or Chinese Medium Schools (CMI), has in practice labelled most secondary schools as incompetent in using English as the medium of instruction. Hence, the exercise has been understood by parents, as well as the international media, as a policy of "forbidding" schools to use English for instruction. In both cases, and indeed in many other cases, there is little sensitivity to the political distinction between what is needed and what is wanted. There is also a lack of sensitivity of the likely confrontation between the teachers and the community at large therefore aroused by government actions.

Second, many of promises were premature. There was a promise of setting up the General Teaching Council within two years. This was an endeavour that was initiated in the late 1980s, but met government prevarication ever since. The General Teaching Council, conceptually non-controversial, is still shelved as this paper is being written in 2002. The speech raised high hopes of raising the qualification of the teachers, by speeding up the achieving of an all-trained, all-graduate teaching force. These were followed, in late 1997, by intensive studies carried out by both the UGC and the ACTEQ (Advisory Committee on Teacher Education and Qualification) in anticipation of drastic and favourable changes. The entire plan was eventually indefinitely delayed with no proper explanation, presumably due to the financial implications. Apparently, Tung was ill-informed of the reality. There was also an obvious lack of coordination among the different players within the government. Hence, many of the policies indicated in his 1997 speech were not echoed in action by the relevant executive arms within the government.

Third, there were dramatic promises of money, which were almost the only items delivered in the end. Apart from the 50 million granted to the Hong Kong Open University as a token of support to continuing education. There was a surprising generosity of a five billion for the Quality Education Fund, which for very good reasons allows schools to develop activities beyond the ordinary, and to move away from equal distribution of funds with no consideration of specificity and effectiveness. There was also a promise in the rise of educational expenditures, which has become a general tone in the subsequent policy speeches. Indeed, in the five years that followed, there was amazing generosity in the money spent on education, but not necessarily bringing out the desired effects. The generosity is even unfavourably received by educators, who see some of the spending as addition to workloads, yet providing no solutions to the issues at stake.

There was, however, a promise in the 1997 speech that there would be a comprehensive review of the education system by the Education Commission. This eventually led to the succession of the chairman of the commission by Antony Leung, a banker known for his loyalty to Tung's policies, and the eventual launching of the Education Reform in 1999.

The Reform: From Launch to Blueprint

The deliberation of the reform started within the Education Commission in 1998. The mission handed down by the Chief Executive was to concentrate on the structure, the curriculum and the assessments.

The Backdrop

The general thinking within the Education Commission at that time was that there were so many *means* for improving education, but the *ends* were often forgotten. Many of such means had been recommended for very good reasons, but the practical implementation often deteriorated into naïve quantitative targets. In the end, money was spent and efforts were paid, but little of the expected improvement came about.

The typical examples include the notorious TOC, or Target Oriented Curriculum, which was launched in 1990. The policy exercise started with the genuine concern for declining students' learning outcomes, and hence designed a curriculum such that the learning targets would guide the teaching. The scheme had a very undesirable start, where the officers in charge of "training" openly declared ignorance about the project. With success in only a few schools, the TOC eventually degenerated into a symbolic conversion of textbooks into worksheets, and a superficial counting of participating schools according to their own declarations.

The second example was SMI, or School Management Initiative that started in 1991, which echoed the world trend of devolution of school management, such that schools would be given more autonomy if they could meet certain management requirements. The scheme was conceptually well received, but attracted mainly schools that were readily effective and innovative. The weaker schools were reluctant to join which defeated the entire purpose of the scheme. The scheme was further promoted partly by coercing new schools to join, and also partly by watering down some of the requirements in order to increase the number of participating schools. No dramatic achievement was visible after all the efforts for implementation.

The third example was the development of information technology in schools. Money was put aside for machines, and there was an ambitious plan of equipping schools with large number of machines envied by other systems. However, there were only vague plans for training and for applications. Many schools received the machines, primary schools in particular, with indifference. A large number of such machines were underused, or not used at all, and soon became obsolete. Delivering the machines and spending the assigned money were almost the only visible target goal when it came to implementation.

In short, there was no shortage of policies and recommendations, and the government had indeed put in the money and effort, but there was little perceivable improvement of the situation. There was therefore a general lack of confidence in all parties. Teachers had no confidence in their students; they complained about students' poor performance and did not think there was a way out. Parents had no confidence in schools; those who could afford voted with their feet and sent their children either to international schools or to schools abroad.[6] Employers had no confidence in local graduates; they preferred returnee-graduates from overseas institutions, or even graduates from Shanghai or Beijing. Above all, people had lost their confidence in government policies in education.

Meanwhile, it is notable that it was a time when the term *reform* was something to be avoided, because it could carry the connotation of "rocking the boat," and would not be welcomed by either civil servants or school practitioners.

The Launch

Against such a backdrop, in January 1999, the Education Commission launched the Education Reform as a campaign. It started with begging the question: *What are the aims of education?*[7] The presentation of the campaign was to provide a list of hypothetical aims for education at all levels and solicit endorsement from the public. It was perhaps the first time ever in the public sector where the launch was managed as a campaign with large-scale public forums and constructive mobilisation of the media. The launch succeeded in reviving people's hope of improving local education. One of the themes of the launch was indeed "*I have a wish: Education should be....*" as a way of attracting responses. A volume of 16,000 responses were received from all walks of life, most of them included criticism of the existing situation as well as suggestions for improvement. It was a successful campaign that mobilised society at large to focus people's minds on a *reform*, a term that has been since accepted.

The eight or nine months that followed were a honeymoon for the Education Commission. Living on the massive support of the campaign, the Education Commission was able to organise a large number of concerned educators and started detailed discussions of concrete goals in order to realise the pledged aims of education. At the height of the discussions, over 100 people were involved in various working groups for the deliberation of the reforms.

During these few months, a number of issues further reinforced the orientation of the reform. In a positive sense, a renewed understanding of the concept of lifelong learning, particularly in the OECD countries,[8] and the association of that to a knowledge society, has convinced the Education Commission to adopt Lifelong Learning as its basic framework of reform. Such a notion has extended the society's commitment to its citizens' learning beyond compulsory education. It has also extended the notion of "education" to include every young person in society. The framework enabled the Education Commission to conceive reforms in different parts of the system in consistency. In a negative sense, the revelation of a large number of failures in the HK Certificate of Education Examination, the school leaving examination, also demonstrated that the system was working against the needs of the society, where few could survive without the ability of lifelong learning.[9]

By September 1999, the Education Commission was able to produce a second report, *Learning for Life*,[10] which laid out the target goals of the reform. These included reforms in examinations, in the curriculum, in admissions at different transitional junctures of the system, and the target goal of reforming tertiary education. Highlights included the abolition of the aptitude test that was part of the allocation system at the end of primary schooling, the revision of the primary one admission, the transformation of the senior secondary system from the British tradition of 2+2 to 3 years, in anticipation of a nominal duration of four years in tertiary degree programmes.

However, the Education Commission's honeymoon in 1999 was also matched by the economic downturn, which was gradually understood to be more fundamental than it was perceived. In particular, the ever-growing serious structural unemployment was early proof of the need of reform in education.

In May 2000, the Education Commission was able to produce a draft of the blueprint,[11] consisting of development plans on various fronts of the reform. With due consultation, the comprehensive blueprint was published in October 2000.[12] The Education Commission made concrete plans for reform in various sectors of the system, but with a two-year window to further deliberate reforms in tertiary education. The blueprint was immediately adopted as government policy and implemented. In practice, the abolition of the aptitude test at the end of primary schools was realised even before the blueprint was published.

Reactions to the Blueprint

However, Education Commission's honeymoon almost came to an end at the publication of the blueprint. The reform, still in full strength, was not always so favourably perceived by the public. There were several dimensions to that.

First, poor co-ordination has led to confusions. There were policies due to earlier decisions prior to the reform, but the actual measures were introduced in parallel with the Blueprint implementations. Such existing policies may or may not be in line with the spirit of the reform. There was little coordination and hence little synchrony. The bureaucrats argued that these were policies in place, and they were only implementing according to schedule. There was little re-examination of whether or not such policies should be given rethink in the light of the overarching reform blueprint, or whether or not they should be implemented with an alternative timetable.

Such measures included the almost mandatory use of Cantonese (Chinese) as the medium of introduction in secondary schools, the language benchmarking of teachers, and the whole series of measures pertaining to "school-based management," which entailed introduction of the notion of "value-added" to schools, continuation of the whole school

Quality Assurance Inspection and the publication of School Profiles. There have also been measures that are created almost *impromptu* as personal decisions of senior officers, such as the requirement of all teachers to undergo training in information technology, yet with no matching applications in curriculum and teaching.

Each of these has aroused controversy of different degrees. One serious example was "mother-tongue" teaching, which has far-reaching implications, but was implemented with little regard to serious intellectual debates and the immediate serious consequences. The implementation was so forceful that foreign media mistook it as Tung's act of decolonisation. The teachers' language benchmarking was handled with little sensitivity and has given the major teachers' union, the Professional Teachers' Union, the opportunity to organise major protests with wide teacher support. The PTU is, incidentally, also perceived as an apparatus of the Democrats, and hence the protest worked to the benefit of the Democrats during the election that came almost immediately after.

All the way, grass-root teachers have been receiving confusing signals about the reform. They are confused about what are parts of the reform blueprint and what are not, and indeed to them such distinctions carry no meaning. All they have experienced are new requirements, coming from diverse directions, each adds to their workload. They are also confused about who is in charge. They hear different if not conflicting messages. One the one hand, there is the call for creating more room for teachers so as to allow them to concentrate on pedagogical matters. On the other hand, there are new additions of work and papers that distract them from helping students' learning. Overall, few teachers have felt the benefits of the reform.

Second, the confusion mentioned above also reflects incompetence in the government or government-related machineries in organising themselves. In policies that pertain to the school sector, often, the Education Commission (an advisory body), the Education and Manpower Bureau (a policy bureau), the Education Department (an executive department) and the Board of Education (another advisory body), and with them the Curriculum Development Council (yet another advisory body with decision powers in matters of curriculum), may often have separate interpretations of the reform, and hence would conduct discussions or exercises that are not always along the same wavelengths.

There was an effort during the deliberation of the reform to pull all these organs together in order to work under the same policy umbrella.

However, when disagreement of interpretation or action arose, little was done to retune the understanding, to reengineer the organisations, or to readjust the personnel in order to achieve a higher degree of consistency. Instead, organisations at the higher level would "conveniently" take direct action or create new set-ups that would override and, at times, undermine the authority or legitimacy of the lower level organisations. Confusion was sustained, and sometimes grew.

Third, related, among decision-makers and leading executives within the government, there is a marked scepticism of directions and conceptualisation of policies. Such directions and conceptualisation are often seen by senior decision-makers and government executives as "high-sounding" or "idealistic," and hence should give way to more pragmatic discussions of the practical means. However, in reality, directions and conceptualisation, or "understanding" of the policies in general, are often essential in mobilising various sectors, such that they could be in a better position to exercise their discretion in facing difficulties and solving problems during implementation. Without such directions and conceptualisation, all parties would remain at the level of concrete measures, and hence would only aim at delivering the "means" without an "end."

Hence, although the reform discussion started with discussion of the aims, which was seen as forgotten in the past years, the aims are again soon forgotten once the reform documents are published. At some lower-level decisions, such as curriculum development, sometimes even the publication of the documents is regarded as an end in itself. It is therefore not unusual to see policy speeches and implementation reports where spending of money is regarded as an achievement. It is also a common observation among educators that, often, implementation of a particular reform project stops short at a grand opening ceremony. There is a culture among decision-makers and executives, that directions and conceptualisation are too idealistic for the realisation of policies. The lack of loftier goals has also contributed to the sluggish process of implementation, where specific difficulties could easily sway the targets or pace of implementation, or where signs of adverse publicity are sufficient to deter actions.

Fourth, and this could be the crux of the issue, the decision processes are often precarious. There are few elements of rational analysis. It is not unusual to hear decision-makers making sweeping remarks on very important issues, but which has no basis on data nor expert analysis. Other times, some particular point of view from a specific stakeholder may catch the decision-maker and cause immediate policy-decisions. There is a detectable sentiment among government officials, for example, against the "elite schools," which is a fussy umbrella term that embraces schools with long tradition and with high achievements. Most of such a sentiment is accumulated over hearsays that are subject to no scrutiny. There was also a visible proliferation of consultants, often from overseas, who could demonstrate little success in their home system, yet could have the ear of the decision-maker, who would then make relevant decisions on important matters. There is simply a lack of expertise in assessing expertise.

Fifth, there is little consciousness of value judgement. A lot of decisions are made with total ignorance of the underlying value choice, and the far-reaching implications of such a value choice. There is little awareness, also, that such a choice should not and could not be made by a single person on behalf of society.

Sixth, in this context, the role of the policy advisory bodies is deteriorating. Such advisory bodies used to play a dual role of a representative of community values on the one hand, and a defender of government policies on the other. Both are ignored. Often, advisory bodies are used not as a think tank, but as an arm for deliberating implementation details, almost replacing the executive departments in their role. As an example, the advisory organ for continuing education is asked to formulate the "regulatory framework" and the "quality assurance framework" which are very much the government's responsibility, and is left no room to deliberate the overarching policies, such as legislation for the rights about lifelong learning, and underpinning principles such as partnership in financing lifelong learning. Meanwhile, essential policies, such as the 60 per cent enrolment target for tertiary education, did not undergo any rational deliberation among any of the advisory bodies, yet was announced and taken for granted. As a consequence, advisory bodies have developed no ownership of the policies, and are not able nor prepared to defend government policies.

The Real Progress

Nonetheless, it would be unfair to see the reform as a failure. The above confusions and incompetence in implementation occur only when one concentrates on *government* implementation. The reform has created a lot of openings for schools to move education in new directions. In the final analysis, in the realm of education, schools matter.

One very visible change among schools is the mushrooming of new ventures and innovations. Although the government machinery is rather clumsy in implementing systemic policies, the reform has indeed created a climate where officers are expected to give room for new ventures, and schools are encouraged to do things on their own initiative. If one is not looking only at what the government has achieved, but realistically looking at what have happened in schools, then the scene is quite encouraging. In the five years of the SAR, there have been quite a number of new schools which were started basing on constructive ideas and alternative models of educating the young. There are new schools that respectively highlight science and technology, personal growth, Chinese culture, social conscience, and so forth. Others concentrate on the deprived. They all start with lofty goals and admirable plans. With few exceptions, they have brought new hope among parents and are hence mostly oversubscribed. Although the reform has yet to restore the community's confidence in the entire system, the delightful offspring do demonstrate that Hong Kong is capable of improving its schools.

Even among the existing schools, changes are taking place, to various extents. An unofficial estimation from some official source paints a picture that around two-thirds of secondary schools and one-third of primary schools have initiated constructive changes respectively. Many of them have moved away from the rigidity of routine activities and devised ways towards students' effective learning. Some of them have changed the mode of operation, such as new ways of time-tabling student activities. Some have included extensive community experience in their school lives. Among others, the past few years have witnessed enormous opportunities for parents' participation and there are signs of the emergence of a territory-wide force from organised parents. Most of above new developments have demonstrated signs of success.

Another front of progress is the decision of some of the best schools to participate in the Direct Subsidy Scheme. As is mentioned earlier, the DSS is to provide schools with the same amount of public subsidy, based on student numbers, but would allow the schools to have more autonomy in admissions and teacher deployment. DSS schools are also allowed to charge a fee in exchange for better facilities or smaller class-size, for example. It took almost five years for the first school, St. Paul's Co-educational School, to breakthrough the ideological boundaries and declare excellence as its goal in joining the DSS. The floodgate is open, and Hong Kong is now to face a higher level of value dilemma vis-à-vis social equity.

All in all, there is an emerging degree of diversity among Hong Kong schools. That is a delightful deviation from the highly conformed school system which was more appropriate for times of quantity expansion. Such a development is very much in line with the contemporary understanding of students' individual construction of knowledge, and is indeed in keeping of the demand of the society for a versatile and adaptive workforce. Such diversity is possible only when there is less unnecessary intervention from the government, although the visibility of the Hong Kong government is still very high in the daily operation of schools.

Such an improvement in school individuality, which is essential to quality education, is also to some extent facilitated by the establishment of the Regional Educational Offices, which is a personnel reorganisation of the Education Department. By way of the REOs, officers are organised by regions for customise services to schools within the region, rather than divided according to their professional expertise. This follows the trend of reorganisation in the private sector at large. Although the effects of such a reorganisation are variedly appraised, and admittedly the disparity among the regions is profound, the constructive contribution of such a move towards school flexibility is unmistakable. Although grassroots educators would still be struggling with bureaucratic barriers on their way to reform, they would also admit that the doors are now wider open.

Hence, although the systemic moves in education reform are disappointingly slow and clumsy, the awareness and initiations for change at the grassroots are encouraging and unprecedented.

New Challenges

However, education works in a larger environment that moves much faster than schools. Even in the three years since the reform was launched, a few fundamental changes in the Hong Kong society is identifiable and will have important impact on Hong Kong.

New Role in China

The first of these changes pertains to the role of Hong Kong in China. Over the first half-a-century after the establishment of the People's Republic, China had largely been closed to the outside world. In that context, Hong Kong was the only window where China interacted with the outside world.

Or, vice versa, it was mainly through Hong Kong that the international community maintained its contacts with the Chinese mainland.

In the last two decades, Hong Kong has continued to play that role during the process where China opens itself up. Hong Kong has brought to China the knowledge and norms that are shared by the international community, and with that help, China has sped up its participation in the international arena.

Now that China is more equipped to play a more active role in the global village, where it is confident that it could acquire the requisites of international participation on its own, Hong Kong has to redefine its role. China's accession to the WTO is a clear milestone that Hong Kong has to find its own identify in the new era.

Second, meanwhile, it has now become more difficult for Hong Kong to maintain its original edge. Hong Kong thrived on its openness, openness that was not only a great contrast to China, but was also unusual in the international market. It was at a time when opening one's own market to foreign investment was to render oneself vulnerable to foreign invasion.

China's opening up is not only a breakaway from the tradition of conservatism, but is also leading a trend of openness that is now believed to be almost the only opportunity a nation could develop amidst keen international competition. In the 1970s, one could not image that countries like China, India, or Russia, Chile, or even North Korea would be so enthusiastic in attracting foreign investments. Now, foreign presence is not only much easier, but also almost inevitable, given the high connectivity enabled by technologies.

In these circumstances, the openness of Hong Kong, which had made it a unique international marketplace, is no longer a privilege. Even if we confine ourselves to the vicinity, Singapore is actively shaping itself as an international hub, and Shanghai is catching up with unbelievable speed.

That Hong Kong's is losing its privilege should have enormous implications to its overall development. Instead of expecting others to come to Hong Kong and use it as a base for activities in the region, Hong Kong should be actively creating its own presence in the international arena. This would mean a change in its general policy orientations. It is of course important to make Hong Kong an attractive place, which is what all the present policies are about, it is even more important to make Hong Kong a major exporter of talents, expertise and quality services. This is what international competition is about in the knowledge society. However, this is yet to be understood by policy-makers in Hong Kong.

In the particular realm of education, there is an emerging tide of international "trade of educational services,"[13] where the exchange of educational activities carries with it the dual consequences of cultural infiltration and economic transactions. From a positive perspective, such a trade will facilitate inter-cultural understanding and will provide complementarities among education systems, such that learners will benefit from the world's best educational programmes. From a pessimistic perspective, however, such a trade will benefit Hong Kong only when its education system is strong enough to maintain its own cultural and quality characteristics, such that it would not become a victim of the international trade war on education, and that its education would not be once again "colonised."

This is not to suggest that Hong Kong should submit to protectionism in education, but it is legitimate to rethink its strategies of educational development. It is not totally inconceivable to allow ample room for international participation, especially in higher education and vocational training, but to create Hong Kong's own edge in specific sectors and selected institutions, yet with wide collaboration with education providers in the mainland and abroad. It is also likely to become a necessity that Hong Kong's education system should also open to a large community beyond Hong Kong. Higher education, in particular, would not see any significant development if its student intake is confined to local citizens.

Concluding Remarks

No one would deny that the first five years of the SAR were difficult years. It was the years where the aggressive opening up of China, the Asian financial crisis and the global economic downturn have all made Hong Kong vulnerable. The vulnerability is to grow, if Hong Kong stays at its past conventions. Moreover, Hong Kong is undergoing fundamental changes towards a knowledge society.

All these have put new expectations on education. Hong Kong's education is therefore facing the double challenges of declining quality and revised orientations. The education reform, dramatic it seemed at its launch, is perhaps only a first step forward on the path towards an education system that could stand the new environments.

In this context, the SAR government inevitably has to face the scrutiny. There are obvious weaknesses in the administration. Perceivably, it is weak in making determined yet consensual value choices, its decision-making is often uninformed, and it often errs on the conservative side. Apparently, this is a new government and the community seems to be prepared to tolerate its immaturity. Such a tolerance, however, is far from endorsement and should not be taken for granted. Regardless of people's attitude towards the government, Hong Kong's education has to undergo fundamental changes, and this is unmistakable.

Notes

1. *A Perspective on the Education System of Hong Kong: Report from an International Panel.* (1992) Hong Kong: Hong Kong Government.
2. The Board of Education was established by the Education Ordinance to advise the governor on education policies. It has evolved into an advisory body for policies in basic education.
3. Established in 1982 to replace the Hong Kong Training Council. It also runs the Technical Institutes and Training Centres.
4. The University Grants Committee, then called University and Polytechnic Grants Committee, oversees development in higher education in addition to its primary function of allocating government resources to higher education institutions.
5. As was estimated by Dr. Tsang Wing-kwong at one of the seminars.
6. By 2001, it has been estimated that in the majority of international schools in Hong Kong, over 70 per cent of their students were ethnic Chinese from local families.
7. Education Commission (1999) *Review of Academic System: Aims of Education (Consultation Document)*
8. This is initiated by the visit of Professor Albert Tuijmann, then from the OECD, now Director of the Institute of International Education, Stockholm University.
9. In the 1999 HKCE Examination, 23,000 (18 per cent of all the candidates, including repeaters) or 9,000 (11 per cent of all the Secondary 5 candidates), scored zero. Few opportunities, both in terms of work and study, were open to these young people.
10. Education Commission (September, 1999) *Review of Education System: Framework for Education Reform: Learning for Life. Blue Print for the 21st Century.*
11. Education Commission (May, 2000) *Review of Education System: Reform proposals. Consultative document.*
12. Education Commission (October, 2000) *Reform Proposals for the Education System of Hong Kong.*

13. This is highlighted by a recent OECD conference on "Trade of Educational Services" held in Washington DC, 23–24 May 2002 in conjunction with the US Department of Education, US Department of Commerce and the World Bank. The conference helped to illuminate the international scene of educational "transactions" in view of the WTO's extension to include GATS, General Agreement on Trade of Services.

8

Policy Blunder of the Century Threatens Hong Kong's Economic Future

Lok Sang Ho*

Director, Centre for Public Policy Studies
Lingnan University

Introduction

8 December 1997 was a fateful day for Hong Kong. The Hong Kong Housing Authority announced a scheme, which it called the Tenant Purchase Scheme, whereby sitting tenants in selected blocks in its heavily subsidized housing estates were given the opportunity to buy at deep discounts the units in which they were currently living. Because the scheme allowed the richer tenants to buy their own units at the same attractive discounts (the discounts were subsequently reduced in 1998) this was obviously against the spirit of the existing policy of reducing and ultimately eliminating the subsidy given to the richer tenants (Ho 1997). By reducing the incentive of the richer tenants to move out of public housing it would lengthen the time for people in the queue to be assigned public rental flats.

I did not realize then that by reducing the incentives for rich tenants to pour their money into private flats, TPS was about to cause a major economic catastrophe.

The fact is that, by allowing the richer tenants to buy their own

* The author would like to thank Gary Wong and Lawrence Ho for research assistance. Support from the RGC Grants Committee (LU3008/00H) is gratefully acknowledged.

units,[1] TPS undermined the prevailing policy to make richer tenants pay higher rents or move out of the subsidized sector altogether. The offer to buy at as much as 88 per cent discount off the estimated market price (if tenants committed to buy within a specified time period) meant that HOS housing by comparison looked extremely expensive and unattractive. As a result, the demand for HOS housing plummeted. Both the turnover and the prices of HOS housing tanked.

HOS owners from now on could hardly hope to resell their units and "trade up" to better units in the private market. Private sector housing owners who had been depending on HOS owners to buy their units similarly found that their principal buyers had "suddenly disappeared." They could not trade up either. These effects filtered up all the way to luxury housing. The entire housing market became paralyzed over night.

These effects were so immediate that they surfaced right away. A statistical study using monthly data showed that there was a discrete, gigantic (60 per cent!), and otherwise inexplicable drop in housing turnover in December.

Many of the homeowners who had posted intentions to sell were not quite aware of it. They just thought it was taking longer for them to sell units after the Asian Financial Crisis. The developers, however, were much more sensitive to the changes in the market place. Their new products — often with modern design and club facilities — used to sell predominantly to second-hand buyers. When these buyers suddenly disappeared, developers were forced to cut their prices aggressively. An amazing phenomenon resulted: newer and better homes were priced lower — sometimes much lower, than older and less attractive homes.[2] For the first time in Hong Kong's history, thousands of HOS buyers forfeited their deposits and withdrew their decisions to buy. This was simply unthinkable given that for every year since 1978 when HOS housing were first put on sale HOS housing had been many times oversubscribed so that being given the right to buy a HOS unit was considered as winning a substantial lottery.

The effects of the TPS on the housing market would reverberate throughout the economy: through a fall in employment, retail sales, and business investment. These effects would ultimately threaten Hong Kong's traditional strong fiscal position and push the SAR government into serious, structural budget deficits (Ho, 24 March 1998). It is unfortunate that neither the government nor the political parties understood the argument or took the argument seriously to act on it.

Predictions Sadly Came True

As explained in my *South China Morning Post* article on 24 March 1998 while Hong Kong's land prices were high and were due for a correction, "this is quite different from saying that Hong Kong's *land policy* was due for a correction. Hong Kong's land prices were high and were rising because the economy was so prosperous, and because Hong Kong's taxes were so low. In a stagnant economy no government can use a 'high land price policy' to keep land prices rising for several years, not to speak decades." Rather than eroding Hong Kong's competitiveness, rising land prices encouraged Hong Kong people to work industriously and to plow their savings into a home or other forms of properties. Because the government collected huge revenues from land premiums, profits tax, and stamp duties, those who could not afford to buy properties benefited from low taxes and generally from the vibrant economy.

The danger for Hong Kong was that all this would change when the TPS goes into full implementation. Given that some public housing estates are quite comparable (indeed identical in some cases) to some Home Ownership Scheme estates, "selling [public housing] cheaply [indiscriminately including the rich tenants] is not only unfair to Home Ownership Scheme (HOS) owners but, most dangerously, by depressing HOS prices, *has eroded the ability of HOS to move up the ladder to better housing*. As potential buyers from among the HOS population disappeared, prices of lower tier private sector housing weaken, again eroding the ability of their owners to move up to middle-tier private housing. The effects will continue further up, finally affecting luxury type buildings."

"The announced policy means that Hong Kong's developers cannot sell their units unless prices are kept very low. In order to survive they can therefore offer very unattractive prices for land bid at land auctions. This is bad news for Hong Kong's taxpayers and homeowners. Homeowners suddenly find that their homes have failed to become a store of value."

I warned that if the public housing privatization scheme is not shelved or amended, it "will have long term implications for Hong Kong's developers, homeowners, and for Hong Kong's fiscal health," and that "the vibrant economy of Hong Kong will become a thing of the past."

Today, as I write this chapter, home prices had fallen 60 per cent off their peak and are continuing to decline. Tens of thousands of homeowners have lost all their equity and have turned into "negative asset homeowners." The government is running huge fiscal deficits and is at a loss trying to find ways to get out of the fiscal crisis. Although home prices and office prices have fallen, Hong Kong's competitiveness rating had fallen from the third position in 1997 to 12th in 2000 (IMD, Lausanne). Although it picked up to 6th in 2001, Hong Kong's ranking slipped again in 2002, to 9th.

Mysterious Setback for Hong Kong

In October 1997 when the Asian Financial Crisis threatened to affect Hong Kong our then Financial Secretary the Hon. Donald Tsang was full of confidence. He assured the public that Hong Kong had strong economic fundamentals and that problems "would be over by Christmas." Hong Kong had gone through so many ups and downs and had indeed proved resilient. Even the American Chamber of Commerce had found in its survey among members the widespread view that Hong Kong should not suffer too badly in the crisis.[3]

The Hon. Donald Tsang was right. Hong Kong was quite unlike any of the countries in the region in that it had been running budget surpluses and had accumulated a huge fiscal surplus. It also had little foreign debt to speak off and boasted the world's largest foreign exchange reserve per capita. Hong Kong did not have much of a current account deficit. Even more impressive is Hong Kong's track record: Hong Kong had gone through the Cultural Revolution and multiple bank failures during the sixties, the most serious oil price shock in human history in 1973–74 accompanied by a 90 per cent decline in the Hang Seng Index that hit bottom in 1975, another oil price shock in 1979, unprecedented interest rate hikes that brought the prime rate above 20 per cent in 1981, political uncertainties that shaved 50 per cent of the value of the Hong Kong dollar from 1982 to 1983, multiple bank failures in the eighties, the 1989 Tiananmen Incident, the Gulf War, and worrying tensions between Britain and Beijing under the Chris Patten Administration. Hong Kong had managed to register positive economic growth, year in, year out, from 1963 right through 1997. Hong Kong's legendary resilience had weathered storms much worse than the Asian Financial Crisis. And in 1997 Hong Kong's fiscal and foreign exchange reserves were the envy of the world and were at their historical highs. What was there to fear?

Yet Hong Kong suffered not only the first yearly economic decline in its officially recorded statistical history. It was a mind-boggling 5.3 per cent decline.

Now consider this list:

- Home prices fell only by 6.85 per cent from their peak reached in May 1997 to November 1997. But from November 1997 to September 2001 home prices fell by 50.6 per cent. The total loss in home prices — not counting the loss in office values which in part must also be related to the loss in the value of homes because of the depressing effect on business activity — amounts to roughly two years of Hong Kong's GDP.
- Second hand transactions plunged 56.1 per cent in December 1997, while first hand transactions plunged 61.5 per cent in the same month. This is strange in view of the fact *that stock prices and the Hong Kong had actually stabilized and had shown an increase in the month* (See Table 4). Moreover, home transactions had shown a recovery in November 1997.
- GDP growth fell by 5.3 per cent in 1998 — something that made history, as in none of the years from 1963 to 1997 did Hong Kong ever experience negative growth.

These discouraging trends continued notwithstanding a number of positive factors:

- Despite the alleged severity of the Asian Financial Crisis, not one licensed bank had failed during or after the Crisis. Much more serious problems had happened during the sixties, seventies, and eighties with multiple bank failures and no major problem resulted. Why was it that this time around the economy can crumble to the extent it did?
- The "property market confidence index" compiled by the Hong Kong Policy Research Institute jumped from 35.5 in January 1998 to 94.2 in February 1998. In 1999 this confidence index actually hit 108.1 in April and remained close to 100 by the end of the year. This suggested that "lack of confidence" was not a factor behind the fall in property prices. Actually many people had a lot of confidence, to the extent that 1998 and 1999 were years of fantastic sales for developers in terms of volumes. Since home prices kept falling, however, people who earlier on had confidence began to lose confidence. Thus, loss of confidence was a result of declining property prices rather than its cause. By the end of 2000 the property confidence index slipped below 70. The property confidence index

jumped from 62 in April 2001 to 76.4 in May 2001 — which was regarded as statistically significant. But property prices continued to sag during the year of 2001. The price decline continued during the year even before the September 11 terrorist attack on the World Trade Center.

- 2000 June to 2000 December Sale of HOS housing was suspended; Then on 3 September 2001 the government announced another suspension of HOS sales (this time for ten months) as well as a freeze on HOS-designated land allocation. An increase of 12,000 home purchase loan quotas was also announced.
- Mortgage rates have fallen from typically "prime or prime plus some percentage" in 1998 to the prime rate by March 1999 and to "prime minus 2" per cent in 2001, while the prime rate itself was also declining sharply.
- The policy of 85,000 a year production target for housing was officially abolished in 2000 (See 1 July 2000, *Economic Times*)[4]
- A mortgage guarantee scheme was introduced in December 1998 by the Hong Kong Mortgage Corporation to provide an additional 15 per cent loan over and above the standard 70 per cent loan on the house price.

What Went Wrong?

I have now assembled plenty of evidence to the effect that the culprit behind all this is really the Tenant Purchase Scheme announced on 8 December 1997 by the Housing Authority. The way it worked in damaging the housing market and then the Hong Kong economy is this. Since TPS allows all sitting tenants, regardless of their income or asset status, to buy their units at very low prices (for the first phase, at as low as only 12 per cent of the estimated market price), TPS effectively kills all interest among the richer tenants to buy Home Ownership Housing. With the disappearance of this main source of buyers from among public housing tenants, HOS owners will have a hard time to sell their units, and if they can sell at all they will have to sell at very low prices. Unable to realize a large equity from their home sales their ability to pay for private housing units will be seriously encompassed. Private housing owners who had depended on HOS owners to buy similarly cannot find buyers with the ability to pay the kind of prices which had prevailed. This is why housing prices and housing market turnover nose dived after 8 December 1997.

How do we know that public housing tenants have huge purchasing power and that they had really been the driving force behind the property price inflation from 1987 to 1997?

Consider the following facts. According to Housing Authority information, one public housing tenant paid $3,950,000 for a HOS housing flat under the HOS Secondary Market Scheme in September 1997 — about two months after the Asian Financial Crisis and already at a discount from the peak prices reached in July. The HOS Secondary Market Scheme allows the owner of an HOS flat to sell his unit without paying back to the Housing Authority implicit subsidy in the price of the land but required that the unit be sold to a public housing tenant or a certified Green Form buyer. That unit was a middle story, 644 square feet flat (usable area) in Fu Keung Court in Wang Tau Hom, Kowloon. This certainly had availed the HOS housing owner over $3 million, probably close to $4 million, of equity to trade up to a better flat in the private sector. It is no wonder that a private sector flat of, say, a thousand square feet fetched over $6 million. The $6 million flat could fetch such a high price only because buyers could sell their own units for a good price. A unit of exactly the same size in exactly the same development and of a similar story sold at $2,560,000 in April 1998 (–35 per cent in seven months) and at $1,880,000 (–52.4 per cent in four years) in August 2001. The buyers again were first public housing tenants. These public housing tenants simply would not pay nearly 4 million dollars for an HOS flat given that public housing flats were being sold at rock bottom prices. Given the much lower price that his flat fetched, the HOS owner could offer only much smaller amount to pay for a private flat.

Proposition One: The injection of money from among public housing tenants caused price appreciation across the board, and provided support even for luxury flats though these latter appear to belong to "a different market."

The Housing Authority had conducted a survey from Oct. 1992–March 93 that showed that 24 per cent of transactions in homes were traceable to public housing tenants. (*Medium Term Review of Long Term Housing Strategy*, Housing Authority, released October 1993).

One may well wonder why public housing tenants were so rich.[5] In truth, many public housing tenants were poor, but a good number of them were quite rich in cash. The reason is largely that they have been paying such low rents that they can save large amounts each month. From 1987 through 1997 both economic growth and inflation were quite high. This not only boosted incomes and savings, but also provided an incentive to buy homes as an inflation hedge.

Yet after 8 December 1997 all of this had changed. Compared to TPS units HOS housing appeared far too expensive. Public rental housing buyers had little reason to spend millions of dollars to buy an HOS flat, when marginally inferior flats sell for extremely attractive prices. That truly irresistible prices were offered the sitting tenants can be inferred from the fact that a flat in Wah Kwai Estate sold for 920,000 dollars in June 2001 and netted a profit of 136 per cent for its sitting tenant who bought the unit in 1998.

Proposition Two: TPS lowers prices across the board all the way to luxury flats. Given the many tiers of housing with one depending on the support of another, the total loss in the value of properties due to a decline in the housing prices at the bottom is a multiple of the value of decline in the price of the lowest tier.

If we assume that the average price of a housing unit was $4 million, which is a very conservative estimate given it was the price paid by a public housing tenant for an HOS unit in the HOS Secondary Market and if the loss in value was 60 per cent, each unit of housing suffered a loss of $2.4 million. Since there are roughly one million private housing units in Hong Kong, the total loss in value amounts to $2400 billion, which is roughly two years of Hong Kong's GDP. While we certainly cannot say that TPS is the only factor behind this loss, there is evidence that TPS was the key factor behind the reversal of the property market.[6] Other factors behind the reversal likely include the unrealistically large production target of 85,000 units a year, which produced a glut of housing (See Tables 1 and 2), and the high interest rates of late 1997 to 1998. For now, the 85,000 units a year target is gone and mortgage rates are the lowest level seen in decades. Housing prices have not yet stabilized notwithstanding the 60 per cent decline since July 1997.

Statistical Evidence and Tests[7]

Referring to Table 3, we can see that there was a sudden drop in second hand residential property transactions in August 1997 as a result of the

Table 1. Private Domestic Property — Supply from 1979 to 2002

Year	Small/ Medium[3]	Large[4]	Total
1979	26300	1500	27800
1980	22700	1800	24500
1981	31000	2500	33500
1982	20600	2500	23100
1983	19000	2600	21600
1984	20900	1400	22300
1985	27950	1950	29900
1986	31550	2550	34100
1987	32400	2000	34400
1988	31350	3150	34500
1989	33800	2700	36500
1990	27400	2000	29400
1991	31650	1750	33400
1992	25140	1080	26220
1993	26690	930	27620
1994	32170	2000	34170
1995	20660	1960	22620
1996	18160	1710	19870
1997	17420	780	18200
1998	20270	2010	22280
1999	33700	1620	35320
2000	23460	[2330]	25790
2001	[24300]	[3500]	[27800]
2002	[28500]	[1200]	[29700]

Sources: *Property Review 1983–1989 Editions*, Rating and Valuation Department, Hong Kong Government Printer.
Hong Kong Property Review 1994, 1998, 1999 and 2001 Editions, Rating and Valuation Department, Hong Kong Government Printer.

Notes: 1. Private Domestic units are defined as independent dwellings with separate cooking facilities and bathroom (and/or lavatory). They are sub-divided by reference to floor area.
2. Supply refer to the supply of private sector premises comprises those premises deemed completed by virtue of the issue of either a temporary or full occupation permit or letter of compliance.
3. Small/ Medium units refer to saleable area less than 100 m^2
4. Large units refer to saleable area 100 m^2 and over.
[ ] = Forecast figures

Table 2. Private Domestic Property[1] — Vacancy[2] from 1979 to 2000

Year	Small / Medium[3]		Large[4]		Total	
	units	% of total stock	units	% of total stock	units	% of total stock
1979	13100	2.9	1500	3.9	14600	2.9
1980	14700	3.1	2000	5.3	16700	3.3
1981	26800	5.3	2900	7.3	29700	5.4
1982	27400	5.3	3800	9.1	31200	5.6
1983	20000	3.7	4400	9.9	24400	4.2
1984	19500	3.5	2900	6.4	22400	3.7
1985	19350	3.2	2750	5.8	22100	3.4
1986	21400	3.4	3300	6.6	24700	3.6
1987	20000	3.0	2300	4.5	22300	3.1
1988	16750	2.4	3450	6.3	20200	2.7
1989	27200	4.1	3100	5.4	30300	4.2
1990	22550	3.2	3600	6.2	26150	3.4
1991	29450	4.1	3550	5.9	33000	4.2
1992	31330	4.2	2740	4.5	34070	4.2
1993	29850	3.9	2390	3.9	32240	3.9
1994	37450	4.7	3220	5.1	40670	4.7
1995	32740	4.0	3460	5.3	36200	4.1
1996	30830	3.7	3220	4.8	34050	3.8
1997	32600	3.8	3380	4.9	35980	3.9
1998	38420	4.3	5400	7.6	43820	4.5
1999	54750	5.9	4390	6.0	59140	5.9
2000	49300	5.2	5650	7.5	54950	5.4

Sources: *Property Review 1983–1989 Editions*, Rating and Valuation Department, Hong Kong Government Printer.
Hong Kong Property Review 1994, 1998, 1999 and 2001 Editions, Rating and Valuation Department, Hong Kong Government Printer.

Note: 1. Private Domestic units are defined as independent dwellings with separate cooking facilities and bathroom (and / or lavatory). They are sub-divided by reference to floor area.
2. Vacancy rate refer to vacancies in respect of all private premises completed during the review year, and those completed earlier but not yet assessed for rating purposes, are determined by inspection at the end of the year.
3. Small/ Medium units refer to saleable area less than 100 m^2.
4. Large units refer to saleable area 100 m^2 and over.

Table 3. Transactions of Second Hand and First Hand Homes by Category

Year/Month	All First Hand	All Second Hand	First Hand Private	Second Hand Private	Second Hand HOS	HOS Secondary Market
9507–9512	**12,752**	**32,112**	**9,697**	**27,260**	**1,843**	—
9601–9612	**23,629**	**115,449**	**19,707**	**101,045**	**6,556**	—
9701	2,935	15,772	1,398	14,213	785	—
9702	3,824	12,211	2,996	11,057	570	—
9703	3,444	11,737	791	10,076	651	—
9704	3,636	20,513	3,250	18,266	1,204	—
9705	2,386	15,412	942	13,499	924	—
9706	1,826	14,093	1,535	12,050	654	—
9707	2,284	18,998	2,147	17,227	984	—
9708	2,721	11,119	2,044	8,595	588	9
9709	3,002	9,635	1,396	7,800	576	142
9710	3,119	9,931	2,174	8,315	671	159
9711	4,422	10,096	1,343	8,653	762	112
*9712**	*1,724*	*4,514*	*364*	*3,804*	*333*	*109*
9701–9712	**35,323**	**154,031**	**20,380**	**133,555**	**8,702**	**531**
9801	2,368	4,286	2,334	3,598	343	81
9802	914	3,597	868	2,883	339	83
9803	5,802	6,594	2,636	5,501	561	99
9804	4,554	5,536	649	4,683	399	79
9805	3,470	5,230	2,429	4,364	394	78
9806	4,510	4,127	3,871	3,413	302	82
9807	1,975	4,060	1,880	3,337	337	84
9808	2,669	4,174	2,603	3,427	362	47
9809	962	3,907	824	3,303	266	72
9810	4,095	3,290	3,724	2,681	265	105
9811	8,783	5,721	6,203	4,974	391	311
9812	6,978	7,002	3,578	5,946	694	487
9801–9812	**47,080**	**57,524**	**31,599**	**48,110**	**4,653**	**1,608**
9901	2,133	6,370	1,999	5,012	851	385
9902	3,067	4,584	1,951	3,268	841	270
9903	4,785	4,945	2,589	3,640	796	241
9904	3,865	5,456	3,507	4,313	543	253
9905	4,750	6,403	4,173	5,063	672	390
9906	1,640	5,949	1,516	4,517	777	434
9907	1,771	5,997	1,394	4,317	946	361
9908	1,046	5,446	777	3,871	867	271
9909	809	4,400	568	3,072	680	253

Table 3. (Cont'd)

Year/Month	All First Hand	All Second Hand	First Hand Private	Second Hand Private	Second Hand HOS	HOS Secondary Market
9910	1,444	4,137	1,400	2,797	569	308
9911	697	4,746	661	3,422	619	275
9912	1,678	4,608	1,022	3,273	543	259
9901–9912	**27,685**	**63,041**	**21,557**	**46,565**	**8,704**	**3,700**
0001	790	5,301	695	4,000	668	255
0002	599	4,720	531	3,590	510	180
0003	2,973	4,561	1,300	3,277	591	275
0004	4,485	4,219	2,487	2,981	569	222
0005	1,169	4,449	1,042	3,188	581	202
0006	633	3,981	582	2,782	471	210
0007	3,360	4,172	2,400	2,929	505	225
0008	5,137	4,723	2,808	3,346	565	335
0009	2,119	5,017	1,780	3,580	659	408
0010	1,873	5,235	1,851	3,785	741	305
0011	1,318	4,728	1,296	3,213	732	115
0012	1,060	3,543	1,058	2,418	389	61
0001–0012	**25,516**	**54,649**	**17,830**	**39,089**	**6,981**	**2,793**
0101	916	3,400	857	2,364	332	80
0102	1,328	3,160	948	2,211	313	129
0103	5,579	5,243	2,676	3,759	481	92
0104	3,282	4,199	1,313	3,031	406	123
0105	1,588	5,416	1,411	3,993	564	460
0106	1,911	5,278	1,611	3,771	687	327
0107	2,052	4,996	1,985	3,500	735	—
0108	1,934	5,557	1,765	3,978	717	—
0109	1,645	4,596	1,109	3,221	625	—
0101–0109	**20,235**	**41,845**	**13,675**	**29,828**	**4,860**	**1,211**

* TPS was announced on 8 December 1997.

Source: Centaline Property Agency Ltd.

breaking out of the Asian Financial Crisis. The drop was a steep 49.6 per cent. But then transactions have stabilized and actually picked up steadily up till November. Strangely, however, another precipitous drop in second hand home transactions occurred in December. This time the drop was more than 56 per cent. Even more shocking was the drop of 61.6 per cent in first hand home transactions in December.

Table 4. Indicators of Changes of Confidence

	The US$ Premium on the HK Dollar in the 1-Year Forward Market	Hang Seng Index Average for The Month
1997.5	161	14021
1997.6	321	14674
1997.7	552	15417
1997.8	1017	15945
1997.9	1117	14454
1997.10	2336	12609
1997.11	4055	10327
1997.12	4036	10807
1998.1	6014	9248
1998.2	3683	10606
1998.3	2396	11315
1998.4	1808	11015

If we look at movements in the Hang Seng Index or movements in the premium of the US dollar on the Hong Kong dollar in the forward exchange market, there is no sign that there was any sudden deterioration in confidence (Table 4). If anything, confidence appeared to have improved a bit in December, as the forward premium narrowed while the Hang Seng Index edged up. The only explanation for the precipitous changes in the property market is the announcement on 8 December of the Tenant Purchase Scheme.

I have conducted various statistical tests to test if my hypothesis that TPS was the key factor behind the property market reversal.[8] I regressed housing market turnover against an instrumental variable for the Asian Financial Crisis, using the premium of the US dollar on the HK dollar in the forward exchange market, and a dummy for the TPS, which took on the value of unity from December 1997 onwards. When confidence in the Hong Kong dollar was weak, the one-year forward exchange rate discount would be high, implying that pressures on the Hong Kong dollar were high. The statistical results showed that the TPS was much more important in explaining the downturn in housing market turnover than the Asian Financial Crisis.

I tested the timing of the TPS by switching a "testing dummy" from zero to unity at different months. I found a discrete jump in the size and the significance of coefficient for this testing dummy in December 1997, the month when the TPS was officially announced (Ho 2001).

I tested the housing market price dynamics by examining whether the causality of housing prices was from lower priced properties to higher priced properties or vice versa. The evidence, based on the Granger Causality Test, clearly shows that the causality runs from lower priced properties to higher priced properties, not the other way round.

I tested a macroeconomic model, trying to explain Hong Kong's private sector domestic demand with such variables as real interest rates, real exports, real government expenditures, and the Asian Financial Crisis instrument. I found large unexplained declines in the growth of private domestic demand from the first quarter of 1998 on. This was so notwithstanding an unprecedented stimulative fiscal budget announced in March 1998.

Fruitless and Misguided Policy Actions

According to my analysis, given the way TPS was designed and implemented, the crumbling of the property market was inevitable. There was no way for HOS housing to attract willing buyers paying the kind of prices that had prevailed before TPS. There was no way for HOS owners to come up with the equity after selling their units to pay the kind of prices for private sector housing which had prevailed before TPS.

Without addressing this central issue, all efforts to "revive peoples' confidence in the housing market" will come to no avail. The $100,000 tax allowance for mortgage interest, which was announced in the 1998 Budget, the enlarged quotas for interest-free loans to help buyers buy homes,[9] the moratorium on land sales,[10] the decision to turn HOS flats into rental flats, the reduction in HOS housing sales targets and then the suspensions of HOS housing sales, the removal of policies for fighting speculation that were implemented in 1994, even the announcement by the Chief Executive that he had abandoned the annual production of 85,000 a year — none of these measures helped stabilize the property market.

It must be admitted that the SAR government made a huge effort to stabilize the market. Under "normal times" any of the measures would have caused the housing market to surge ahead. But none of the measure dealt with the central problem: which is the drying up of money that had been flowing into the market from among the public housing tenants. To reopen the "tap" will not cost the government anything, and indeed will bring back much of the revenue that had been lost. Instead the government pumped money into the market. But all the money that was being pumped into the market really went down the drain, because TPS was telling people that HOS housing was not worth much, and because the richer tenants can hang on and wait for their housing blocks to be sold at bargain prices.

One may well question the equity and the logic in subsidizing and resubsidizing the rich tenants at the expense of taxpayers. Allowing rich tenants to buy their flats at favourable terms is tantamount to putting an end to the Housing Subsidy Policy. Allowing only tenants in selected blocks this option and not offering the same option to other rich tenants is arbitrary and unfair. Giving the Green Form applicants, who are certainly much better positioned than White Form applicants, extra hand-outs (as much as $5,100, non-repayable) per month for buying homes in the name of supporting the housing market contravenes any sense of justice, when unemployed people in dire straits are looking for $5000 a month jobs.

Should We Hold Tung Chee-hwa Responsible?

It will not be totally fair to Tung Chee-hwa if we say that it is *his* TPS policy that led to the collapse of the Hong Kong property market and the overall demise of the Hong Kong economy. The TPS was not entirely his making. Actually back in July 1991 the Home Ownership Committee had approved a trial scheme under which selected public rental housing blocks were given some upgrading and then offered to eligible applicants under the Option to Rent or Buy Scheme (ORBS). The Scheme was launched as a pilot scheme in December 1992 and attracted 1,543 applications. Then there was also the direct precursor of TPS, the Sale of Flats to Sitting Tenants Scheme (SFSTS), which was launched in August 1991. That scheme was coldly received by tenants. The scheme was later revised to offer more attractive prices and to provide some guarantees on repairs. The Executive Council however did not endorse the revised scheme.[11] The rudiments of the TPS were there. The seeds of an economic disaster were there — well before Tung came into office. We cannot blame him for not understanding the dynamics of the housing market. After all, few housing scholars realized the negative implications of TPS, let alone the magnitude of the damage, ahead of time. Nevertheless we cannot say that Mr. Tung had no responsibility in this matter.

I had spelled out the pitfalls in the design of the scheme in December 1997 (Ho 1997). and had spelled out in detail and graphically the damage the TPS was doing the economy in March 1998 (See my 24 March 1998 *South China Morning Post* article). I had written to Mr. Tung and to senior officials (The Hon. Mrs. Anson Chan, Chief Secretary, the Hon. Donald Tsang, Financial Secretary, and the Hon. Wong Sing Wah, the Secretary of Housing) in March. And I wrote Mr. Tung another letter in July. I was there to offer free advice and free consulting, but I received no more than an acknowledgement. The issues were so important and so crucial to Hong Kong, and the situation was so urgent, that I felt like a doctor administering a life-saving medication to a patient, when the patient simply refused to take the medication.

I am glad that Mr. Tony Miller, the Director of Housing, did respond to my *South China Morning Post* article with his own article telling his version of the story (Miller 1998). But this is on reflection quite unlucky. Once the official line has been stated in the public there was little room to retract. I wished there had been a direct dialogue between him and myself. More important, Mr. Miller was only implementing policies decided upon by the government. I wished there had been a serious dialogue between senior government officials on the one hand and myself.

Similarly it will be unfair to lay the blame of 85,000 units a year production target entirely on Mr. Tung. We must remember how legislators rallied and demonstrated on behalf of "shelless snails" when many would-be homebuyers were unhappy missing the boat when home prices kept on rising relentlessly. We must remember how legislators welcomed the TPS when it was announced and wanted the plan to be extended. We must remember how some legislators tried to undermine the "richer tenants pay more rent" policy.

Finally, I had faxed my urgent call for amending the TPS scheme in 1998 to all the political parties. None of these political parties ever seriously considered the matter and made it a priority in their regular exchanges with the government. If we accuse Mr. Tung for being heartless or for lacking insight, all the political parties should also share the blame.

In my mind, Mr. Tung is an honest man with a keen interest to serve Hong Kong and China. But good intentions are not enough. Good and honest intentions may even become highly dangerous when they go hand in hand with grand visions. The vision of raising the homeownership rate in ten years from 50 per cent to 70 per cent, which was announced in Mr. Tung's 1997 Policy Address, would not have done much damage if Mr. Tung had held it as just a wish rather than a policy target. But Mr. Tung meant what he said. He went about an ambitious public housing privatization scheme (still in full force, see Table A1), asked his officials to come up with a schedule of land sales in line with his 85,000 units a year target, and enlarged home purchase loan quotas.

In my mind, Mr. Tung had a number of serious misconceptions about the housing market, which led to his misguided housing policies. He thought the housing market was a bubble ready to burst any time by the time he became Chief Executive of the SAR government. He thought the price rises were due to a high land price policy under the British rule and that high land prices would erode Hong Kong's competitiveness. The "high land price policy" consisted of restrictions in land supply which had led to a gross imbalance between supply and demand. He did not realize that no government can ever implement a high land price policy against economic fundamentals and succeed in bringing about high land prices. He also thought that Hong Kong had depended on the property market excessively and that this was unhealthy, when in actual fact Hong Kong had never depended on the property market alone to maintain its prosperity. The property market was at best a catalyst or a bridge that allows people working in the internal sector of the economy share the economic gains achieved by the external sector in the first instance. Mr. Tung is certainly not alone in failing to understand these relationships. Mr. Tung is not alone in presuming that the Asian Financial Crisis caused the mess in Hong Kong. How can we put all the blame on him alone?

What We Should Know about the Property Market

Actually, call it a bubble or not, the secular price increase from 1987 to 1997 was inevitable, as much as the secular price decline after 1997 was inevitable. The earlier price increase was dictated by the high savings accumulated among public rental housing households, high inflation rate, and the policy of making richer tenants pay higher rent. To blame the price increases to speculators would be a big mistake, because speculators cannot sustain a market increase against the economic fundamentals.

While the median rent to income ratio for public housing households rose from 6.9 per cent in 1986 to 8.6 per cent in 1996, per capita GDP jumped from $56576 a year to $188,859 a year. The increase was 334 per cent. That many public housing tenants were cash-rich was unquestioned. The "richer pays more" policy (called the "Housing Subsidy Policy") had led to huge amounts of money pouring into the housing market, buoying up home prices all the way to luxury buildings because of the "housing ladder effect" — any homeowner able to sell his unit at a good price is ready and able to pay a good price for the better home. A survey conducted by the Housing Authority in 1992–93 showed that 24 per cent of all transactions in homes were traceable to public housing tenants.

The secular increase in the values of homes made homeownership increasingly inaccessible to first time buyers from among private housing renters, because they could not compete with the cash-rich public housing tenants, nor could they compete with those who sold their homes at handsome profits. The HOS programme and the sandwich housing programme could help these people and would not have been too costly for the government to provide — as long as the government could tap the huge profits directly or indirectly arising from the property market itself. It must be noted that the purchase-to-rent ratio among housing transactions in 1997 was 75:25. Quite contrary to the Chief Executive's wish, it had fallen to 43:57 by August 1999 (See *Oriental Daily*, 4 September 1999) — testifying to the Chinese adage: "desiring to go fast, you fail to arrive."

While home prices were rising dramatically during the ten years from 1986 to 1996, the homeownership ratio rose from 38 per cent to 50 per cent. This is a very impressive rise, achieved without an explicit call to raise the ownership ratio.

During the ten years from 1986 to 1996, the proportion of over-crowded households fell from 13.9 per cent to 2.0 per cent. People were living in bigger and better homes, notwithstanding (or because of) the secular rise in home prices.

In 1985–86, the over-subscription rates for HOS/PSPS housing were 3.4 and 9.1 respectively for Green Form and White Form Applicants. In 1995–96, the over-subscription rates were 4.7 and 20.8. Public housing tenants who could not wait for a successful turnout in HOS applications were paying, in 1997, as much as $5000 plus a square foot for a flat that was three years old or over.

The fact is: if the public rental housing tenants were not so cash rich Hong Kong's property prices would not have been so high. But this is not a problem. High property prices made Hong Kong people work harder, gave the government the revenue to help the poor — particularly in building them low rental flats.

The high turnover in the housing market had helped create lots of jobs throughout the economy: decorators, movers, bankers, lawyers, brokers, furniture makers. The spending of these in turn create jobs in the restaurant business, personal services, entertainment, etc. The government collected plenty of revenue through land premiums, profit taxes, salaries taxes, stamp duties. With a strong revenue, it was in the position to hire more people and provide more services.

Did this hurt Hong Kong's competitiveness? Yes and no. Yes, to the extent that as a high cost location some industries could not survive in Hong Kong. In particular, high wages and rents mean that labour-intensive assembly-type manufacturing could not survive in Hong Kong. Some landowners charged exorbitant rents that drove restaurants and retailers out of business. But they could not do this forever. The market would discipline them and punish them by making their premises vacant for a long time.

High wages and high property prices need not hurt Hong Kong's competitiveness to the extent that Hong Kong had a motivated labour force. High incomes also meant that Hong Kong could attract international retailers. With high incomes gone, even though Hong Kong's retail sector rent has come down, its ability to compete for international investment in the retail sector has faded.

Hong Kong's Economic Future

Today, Hong Kong's economic future hangs in the air. With each phase of TPS housing sold, recovery of Hong Kong's property market and the Hong Kong economy becomes more and more remote. In principle, the cash rich tenants, having bought their own units, may still trade their TPS units for a better home in the private market. Some of them are indeed doing this. One may complain about the gross unfairness for public housing tenants long subsidized by taxpayers pocketing handsome profits yet again by a Scheme that destroyed the wealth of the very taxpayers who had subsidized these tenants in the first place. But given TPS in place, it would still be better for the TPS owners to trade up to better homes in the private market.

Unfortunately, this is the exception rather than the rule. First, the interest of TPS owners in buying homes for investment purposes is quite low, given that the Tung Chee-hwa Administration has made it clear that it does not want to see home prices rise rapidly. If they have money to put away, they would rather put it in the various resort type homes available throughout the Pearl River Delta at very low prices. Indeed many of them do so. This becomes a drag on the HK economy in two ways. Every weekend as these households go to their resorts in Guangdong Hong Kong's retail and restaurant sector suffer. The outflow of capital also directly implies a loss of land revenue for the Hong Kong SAR government.

Second, home prices are still declining because it will take quite some time before a new equilibrium is reached that is compatible with the very low prices of TPS units. To the extent that TPS has destroyed the main revenue base of the SAR government, it is a foregone conclusion that the SAR government will run into serious structural deficits. The increasing unemployment brought about by the government's "productivity enhancement" initiatives and by the decline in domestic demand due to the property market reversal will further accentuate the property market decline. This will become a vicious circle with serious consequences for the Hong Kong economy.

In 2000 the Hong Kong economy grew at 10.5 per cent, an impressive growth rate. Yet home prices fell by 8.5 per cent in the year. This is most inexplicable — until we understand the story about how TPS has destroyed the homeownership ladder.

The Tenants Purchase Scheme Q&A in the Housing Authority's website explains the thinking behind the scheme as follows: "The government has set a target of increasing homeownership to 70 per cent by 2007. Home ownership helps foster a sense of belonging and gives owners greater security. It also provides purchasers with a first step on the housing ladder, and by providing added opportunities for upward mobility promotes the release of scarce public housing resources for those in need." (http://www.info.gov.hk/hd/hiosk/tps/faq.htm) In point of fact, the first step is low cost rental housing. In 1996 and 1997, each year close to 10,000 households moved out of public rental housing to become owners in HOS housing or private housing. This was made possible by the accumulation of savings. TPS gave public housing tenants an alternative, and took away the attraction and the support for HOS housing. Mr. Miller, the Director of Housing, in a rebuttal to my *South China Morning Post* article, doubted that selling no more than 27,000 units of TPS would cause the kind of effects that I described in my Policy Blunder article. We have now witnessed the destructiveness of the policy. The evidence is for everybody to see.

I have one more prediction to make today. If TPS is not changed (See Table A1), we may as well write off Hong Kong's economic future. Some analysts think that Hong Kong's housing market will be salvaged by putting an end to HOS housing all together. But I must say that this is wishful thinking. The housing market is suffering from a drying up of funds from the bottom up. This has disabled tens of thousands of households from trading their homes for better homes and has destroyed the equity of homeowners. Putting an end to HOS housing only reduces supply but will not boost demand. Putting an end to HOS housing will not bring back the "water" that had stopped flowing. This means that property developers will continue to sell mainly to first time buyers. Since the purchasing power of first time buyers must decline over time as the richer buyers are "consumed" or committed in the earlier purchases, home values can only go down. With further declines in home values the SAR government will go bankrupt. Hundreds of thousands of Hong Kong people will go bankrupt. Hong Kong's competitiveness will go down the drain as the economically viable middle-class people go bankrupt one by one.

I hope I will be proven wrong.

Notes

1. This is the single most serious policy reversal under the Tung Administration. Allowing rich tenants to buy at subsidized prices means that these tenants can realize the capitalized implicit rental subsidies "at one go" — which is clearly equivalent to reversing the policy to make richer tenants pay higher rent.
2. Notice the sudden jump in transactions in first-hand homes in March 1998. The increase in transactions in second-hand homes was much smaller. See Appendix.
3. According to *Mingpao* (5 December 1997), 96 per cent of members surveyed by the American Chamber of Commerce believed that the investment climate in Hong Kong over the next five years were either very good or excellent.
4. The 85,000 a year production target was prescribed on a wrong diagnosis. There had never been any serious imbalance between supply and demand prior to 1997, despite large jumps in housing price. The asset price inflation was driven by the injection of accumulated savings from the richer public housing tenants. The 85,000 a year target led to excessive production starting in 1999. See *Mingpao* (14 September 2000).
5. Watanabe (1998) found that, of the four categories of households in Hong Kong, namely public housing tenants, HOS housing owners, private housing tenants, and private housing owners, public housing tenants saved by far the most in both absolute and relative terms
6. Let it be known that I am not against privatizing the public housing stock as such. But I maintain that the units should only be sold to those who meet the criteria for public housing assistance, and that any subsequent resale of the units should be restricted to buyers who meet the same criteria. As long as

such criteria are maintained, the price should be allowed find its own level in the market place and will not affect the housing market adversely, because the richer tenants must still either pay the higher rent or buy in the HOS or private market (Ho 1995).

7. See also Yeung (2001). Yeung did a survey among public housing tenants in 18 TPS estates and found that the introduction of TPS affected interest in buying HOS housing greatly.
8. See Ho (2000: Chapter 18).
9. For example, on 13 June 1998 the Director of Housing announced a plan to increase the quota for the Home Purchase Loan Scheme from 4,500 to 10,000 to allow more middle class families to fulfill their dreams of owning a home. In June 2000 the Home Purchase Loan Scheme was extended to single persons. According to a press release (19 June 2000) successful White Form applicants can borrow an interest-free loan up to $500,000 while Green Form applicants can borrow up to $800,000. Alternatively they can choose a non-repayable monthly subsidy of $3,400 (WF) or $5,100 (GF). Single-person applicants will be granted loans/monthly subsidies at half the family rate. GF applicants can use the loan to buy flats sold under the Home Ownership Secondary Market Scheme or re-finance flats they have already bought.
10. On 22 June 1998 the SAR government announced a nine-point package to stabilize the housing market, including a moratorium on land auctions for nine months through the end of the fiscal year ending in March 1999.
11. See Leung Wai Tung (1993). "Housing," in Ho Lok Sang and Choi Po King (eds.), *The Other Hong Kong Report 1993* (Hong Kong: The Chinese University Press).

References

Ho, Lok Sang (1995). "Privatization of Public Housing: an Analysis of Policy Alternatives," *Contemporary Economic Policy* (USA), Vol. 8, No. 3 (July), pp. 53–63.

Ho, Lok Sang (1997). "Flaws in Housing Policy," *South China Morning Post* (Analysis), 30 December.

Ho, Lok Sang (1998). "Cost of Bursting Property Bubble," *South China Morning Post* (Analysis), 15 June.

Ho, Lok Sang (1998). "Depressing Home Truths," *South China Morning Post* (Analysis), 18 May.

Ho, Lok Sang (1998). "Largest Threat to the Economy Comes from the Largest Action of the government," *Mingpao*, 26 March.

Ho, Lok Sang (1998). "Policy Blunder of the Century," *South China Morning Post* (Analysis), 24 March.

Ho, Lok Sang (2000). "Address housing before raising tax," *South China Morning Post* (Analysis), February.

Ho, Lok Sang (2000). "Bringing competitiveness home to people," *South China Morning Post* (Analysis), 24 July.

Ho, Lok Sang (2000). "Economic Ecology: the Case of Hong Kong," *Principles of Public Policy Practice* (Boston: Kluwer Academic Publishers).

Ho, Lok Sang, and Wong, Gary (2001). "Equity Effects, Housing Market, and the Macro Economy: the HK Case," mimeo.

Miller, Tony (1998). "Time for a strong dose of economic realities," *South China Morning Post*, 7 June.

Watanabe, Mariko (1998). "The Impact of the Public Housing Policy on Household Behaviour in Hong Kong," M.Phil. Thesis, Hong Kong: University of Hong Kong.

Yeung, Fai Yip (2001) "A Study of the Impact of the Tenants Purchase Scheme (TPS) on the Hong Kong Housing Market," M.Phil. Thesis, Hong Kong: Lingnan University.

Appendix Tables

Table A1. Six Phases of TPS

Phase One	1998	26896 units
Phase Two	1999 March	27161 units
Phase Three	2000 Feb.	27415
Phase Four	2001	26414
Phase Five	2002	26486
Phase Six A	2003	26312
Phase Six B	2003	23451

Source: Housing Authority

Table A2. Housing Price Index (Overall)

Year & Month	Price Index	Percentage Change
9701	142.7	6.0967
9702	154.3	8.1289
9703	162.2	5.1199
9704	157	–3.2059
9705	172.3	9.7452
9706	172	–0.1741
9707	167.2	–2.7907
9708	171.1	2.3325
9709	170.3	–0.4676
9710	172.9	1.5267
9711	160.5	–7.1718
9712	155	–3.4268
9806	*112.5*	*–27.4194*
9812	*104.6*	*–7.0222*
9906	*102.3*	*–2.1989*
9912	*95.7*	*–6.4516*
0006	*86*	*–10.1358*
0012	*81.8*	*–4.8837*
0106	*79.6*	*–2.6895*

Source: Rating and Valuation Department

Note: From 1998 the percentage price changes are reported for every six months. Note that in 2000, a year of super strong growth, Hong Kong recorded more than 14 per cent decline in home prices.

Table A3. Employment Situation Since the Asian Financial Crisis

Period	Labour Force	Employment	Jobs Gained or Lost ('000)	Unemployment Rate
1997:4	3.297	3.2214	77.7	2.2
1998:1	3.247	3.1414	–80	3.3
1998:2	3.258	3.1177	–23.7	4.3
1998:3	3.290	3.1143	–3.4	5.2
1998:4	3.310	3.1154	1.1	5.9
1999:1	3.297	3.0928	–22.6	6.3
1999:2	3.326	3.1235	30.7	6.1
1999:3	3.316	3.1016	–21.9	6.3
1999:4	3.340	3.1313	29.7	6.3
2000:4	3.402	3.2524	121.1	4.4
2001:Jun-Aug	3.428	3.256	3.6	4.9

Source: Census and Statistics Department

Note: This Table shows that even after the Asian Financial Crisis, in the last quarter of 1997, employment grew by 77,700. In the following quarter 80,000 jobs were lost. There is statistical evidence to suggest that job creation is very much related to housing market turnover. The loss of housing market turnover subsequent to TPS translates into a loss of jobs.

9

The Social Welfare Reform: A Way to Reduce Public Burden?

Kenneth L. Chau*

Professor of Social Work, Department of Social Work
The Chinese University of Hong Kong

Chack-kie Wong*

Professor, Department of Social Work
The Chinese University of Hong Kong

Synopsis

The social welfare reform will be reviewed in terms of the nature of the reform policies, the progress and foreseeable trends for social welfare. Basing on this review as a context, an analysis will be made to unravel key motivating factors and societal forces (within the realm of the economic, political and social arenas) that may have been instrumental to this reform effort. Since the Basic Law has excluded the possibility of political reform as a response to emerging changes and governance crisis, the social welfare reform appears politically motivated to meet the high public expectation of the post-colonial state, as well as to enhance the state's legitimacy and capacity. In the final analysis, however, evidences suggest that the social welfare reform is more than taking the interest of the public's political and social rights. It is driven by an emphasis on market mechanism, cost-effectiveness, competitiveness and social morality. The social welfare reform thus mirrors the New Right ideology and the images of a

* The authors would like to acknowledge Miss Chan Wai Yin, Rachel, for her research assistance and administrative support.

managerial state, and serves the ultimate aim of reducing the state role and public spending in social welfare. It hence reveals the unenviable dilemma of the government: the need for cost-containment for capital accumulation and the need for legitimization. Empirical data will be used to complement the theoretical analysis, and to shed light on the impact and contributions of Tung Chee-hwa regime to the social welfare landscape.

Introduction

The 1997 handover ushers in a new era for Hong Kong. Despite the smooth transition, the newly established HKSAR government was not spared of internal governance problems. On the area of social welfare, the government faces an awkward dilemma. On one hand, given the ageing population, the widening wealth gap, the growing political consciousness of the people, the transition into a knowledge-based economy and other formidable challenges, the government has to meet the rising social demands by better and more service provision in order to maintain social stability and government credibility. On the other hand, it has to tighten its budget for financial sustainability and economic competitiveness in view of global economic downturn. The government is inevitably under pressure and scrutiny and is facing an emerging governance crisis.

It has been noted that the provision of social services serves to maintain social harmony so as to legitimize state rule (O'Connor 1973: 6–7). Traditionally, Hong Kong people think that the government is responsible for the well-being of local citizens (Ho 2001: 38), however, the post-colonial social welfare policy appears to be more important to further legitimize the governance of the HKSAR government in times of economic difficulty and governance crisis. Although in broad terms, welfare includes social welfare (the public social welfare), fiscal welfare (tax allowances and reliefs) and occupational welfare (benefits and services provided by employers) (Titmuss 1963: 42–52; Walker 1984: 28), this chapter will confine its analysis to social welfare provided or subsidized by the Social Welfare Department (SWD) because of space limitation. The attention is paid to the social welfare reform as a way to reduce public burden in the post-colonial Hong Kong in particular. In this respect, the measures introduced to achieve productivity gain, to revamp the subvention system for the non-government organizations (NGOs), to enhance service performance and to review the Comprehensive Social Security Scheme (CSSA) and related services, all reflect elements of a new public management ethos. There emerges a changing social welfare landscape in Hong Kong. The HKSAR government is seen to be responding to popular demands through these reform measures, yet questions have been raised as to its real motives and the Chief Executive's achievements in these reform initiatives.

What motivates the HKSAR government to introduce the social welfare reform? Is cost containment the major purpose of the government? Is the social welfare reform able to cater for the rising demand for social welfare? What are the political and social implications of the reform? In this chapter, we seek to answer these questions by studying the ideological and theoretical foundations on which the social welfare reform rests and the distinctive socio-economic and political contexts which shape the reform. The implications of the reform will be discussed. In the final analysis, the social welfare reform seems to have been designed for meeting the requirement of a managerial state that is emerging in Hong Kong.

Socio-economic and Political Context of the Post-colonial Hong Kong

Since the 1997 handover, Hong Kong has not only experienced sovereignty change, but also faces multiple transformations in the social, political and economic arenas. These changes precipitate public demand for social services, and in turn, impose unprecedented challenges on the Hong Kong government.

Socio-economic Context

Soon after the handover, the Hong Kong economy was cracked by the Asian Financial Crisis (See Figure 1). The economic bubble was exposed. Hong Kong economy can no longer be sustained only by the property market and financial investment. Under the wave of economic restructure, many organizations in both private and public sectors either streamline or even shut down their operations. Middle aged, low-skilled, general, operative staff, and even technical staff as well as white collars at the medium level are vulnerable to layoffs. Fresh graduates and mainland immigrants experience difficulties to find a job. The unemployment and underemployment rate has reached high levels (Figure 2). Other negative effects of economic downturn include poverty, the widening wealth gap and negative equity problem (Ho 1999; Chow 1999).

Figure 1. Real Growth Rate of GDP and Per Capita GDP (at Constant 1990 Market Prices), 1996–2001

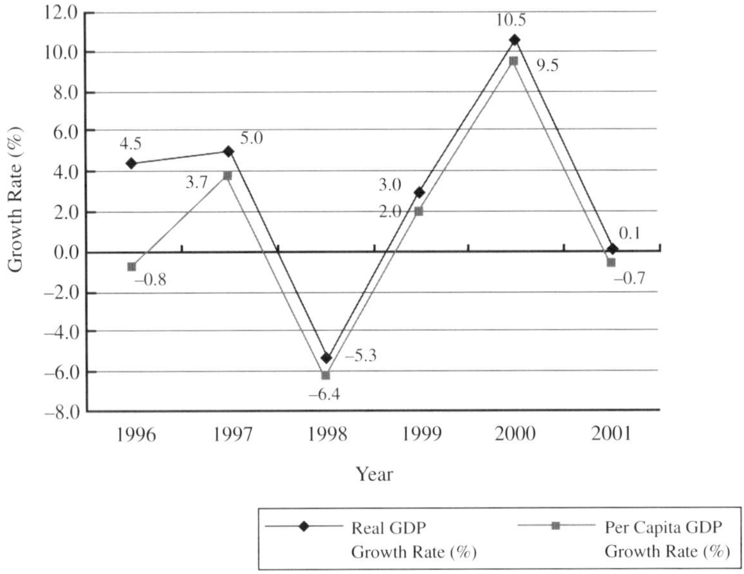

Sources: Census and Statistics Department (2001), Leung (2002).

Figure 2. Unemployment Rate and Underemployment Rate 1996–2001

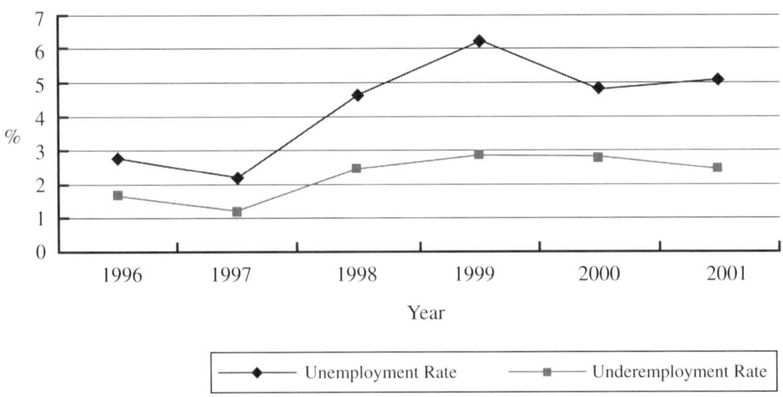

Sources: Tsang (1999), Tsang (2000), Leung (2002).

Meanwhile, Hong Kong is undergoing substantial demographic changes and is becoming a city with an aging population. According to government figures, the median age of the population rose from 34 in 1996 to 37 in 2000. The proportion of people aged under 15 fell from 19 per cent in 1996 to 17 per cent in 2000, while the proportion of people aged 65 and over increased from ten per cent to 11 per cent (Hong Kong Government 2001: 415). A recent population report of the United Nations also reveals that Hong Kong is one of the places which have the largest decline in the fertility rate in the world between 1950 and 2000. In 2050, it is projected to have at least ten per cent of its population aged 80 years or over, becoming one of the oldest old in the world (United Nations Population Division, 2002). Mainland immigrants pose another source of demographic change. With 150 mainlanders permitted to come to Hong Kong each day, about 55,000 people will be added to Hong Kong every year. They are most likely from lower socio-economic backgrounds and rural areas (Chau and Ngai 2000: 149).

As in other metropolis, the social function of the family in Hong Kong has undergone some changes. Traditional families have been gradually substituted by nuclear families. The size of families is getting smaller. Meanwhile, divorce, single parenthood, cohabitation and two-earner families are becoming more common (Chau and Ngai, 2000: 151).

In fact, the welfare of Hong Kong people is far from secure. In 1999, a comprehensive study of Hong Kong's social development between 1986 and 1998 was conducted. It was measured using a specially created Social Development Index which consists of 47 social, political and economic indicators. According to the data, Hong Kong has recorded a substantial and stable social progress during the period studied. However, there are serious disparities in social development. That is to say, Hong Kong's social development was not uniform across all sectors of the society. The social performances of Hong Kong's vulnerable population groups, that is women, the elderly, low income households, youth and children, are disappointing. High negative social developments are found in the groups of low income households, youth and children. While women and the elderly have received social gains, their social advancement is still insignificant to achieve a secure welfare (Estes 2000).

In fact, the public spending on social welfare, housing, health care and education has been increasing since the mid-1990s. Expenditure on these policy areas still takes a large share of recurrent public expenditure after the handover (See Table 1 and Figure 3). Despite of this, however, the

Table 1. Recurrent Public Expenditure by Policy Area Group 1996/1997 to 2002/2003

	97/98 (%)	98/99 (%)	99/00 (%) (Revised Estimate)	00–01 (%) (Estimate)	01–02 (%)	02–03 (%)
Education	21.2	21.8	22.0	22.3	21.8	22.4
Health	15.1	15.3	15.3	15.4	15.0	14.8
Social Welfare	11.8	13.5	13.7	13.8	13.9	14.6
Housing	6.6	6.3	6.0	5.8	5.9	5.6
	$ Mn	$ Mn	$ Mn	$ Mn	$ Mn (Revised Estimate)	$ Mn (Estimate)
Total Recurrent Public Expenditure ($Mn.)	172,419	187,857	195,272	198,619	213,220	219,705

Source: Leung (2002).

Figure 3. Recurrent Public Expenditure by Policy Area Group 1996/1997 to 2002/2003 ($ Mn)

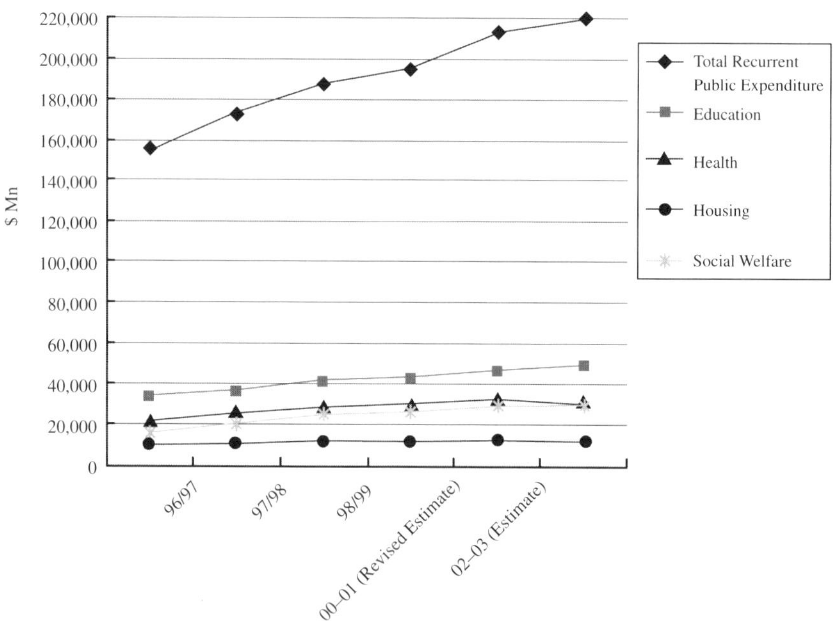

Source: Tsang (2001), Leung (2002).

public demand for better and more social protection is still accelerated because of the disappointing economic performance, rapid social changes and the unbalanced social development. New agenda is urgently needed to cater for the social needs of the vulnerable population groups in particular.

Political Context

Under the notion of "Hong Kong people ruling Hong Kong," the Hong Kong public harbors a high expectation of the post-colonial government. However, the political, economic and societal framework of the colonial era, which is preserved by the Basic Law, is no longer compatible with the socio-economic and political development of the post-colonial period. With the chief executive not directly elected, the government is lacking in political legitimacy. There is inadequate check and balance between the legislative and executive branches under the executive-led system (Lee 1999).

In the light of the growing political consciousness among the people, the government likewise has become more sensitive of its performance legitimacy. However, the ideology of a small government, the non-interventionism and bureaucratic dominance that the government adopts, all fall short for tackling the emerging socio-economic challenges. Successive policy and administrative failures which surfaced soon after the handover revealed the mediocre policy-making capacity of the civil service and its incompetence in crisis and risk management, hence the ability and the quality of the civil service was cast in doubt. The lack of political accountability, however, has immunized high officials from political accountability and personal responsibility for their negligence or policy failures (Lee 1999: 950). Few examples will suffice. The slow responses and inappropriate policies of the government in incidents like the "bird's flu" crisis in late 1997 and the new Hong Kong International Airport fiasco in mid-1998 exposed the civil service's lack of knowledge and skills in crisis management (Ho 2001: 34).[1]

Governance mistakes and economic hardship intensify the general citizens' discontent with the Hong Kong government (Chow and Fan 1999: xxxvii). A Home Affairs Bureau survey in August 1998 shows that the public discontent has reached a record high. It shows that most people were not happy with the "present situation". The public's satisfaction with the government's performance was at the lowest since 1991. At the top of the public's complaint was, however, the low efficiency of the civil service

(Yeung 1998b). The public opinion survey of the University of Hong Kong also reveals that, in as short as in one year's time, the public confidence over the government has dropped significantly from 67.7 per cent in September 1997 to 54.5 per cent in August 1998 (*Ming Pao* 12 October 2001).

Public Sector Reforms as a Response to Governance Crisis

The major factor of the emerging governance crisis is, as Lee observes (1999), the problematic constitutional design. Although political and administrative reforms such as democratization and ministerialization may be a solution, the Basic Law has excluded the possibility of these reforms in the near future, if not indefinitely. The reshuffle of the legislative and the executive branch, likewise, appears strictly restricted (Lee 1999: 53).

With the unlikelihood of political and administrative reforms, the post-colonial government resorts to public sector reforms, which had been initiated in late 80s by the then Finance Branch, for strengthening the government's capacity to deal with public demands and challenges and, hence, retaining its legitimacy (Lee 2000). Among these reform initiatives, social welfare reform is one of the targeted areas. Under the context of these transitions and changes, how has Hong Kong's system of public social welfare been transformed to satisfy public needs and simultaneously fulfill the legitimatization function of the state?

Social Welfare in the Post-colonial Hong Kong

"Hong Kong is not a welfare state," so states the Social Welfare Department (1999: 5). Social welfare provision in Hong Kong is, at best, residual in nature, in other words, as the last resort for the needy (Wong, et al. 2001: 2). The rapidly emerging contextual changes have rendered the existing social provisions inept to meet the rising social demand. Yet, in Tung's reform package, the government has no intention to turn Hong Kong into a "western style" welfare state[2] because of the budgetary constraint and the need to maintain economic competitiveness.

Social welfare provided or subsidized by the SAR government in Hong Kong comprises nine kinds of services, namely social security, family and child welfare services, medical social services, group and community work services, rehabilitation services, services for young people, the elderly and offenders, and lastly legal aid services. Starting from the 1997 Policy Address, the SAR government has either proposed or implemented various reforms in its social welfare programs, including enhancement of care for the elderly, review of the CSSA Scheme, introduction of the Lump Sum Grant Subvention Scheme and competitive bidding in social services. Social welfare in Hong Kong will be reviewed in the following, and the focus is typically centred on these reform programs (Tung 1997).

Social Security System

In general, social security in Hong Kong is a non-contributory scheme, which provides financial and material assistance to people to meet their basic and special needs. There are five types of assistance packaged under the system. The CSSA scheme is a means-tested financial assistance designed for needy individuals or families to meet their basic needs. The Social Security Allowance Scheme consists of Old Age Allowance and Disability Allowance for the elderly and severely disabled persons respectively. The Criminal and Law Enforcement Injuries Compensation offers cash payments to victims, or their dependants in case of death, of crimes of violence and law enforcement acts on a non-means-tested basis. The Traffic Accident Victims Assistance Scheme is a non-means-tested cash assistance for road traffic accident victims or their dependents in case of death. Emergency relief is a financial and material assistance for victims of natural and other disasters (Information Services Department 2000; Census and Statistics Department 2000: 295). Government figures show that welfare budget (Table 2) and public expenditure of social security schemes (Table 3) after the handover have been rising.

Reform of the Comprehensive Social Security Assistance Scheme

In his first policy address, the Chief Executive Tung Chee-hwa outlined the need for CSSA review in the hope that the scheme would provide assistance to the needy without reducing their incentives to work (Tung 1997). In view of the rising CSSA expenditure, Tung further prescribed the reform in his policy address in 1998. Adopting the residual approach, he intended to direct valuable resources to people with real need to ensure an efficient and effective use of public funds (Tung 1998).

In December 1998, the government released *Support for Self-reliance: Report on Review of the Comprehensive Social Security Assistance*

Table 2. Expenditure of Social Welfare Department 1996/97 to 2000/2001 ($Mn)

	96/97	97/98	98/99	99/00	00/01
Departmental Expenditure	1,686	1,925	2,228	2,310	2,352
Payments for Social Security Schemes[1]	11,183	13,877	17,784	18,519	18,700
Subvention to Non-governmental Organizations	3,991	4,598	5,419	6,065	6,453
Total	16,860	20,400	25,431	26,894	27,505

Source: Census and Statistics Department (2001).

Note: 1. Payments for Traffic Accident Victims Assistance and payments for Fee Assistance for Child Care Centres are excluded.

Table 3. Social Security Schemes 1996/97 to 2000/2001

	96/97	97/98	98/99	99/00	00/01
Comprehensive Social Security Assistance					
Number of Cases	166,720	195,645	232,819	228,015	228,263
Amount ($Mn.)	7,127.8	9,441.3	13,028.7	13,623.4	13,599.8 5
Social Security Allowance					
Number of Cases	510,091	517,865	526,742	535,452	550,585
Amount ($Mn.)	4,041.6	4,420.2	4,737.3	4,883.3	5,129.6
Disability Allowance					
Number of Cases	72,264	77,051	81,741	89,617	96,851
Amount ($Mn.)	1,036.6	1,181.8	1,321.0	1,419.8	1,567.1
Old Age Allowance					
Number of Cases	437,827	440,814	445,001	445,835	453,734
Amount ($Mn.)	3,005.0	3,238.4	3,416.3	3,463.5	3,562.5
Criminal and Law Enforcement					
Number of Cases Authorized for Payment	568	604	557	447	427
Amount ($Mn.)	11.4	14.3	16.8	12.2	10.0
Traffic Accident Victims Assistance					
Number of Cases Authorized for Payment	5,558	5,655	5,809	5,797	5,998
Amount ($Mn.)	122.8	137.4	164.8	133.5	130.0
Emergency Relief					
Number of Victims Assisted	807	1,082	1,097	2,643	868
Amount ($Mn.)	2.2	1.3	1.6	0.6	0.9

Source: Census and Statistics Department (2001).

Scheme. The new arrangements of CSSA scheme have been implemented since June 1999, in which most suggestions of the review are adopted.

The government stated that growing public concern on the CSSA scheme was the main reason for the reform (SWD 1998: 3). The public worried about the "rapid growth in the CSSA caseload and its expenditure, high levels of CSSA benefit for larger families as compared with market wages, the sharp increases in the number of people of working age turning to CSSA," as well as the abuse and fraud of the system (Ibid.).

According to the document, there was 146 per cent increase in the number of CSSA cases from 1993 to 1998, with "unemployment" and "single parent" cases registering a disproportionate increase (SWD 1998: 3–6). It highlights the public's concern that the growing caseload and expenditure were due to "the increasing attractiveness of the benefit levels vs. a relatively slow growth in wages over the past few years". The government stressed that "the ever-increasing growth in CSSA expenditure is worrying and unsustainable in the long term, given that it is a non-contributory scheme, financed by general revenue obtained from a low tax base" and that the possible emergence of a dependency culture should be avoided (SWD 1998: 4–5). At the same time, although the cases of abuse and fraud of the scheme were extremely small, the SAR government believed that measures should be stepped up "to ensure prudent and defensible use of public funds" (SWD 1998: 9–10).

The main purpose of the HKSAR government was to prevent dependency on CSSA. It expected the reform to provide a safety net to "help the truly needy and disadvantaged members of the community", to offer "temporary assistance for people of working age who are genuinely unable to find work, and to encourage and help them to rejoin the workforces so that they can lead independent and productive lives" (SWD 1998: 13). As stated in the review, the main strategies place emphasis on social responsibilities, re-establishment of self-reliance and work ethics among unemployed able-bodied recipients. To avoid creating disincentives to work, the CSSA benefits will be commensurate with the economic situation so that recipients will not be better off than those who are employed, and controls will be strengthened to prevent fraud and abuse. Meanwhile, the SAR government emphasized that "any measure to tighten existing arrangements should not affect the elderly, the disabled and those in ill-health" (SWD 1998: 14–15).

Various measures are taken according to the reform objectives and strategies. Support for Self-reliance Scheme (SFS) is one of the elements of the reform. It includes three parts. The first is the Active Employment Assistance program. Counseling, job assistance and retraining are provided by the Labor Department, the Employees Retraining Board and some non-governmental organizations (NGOs). Unemployed recipients receiving CSSA assistance have to apply for at least two jobs every two weeks. Meanwhile, interviews are arranged by the social security field unit every two weeks in order to monitor the progress of recipients' job search and to render appropriate assistance. If an unemployed recipient does not actively seek work in accordance with the requirements or refuses a reasonable offer of job interview without a good reason, the assistance will be terminated (SWD 1998: 16–18). The second part of SFS scheme is the additional help by way of community work. Recipients are assigned to unpaid community work, such as cleaning up of beaches and rubbish collection, in order to help them build up their self-esteem and work habit and to prepare them for rejoining the workforce in the future (SWD 1998: 18–20). The SFS scheme disregards earnings from new full-time job so as to give unemployed recipients the incentives to work (SWD 1998: 20–21).

At the same time, CSSA payments for able-recipients have been adjusted. Standard rate payments to able-bodied adults/children in households comprising three or more are trimmed down. In the case of the payments to a family of three, there is a ten per cent reduction, while a family of more than three will receive 20 per cent cut. Able-bodied recipients can still get special grants, but they are no longer eligible for long-term supplements which are only available for the elderly, the disabled and the infirmed who have received the assistance continuously for 12 months (Wan 1999).

The eligibility criteria for able-bodied applicants are also tightened. Asset limits for able-bodied recipients are scaled down by 35 per cent for a single recipient and 31 per cent for a family of four. Meanwhile, the values of self-occupied residential property for able-bodied recipients aged under 50, which was totally disregarded in the past, are now included in the asset test. There is a grace period of 12 months for the property owners, during which the value of the property will be totally disregarded to allow them to make alternative arrangements, including selling the property. The period can be extended for exceptional cases (SWD 1998: 28–30; Wan 1999).

To ensure prudent and defensible use of public resources, the HKSAR government has strengthened investigation teams and resumed home checks for all new CSSA cases. In 1999, SWD spent $40 million on investigation teams, home checks and also telephone hotline in order to fight against abuse and fraud of the system (*Ming Pao* 21 April 2001).

Services for the Elderly

The HKSAR government provides community support services and residential care mainly for people aged 60 or above either directly through SWD or through subvented NGOs. These services include social centres, multi-service centres, day care centres, home help services, Senior Citizen Card Scheme, care-and-attention homes and so forth (SWD 1999: 74–80).

Soon after the establishment of HKSAR, the Elderly Commission was set up under the chairmanship of Mr. Tam Yiu-chung, an Executive Council member. The Commission advises the government on elderly policies, coordinates the planning and development of programs and services for the elderly, and monitors their implementation (SWD 1999: 75).

Caring for the elderly was one of the main themes of Tung's 1997 policy address. He announced three objectives of elderly policies: they are to provide the elderly with (1) a sense of security, (2) a sense of belonging, and (3) a feeling of health and worthiness (Tung 1997).

The first objective is to be accomplished through offering financial security to the elderly, including the introduction of the Mandatory Provident Fund (MPF) scheme and the increase in the monthly payment to elderly CSSA recipients. The MPF scheme has been implemented since 2000, which marks the establishment of forced saving for retirement protection in old age in Hong Kong. However, the Chief Executive said in his 2000 Policy Address that the government would complete the review on the old-age allowance (Tung 2000). A means-test for eligibility and cutbacks was considered. These proposals had given rise to controversy and protests (So and Yiu 2000).

As stated in the 1997 Policy Address, through providing "a place to call home and the effective delivery of good services" the HKSAR government seeks to instil a sense of belonging among the elderly. Various proposals were introduced to enhance community support and residential care. They include tax incentives and public housing privileges, all aim to encourage family support and to help those elderly who have no family but want to live in their own homes (Tung 1997).

For the third objective — to promote a feeling of health and worthiness, the government seeks to improve medical care, social services and opportunities for the elderly to participate in community life. Means such as setting up elderly health centres and introducing an Elderly Volunteer Program have been proposed.

Recently, the Director of Social Welfare, Mrs. Carrie Lam Cheng Yuet-ngor, revealed that the government planned to provide allowance for the elderly who, for personal reasons, did not apply for the CSSA. However, details of the plan has not been decided (*Hong Kong iMail* 27 August 2001). There is a report that the Chief Executive will announce an increase in the Old Age Allowance for those aged 70 and over (*South China Morning Post* 24 September 2001).

Other Social Services

Apart from targeting the elderly and people with financial need, the social welfare system in Hong Kong also provides services to family and children, young people, disabled people, offenders and people who need medical social services and legal assistance. Reform programs have not been extended to these service areas comparable to the magnitude of the new policies introduced in the area of social security and services for the elderly.

SWD is solely responsible for medical social services. Up to January 2000, there are 114 medical social service units in public hospitals and specialist clinics under the Hospital Authority, and in some out-patient clinics under the Department of Health. These working teams provide various kinds of assistance to patients and their families, such as counseling, financial and housing assistance (Information Services Department 2000).

SWD also provides services for offenders. It adopts social work approach in the treatment and rehabilitation of offenders through probation service, residential training and aftercare services (Information Services Department 2000).

Like services for the elderly, SWD and NGOs jointly offer family and child welfare services, group and community work services, services for young people and rehabilitation services. For the family and child welfare services, the government intends to preserve and strengthen the family unit, and help them to prevent and solve problems through such measures as family services centres, the Family and Child Protective Services Units and 24-hour hotline service. Under the group and community work services, group work units are operated in community centres with an objective of "developing character, self-reliance, and responsibility of individuals and groups, and improving their ability in tackling community problems as well as the quality of community life. The aim of services for young people, such as school social work and outreaching social work services or integrated teams, is "to encourage young people to involve themselves in worthwhile activities for the development of character, personality, leadership and social skills." Rehabilitation services are provided for the disabled through sheltered workshops, day activity centres, supported employment units, social and recreational centres and so forth (Information Services Department 2000).

Legal aid services are delivered by the Legal Aid Department. Residents and non-residents in Hong Kong who meet the financial eligibility and justification for taking legal action in the Hong Kong courts can receive legal aid services (Census and Statistics Department 2000: 297).

Reform of the Social Welfare Subvention System

NGOs have long been regarded as partners with the government in the provision of welfare services. They are major providers of services, especially in the area of family and children services, services for young people and the elderly, as well as rehabilitation services (Census and Statistics Department 2000; SWD 1999: 98). The government provides NGOs with financial support on the basis of input-control either through subvention under recurrent expenditure, or Lotteries Fund grants for capital expenditure and experimental welfare projects (SWD 1999: 97; Legco Panel on Welfare Service 1999). As shown in Table 2, there was an increasing trend in the amount of government subventions to NGOs throughout 1996 to 2000. It accounts for about 75 per cent of total government expenditure on social welfare services if social security is discounted. More than 25,000 staff are employed by NGOs, which stands for about 80 per cent of all social welfare personnel in Hong Kong (SWD 1999: 98–9). In order to monitor the performance of NGOs, the evaluation unit of the SWD carries out quarterly service assessment on and regular visits to subvented organizations, in-depth study on selected social welfare services and assessment of experimental projects (SWD 1999: 98–99).

In the financial year 1997–98, the social welfare subvention system underwent a review with an objective of ensuring NGOs to manage public resources effectively to meet the performance standard (SWD 1999: 16). In

April 1999, the Service Performance Monitoring System (SPMS) was launched. Under SPMS, individual service units have to conduct an annual self-assessment while SWD carries out a performance audit of each NGO every three years. Accompanied with it were the introduction of the Funding and Service Agreements (FSA) and Service Quality Standards (SQS). The FSAs "include the objective and nature of service to be provided, the output indicators and funding arrangements", and the SQSs "define the policies, procedures and practices which a service unit should have in place in order to deliver quality service to its clients". Meanwhile, the Lump Sum Grant Subvention Scheme (LSGS) which has gone through various stages of consultation with NGOs and different levels of modifications, was put into effect in December 2000. As a result, the government's financial relationship with NGOs shifts from an input-control basis to an output/outcome monitoring and evaluation with flexibility in financial and personnel management. It was said to provide NGOs with incentives to be accountable and to use resources efficiently and effectively, hence, to achieve Enhanced Productivity Program (EPP) targets in the coming years (Legco Panel on Welfare Services 1999; Lee 2000: 7). EPP is a public management reform announced by the Chief Executive Tung in his 1998 policy address. Under the program, the government sets targets and requires subvented organizations to review their baseline expenditure regularly so as to ensure it is directed to main priorities of the government. Meanwhile, subvented organizations also have to achieve a five per cent productivity gain of their operating expenditure between 1998 and 2002.

Competitive Bidding

In order to attain efficiency and cost-effectiveness in delivering social welfare services, the government has contracted out several projects for competitive bidding among NGOs and the private sector. In 1999, a pilot test on competitive bidding in the area of meal services for the elderly was launched amidst objections from many NGOs (Chan and Wong 2000).

Subsequently, the government has further contracted out other home care services for the elderly through competitive bidding. It plans to extend the competitive bidding to day care services and residential care services for the elderly, as well as child care centres in the coming two years (Wu 2001). This marks the entry of the private sector into the public domain of welfare provisions and the beginning of what otherwise would be the commercialization of welfare, that is, the public service market.

The Emergence of Post-colonial Managerial State

Evidently, the social welfare reform has introduced significant changes in both actual practices and ideology of social services. In many ways, the supremacy of market mechanism, cost-effectiveness, competitiveness and social morality which underlie the design, planning and provision of services, mirrors the major tenets of the ethos of new managerialism. The movement of new managerialism, or the new public management, is making sweeping changes to the public sector in Western countries in recent years. Its global effect has been felt in the field of social welfare. A brief recap of the emergence of new managerialism in Western democracies should provide a basis for understanding the consequences that were brought to bear on our welfare reforms in Hong Kong.

The Emergence of New Managerialism in Western Liberal Countries

The Keynesian welfare state has enjoyed its golden age in western liberal countries during the two decades after the end of the World War II. Under the welfare state, the states have extensively intervened into social and economic affairs, such as providing social and economic rights, securing full employment and promoting collective consumption, with an objective of establishing political legitimacy (Midgley 1997: 137; Lee 1998: 627). Social welfare was widely believed to be a social right under the entitlement of citizenship (Marshall 1950; Morris 1994: 44). This positive attitude toward social welfare resulted in the "welfare state consensus". Political parties converged on the point that Keynesian economic model and extensive welfare provisions were essential for prosperity and minimum social standards (Midgley 1997: 137).

Since the 1970s, however, the welfare state consensus has begun to fade out (Esping-Andersen 1996). As in the post-colonial Hong Kong, a severe global downturn in the economy following the 1973 oil crisis has presented many countries with stagnant economic growth, high levels of unemployment and increasing list rolls of welfare (Midgley 1997: 139; Cass 1997). Meanwhile, social welfare and the rising welfare expenditure began to be viewed as a source of high taxes, and hence, a public burden.

People complained that social services have gone too far, that they benefited the better off to a greater extent than the poor (Taylor-Gooby 1985: 15 and 23). Their support for welfare has become selective, more for central and virtually universal programmes such as pensions and health, whilst less for peripheral and residual programmes like unemployment and social assistance benefits (Ferrera 1993: 4). There was a wide coverage on "welfare scroungers" in the press reports (Golding and Middleton 1978 and 1982).

In the academic field, the New Right theories represent the public burden view of social welfare. They advocated neo-liberalism and neo-conservatism, with the former stressing on the supremacy of market mechanism, while the latter emphasizing on traditional morality, social authority and self-sufficiency. They classify the poor into moral categories of merit or individual misbehaviour: worthy and unworthy, deserving and undeserving, poverty and pauperism. The deserving poor are those who do not possess the ability of self-reliance, such as the elderly who have lost working ability, patients and the handicapped. The able-bodied poor are considered the undeserving poor because they are lazy, dishonest and individually responsible for their poor conditions (Katz 1993: 5). In short, the cause of poverty of the deserving poor is exogenous, i.e., a social problem, while that of the undeserving poor is endogenous, i.e., an individual problem.

New Right theorists, such as Charles Murray, criticize the welfare system homogenizing the poor, that is, it is unable to distinguish the undeserving poor from the deserving poor and that it stigmatizes dependency. Too much welfare induces dependency culture and undermines social order, including illegitimate births and lone parenthood (Murray 1984; Hanson 1998; Becker 1997: 15). Therefore, the New Right calls for a limited government. Public policy should encourage self-reliance. Public welfare should be only provided for the deserving poor. Meanwhile, the role of private charities in welfare provision has to be enhanced (Murray 1999; Hanson 1998; Siegel 1998). From the view of the New Right, it is good dependency on the family but bad on the state.

The new managerialism underlying the managerial states is the administrative practice of the New Right politicians. It is the combination of public choice theory and business management techniques. That is to say, on the one hand, it advocates the supremacy of market mechanism over the state and uses personalized incentive system to motivate self-interested individuals; on the other hand, it emphasizes business values such as productivity, efficiency and entrepreneurship. Hence, under the new managerialism, management ethos replaces political values of social and economic rights and is regarded as an indispensable element for national strength (Lee 2000: 1–2).

Clarke and Newman (1997) see the institution of the managerial state as involving a dispersal of power. The strategic centre of the state delegates its authority to subaltern organizations so that the latter are empowered to act on its behalf through practice such as contracting out and setting up quangos, these are "public bodies having appointed boards with executive and financial authority operating at arm's length to the government" (Lee 2000: 4). It results in "a more mixed economy of welfare with expanded roles for the private, voluntary and informal sectors" (Clarke and Newman 1997: 25). Nevertheless, it by no means suggests that the state has substantially lost its power. Instead, new forms of state power are available for the state through regulation, contracting, monitoring and surveillance (Ibid.: 26). While empowered subaltern organizations have autonomy to manage resources, they are subjected to constant result-oriented evaluation by the state which emphasizes on actual achievements, efficiency and cost-effectiveness. Therefore, the state power has been extended since "dispersal has meant the simultaneous shrinking of the state and the enlargement of its reach into civil society (through its engagement of non-state agents)" (Ibid.: 29). Power and control are centralized by "tighter fiscal control, new policy directions and an expanding apparatus of audit and evaluation" (Ibid.: 29). For Clarke and Newman, it is a Foucauldian form of power that the state "relies less on direct control through state apparatuses of the conventional kind and more on 'productive subjection' through new discourses and practices" (Ibid.: 30).

The relationship between the state and citizens also changes under the new managerialism. Replacing the political value with managerial one, the state posits itself as an entrepreneur while citizens as consumers. The prime objective of the managerial state becomes offering choices for consumers and satisfying their demands in the public service markets (Clarke and Newman 1997: 29; Lee 2000: 2).

The victories of Margaret Thatcher of Britain and Ronald Reagan of the United States represented the retreat of the state in Western liberal countries from welfare state to managerial state. These two leaders supported traditional social values, including family order, religion and authority. They were in favor of economic liberalism, anti-statism, and traditionalism underlying the managerial state, as well as populist authoritarian leadership (Midgley 1997: 140). In retrospect, the social welfare reform initiatives introduced by the governments in Britain and the United States in the time of economic hardship, bear resemblance to those of the post-colonial SAR government, notably in their aims at alleviating government's financial burden, enhancing efficiency and cost effectiveness in using public resources. It shows that the role of the western liberal states in social protection has changed, since the restructure "attempts to realign a series of relationship — between the state and the citizen; between the state and the economy; and between the state and its institutional or organizational forms" (Clarke and Newman 1997: 24).

The Post-colonial Managerial State

In post-colonial HKSAR government, it was clearly not the crisis of the welfare state (as in western liberal countries) that brought about the new management measures in the public sector. Neither was the public sector reform in Hong Kong built entirely on financial grounds. Looking back to the tenure of the Chief Executive's first term of office, the welfare reform measures (as part and parcel of the larger public sector reform) were carried out within a specific socio-economic and political context marked by changing demographic make-up, a faltering economy and declining political legitimacy.

Ideas of new managerialism have been applied, in broad stroke, to enhance cost efficiency and alleviate long-term public burden, which can be revealed from the welfare reforms in four aspects. Firstly, the New Right ideology plays an influential role in the making of social welfare policies designed to prevent a dependency culture. Social welfare services have been restricted to the "deserving poor" and the "truly needy". The message was clearly expressed in the reform of the CSSA scheme, in which welfare assistance is reduced and measures are introduced to encourage self-reliance among able-bodied recipients. On the other hand, the government has proposed to enhance services for the elderly, disabled, a group of deserving poor and truly needy. Evidently, financial consideration seems only a small part of the motivation.

Secondly, a devolution of responsibilities is manifested in the welfare reforms. The HKSAR government's retreat from its role in social welfare provision and relegating its responsibilities to the NGOs, the private sector, individual and the family reflects the anti-welfare sentiment. As mentioned, welfare cut and self-reliance were already a key feature emphasized in the CSSA reform. The implementation of MPF mandates individual contributions towards their own retirement protection. Meanwhile, at the same time the government proposes to enhance services for the elderly, it also encourages family care and support of senior citizens with tax incentives and public housing privileges. The competitive bidding for provision of selected social services has open up an important avenue that permits the participation of private sector in the provision of social services in scopes not hitherto available.

Thirdly, as expected by Clarke and Newman (1997), a managerial state with the accompanying standardized managerial measures, often expands more than reduces the state's power and control of non-governmental agencies. In SAR Hong Kong, the welfare reforms have changed the relationship between the government and the NGOs, from a partnership to a contractual one characterized by a relationship between principal and agent. As more social services are opened up for competitive bidding, NGOs have to confront competition within the non-government sector and with the private sector. Furthermore, while NGOs enjoy a greater autonomy in managing resources under the new performance-based funding model — LSGS, they have been put under tightened monitoring for efficiency, performance and outcome quality. Initially, the new subvention mode was met with opposition from NGOs for the constraints and adverse effects imposed on the agencies. The funding model was finally implemented in December 2000 after much negotiation and concessions from the SWD, with only 93 of the 181 subvented NGOs joining the scheme initially (Wong 2000). In short, the government has since become a buyer of service engaging in a principal-agent relationship with the NGOs. It relies less on direct input control or on service delivery for performance monitoring. Paradoxically, its power has been centralized with new modes of control (e.g., by performance indicators and targets, pre-set output measures, etc) instituted for performance audits. The government, as buyer of service and principal, is thus in a strategic position to leverage the various producers (the NGOs, the private sector), as agents, for enhanced performance quality, standard, and economy of social services (Clarke and Newman 1997: 30; Lee 2000: 9).

Fourthly, the adoption of private business management practices in public services such as social welfare has been fuelled by the concern for economic efficiency and utilization maximization (Hood 1998; Yeatman 1997). An economic value framework that emphasizes efficiency, productivity and cost-effectiveness seems to dominate the welfare reform of HKSAR government. Ostensibly, the LSGS and competitive bidding were introduced on the basis of cost analysis, results and performance. In fact, the result of competitive bidding of meal service for the elderly was so impressive that the costs was cut by 20 per cent and the number of meals served exceeded estimation by 26 per cent (Chan and Wong 2000). Meanwhile, the strategies for welfare cut, by means of distinguishing deserving and undeserving poor and promoting the sense of self-reliance among recipients of social assistance, emerge to be a preferred tactic. For instance, while the growing trend of the CSSA expenditure has not stopped, the CSSA caseload has decreased in 1999–2000 (See Table 3 and Figure 4). In January 2000, SWD has not sought additional funding from the Legislative Council for CSSA scheme for the first time in six years (*Hong Kong Standard* 22 January 2000). Most importantly, the reform seems to be quite effective to achieve the goal of the government that the cases of single parent family and unemployment fell (See Table 4). Meanwhile, in the light of aging population, the introduction of MPF is seen as a means to alleviate the financial burden of the government in the long run.

The adoption of new managerialism in the welfare reform initiatives further reinforces the residual view underlying the SAR government's social welfare policies. It has never been Hong Kong's intention to treat social welfare as an unconditional social right or a citizen insurance granted by the government. Nor is the social welfare system built to maintain social justice or redistribute resources from the rich to the poor.

Figure 4. Total Expenditure Under the Comprehensive Social Security Assistance Scheme 1996–97 to 2000/2001 ($ Mn)

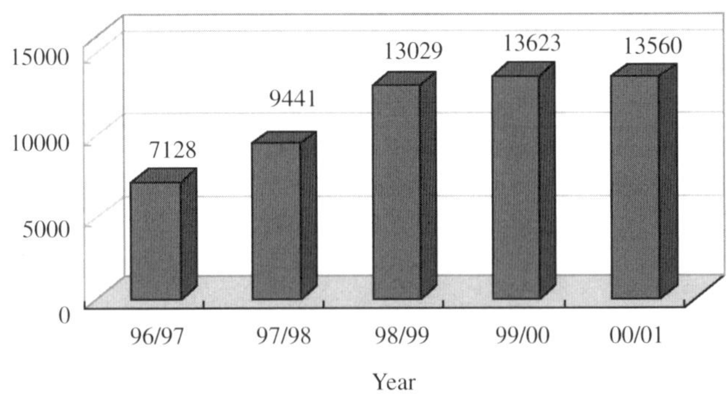

Source: Census and Statistics Department (2001).

Table 4. Comprehensive Social Security Assistance Cases by Type 1996/1997 to 2000/2001

	96/97	97/98	98/99	99/00	00/01
Old Age	98,765	112,067	124,304	133,070	135,409
Disabled and Ill Health	29,760	34,519	39,782	31,693	31,534
Single Parent Family	13,303	17,161	25,613	25,146	26,078
Low Earnings	3,102	4,714	7,562	8,002	8,319
Unemployment	14,964	19,108	31,942	26,185	23,250
Others	6,826	8,076	3,616	3,919	3,673
Total	166,720	195,645	232,819	228,015	228,263

Source: Census and Statistics Department (2001).

Instead, the HKSAR government intends to establish the system as a last resort for the people when they can no longer be self-sufficient (Chau and Ngai 2000).

Evidently, the HKSAR government has put economic rationalism above social welfare. The level and sophistication of social welfare is dependent on the economic policy. As stipulated in the Basic Law, the HKSAR government "shall follow the principle of keeping expenditure within the limits of revenues in drawing up its budget, and strive to achieve a fiscal balance, avoid deficits and keep the budget commensurate with the growth rate of its gross domestic product" (Article 107). In the 1999–2000 Budget, the former Financial Secretary Donald Tsang regarded keeping the overall growth in government spending within the rate of economic growth as a prudent fiscal management principle (Tsang 1999: 25). He also expressed his worry on the increasing expenditure on social welfare: "[i]n the past five years to 1998–99, we have increased recurrent spending in these spending in these areas in real terms by … 103 per cent for social welfare … This significant growth in expenditure on welfare over the years has increased the share of social welfare recurrent spending from 8.7 per cent in 1994–95 to its current 14.1 per cent. Under our existing policies, demand for services and support in all these areas is bound to increase owing to rising unemployment and an aging population. An anticipated large inflow of people from the Mainland who have the right of abode in Hong Kong creates added pressure … We cannot afford much longer double-digit growth in welfare spending each year" (Tsang 1999: 28–29).

Hence, the government put emphasis on individual obligation to the society. In addition to social welfare reform, the words of the Financial Secretary Antony Leung reflects such economic rationality. He has repeatedly stressed that the local economy is undergoing a "paradigm shift" to a knowledge-based economy which put Hong Kong into a difficult time. However, believing in free market mechanism and his "fishing philosophy" that the government had better not to give fish to people but teach people how to fish, Leung has clearly stated that the government would not use its huge foreign reserves to offer a direct financial relief to the public to overcome the economic difficulties. While a survey showed that over 30 per cent of Hong Kong people called for tax rebate, Leung has turned down the request. Instead, the government has revealed it would put efforts to improve business environment and create business opportunities through promoting intelligent technology, tourism, film industry and so forth. Leung has also delivered a clear message to Hong Kong people that they should not rely on the government, but to be self-sufficient through methods such as life-long learning (*Hong Kong iMail* 16 August 2001; *South China Morning Post* 29 August 2001; *Ming Pao* 28 August 2001).

The Implications of the Social Welfare Reform

It is clear the HKSAR government is going toward a managerial state. The adoption of the new managerialism is accelerated by the distinctive socio-economic and political developments after the handover. Social welfare reform serves to enhance efficiency and cost-effectiveness, to improve service quality and to maintain government's financial sustainability and, most importantly, to achieve its political goal, that is, performance legitimacy. Then, how far does the reform achieve its aims?

Public opinion can be a key indicator to measure the achievement of the government. In theory, public opinion should be the basis of public policies and thus, it can serve as a barometer for the popularity of public policies and the government (Wong, et al. 2001: 3). A generally held assumption is that if the public policy is consistent with the social value of the people, it is more likely to receive a positive appraisal from the public. In view of this, we will draw upon public attitudes toward welfare and social welfare policy between 1999 and 2001 as potential evidence of the Chief Executive's performance in the social welfare reform.

Statistics show that Hong Kong people still adopts the traditional, instrumental view towards politics. In this view, the government is considered to be liable for the well-being of the people. Accordingly, the ability of the government in satisfying the needs of the people greatly underlie the legitimacy of the government. In view of this, the government should prioritize the welfare of the people in its policy agenda (Ho 2001: 37–38).

Generally, the perception of social welfare of the people is consistent with those underpinning the government social welfare policy (Wong, et al. 2001: 33). Survey results show that the government and the people converge on the point that self-reliance can best meet individual demands (Wong, et al. 2001). They place emphasis on individual obligation to the society and work ethics. Most people also believe that the responsibility of the government lies on helping the truly needy, including the elderly, the sick and the unemployed. The people's priority for the government remains in the reduction of unemployment and poverty (Wong, et al. 2001: 32; Ho 2001: 38).

Unfortunately, the public rating of the government's performance in ensuring economic and social well-being of the people is rather low. According to the data, most people regard poverty, income inequality and unemployment as serious problems and tend to negatively evaluate the government's governance accordingly (Wong, et al. 2001; Ho 2001: 40). In addition, more people considered that public welfare and government expenditure in social welfare are insufficient (Wong, et al. 2001: 21).

With regard to the reform initiatives of the government, they are generally backed by the Hong Kong people, including the pace and quantity of these reform initiatives. Hong Kong people do agree that reforms are needed in times of economic difficulties and it is appropriate to launch welfare reform. Most people expect the government to lead Hong Kong to a better future (Lau 2002; Ng and Li 2002; Wong, et al. 2001).

However, there are doubts over Tung's ability to achieve the betterment of Hong Kong. Public concern has been raised over the inadequate consultation on the reforms. More people believe that reform packages are more beneficial to the business sector than to the collective interests of the general public (Lau 2002).

In terms of social welfare reform, the data shows that an average support was obtained from the people, in which, the initiative that scores the highest support from the sample is the CSSA reform (Wong, et al. 2001). However, it is worthy to note that most people attribute poverty and the rise of CSSA cases to socio-economic factor, a view which is contradictory to the contention of the government and the position of the New Right theorists.

There has not been other social welfare reform items that have been applauded as high by the people. According to the data, most people doubt the effectiveness of MPF. They also oppose welfare cut and contracting-out of social welfare services for want of quality assurance (Wong, et al. 2001; Lau 2002). While evidence shows that social services have been provided in more economized ways, the government is being criticized for putting too much emphasis on economic rationality, that is on efficiency, cost-effectiveness and financial sustainability while shrugging its obligation for social welfare provision, and the assurance of fairness and equity to the vulnerable groups. In fact, the New Right's advocacy for a small government and welfare retrenchment is at odd with the rising public sentiment and demand for more and better social provisions at times of economic downturn (Chau and Ngai 2000: 151).

In fact, there are oppositions against various welfare cut from social workers and service recipients. They are typically against the introduction of measures to reduce welfare provisions in times of economic difficulty. Employees of companies that have taken on government contract work have protested against unfair treatment, such as long hours and low pay (*Ming Pao* 24 September 2001). A survey reportedly shows that the work pressure of social workers has increased under the newly introduced LSGS (*Ming Pao* 27 August 2001).

Based on his survey conducted between May and August 2001, Lau (2002) holds that although most Hong Kong people support public sector reforms, they are not ready to make major sacrifices. They believe that the government should take up the main responsibility for the well-being of people. Hence, Hong Kong people are unlikely to agree with measures and policies, such as welfare cut and contracting-out of social services, that would undermine their entitlements. This public attitude has become the biggest obstacle for the government in carrying out its reforms.

Meanwhile, the survey of Wong, et al. (2001) in June 2001 finds a shift in public attitude toward social welfare or seeking help for personal difficulties. It also reveals that some Hong Kong people, particularly in the lower classes, appear to be less reluctant to apply for CSSA in times of financial difficulties. It may indicate that the social value among Hong Kong people has changed; or perhaps, this is a pragmatic choice because of financial uncertainties and hardship for some who have encountered lower wages. Henceforth, the need for institutional support in time of adversity has increased. It is time that the government should take steps to consider a strategic and long-term plan for the local social security system (Wong, et al. 2001).

Analysis above shows that business management principles cannot completely replace political values. As Clarke and Newman (1997: 31) show that while the power of the state has been centralized under the new managerialism, the state is exposed to more potential cooption and resistance. The restructured power relation is therefore unstable. Generally speaking, the social welfare reform has yet to receive a wider support from the people. The public's less than enthusiastic support has not enhanced the government's performance legitimacy.

Conclusion

Hong Kong is undergoing various changes and transitions in socio-economic and political aspects, including population aging, economic restructuring and a high expectation with the post-colonial government. Accompanied with these is a rising public demand for more and better social services. In the view of this, social welfare reform is politically motivated by the HKSAR government to meet public demand and to enhance the state's legitimacy and capacity.

Focusing on the social welfare reform, this chapter has pointed to a new governing ideology of the HKSAR government. The cutback on social welfare has not retrenched the government's control over the society. Under the new managerialism and the New Right ideology, the government's influence has been enhanced through the new result-oriented control measures. Market mechanism, cost-effectiveness, competitiveness and social morality are prime considerations. In fact, such practice is not unique in the social welfare arena but is an integral part of the larger, public sector reform requirements.

As a political response to the economic downturn and the governance crisis, the social welfare reform was motivated to enhance government's capacity, to retrieve public confidence and, hence, the legitimacy of the government. However, the adoption of the New Right ideology and the new managerialism invites suspicion that the social welfare reform is not committed to the best interests of the public, but to reducing the state role and public spending in social welfare instead. Evidences show that the reform cannot cater to the requirements unique to Hong Kong's socio-economic development, nor can it meet with the public's expectations.

Given the bleak economic prospect, however, the public demand for welfare services is expected to grow. While it has yet to recover from the Asian Financial Crisis, the Hong Kong economy is further shadowed by the economic downturn of the United States, and by the likely global economic recession after the terrorist attack in the United States on September 11, 2001. The unemployment and underemployment rates remain high, as the seasonally adjusted unemployment rate in December 2001–February 2002 has reached 6.8 per cent which is forecasted to continue to rise ("Unemployment and Underemployment Statistics," 2002). A survey also shows that 17.8 per cent of the population were living below the poverty line in 2000 with an average income of less than $2,550 a month (Lam 2001). The widening wealth gap, hitting the record of the local Gini Coefficient at 0.525, is causing no small alarm (Census and Statistics Department 2001).

At the same time, attention was paid to the financial capability of the government. Although prudent management continues to be the guiding principle of public finance management, the government has recorded three budget deficits since the handover (Leung 2002). The narrow tax bases and depressed property market, which implies disappointed land-related revenues and performance of many related industries such as banking and construction, have dragged down the government revenues. The rigid operating expenditure, including the major component of civil servants' salaries, as well as the rising welfare expenditure with the surging unemployment rate and the aging population have kept the government expenditure increasing (Xu 2002). In its two-year study, the Task Force on Review of Public Finances, headed by the Treasury Secretary Denise Yue, warned that Hong Kong was facing a structural deficit. The HKSAR's $369 billion fiscal reserve would be wiped out by 2008–09 and the reserves would be transformed into a $2.66 trillion debt by 2021 if the government does not cut spending or raise taxes. The Task Force suggested to control the growth of government expenditure by aligning it with the growth of the economy ("Task Force," 2002).

Some critics worry that the study opens the door for the government to cut welfare spending. Beyond expectations, however, the public expenditure continue to grow without significant measures to increase government revenues in the 2002–03 budget. Recurrent expenditure for social welfare in 2002–03, estimated to be $32.1 billion, receives the largest percentage growth of nine per cent with most increases in payments for social security and services for the elderly. The government also offers measures to help the community ride out the adversity, including reducing rates payments, reducing water and sewage charges and trade effluent surcharge, as well as freezing government fees and charges (Leung 2002; Moy 2002). However, there are doubts that the government might have underestimated the number of people seeking welfare in the time of economic difficulty (Moy 2002).

It has been the hope of the government to reduce public spending in order to achieve fiscal balance in the long run. In his maiden budget, Antony Leung states that the government will restore fiscal balance step by step. His target is, by 2006–07, the fiscal budget will record a balance and public expenditure will be reduced to 20 per cent of GDP or below (Leung 2002). Cutting pension and social security payments is one of the possible ways. As Antony Leung tells, "[p]rice movement in government expenditure does not follow that of the economy. This is mainly attributable to the higher wage content of government expenditure. Wages tend to increase faster than the general price level in the economy, which means that the price of government expenditure grows faster than the general price. Government expenditure also includes pensions and social security payments, and these have not adjusted downwards with the general price level in times of deflation. The differential between the government expenditure price level and the general price level thus widens further" (Leung 2002).

The economic downturn, deteriorating living standard, undemocratic system, doubts on the administrative and fiscal capability of the government all continue to cast negative effects on public confidence over the government. Surveys of the Home Affairs Bureau show that the public's satisfaction with the government performance was low (Figure 5).

Figure 5. Public Satisfaction with the Government's Performance, July 2000 to July 2001, Conducted by the Home Affairs Bureau

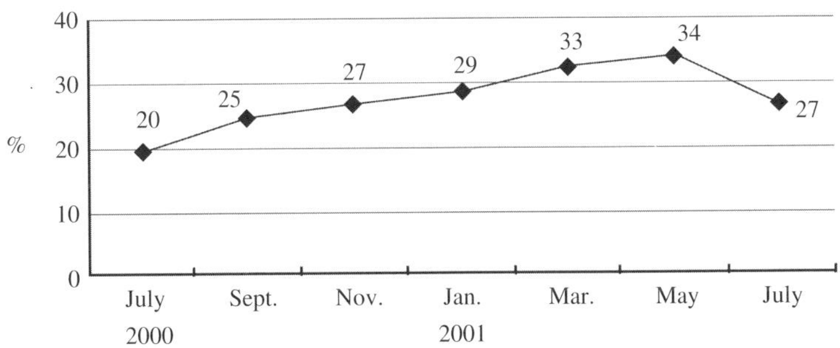

Source: *Hong Kong Economic Journal* (2 August 2001).

The creditability of the Central Government was ahead of the HKSAR government since December 2001 (*Ming Pao* 18 December 2001). The Coalition Against Second Term was founded to protest against Tung's leadership (Leung 2001). Despite of these, being the only validly nominated candidate, Tung was re-elected uncontested under the Chief Executive Election Ordinance in March 2002 (Lee 2002). However, according to the survey of the Hong Kong Institute of Asia-Pacific Studies, before the nomination exercise ended, only 49 per cent of the people supported Tung to serve for a second term. The actual popular support of Tung may be even lower given that some support Tung merely because they have no choice. The re-election of Tung is mainly attributable to the election system, not to consolidated public support (Wong 2002). An opinion poll of the Faculty of Social Science of the Chinese University of Hong Kong reveals that only a small fraction (8.2 per cent) of respondents believe Tung could best represent Hong Kong's interest, while the majority (60.9 per cent) thought he was more accountable to the Central Government than to the HKSAR. Almost one out of two respondents (48.3 per cent) believed Tung would not place Hong Kong's interests first if there was a clash with Beijing on the issue. Moreover, the rating of the HKSAR government's ability (51.6 per cent) was below that of the Central Government (57.9 per cent) and the Macau SAR government (57.5 per cent) (Leung 2002).

How to enhance public confidence on the government, and thereby the governance legitimacy, remains an unsolved concern. Due to the vital legitimatization function of social welfare, the government had spent more on social welfare in the years under study. It is doubtful that cost-containment was government's primary objective. Nevertheless, cost-containment and legitimization function for social stability has been a two-fold objective in social welfare.

Hence, in the social welfare reform, the government is caught in an unenviable dilemma. There is the need for squaring the welfare circle on the one hand and the need of legitimizing for social stability on the other hand, if we use neo-Marxist analytical framework (O'Connors 1973). Even though the government might conceive of social welfare as a public burden, it also regards social welfare indispensable for social stability. In the process of coping with this two-fold objective of social welfare, despite of its internal contradictory nature, it is not surprising to notice substantial increase in social welfare spending while managerial measures, such as value-for-money principles, were also applied at the same time.

Thus, it remains a central concern for the government to ensure political and social feasibility of its reform initiatives. In view of this, professional advice is crucial in formulating public policy. Unlike in Western countries and some Asian nations, the HKSAR government does not have a tradition of using policy research for gauging the political and social implications of a new policy or reform initiative. Neither is the HKSAR known for tapping on the expertise of the academic communities as think tanks or consultants for social policy making. It was revealed that of the 150 million dollar the HKSAR government spent on consultancy on policy related research in 2001, only a negligible amount (4.8 per cent) was contracted out to local institutions of higher education (*Ming Pao* 26 March 2002). We think there is a need for the HKSAR government to promote policy research and broader engagement of the local academic community in policy research and social policy development. An important first step would be for the government to facilitate better access to government information for systematic policy research. Equally necessary is the need for the government to step up measures to enlighten the public and to better assess public response and reaction on policy or reform initiatives.

It is an indisputable fact that social welfare policy affects all people of the community. As a social institution, social welfare has the objective of satisfying the basic human needs to all. In affluent society like Hong Kong, social welfare provisions and benefits do not only concern about absolute poverty or destitution, but also basic living standard in comparative terms, that is, the broader concern for social equity, social justice and balanced development. In initiating social welfare reform, there are implications far beyond the confine of social welfare that must also be attended to.

Notes

1. In late 1997, the "bird flu" broke out and stirred up a widespread public concern. Officials made slow responses to the inflection matter at first. But few days later, a hasty slaughter of all the local chickens, the source of the influenza virus, was launched. The operation was poorly leaded without proper coordination among government departments. In spite of widespread critics, the then Chief Secretary Anson Chan defended that no official would be held responsible (Lee 1999: 950.). The new Hong Kong International Airport fiasco is another infamous case. Without comprehensive assessment of computer system, a system breakdown on 6 July 1998, the first day

operation of the new airport, led to messes including baggage mishandling and flight delays. The airport operation has not been turned to normal until almost two months later causing considerable economic loss and unfathomable damage of Hong Kong's reputation. However, officials declined to assume the responsibility. Anson Chan apologized only because of a great political pressure (Ibid.; Yeung 1998a).

2. In fact, according to some authority (e.g. Walker and Wong 1996), Hong Kong is a neo-liberal welfare state. It has universal basic education, universal health services, universal old age allowances; as well as strong role of the state in public housing.

References

Becker, Saul (1997). *Responding to Poverty: The Politics of Cash and Care* (London and New York: Longman).

Cass, Bettina (1997). "Questioning The Very Idea of Dependence? Public Policy Responses to Unemployment and Marginalization," *The Jobs Letter* 57. Retrieved on 6 October 1999, from http://www.jobsletter.org.nz.

Census and Statistics Department (2001). *2001 Population Census* (Hong Kong: Hong Kong Government Printer).

——— (2001). *Hong Kong Annual Digest of Statistics 2001* (Hong Kong: Hong Kong Government Printer).

Chan, Quinton, and Wong, Martin (2001). "Welfare's Bottom Line," *South China Morning Post*, 12 March, p. 14.

Chau, Kenneth Kin-lam, and Ngai Ngan-pun (2000). "Xinjiyuan de Xianggang shehui fuli" (Social Welfare of Hong Kong in the New Millennium), in Lau Sui-kai (ed.), *Xianggang 21 shiji lantu* (Hong Kong: The Blueprint for the 21st Century) (Hong Kong: The Chinese University Hong Kong).

Chow, Chuen-ho Larry, and Fan Yiu-kwan (1999). "Introduction," in Chow Chuen-ho Larry and Fan Yiu-kwan (eds.), *The Other Hong Kong Report 1998* (Hong Kong: The Chinese University Press).

Chow, Nelson (1999). "Social welfare," in Chow Chuen-ho Larry and Fan Yiu-kwan (eds.), *The Other Hong Kong Report 1998* (Hong Kong: The Chinese University Press).

Clarke, John, and Newman, Janet (1997). *The Managerial State: Power, Politics and Ideology in the Remaking of Social Welfare* (London: Sage Publications).

Efficiency Unit (1995). *A Management Guide for Civil Servants* (Hong Kong: Hong Kong Government).

Esping-Andersen, G. (ed.) (1996). Welfare States in Transition: National Adaptations in Global Economies (London: Sage).

Estes, Richard J. (2000). *Social Development in Hong Kong: The Unfinished*

Agenda. Executive Summary of the Report of the Project on Social Development Index for Hong Kong of the Hong Kong Council of Social Service (Hong Kong: The Hong Kong Council of Social Service).

Ferrera, Maurizio (1993). *EC Citizens and Social Protection: Main Results from a Eurobarometer Survey* (Brussels: The Commission of the European Communities).

Golding, Peter, and Middleton, Sue (1978). Why is the press so obsessed with welfare scroungers? *New Society* Vol. 46, No. 838, pp.195–97.

——— (1982). *Images of Welfare: Press and Public Attitudes to Poverty* (Oxford: Martin Robertson).

Hanson, F. Allan (1998). "How Poverty Lost its Meaning," *The CATO Journal* Vol. 17, No. 2. Retrieved on 1 April 2000, from http://www.cato.org/pubs/journal.

Ho, Kwok-leung (2001). "Popular Support for Effective Government," in Lau Siu-kai, Lee Ming-kwan, Wan Po-san and Wong Siu-lun (eds.), *Indicators of Social Development Hong Kong 1999* (Hong Kong: Hong Kong Institute of Asia-Pacific Studies).

Ho, Lok-sang (1999). The Rise and Fall of the Economy," in Chow Chuen-ho Larry and Fan Yiu-kwan (eds.), *The Other Hong Kong Report 1998* (Hong Kong: The Chinese University Press).

Hong Kong Government (2001). *Hong Kong 2000* (Hong Kong: Information Services Department).

——— (2002). "Hong Kong Facing a Structural Fiscal Problem and Decisive Actions Called For," 21 February, press release retrieved from http://www.info.gov.hk/gia/general/200202/21/0221187.htm.

——— (2002). "Unemployment and Underemployment Statistics for December 2001–February 2002," 18 March, press release retrieved from http://www.info.gov.hk.

Hood, Christopher (1998). *The Art of the State: Culture, Rhetoric, and Public Management* (Oxford: Clarendon Press).

Information Services Department (2000). "Hong Kong: The facts — Social welfare," Hong Kong: Information Services Department, retrieved from http://www.info.gov.hk/swd.

Katz, Michael B. (1993). "The Urban 'Underclass' as a Metaphor of Social Transformation," in Michael B. Katz (ed.), *The "Underclass" Debate: Views from History* (Princeton, N.J.: Princeton University Press).

Lam, Agnes (2001). "Alarm Sounded on Poverty," *South China Morning Post*, 24 September, p. 8.

Lau, Siu Kai (2002). "Hong Kong People Support Reforms, but Questions the Capability of the Tung Administration" (Xianggangren zhichi gaige, wei zhiyi Dong zhengfu nengli) *Ming Pao*, 10 January, p. C15.

Lee, Eliza Wing-yee (1998). "The Political Economy of Public Sector Reform in

Hong Kong: The Case of a Colonial-developmental State," *International Review of Administrative Sciences* 64, pp. 625–41.

——— (1999). "Governing Post-colonial Hong Kong: Institutional Incongruity, Governance Crisis, and Authoritarianism," *Asian Survey* 39 (6), pp. 940–59.

——— (2000). "The Politics of Public Sector Reform in Post-colonial Hong Kong" Paper presented at the Eastern Regional Organization for Public Administration (EROPA) Hong Kong Conference, 4–5 October 2000.

Lee, Jikjoen (1997). *Jinnian Xianggang shehui fuli zhengce de fazhan: yi Peng Dingkang de shizheng wei anli* (Recent Social Welfare Policy Development in Hong Kong: The Case of Christopher Patten) (Hong Kong: Hong Kong Institute of Asia-Pacific Studies).

Lee, Mathew (2002). "Unopposed Tung Vows to Think Like the People," *Hong Kong iMail*, 1 March, p. A2.

Legco Panel on Welfare Service (1999). "Review of welfare subvention policy," 8 November. Retrieved on 28 April 2001, from http://www.info.gov.hk/hwb.

Leung, Ambrose (2001). "Protesters Give Tung Marching Orders," *South China Morning Post*, 26 November, Hong Kong, p. 6.

——— (2002). "Only eight in 100 believe Tung is the best," *South China Morning Post*, 4 April, Hong Kong, p. 1.

Leung, Antony (2002). *The 2002–03 Budget*. Retrieved on 7 March 2002, from http://www.budget.gov.hk/fb/2002/budget/english/e_budget.htm.

Marshall, T. H. (ed.) (1950). *Citizenship and Social Class and Other Essays* (Cambridge: Cambridge University Press).

Midgley, James (1997). *Social Welfare in Global Context* (Thousand Oaks: Sage Publications).

Morris, Lydia (1994). *Dangerous Classes: The Underclass and Social Citizenship* (Routledge: London and New York).

Moy, Patsy (2002). "Elderly Services and CSSA Funds Boosted," *South China Morning Post*, 7 March, IV Budget 2002.

Murray, Charles (1984). *Losing Ground: American Social Policy 1950–1980* (New York: Basic Books).

——— (1999). "What Government Must Do? Make Welfare Unappealing or Reform Will Fail," retrieved on 1 April 2000 from http://www.theamericanenterprise.org.

Ng, Kang-chung, and Li, Angela (2002). "Tung's Personal Popularity Trails Support for Policies, Survey Finds," *South China Morning Post*, 5 January, Hong Kong, p. 2.

O'Connor, James (1973). *The Fiscal Crisis of the State* (New York: St. Martin's Press).

Siegel, Charles (1998). "Welfare Reform: Why the Left Failed," retrieved on 1 April 2000 from http://www.preservenet.com.

So, Antoine, and Yiu, Enoch (2000). "Nearly Half of Employers Miss MPF Deadline," *South China Morning Post*, 1 December, p. 1.

Social Welfare Department (SWD) (1999). *Departmental Report 1997/98* (Hong Kong: Hong Kong Government Printer).

——— (1998). "Support for Self-reliance: Report on Review of the Comprehensive Social Security Scheme," retrieved from http://www.info.gov.hk/swd.

Taylor-Gooby, Peter (1985). *Public Opinion, Ideology and State Welfare* (London: Routledge).

Titmuss, Richard M. (1963). *Essays on "The Welfare State"* (London: Unwin University Books).

Tsang, Donald (1999). *The 1999–2000 Budget: Onward with New Strength* (Hong Kong: Government Printer).

——— (2000). *The 2000–01 Budget: Scaling New Heights* (Hong Kong: Government Printer).

——— (2001). *The 2001–2002 Budget: Honing Our Strengths, Striving to Excel* (Hong Kong: Government Printer).

Tung, Chee-hwa (1997). *Building Hong Kong for a New Era* (policy address to the Provisional Legislative Council) (Hong Kong: Government Printer).

——— (1998). *From Adversity to Opportunity* (policy address to the Legislative Council) (Hong Kong: Government Printer).

——— (2000). *Serving the Community, Sharing Common Goals* (policy address to the Legislative Council) (Hong Kong: Government Printer).

United Nations Population Division (2002). "*World Population Prospects: The 2000 Revision*. Retrieved on 3 April from http://www.un.org/esa/population/publications/wpp2000/wpp2000h.pdf.

Walker, Alan (1984). *Social Planning: A Strategy for Socialist Welfare* (Oxford: Basil Blackwell).

Walker, A., and Wong, Chack-kie (1996). "Rethinking the Western Construction of the Welfare State," *International Journal of Health Services* 26 (1), pp. 67–92.

Wan, Cynthia (1999). "Sharp Rise in Payments to 15.5 billion," *South China Morning Post*, 25 February, Hong Kong, p. 4.

Wong, Chack-kie, Chau, Kenneth Kin-lam, and Wong, Timothy Ka-ying (2001). *Tequ zhengfu shehui zhengce de pinggu: Xianggang shimin de guandian* (Evaluation on HKSAR Government Social Welfare Policy: Public Perception (Hong Kong: Hong Kong Institute of Asia-Pacific Studies).

Wong, Martin (2000). "Welfare Funding Scheme Dodged," *South China Morning Post*, 5 December, Hong Kong, p. 6.

Wong, Timothy Ka-ying (2002). "*Cong minyi kan lianrenhou de guanzhi*" (The Governance of the Chief Executive's Second Term from the Perspective of Public Opinion), *Hong Kong Daily News*, 2 March, p. A11.

Wu, Wensui (2001). "Elderly services should not be privatised" Anlao fuwu buying siyinghua), *Ming Pao*, 17 March, p. B12.

Yeatman, A. (1997). "The Reform of Public Management: An Overview," in Mark Considine and Martin Painter (eds.), *Managerialism: The Great Debate* (Victoria: Melbourne University Press).

Yeung, Chris (1998a). "Flying in the Face of the Facts," *South China Morning Post*, 11 July, p. 15.

——— (1998b). "Survey Shows Growing Discontent," *South China Morning Post*, 4 August, p. 6.

Xu, Steven (2002). "Key Deficit in Flexibility," *South China Morning Post*, 25 February, online.

10

Separation and Integration: Hong Kong–Mainland Relations in a Flux

Chris Yeung

Associate Editor and Political Editor
South China Morning Post, Hong Kong

Introduction

Chinese Premier Zhu Rongji caused more than a stir on 4 September 2001 when he was questioned by a Hong Kong journalist during his visit in Ireland. Hong Kong, he said, should not "discuss without decision, make decision without execution."[1] His off-the-cuff comment has been widely seen as a true reflection of Beijing's dismay with the governance of the Hong Kong Special Administrative Region (SAR). Speaking to Hong Kong journalists again one day later, he clarified that he had no intention of criticising the SAR government.[2] The rare comment made by the top Beijing leader on the way Hong Kong people was ruling Hong Kong could have whipped up a political storm before the handover or in the early years of the SAR. This is because any overt criticism on how the SAR is governed could have provided the ammunitions for China critics to accuse Beijing of interfering with the SAR affairs. The fact that that had not happened, and that, quite the contrary, the community has responded positively to Mr. Zhu's remarks speaks volumes of the changes in Hong Kong–Mainland relations five years after the sovereignty changeover.

Much to the credit of Beijing leaders for exercising great self-restraint uncharacteristic before 1997, the worst fear of Chinese interference with the internal affairs of the SAR after the handover had not come true. Opinion surveys conducted by various organisations show a high degree of public approval of the performance and trust in the Central Government. Within the Hong Kong society, there is a general public awareness of the utmost importance of a cordial and harmonious relationship with the mainland. Although some activities such as the 4 June commemorative events remain divisive within the society, they have not caused major frictions in Hong Kong–Mainland relations. There was no serious political crisis in the tricky relations in the past few years. In the face of sharp differences between the mainland's socialist systems and Hong Kong's capitalist systems, political leaders from both sides of the border have reckoned the need to be more flexible, pragmatic and understandable so as to allow more room for brinkmanship in handling political issues such as Article 23 in the Basic Law and the Falun Gong activities in Hong Kong. Notwithstanding a spate of political controversies, the two systems co-existed peacefully in the past five years.

It is on the economic front where drastic changes in the Hong Kong–Mainland relations are taking place. Over the past year, Tung and his new team — Chief Secretary Donald Tsang Yam-kuen and Financial Secretary Antony Leung Kam-chung — have stepped up efforts to forge closer economic ties with Guangdong and the Pearl River Delta region. Leung has underlined the importance of the need for a paradigm shift in the mindset of Hong Kong people towards the mainland. In the wake of the sharp economic downturn in the US following the terrorist attacks on 11 September, senior Chinese leaders have pledged to give full support to Hong Kong and strengthen economic cooperation between the two places to help maintain Hong Kong's economic prosperity. Officials from both sides are holding discussion on a Closer Economic Partnership Arrangement (CEPA) within the parameters of the World Trade Organisation. Within the community, there is a growing awareness that the future of the Hong Kong economy lies with the mainland. Businessmen, professionals and people from other walks of life are in one voice calling on the SAR government to talk to the mainland authorities for new economic opportunities. They include allowing more mainland visitors to visit Hong Kong, enabling Hong Kong professionals such as lawyers to practise in the mainland, using Hong Kong as a centre for mainland firms to raise capital and easing restrictions for mainland capital in Hong Kong's stock market.

At the community level, interactions and exchanges between the two peoples have increased significantly. Government figures show more people now own their property in the mainland. The number of people who are working or plan to work in the mainland is also on the rise.[3] This is despite the fact that opinion polls found no major change of public perception about their identity under the new constitutional order. Results of tracking polls on attitude towards China shows more than half of young people identified themselves primarily as Hong Kongers. Only 18.6 per cent out of 623 Form Three to Form Six students consider themselves Chinese.[4] According to the Hong Kong Transition Project, 45 per cent of respondents consider themselves to be Hong Kong people. 26 per cent described themselves as Hong Kong Chinese. Only 22 per cent say they are Chinese.[5] Morever, discrimination against mainlanders remains deeply rooted in the society as manifested in the right of abode saga in 1999 and alleged reliance of mainland migrants on government welfare benefits. Some people also blamed the one-way permit policy, under which 150 mainlanders are allowed to migrate to Hong Kong each day, as one of the major causes behind the chronic problem of unemployment. Speaking in Singapore in April, 2002, a senior Hong Kong official Mike Rowse said a skill-based policy on migrants from the mainland must be adopted to enhance quality of manpower in the long-run.[6]

Under the policy of "one country, two systems," the political relations between the SAR and the mainland are marked by a high degree of separation. Except for defence and foreign affairs, the SAR is allowed to exercise a high degree of autonomy. The SAR government is constituted by the people of Hong Kong. The Chief Executive is elected by an Election Committee entirely composed of Hong Kong people. Events in the past five years show Hong Kong people remain highly sensitive to the visible and invisible hands of Beijing in SAR affairs, as they have been before the handover. Yet on the economic and socio-cultural areas, integration and interaction have become the order of the day. The trend of "go north" has seemingly become irresistable.

According to a survey on the "Political Linkage and Interaction between Hong Kong and China" conducted by the Chinese University of Hong Kong in April 2002, 54 per cent are satisfied with the policies of China towards Hong Kong.17.9 per cent are dissatisfied and 14.3 per cent chose "half-half." But in another finding, 55.3 per cent of respondents do not think that Hong Kong people have the ability to influence the policies of China towards Hong Kong. In a separate finding, 52.5 per cent do not believe Hong Kong people have the ability to influence the Central People's Government (CPG) on its policy on democratisation in Hong Kong.[7] The findings best reflected the mixed feelings of Hong Kong people towards the CPG since the handover. The overall perception of people towards China has been good mainly because the CPG has not meddled with domestic affairs of the SAR. But on the other hand, there is an equally strong feeling that the China factor, or specifically the views of Beijing, is crucial in the democracy development of Hong Kong. The political, economic, socio-cultural cross-currents have made an impact on the developments of Hong Kong in the past five years. There is no doubt they will bring about more complexities, challenges and opportunities in the Hong Kong–Mainland relations in the next five years.

Beijing's Perspective

The policy of "one country, two systems" was primarily designed to achieve the dual objectives of preserving prosperous Hong Kong while securing China's wide national interests of territorial sovereignty. It was mooted in the early 1980s by late patriarch leader Deng Xiaoping with an ultimate goal of reunifying Taiwan. The basic ideas of the policy, which were further defined in the Basic Law of the Hong Kong Special Administrative Region promulgated in 1990, are:

- Adhering to one country and safeguarding national sovereign
- Upholding the arrangement of keeping the system basically unchanged and;
- Safeguarding stability and prosperity.

A three-part strategy was adopted. First, a Basic Law in the form of a national law was enacted to separate the two systems. It is binding on both the SAR and China. Under the Basic Law, Hong Kong is empowered to handle domestic affairs with a high degree of autonomy while Beijing retains power over defense and foreign affairs. The delineation of powers is designed to prevent mainland interference. Secondly, a minimalist approach has been taken to realise the concept of "one country." This is symbolised by, among others, a change of flag and emblem, and Beijing's power in the endorsement of the SAR's chief executive and principal officials. Thirdly, there has been a general understanding and recognition of the need for mutual tolerance and mutual respect when dealing with differences that may emerge over practical problems when the two systems interact.[8]

The Taiwan factor aside, there are good reasons for China to preserve the "duck that lays golden eggs." A prosperous and stable Hong Kong plays an important supporting and facilitating role in China's modernisations.

"Our country is undergoing modernisations. But we are still lagging behind on the question of funds, skill and technology and management method. By retaining its capitalist system, Hong Kong can maintain its stability and prosperity and function as a conduit of communications between us and foreign capitalist countries."[9]

Hong Kong can directly and indirectly provide a channel for China to lure foreign funds, advance technology and economic management knowledge. On the other hand, the opening of Chinese economy in the late 70s was a crucial factor for Hong Kong's economic boom in the past two decades, not to mention the heavy reliance of Hong Kong on daily necessities including water and food from the mainland.

Chinese Premier Zhu Rongji said in March 2002 Hong Kong had played a leading role in contributing to China's open door and reform in the 80s. He said: "As the world economy develops, I think there should be some adjustments to the role of Hong Kong. All elites in Hong Kong are looking at the issue. We are also willing to discuss the issue with the SAR government and people."[10]

Following China's further opening to foreign investments in the post-WTO era, the unique role of Hong Kong and its specific economic relationship with the mainland are bracing for major changes. The Central Government has earlier given its blessing to a proposal by the Chief Executive for a free trade zone agreement between the SAR and the mainland. (It was later renamed as CEPA). The Hong Kong/Guangdong Cooperation Joint Conference has also since mid-2001 speeded up discussions on ways to harmonise infrastructure development and speed up the flow of goods and people across the border. Guangdong vice-governor Ou Guangyuan said on 15 March 2002, greater cooperation between the province and Hong Kong would avoid adverse competition that might be harmful to the interests of both sides.

While Beijing leaders reckoned the need not to meddle with SAR's internal affairs — and to be seen as such — that does not mean it has adopted a totally hands-off approach. Over the past five years, the Central Government has adopted a strategy of "zhuada fangxiao" (taking a firm grip of the major things and letting the minor ones go).[11] With high autonomous powers delegated to the SAR, the Central Government holds a firm grip on the post of the Chief Executive to make sure their interests are safeguarded in the SAR. The blessing of Beijing was symbolised first by Chinese President Jiang Zemin's famous handshake with Tung in 1996, after which Tung has emerged as a leading contender for the post of first

Chief Executive. He won the first CE election with a big margin. Beginning mid-2000, Jiang and other senior Beijing leaders including Vice Premier Qian Qichen spoke publicly in support of the candidacy of Tung for the second term. Tung was re-elected uncontested on 28 February 2002. Pro-democracy activists maintained Tung was anointed by Beijing.

As its stakes in the success of "one country, two systems" are high, Beijing needs full confidence in the chief executive that he or she will safeguard national interest in the SAR. This is particularly important in view of the strained relations between Hong Kong and the mainland after the 4 June Tiananmen Square crackdown. Shocked by scenes of over one million people taking to the streets to oppose the bloody crackdown of student protestors, Beijing has warned Hong Kong not to interfere with the mainland's systems and way of life. Professor Xiao wrote both the SAR and the central authorities must respect the reality that each practised a different social system.[12]

> (One) should not be allowed to use one system to change the other system. The Central People's Government will not change the capitalist system in Hong Kong within 50 years. It will not introduce the socialist system and policies in Hong Kong. Hong Kong should also not interfere or try to change the socialist system and introduce the capitalist system in the mainland ... Turning Hong Kong into a subversive base against the Central People's Government and socialist system is not allowed.[13]

The active role of Hong Kong in the 1989 pro-democracy movement prompted the Chinese government to insert a last-minute provision in the Basic Law, or the so-called Article 23. Under the article, Hong Kong has to enact its own law to, among other things, ban subversive activities.[14] Given the sensitivity of the issue and the fact that there has been no serious subversive threat, the Central Government and SAR government have apparently had tacit understanding that the legislative task should be put aside in the early years of the SAR. By doing so, it has avoided a potentially divisive debate within the society and tension between the SAR and the mainland at a time when local and international confidence in the future of Hong Kong remains fragile. Remarks given by a senior National People's Congress official Qiao Xiaoyang and Secretary for Justice Elsie Leung Oi-sie in February 2002 indicated the issue of Article 23 could no longer be further delayed. Qiao said legislative work should begin as soon as possible.[15] Failure of the SAR government to address the issue may cause political unease in the SAR–Mainland relations.

Tung Chee-hwa and Mainland–Hong Kong Relations

Under the Basic Law, the Chief Executive shall be accountable to the Central People's Government and the SAR. This is no easy task as the interests of Hong Kong and China are not always congruent, if not potentially conflicting in some areas.

Having delegated a wide range of autonomous powers to the SAR, Beijing is keen to have a chief executive who can safeguard their interest in Hong Kong. He or she must be someone whom Beijing can trust. Known for their political pragmatism, Hong Kong people accept the notion that the trust of Beijing is a must for the chief executive. This will reduce uncertainty and ensure harmony in Mainland–Hong Kong relations under the policy of "one country, two systems." That said, they also expect the SAR leader to be a defender of their interests and systems and a good interlocutor between the SAR and Beijing. He or she should dare to speak up and fight for the interests of the people of Hong Kong without fear on matters that Beijing might not feel happy with.

Despite the decline of public support for Mr. Tung in the past few years, there have been no clear signs that he has lost support from Beijing leaders. Publicly, senior Chinese leaders have hailed Mr. Tung's ability to tackle the complicated issues that have emerged after the handover such as the Asian financial crisis. Taking a deeper and wider perspective of the development of Hong Kong, senior Chinese officials have expressed satisfaction over the performance of Mr. Tung. Obsessed with fears of instability in the early years of the SAR, they maintain Mr. Tung has already accomplished a smooth transition. To Beijing, this is no small achievement. Nor this could be taken for granted. Furthermore, any signs of weakened support for the Chief Executive by Beijing will create political uncertainties.

More important, Mr. Tung has been able to demonstrate to Beijing his tactful grasp of the complexities in seeking a fine balance in the policy of "one country, two systems" and his determination to push Mainland–SAR relations to a new height. In his Policy Address in October 1997, he said:

> Our country has bright prospects from which Hong Kong is sure to benefit. Hong Kong has finally broken free from the psychological constraints brought about by the colonial era. We should have the courage to set aside past modes of thought and plan Hong Kong's long-term future with new vision.
>
> In recent decades, Hong Kong and the mainland have established broader and closer relationships in many areas. Whereas previously they had mainly been

> confined to non-governmental level, with reunification and with government support, the relationship between Hong Kong and the mainland should flourish comprehensively in all fields such as the economy, finance, trade, transport, culture, education, science and technology, tourism and sports.[16]

From the perspective of Beijing, Mr. Tung has managed to uphold and promote the concept of "one country" and impress the local and international community that the "two systems" are working well. On the socio-political front, he has repeatedly called on Hong Kong people to enhance their understandings about China's development. Taking the risk of being criticised as apologetic during overseas visits, he spoke positively of the economic achievements and potentials of China in the medium and long-run. Meanwhile, he treaded carefully on matters that have political and diplomatic implications.

Without condemning the 1989 Tiananmen protestors as the communist regime had done, he sought to convince the local dissidents it was imperative for Hong Kong people to look forward and drop the "historical baggage." On the economic arena, greater integration with the mainland economy has been a constant theme in his past five policy blueprints. Rhetoric aside, Mr. Tung has set up new joint institutional forums with the Guangdong counterparts to discuss wider economic integration in the Pearl River Delta region. The process of "go north" in the economic front has been given a big boost following the teaming up of Mr. Tung with Donald Tsang Yam-kuen and Antony Leung Kam-chung in May 2001. Mr. Tsang has succeeded the retired Anson Chan Fang On-sang as the Chief Secretary for Administration. Mr. Leung, a prominent banking executive, took over from Mr. Tsang. A flurry of visits have been paid by the pair to Guangdong in summer 2001 to speed up the process of greater integration of Hong Kong into the Pearl River Delta region. Opening hours at the immigration border points have been lengthened. 24 hours opening of the border checkpoints is no longer a question of if, but when. New regional express rail network linking Hong Kong, Shenzhen and Guangzhou are being examined. With the access of China into the World Trade Organisation, the economic integration between Hong Kong and the mainland are set to enter a new era.

A trend in the long run aside, the September 11 shockwave has deepened public anxiety about the economic viability of Hong Kong and prompted a significant change of set minds. A chorus of calls have been made by a cross section of society for China to help Hong Kong tide over the crisis. Among the litany of proposals including allowing more mainland visitors to come, exploring more business opportunities and opening up some sectors such as retail for Hong Kong investors. In addition to economic factors, there are good political reason for Beijing to lend a helping hand to Hong Kong. Beijing's strong support for Hong Kong could bolster the authority of Tung at a time of severe criticism against his leadership. Some senior officials have indicated that the trust of Beijing towards Mr. Tung is vitally important for the success of "one country, two systems." Speaking at a luncheon hosted by the American Chamber of Commerce on 15 October 2001, Mr. Donald Tsang said:

> ... the calm and measured stewardship of C H Tung which has earned the respect and support of those who have entrusted him with turning the concept of One Country Two Systems into a reality. Without that trust and respect, nothing else is really possible. And when people air their grievances and complain about how badly things have gone since the Handover — as people are wont to do in a free and open society like ours — we should occasionally take time to remind ourselves of that simple fact of life.[17]

Tung, however, has to pay a price for the strong backing of Beijing leaders. Hong Kong people do not view the Chief Executive as a good representative of the interest of Hong Kong. 60.9 per cent of respondents in a survey conducted by the Chinese University of Hong Kong found the Chief Executive is more accountable to the CPG rather than the SAR government. A separate question shows only 8.2 per cent of the respondents choose the Chief Executive as the best representative of the interest of Hong Kong, ranking behind all other given major institutions including the legislature, media and judiciary.[18]

Although there is no fundamental conflict in the Mainland–Hong Kong relations in the first five years of the SAR, new political and economic issues have posed fresh challenge to the two places. Political controversies had strained relationship at times and raised concern about the policy of "one country, two systems." The drastic changes in the mainland and Hong Kong economy have given new momentum for greater economic integration on one hand. On the other hand, it triggered fears that those rapid changes would blurr the lines of "two systems" in the long run. The cross-currents undercut the dynamics of Hong Kong–Mainland relations since the handover and posed a difficult task to the Chief Executive.

Political Controversies

Prior to the handover, the issue of future political relations between the SAR and the mainland had been boiled down to one question — whether Beijing would interfere with Hong Kong's internal affairs. As events unfolded since 1997 show, the political complexities and cross-currents in the Hong Kong–Mainland relations have turned out to be far more subtle. They are clearly reflected in several post-handover controversies.

Democracy and Human Rights

The Democrats-led Hong Kong Alliance in Support of Patriotic Democratic Movement in China (Alliance) has been a thorn in the eyes of Beijing. Well before the handover, China-friendly businessmen including Shui On Group chairman Vincent Lo Hong-sui has made an open appeal for the Alliance leaders to disband the group to avoid irritating Beijing. Mr. Tung has also, in more than one occasion, urged Alliance's core leader Szeto Wah to cancel the annual activities to commemorate the 4 June bloody crackdown. The Alliance has ignored their advice and continued to organise the annual commemorative activities. That said, it is also true that the pro-democracy flagship formed at the heyday of the 1989 Beijing protests has significantly scaled down its activities as time went by. Its campaign for a democratic China has become more symbolic than substantive.

Dissident Frank Lu Siqing, who runs a one-man operation in Hong Kong — the Information Centre for Human Rights and Democracy — has attracted much publicity in local and foreign media. Although a mainland court has described him as a "hostile foreign element" and the centre a hostile "overseas organisation," his operation remains lawful in the SAR. Lu has also been granted the permanent residency status after he fulfilled the seven-year residency length requirement.[19] Ostensibly, he faced no political pressure for him to stop his work.

Contrary to some pessimistic forecast made before 1997, the Hong Kong-based campaign for greater democracy and human rights in China has not caused major frictions in Hong Kong–Mainland relations. This is largely due to the fact that these activities had not brought about substantive impact on developments in the mainland. Nor the activists had created great embarrassment to the SAR government in their activities.

Slogans such as "Down with the communist leadership" had disappeared in democracy protests.

On the surface, the SAR government has adopted a relaxed attitude towards local dissident activities. But there are clear indications that security officials remain hyper-sensitive about activities that might cause tension and political embarrassment in Mainland–Hong Kong relations. In April 2002, US-based human rights activist, Harry Wu, who holds a US passport, was denied entry into Hong Kong. According to the *South China Morning Post*, security officials fear that Wu's trip was related to a joint plan with a locally based dissident group on a campaign on China's human rights. Officials are worried it could turn Hong Kong into a subversive base.[20] In January 2000, prominent dissident-in-exile Wang Dan was also denied a visa to visit Hong Kong to attend a symposium to commemorate the May Fourth Movement and the June Fourth1989 crackdown.[21]

Realistically, the SAR government can do nothing on the Alliance and activists such as Mr. Lu even if it wants to so long as their activities are within the law and held in a non-provocative and low-key manner. As a matter of fact, SAR officials have also had to take into account the fact that those activities are living proof of the policy of "one country, two systems."

That said, the relationship between Beijing and the Democrats worsened after the 1989 Tiananmen Square protests remains hostile. About 30 core members of the Democratic Party and some prominent small "d" democrats are not allowed to visit the mainland. Despite repeated requests made by them, Mr. Tung does not appear to have put a strong case for them to the Beijing leaders for their rights to visit the mainland. Failure of Mr. Tung to bridge the gap between Beijing and the democrats resulted in a lose-lose situation. Democrats put the blame on Mr. Tung for his reluctance to fight for their interests. The deadlock between Beijing and the democrats has made it more difficult for Tung to help ease the strained ties.

Over the past five years, the icy relationship between democrats and Beijing has shown no significant improvement. Nor there are indications of deterioration in their relationship. But given the fact the democrats remain a powerful political force in the SAR, such relationship can hardly be seen as a healthy sign. The fragile relationship will continue to become a source of instability in Hong Kong–Mainland relations if Tung remains coy in taking a more active role in seeking long-term improvement. Issues such as Article 23, Falun Gong and press freedom will put their unsettling relationship to a real test.

Falun Gong

The Falun Gong spiritual movement has and will remain the stickiest challenge for the leadership of Mr. Tung and the whole society in handling its relations with the mainland. Outlawed in China, it was first labelled as "cult," later as subversive since 1999. Despite massive suppression by the Chinese government, the group remains defiant and has posed persistent challenge to the communist leadership through well-organised campaign. In Hong Kong, the group was registered under the Societies Ordinance in 1996. Few people were aware of their activities not until 1999 when the group became the subject of a nationwide crackdown in the mainland. Their activities in Hong Kong had become extremely sensitive. The government was under pressure to ban the group. Officials were criticised by pro-China factions for their soft-handedness and insensitivity to Beijing's fears. Nellie Fong Wong Kut-man, who sits on the quasi-cabinet Executive Council, said the Falun Gong activists caused embarrassment to the SAR. She said at a Cable Television News interview:

> I feel that the existence of Falun Gong in Hong Kong makes us very embarrassed. Our country says it is illegal, but they are registered in Hong Kong. It is not helpful to relations with our neighbours. It makes it worse. The SAR has to think of ways to deal with it. I hope both sides will develop a better mutual understanding.[22]

The government initially emphasised that any groups would be allowed if they stuck to the law. As political pressure built up, there was a subtle shift of emphasis. While ruling out "fast-tracking" an anti-subversive law and introducing a new "anti-cult" legislation, Mr. Tung and his senior aides sharpened their words and warned there are limits to civil liberties. Mr. Tung said in Tokyo in March 2001, "I want you to be aware of the social unrest caused by Falun Gong in the mainland … From Hong Kong's perspective, we cannot allow our freedom and tolerance to create social unrest. We also cannot allow our freedom and tolerance to create social unrest in the mainland." Unlike the initial government line, Mr. Tung put more emphasis on the need to consider China's interests, not just the SAR's interest in the issue of Falun Gong.

The Falun Gong case has raised important issues. First, it reflected the predicament of the Chief Executive and SAR government in maintaining harmonious relations with the mainland when their interests conflicted with each other. Beijing sees the Falun Gong as a severe challenge to the leadership and a threat to stability. The high-profile presence of their activists in the SAR could be a great embarrassment, not to mention their strategic importance in influencing public opinion — through their base in Hong Kong — in Western countries. For people in Hong Kong and overseas, it is hardly surprising that the Falun Gong movement is seen as a major test case of the imaginative concept of "one country, two systems. " It will test the tolerance of Beijing and, equally importance, the resolve of the SAR leadership in safeguarding the "Hong Kong systems" in the face of direct and indirect pressure from Beijing. A fine balance has to be struck between the need to allow the lawful activities of the Falun Gong to continue and the need to minimise the political shock to the Mainand–Hong Kong relations that will inevitably emerge. Beijing's self-restraint in not to make high-profile remarks on the activities of the Falun Gong in Hong Kong has eased the pressure on the SAR government. On the other hand, the "talk but not act" tactics of the government in handling the Falun Gong has worked in managing the otherwise no-win situation. The fact the tolerance of the Falun Gong in Hong Kong has been cited as concrete example of the policy of "one country, two systems" shows a "no-win" situation can be turned into a "win-win" situation for Hong Kong and Beijing. That said, uncertainties remain as there will be spillover impact on Hong Kong if tension between the Central Government and the Falun Gong in the mainland grows. The SAR government will also come under growing pressure if the local activists step up their campaign and attempt to test the tolerance of the SAR government and the CPG.

The Li Shaomin Case

Like the Falun Gong case, the Li Shaomin saga has also emerged as a positive case of how a political crisis between Beijing and Hong Kong could be averted. Expelled to the United States after convicted of espionage charges in 2001, Dr. Li of the City University was presumably not allowed to return to Hong Kong as it is part of Chinese sovereignty. He holds a US passport. Even though he holds a valid work visa and might have a case in law, under which Hong Kong can be interpreted as "outside China," for him to be able to return to Hong Kong, it could be seen as political incorrect for the government to allow him in. It therefore came as great surprise in late July when he was allowed to re-enter Hong Kong from the US. The university's council also decided later he could resume his teaching job.

The government decision has won applauses from the community.

Known for their criticism against the Chief Executive for being too compromising towards the Central Government, the Democratic Party has hailed the move as a good sign of Hong Kong's autonomy. Regardless of whether the US government has exerted diplomatic influence in this case, the fact remains the Chinese government has turned a blind eye to the presence of a convicted spy on Chinese soil. Beijing's decision is not without cost. Some pro-China political figures and Hong Kong-based mainland legal experts have seriously challenged the legal grounds and the political rationale for allowing Dr. Li in.

Two mainland legal experts at the City University Zhu Guobin and Gu Minkang wrote in the Chinese-language *Apple Daily*: "If Hong Kong can be excluded as outside the country, is not Hong Kong becoming another sovereign? Is not 'one country, two systems' becoming 'two countries, two systems'? What is 'one country, one systems' all about" What is rule of law? We are confused."[23]

One of the sharpest attacks came from Ma Lik, a local deputy of the Chinese National People's Congress, who asked whether the government's decision amounted, in effect, to a declaration of independence for the SAR.[24] He was virtually the lone critic, however, as most of the pro-Beijing figures kept silent.

Most analysts are cautious about the implications of the Li Shaomin case in light of the unique factor of China–US diplomatic tussle. At a time when China was anxious to improve relations with the Bush administration in the US, any mishandling of the case would needlessly create frictions. But the political cost has been high. The authority of the Chinese courts has been severely undermined and its image tarnished. Some conservative figures in the pro-China camp have challenged whether fundamental principle behind the "one country, two systems" formula had been compromised for national interest in international power politics. The implications of the Li Shaomin case on Mainland–Hong Kong relations in the long run are yet to be ascertained. One clear sign is that the SAR and Beijing appear to have taken a more flexible and relaxed approach in handling politically sensitive issues. A senior Justice Department official said they have gone through the relevant laws and found none could provide a legal basis for banning the re-entry of Dr. Li.[25] By sticking to the rule of law, the government has attempted to distance itself from the intricate political and diplomatic wrangle between China and the US. On the other hand, the government has reiterated in a high-profile manner that it is not their policy to allow Hong Kong being used as a base for spying activities. The strategy of "talk tough, but act soft" has achieved the dual goals of keeping Hong Kong's autonomy and avoiding political embarrassment to the sovereign.

Press Freedom

In contrast with the aggressive tactic of Hong Kong-based Chinese officials in the propaganda war with the British sovereign before the handover, representatives of mainland bodies have exercised self-restraint over domestic Hong Kong issues after 1997. One glaring exception, however, hinged upon the sensitive question of press freedom. As government-funded public broadcaster, Radio Television Hong Kong (RTHK) came under fire in 2000 when former Taiwan envoy Cheng An-kuo defended on the air the "two-state notion" advocated by former president Lee Teng-hui. The notion was condemned by Beijing as "splittist." Pro-China forces have mounted a intensive campaign against RTHK and some of its controversial programmes.

The RTHK programme Headliner was no stranger to controversy. Its approach in handling current affairs in a satirical way has come under strong criticism in numerous occasions since the handover. One major controversy erupted in October 2001. On 13 October 2001, a segment of the programme — Superman's Special Report — poked fun at the Tung administration by linking it with the oppressive Taliban regime in Afghanistan. The Chinese-language *Ta Kung Pao* carried a letter to the editor a few days later with strong hints that the programme was anti-Tung. Mr. Tung did not react directly, but only said he did not comment on "bad-taste productions." A few days later, the China's official *People's Daily* website carried articles criticising the programme and RTHK. Publicly, mainland officials have refrained from making comment.

A related incident happened in April 2000, when a deputy head of the Central Government's Liaison Office in Hong Kong, Wang Fengchao, warned local media not to report views that advocate Taiwan independence as normal news. Media, he said, were obligated to uphold the integrity and national sovereignty of the country. Wang called for an early enactment of the anti-subversive provisions in the Basic Law. According to a senior journalist who has talked to Wang, Wang said he was ordered by the CPG to declare Beijing's stance on the issue. A veteran mainland cadre on Hong Kong policy, Wang understood well his remarks would be seen as interference with SAR affairs.

In spite of a stir in the wake of the controversy, there has been no serious damage, not to mention crisis, in Mainland–SAR relations. One important factor is that the mainland interest has been sufficiently represented by the pro-China circle in Hong Kong. Some vocal pro-China figures and leftwing media have been active in championing the viewpoint of China in public opinion battle. In some cases such as Falun Gong and role of RTHK, they are more Catholic than the Pope. As a result of which, Beijing does not have to come out often to defend its interest publicly.

Tung Chee-hwa: A Source of Friction

Under the Basic Law, the Chief Executive is elected by an Election Committee that is composed of Hong Kong residents and appointed by the Central People's Government (CPG). He or she is accountable to the CPG and the people of Hong Kong. The dual accountability of the Chief Executive has not caused any major problem on issues where the interests of Hong Kong and the CPG are concurrent. But sharp conflicts could emerge on matters that there are different opinions and standpoints. The leadership and the re-election of Mr. Tung has become a source of friction in his first term.

A prominent businessman but an unknown in political circles, Mr. Tung romped into victory in the first Chief Executive election. He defeated heavyweight competitors including tycoon Peter Woo Kwong-ching and former chief justiceYang Ti Liang by a big margin in the poll among the 400-member Selection Committee. Opinion polls conducted at that time also showed he was widely accepted by the community. He was seen as a honest person who was committed to lead Hong Kong. His honeymoon was, however, short-lived. Beginning in mid-1998, he encountered a range of economic and political troubles following the outbreak of the Asian financial turmoil and a spate of policy blunders such as the outbreak of an avian flu in late 1997. A significant drop in voter turnout in the 2000 Legislative Council elections reflected the depth of public discontent, particularly among the middle-class people. In spite of a short period of economic recovery in 2000, the economy headed towards a recession in late 2001 with negative growth. Unemployment rate hit a record high of seven per cent in April 2002. The problem of unemployment was no longer limited to low-skilled labourers, but middle and senior-level professionals. The September 11 terrorist attacks in the United States and the war at Afghanistan have dealt a severe blow to the world economy and the Hong

Kong economy. Although many people resigned to the reality that the grim external economy was largely to be blamed, they are adamant poor leadership, inefficient civil servants and bad policies have made things worse. Following the announcement of his fifth — last in the present term — policy address on October 10, there have been more public calls for him not to seek re-election. A plea made by a woman caller at a RTHK radio phone-in programme for Mr. Tung to stand down has summed up the sentiments of many people. She said:

> This year's policy speech is the best so far, particularly the accountability system. But why can't it make Hong Kong people feel confident and vibrant as we were four years ago. We Hong Kong people only want to hear one remark from the Chief Executive. (That is:) 'For the betterment of Hong Kong and Hong Kong people, I will not run for another term.' This is more practical than the accountability system.[26]

Opinion polls conducted by independent media and research bodies have also found a continuing fall in Mr. Tung's popularity. If there has been no major "down with Tung" political campaign, it is because most Hong Kong people have resigned to the reality that their voices do not count. Beijing leaders have made clear as early as the summer of 2000 that they want Mr. Tung to serve another five-year term for the sake of stability.[27] Influential tycoons including Li Ka-shing and Peter Woo Kwong-ching have leapt to give their full support. Cynics cast doubts if the support from prominent businessmen was given whole-heartedly. Some speculated that most businessmen dare not to antagonise China in view of their enormous business interest in the mainland.

Controversy surrounding the leadership and governance of Tung in the past two years has reflected a wide gap between the expectations of Hong Kong and Beijing for the SAR chief. To Hong Kong people, the Chief Executive is evaluated according to concrete results. They have given him a fail grade, not solely because of policy failures, but his style and approach of leadership. He has been sharply criticised as indecisive, incompetent and out of step with the rest of the society. Businessmen lambaste him for his lack of ideas and ability in reviving the economy. Grass roots groups attack him for as overly pro-business. Middle class residents consider him to be too conservative and too inclined to please Beijing when handling matters such as Falun Gong.

Beijing does not put all the blame of policy failures on Tung. Beijing leaders and some Tung supporters have argued the social and economic malaise was left over from the former British Hong Kong administration. There is some truth in the assertion. To Beijing, stability in the first decade after the handover is a top priority task and Tung has succeeded in securing a smooth transition. He weathered a financial crisis, maintained international confidence and dissipated local jitters about "one country, two systems." Judging from remarks made by Premier Zhu Rongji about the problem of governance in Hong Kong, it is plausible that Beijing is also concerned about the leadership style of Tung.[28] But given five more years, top leaders are confident Mr. Tung will be able to lead Hong Kong out of doldrums.

Remarks made by Chinese leaders as the second CE election drew near indicated Beijing did not want a genuine competition for the top post. On the other hand, Beijing leaders have attempted to be sympathetic towards the feelings of discontent in the society. President Jiang Zemin spoke to reporters before meeting with Mr. Tung in December 2001, "I noted that he (Tung) has made some self-criticism in his speech.. No one is perfect. We found Mr. Tung is good on the whole." Jiang gave his backing for Mr. Tung to seek re-election. Mr. Jiang was referring to self-confession made by Mr. Tung on the deficiencies in his governance in the past five years on December 13, 2001, when he formally declared his candidacy for the second CE election.[29] Beijing's strong support has made no impact in one way or another on the popularity of Mr. Tung. Pro-democracy leaders have severely criticised Beijing for meddling with the internal affairs of Hong Kong by making high-profile comment on the candidature of Mr. Tung. But the community has seemingly accepted the political reality that the blessing of Beijing is vitally important to the future CE. Whether that was explicitly declared in open makes no difference.

While public ratings of Mr. Tung's performance in social policies were low, the community generally agreed that he plays an important role in strengthening closer economic ties with the mainland. Top Beijing leaders have also pledged to do everything it could to help revive Hong Kong's economy. By opening up more opportunities for businesses and professionals, Beijing is hoping that it would improve Hong Kong's economy and ease the political pressure on Tung.

Judging from Mr. Jiang's reference to Mr. Tung's confession of deficiencies, it is plausible that Beijing has shared some of the criticism against Mr. Tung. But overall speaking, Beijing leaders firmly believe Mr. Tung is still the best person for the top job in the first ten years of the SAR. They also fully endorsed the broad direction of Mr. Tung's policies. They include full-speed integration with the mainland economy and Pearl River Delta region, a conservative approach in dealing with democracy aspirations and dissident views and a sensitive touch on matters that hinged upon the interest of "one country." Equally important, Beijing sees the CE as an institutional authority with legitimacy coming from the central government through a process of appointment. Fierce opposition against the CE could be construed as an affront to the authority of the Central Government. With no sign of early recovery of the economy, public approval rate of Mr. Tung is likely to stay at a low point. Any major policy blunder or political scandal at the SAR leadership in the next five years might trigger a political crisis on the authority of Mr. Tung. If that happens, the political relations between the mainland and the SAR will be drastically upset.

Right of Abode Saga

The "right of abode" case in 1999 has posed the most severe challenge to Mainland–Hong Kong relations. In late 1999, the Court of Final Appeal (CFA) declared some provisions in an immigration ordinance unconstitutional and ruled children born out of wedlock in the mainland were entitled the right of residency in Hong Kong. The CFA also asserted its power to review the constitutionality of laws passed by the Chinese National People's Congress Standing Committee (NPCSC). A NPCSC spokesman said in a statement the ruling was not in line with the Basic Law, but stopped short of telling the government what to do. Claiming a possible influx of 1.67 million mainland people to Hong Kong as a result of the ruling, the government asked the NPCSC to interpret two relevant sections of Article 23 in the Basic Law. An NPCSC resolution overturned the judgment. SAR officials reiterated they took the initiative to ask for assistance from the NPCSC, who was unwilling to do so.

The community appears to be convinced that Beijing did not want to get involved. Critics fingered at the government for "inviting interference" by the Chinese legislature with a case about permanent residency that clearly falls within the autonomous powers of the SAR courts. Pro-democracy politicians and legal experts have repeatedly pressed the government for an assurance that they would never take similar measures again in future. The government has refused to do so.

A further challenge took place in 2000 when the CFA ruled a separate case concerning another provision in the article on permanent residency.

The Court reaffirmed its stance that it has jurisdictions over the provision. This time, the NPCSC has reacted more cautiously and did not indicate further action. Meanwhile, the government indicated it has no intention to seek another NPCSC interpretation. A constitutional crisis had never happened.

In spite of the potential damage to Hong Kong's judicial autonomy, the majority of the community has indicated their support for the Central Government's position on the right of abode case. Many people praised Beijing for making the right decision in the overall interest of Hong Kong. As Hong Kong was facing a severe economic downturn, a mass influx of mainland migrants would worsen unemployment. Rightly or wrong, some people have stigmatised mainland migrants as low-skilled people who might have to rely on government welfare payment after they are allowed to stay.

By reiterating its initiative of seeking an NPCSC interpretation move, the government has effectively eased the political fallout over the sensitive issue of Beijing interference — though at a huge political cost. Critics have lambasted the Tung leadership of giving up the SAR's autonomy on their own. Some legal experts have pointed out the more appropriate solution was to amend Article 24 in the Basic Law. But in light of the Chinese opposition to an early amendment of the Basic Law, the government dares not to confront with the central authorities on the issue. By doing so, it has averted a constitutional and political crisis.

External and Foreign Affairs

Hong Kong thrives on its unique status as an international city that is different from other parts of China. Although the Basic Law stipulates that foreign affairs should be handled by the CPG, it provides autonomous powers to the SAR in dealing with a wide range of external affairs. Hong Kong is also able to maintain its own identity in some international organisations either as a non-sovereign member or as part of the Chinese delegation. In real world issues, the SAR has been given more flexibility in handling matters that have sensitive implications on China's foreign policy. These matters could have caused frictions in Mainland–SAR relations if they had not been handled with political skills.

In July 1999, the Central Government blocked a proposed papal visit to Hong Kong on grounds that they considered it as visit by the head of state rather than one by a religious leader. Tung commented in August that it was "unfortunate" that the Pope could not visit Hong Kong because of foreign policy concerns. China has no official ties with Vatican. Meanwhile, Hong Kong church has been allowed to maintain ties with Vatican and contacts with underground churches on the mainland. Local church was caught in the middle when Beijing and the Vatican were locked in a row over the latter's decision to cannonise 120 Chinese and foreign missionaries killed in China during the Boxer Rebellion in the early 20th century. Local churches went ahead with its celebrations after being advised by mainland officials in Hong Kong to keep a "low profile." In 2001, church leaders said the incident was over and their relations with the mainland have improved.

A public auction of two Chinese antiques looted by Western imperial troops during the Boxer Rebellion in Hong Kong in 1999 has caused more than a stir in the community. Some pro-China figures have condemned the move by a private auction company. They called on the government to intervene on grounds that auctioning of national relics constituted "foreign affairs." Mainland officials in charge of cultural relics also said in public the auction was inappropriate. The State Council's Hong Kong and Macau Affairs Office and Foreign Ministry have kept silent and did not exert pressure on the SAR government. The government has decided not to intervene. The two pieces of relics were later purchased by bidders representing mainland companies, resulting in a win-win situation for both the SAR and Beijing.

Hong Kong's engagement with the outside world has always been a hyper-sensitive issue in light of Beijing's sensitivity about sovereignty. Many issues could easily be raised to the high plane of sovereignty. The fact that they had not indicates both the Chinese and SAR governments are conscious of the need to be flexible, pragmatic and to avoid "pan-politicisation" in dealing with practical issues.

Economic Integration

The most drastic change in Mainland–Hong Kong relations after the handover took place in the economic arena. The 1998 financial turmoil and the sharp fall of property prices dealt a severe blow to the economy of Hong Kong. Following the downturn in the US economy in 2000 and the terrorist attacks in the US on September 11, 2001, the Hong Kong economy faces the worst crisis for decades. Against the background of the worst economic circumstances in decades, calls were looming for Hong

Kong to fully embrace the mainland economy. Recommendations are abound. Among others, some say border crossing should be opened 24 hours a day. Infrastructure links between Hong Kong and the neighbouring Pearl River Delta region should be greatly boosted. Mainland talents and investors should be lured to come to Hong Kong. Restrictions for mainland visitors should be lifted. The government should take the lead to explore investment opportunities for Hong Kong businesses in the mainland. In short, people from various sectors agree a full integration with the mainland economy is the only way forward for Hong Kong.

Before 1997, the mainland had been largely portrayed as poor and backward. The pace of changes in the past few years has shocked many people. The Chinese economy has defied unfavourable external environments in the past few years and managed to grow at a rapid pace. After years of negotiation, it formally acceded to the World Trade Organisation in late 2001. The country's overall political and diplomatic strengths have grown. 2001 will also be remembered as a watershed year with the successful bid by Beijing to host the 2008 Olympics and the national football team's victory in the 2002 World Cup Qualifier. Under such circumstances, public perception of China has changed. The image of China has become more complex, with both positive and negative signs of development. Even though most of the inland provinces remain poor, several coastal and major cities such as Shanghai, Guangdong and Beijing are narrowing their gap with Hong Kong. Some economists and businessmen predicted Shanghai would be able to catch up with Hong Kong in ten years. Others are less sanguine and estimate it might take two to three decades. The bid by Shanghai for a Disney theme park in the metropolis earlier has deepened fears that Shanghai — not Singapore — would be the major competitor for Hong Kong for the premier status in the mainland.

Hong Kong served a pivotal role in China's modernisations since 1979. Its importance as a direct and indirect investor, a trade intermediary and a window for mainland firms increased in the past two decades even as China opened its door wider to the world. Even though China's economy is expected to grow much faster after its entry into the WTO, many economists and businessmen are adamant Hong Kong still has a unique role in the post-WTO Chinese economy. But the need for a major adjustment is also seen as a must. Speaking at a press conference held at the end of the annual National People's Congress plenum in March 2002, Premier Zhu Rongji spoke positively about Hong Kong's contribution to the mainland economy in the past decades. He emphasised, however, there is a need for Hong Kong to adjust its role. The Central Government, he said, could give fully support if need be.

The economic vitality of Hong Kong has been one of the basic considerations behind the guiding principle of keeping Hong Kong's prosperity and stability for China's modernisations. Late patriach Deng Xiaoping, for instance, urged the building of more "Hong Kongs" in the mainland. With the drastic restrucuturing of the Hong Kong economy and the rapid growth of a more diversified mainland economy, the economic relations between the two places are heading for major changes in the next five to ten years.

The "double dip" and the major restructuring in the Hong Kong economy have made tremendous impact on the mind-set of people. With the bursting of the bubbles of property-dominated economy and the disillusionment of technology-led new economy, Hong Kong people are looking towards the booming mainland economy for hope and opportunities. A sense of dependency on mainland support to bring the SAR out of recession grew. Instead of advising Beijing to stay away from Hong Kong affairs, people are asking for all sorts of assistance and favours from Beijing to help enliven the Hong Kong economy. In July 2001, Chief Secretary for Administration Donald Tsang has led a high-level business delegation to tour the less-developed Western region. In October 2001, Financial Secretary Antony Leung took another delegation of businessmen and professionals to attend business conferences in Beijing. The new "Tsang–Leung" team, formed after Anson Chan quit in May 2001, has since then given top priority to the issue of Hong Kong–Guangdong economic cooperation. Secretary for Justice Elsie Leung, whose primary duty is to advise the government on legal matters, has strongly lobbied for new opportunities for the legal profession in China's legal development such as arbitration in the post-WTO era. A policy tilt towards greater integration with the mainland has become more obvious since the year 2000.

Speaking at the end of a six-monthly meeting of the Hong Kong–Guangdong Economic Cooperation Conference in early 2002, Mr. Tsang envisaged a fuller and speedier integration of the Hong Kong economy with the Pearl River Delta region. Some business leaders and economists envisioned the emergence of two economic powerhouses in the mainland in the long-run — one will be the Pearl River Delta region with Hong Kong as the dragonhead and the other will be the Yangtze River Delta region with Shanghai as the engine of growth. A fuller picture of the Hong Kong economy in the post-WTO Chinese economy remains unclear. Suffice to say that the greater economic integration is set to bring about drastic changes in the Hong Kong economy and lifestyles, the economic relations as well as the wider relationships between the mainland and the SAR.

Conclusion

As Hong Kong people took comfort from the fact that Beijing had not overtly interfered with the SAR's internal affairs, they found themselves at a loss about their new identity and relations with the mainland. On one hand, the Basic Law provides a buffer that separates the two systems. To a certain extent, some existing policies such as border control and mainland visits have separated the two peoples. In spite of the rapid changes in the mainland in the past two decades, the political, legal and administrative systems between the two places remain sharply different and separate. But on the other hand, the economic interactions between the two places have grown and economic forces have pulled the two peoples closer. Tens of thousands of people flocked to the neighbouring cities such as Shenzhen for playing golf and shopping during long weekends. Many have bought a second home in the region for leisure or investment. In a nutshell, the Hong Kong economy and the whole society are at the threshold of a new phase of integration with the mainland.

An article published in the China-watching magazine Mirror Monthly in October 2001 said: "More and more people began to understand that it is imperative to keep the two systems in political, legal and administrative areas separate. But in the areas of economic cooperation and trade, it's better for the two sides to strengthen division of labour and cooperation, coordination, provide mutual support and avoid negative competition. This will be good for both sides."

The line between separation and integration cannot be clearly delineated. This is particular the case for the international community. Perception is reality. US Consul General in Hong Kong Michael Klosson has cautioned that although the desire of Hong Kong business to tap even further its hinterland on the mainland as a new source of economic growth is understandable, some of these initiatives will take Hong Kong — and the "one country, two systems" relationship — into new territory. He cited as a case in point a proposal to speed border crossings by placing Hong Kong and mainland customs and immigration officials under one roof. Mr.

Klosson said such arrangement will raise hard questions about jurisdiction and the relationship between the two separate legal systems. He said border streamlining and the CEPA talks pointed to the fundamental dilemma Hong Kong is facing: how to strike the proper balance between deeper economic interdependence with mainland China and maintaining Hong Kong's political, cultural and economic distinctiveness. He said Hong Kong needs to avoid create international perceptions that Hong Kong has become just another city to China.[30] The separation versus integration debate will continue to be major topic among elites in the political, business, academic circles and foreign community. As politics and economics are mingled with cultural affinity and patriotic feelings, the debate on Hong Kong's uniqueness and integration will be divisive and, at times, emotional.

In her farewell speech at an Asia Society lunch held on April 19, 2001, Anson Chan has attached greater importance for Hong Kong to maintain a separate and unique identity. She said:

> I have become increasingly concerned since the Handover that too many Hong Kong people have become more inward looking. Understandably perhaps, they have looked towards the mainland at the expense of our traditional links with the rest of the world. Some are so concerned about integration that they seem to forget that our strength lies in the separation which is fundamental to the success of One Country Two Systems — not just for Hong Kong, but for China as well. By contrast, I have watched with admiration as the mainland has increased its outreach to the international community.[31]

Critics cited the spread of the so-called "culture of subservience" as evidenced from the University of Hong Kong polling saga as a case of a worsening trend of Hong Kong getting more like the mainland.[32]

With clear emphasis on the "one country" notion, Mr. Tung has underlined the utmost importance for Hong Kong to strengthen ties with the mainland. He said in his Policy Address on 10 October 2001:

> Following comparative studies, the Commission on Strategic Development has clearly set out Hong Kong's positioning as a window on the world for the mainland, a major city in China and Asia's world city excelling in high value-added services.
>
> ... Hong Kong's future development hinges on the economic growth momentum in the mainland ... Enhancing co-operation with the Pearl River Delta (PRD) is of particular importance. Over the past two decades, Hong Kong and the PRD have complemented each other, and together developed into a highly

> productive economic region. With a population of 40 million and many affluent consumers in a number of cities, the PRD is an enormously attractive market. Following China's accession to the World Trade Organisation, cooperation between Hong Kong and Guangdong will rise to new heights. The government is determined to actively promote economic co-operation between Hong Kong and the PRD region with a view to achieving a 'win-win' situation[33]

Few people disagreed with the strategy of strengthening economic relations with the mainland. Given Hong Kong's proximity to China, the government is under strong pressure for it to ensure Hong Kong businessmen will benefit from a more open and vibrant Chinese economy. The old strategy and mindset of keeping a buffer between Hong Kong and the mainland under the grand design of "one country, two systems" face severe challenge under the new economic and political environments. Greater economic integration between the mainland and Hong Kong has been seen as an irresistible trend and, perhaps, the only way out. At issue is a question of striking a balance between separation and integration. Shocked and rocked by the sharp deterioration of the economy, Hong Kong people are undergoing a period of psychological trauma. Their self-confidence in the superiority of Hong Kong people, the Hong Kong systems and ways of doing things has been eroded, if there is any at all. Seeping through the society has been a deep feeling of doomsday pessimism. This is in stark contrast with the "get-up-and-go" spirit in some Chinese cities such as Shanghai and Shenzhen. Fears that Hong Kong is slipping from the international competitive ladder have never been so intense in the past decades. Optimistic remarks made by SAR leaders such as Donald Tsang that "Hong Kong, once again, will win the day" have been seen by cynics as whistles in the dark.[34] Opinion polls show more people are worried about the competition from mainland cities.

With fears about Chinese interference largely dissipated, the worries of marginalisation of the Hong Kong economy under a broader picture of a rising China have loomed. This has brought about tremendous impact on the set minds of the SAR elites and the society as a whole. There have been more soul-searching and public debate about the long-term positioning of Hong Kong in the past two years. More people have changed their set minds and taken a more realistic view about mainland China. The issue of positioning hinges upon the fundamental question of how Hong Kong people and the society as a whole relate themselves to the developments of China under the parameters of "one country, two systems." Mooted in more than two decades ago as a long-term solution to solve the question of

Taiwan, the policy has created both constraints and opportunities for the SAR and the mainland. Mr. Tung should be given credit for his effort to give new impetus to greater economic integration across the border in the past five years. But on the other hand, he has been increasingly seen more as the representative of the interest of Central Government instead of the interest of Hong Kong people. His values, set minds and style of governance have been seen as "too Chinese." Fairly or not, the Tung complex has deepened the perception among some quarters in the society that Hong Kong is heading towards a trend of "Mainlandisation." To them, Hong Kong is more like China while China is more like Hong Kong. There are growing fears, particularly among Western-minded middle class professionals, that Hong Kong is losing its unique characteristics and values under the reign of Mr. Tung.

Events and developments since the handover have shed light on the real-life problems and challenges when the two systems are interacted under the tenet of "one country." Regardless of the mode of economic interdependence in the post-WTO era, economic dynamism is set to bring about even more drastic changes in the Mainland–SAR relations. On the political front, the ruling Chinese Communist Party is bracing for leadership change at the party plenum in autumn 2002. Whether the fourth generational leadership will speed up the process of political liberalisation remains unclear. Even though Beijing's policy towards Hong Kong has been laid down in the Basic Law, a more liberal approach and relaxed attitude among the new communist leaders on Hong Kong affairs could make much difference in how the principle of "one country, two systems" is applied in real-life issues and Hong Kong–Mainland relations are defined and re-defined. On the societal level, the process of interactions between the two societies at all levels is set to grow wider and deeper. The rapid changes in the political, economic and socio-cultural spheres will take the Hong Kong–Mainland relationship to a new phase in the next five years.

Notes

1. *South China Morning Post*, 5 September 2001.
2. *South China Morning Post*, 6 September 2001.
3. See "Hong Kong Residents Experience of and for Aspirations of Taking Up Residence in the mainland of China," Planning Department, Hong Kong Government, December 2001, www.info.gov.hk.

4. *South China Morning Post*, 1 October 2001.
5. See "Winter of Despair," Hong Kong Transition Project, December 2001, www.hkbu.edu.hk/~hktp.
6. *South China Morning Post*, 22 April 2002.
7. *Ming Pao*, 4 April 2002.
8. See "The Hong Kong Policy of the People's Republic of China, 1949–1997, " Lau Siu-kai, *Journal of Contemporary China* (2000) 9 (23), 77–93. See also "Hong Kong Under One Country Two Systems: Promises and Realities," Brookings Working Paper, 2000-01, Chris Yeung, Brookings Institution. The paper is available at www.brookings.edu.
9. Xiao Weiyun (ed.), *One Country Two Systems and the Basic Law of Hong Kong Special Administrative Region* (Hong Kong: Hong Kong Culture and Education Publishing Company, 1990).
10. *Hong Kong Economic Journal*, 16 March 2002.
11. Chris Yeung (ed.), *Beijing's Hong Kong Policy In the First Year of Transition, Hong Kong China: The Red Dawn* (Sydney: Prentice Hall, 1998).
12. Xiao Weiyun (ed.), *One Country Two Systems and the Basic Law of Hong Kong Special Administrative Region* (Hong Kong: Hong Kong Culture and Education Publishing Company, 1990).
13. Ibid.
14. Article 23 of the Basic Law says, "The Hong Kong Special Administrative Region shall enact laws on its own to prohibit any act of treason, secession, sedition, subversion against the Central People's Government, or theft of state secrets, to prohibit foreign political organizations or bodies from conducting political activities in the Region, and to prohibit political organizations or bodies of the Region from establishing ties with foreign political organizations or bodies."
15. *South China Morning Post*, 28 February 2002.
16. The Chief Executive's Policy Address, October 1997.
17. Speech given by Chief Secretary Donald Tsang at American Chamber of Commerce, 15 October 2001. Text is available at www.info.gov.hk.
18. *South China Morning Post*, 4 April 2002.
19. *South China Morning Post*, 18 August 2000.
20. *South China Morning Post*, 20 April 2002.
21. *South China Morning Post*, 4 January 2000.
22. *Sunday Morning Post*, 4 February 2001.
23. *South China Morning Post*, 5 August 2001.
24. Ibid.
25. Based on the author's own interview with officials.
26. *Sunday Morning Post*, 21 October 2001.
27. *South China Morning Post*, 22 September 2001.
28. *South China Morning Post*, 5 September 2001.

29. *South China Morning Post*, 20 December 2001.
30. "1997 Plus 5," US Policy towards Hong Kong Today, remarks by US Consul General Michael Klosson to the Hong Kong Association of New York, New York, 16 April 2002. Speech is available at www.usconsulate.org.hk.
31. *South China Morning Post*, 20 April 2001.
32. See Sin-ming Shaw "Back to a Culture of Subservience," *South China Morning Post*, 27 August 2000.
33. The Chief Executive's Policy Address, 10 October 2001.
34. *Asiaweek*, 2 November 2001.

11

Civil Service Reform in the Hong Kong SAR

John P. Burns*

Professor of Politics and Public Administration
The University of Hong Kong

Introduction

During the 1990s the Hong Kong government initiated major reforms of the civil service on at least two occasions (1995 and 1999). During the intervening years public sector reforms of various kinds such as the Finance Branch (now Bureau)-initiated reforms of 1989, the establishment of the Hospital Authority in 1990, and the Enhanced Productivity Programme (EPP) in1998 have also impacted the civil service (See Lee and Cheung 1995). In the 1990s government-initiated civil service reform followed periods of economic decline during which the business community pressed government to cut public expenditure. Still, civil service reforms in Hong Kong have been piecemeal and have left the traditional civil service system largely intact. Absent have been the thorough and searching reviews that characterized reform movements in many countries overseas, such as Australia, Canada, New Zealand, the UK and the USA or, indeed, the rest of China (See Lane 1997).

Context

In April 2001 the Hong Kong civil service numbered about 180,000 people

* The author is grateful to Ian Scott for comments on an earlier draft of this paper and suggestions for revision and to the UGC Research Grants Council for its support.

(Civil Service Bureau [CSB] 2001c: 6) organized into approximately 400 different occupational grades. Of these, less than one per cent were directorate officers, about two per cent were senior management/ professional officers, and 21 per cent held junior or middle manager/ professional positions (CSB 2001c: 7). The civil service employed about 2.7 per cent of the population or 5.3 per cent of the total labor force, was relatively young (nearly half of all civil servants were under the age of 40) and mostly local (officers on overseas terms of service still held 8.7 per cent of directorate positions in 2001, however) (CSB 2001c: 7). Women held about a third of all civil service positions, concentrated largely in lower ranking jobs. Still, women made up about half of the HKSAR's elite 530-strong Administrative Officer grade. By 1998, civil servants had established more than 200 staff associations or unions. The government estimates that about 70 per cent of civil servants belong to such associations. The government has pledged to consult civil servants through these associations before making any "considerable change in conditions of service which affects a substantial part of the service as a whole" (CSB 1998).

Hong Kong's centralized pay and benefits system places most civil servants on one of eleven uniform pay scales, the largest of which, the Master Pay Scale (MPS), covers more than 60 per cent of the civil service. Pay scales are set centrally and adjusted annually based on an official pay trend survey. Pay level surveys are rarely carried out (the last one was in 1986 for the government as a whole). In 2000–01 pay and other personnel related expenses for the civil service accounted for about 34.5 per cent of recurrent expenditure (CSB 2001c: 37). Personnel costs of subvented organizations took another 34.7 per cent of recurrent expenditure (*SCMP* 11 December 2001), so that personnel costs of all public bodies supported by the government accounted for nearly 70 per cent of total recurrent expenditure.

The Chief Secretary for Administration heads the civil service. Together with the Chief Executive, he and the other 26 principal officials identified in the Basic Law (Article 48), all appointed by the central government in Beijing (Basic Law, Articles 45 and 48),[1] lead the executive branch. That is, neither the people of Hong Kong nor the legislature plays any significant role in the selection of the government (Scott 2000; Ghai 1999).[2] However, the people do elect by universal suffrage 24 members of a 60-member Legislative Council. Another 30 members are returned by functional constituencies that represent employers, labor, and professional groups and that could have as few as 100 electors. Because their support is constitutionally required to pass bills in the legislature (Basic Law, Annex II, Section II), these groups which represent narrow sectional mostly business interests exercise substantial veto power. An additional six members are currently selected by an 800-member Election Committee, a practice that will cease in 2004 when the number of elected non-functional constituency members will increase to 30 (Basic Law, Annex II, Section I (1)). Hong Kong's constitution, then, while providing for a separation of powers system (See Ghai 1999: 262–64), weakens the legislature to accommodate "executive-led government" or rule by the bureaucratic elite.

Popular perceptions of the performance of the Hong Kong government have varied over the years, to a certain extent with the performance of the economy (See Figure 1). Thus, when growth of GDP rose from 1996 to 1997 so too did satisfaction with the performance of government and when GDP fell from 1993 to 1996, so too did satisfaction with government performance (See Figure 2). The Asian financial crisis, however, hit Hong Kong hard beginning in late 1997. The economy contracted by more than five per cent, unemployment rose to historic highs of over six per cent,

Figure 1. Growth of GDP, 1983–2001

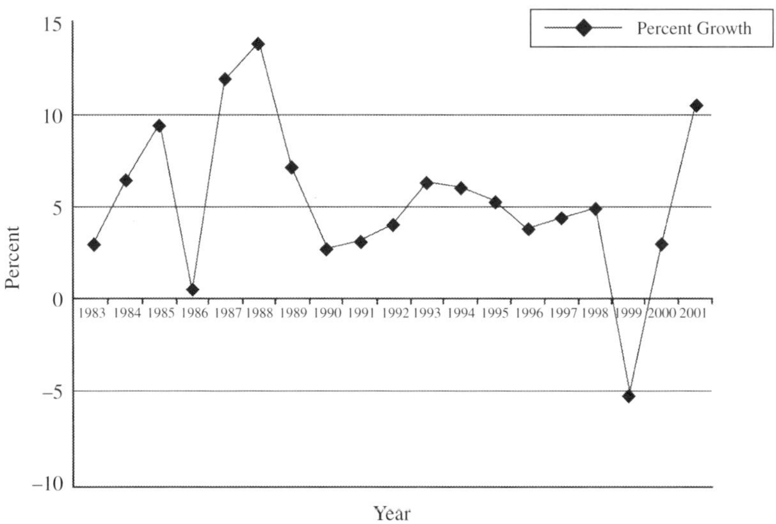

Source: Hong Kong Government (various years), *Hong Kong Report* (Hong Kong: Government Printer).

Figure 2. Perceptions of Hong Kong Government Performance, 1993–2001

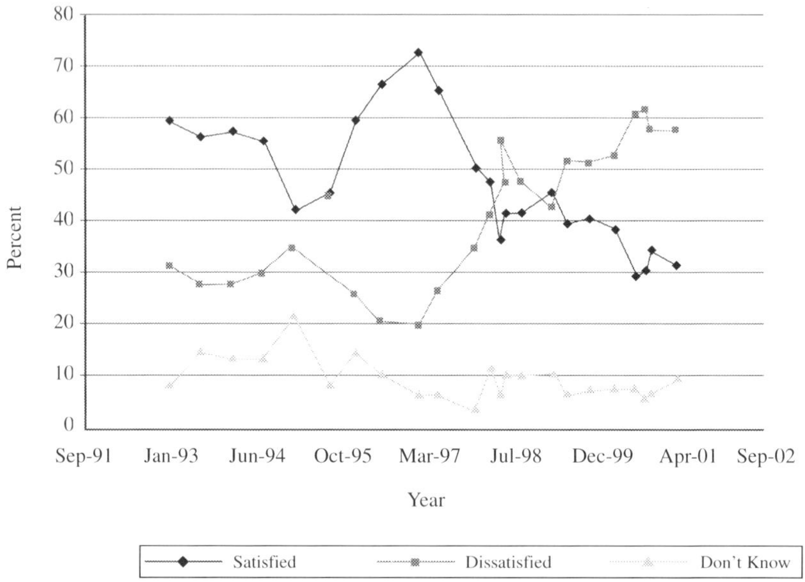

Source: The Hong Kong Transition Project (2001), "Becoming China: the Public State of Mind on Hong Kong's Integration with the Mainland" Hong Kong: Hong Kong Baptist University, p. 17.

employers froze or cut wages, and prices fell. Indeed, by the end of 2001, Hong Kong had witnessed 35 months of continuous deflation. Hong Kong's property price bubble burst, and by 2001 property prices had fallen by about 60 per cent over their 1997 peak levels. The economic bad times have been accompanied by growing dissatisfaction with the performance of the government.

In addition to Hong Kong's poor economy government policy blunders have driven satisfaction levels down. The media and government itself have revealed examples of serious misconduct, dereliction of duty, failure to take responsibility, and corruption. First, the chaotic opening of Hong Kong's new International Airport in July 1998 prompted three investigations (one each by a Legislative Council Select Committee, a Commission of Inquiry appointed by the Chief Executive, and the Ombudsman). The Legco Select Committee concluded that the Chief Secretary for Administration Anson Chan Fang On-sang, who chaired the Airport Development Steering Committee [ADSC], should "shoulder special personal responsibility" for the chaotic opening, that she failed to ensure that all signs of risk were considered, and that she failed to lead the ADSC in assessing the readiness for the opening (Report 1999: 187; *SCMP* 28 January 1999). The Select Committee also criticized the Secretary for Works Kwong Hon-sang for misleading the ADSC and failing as a professional advisor (Report 1999: 189–90). Further, Legco criticized directors of the New Airport Project Coordinating Office for failing to act as the government's watchdog, "dangerously misunderstanding the situation" and having little appreciation of their duties (Report 1999: 192–96; *SCMP* 28 January 1999). Although the Chief Executive apologized to the people of Hong Kong, he concluded that there was "no *prima facie* evidence to support disciplinary action against any of the officers concerned since there was clearly no question of misconduct." "The officers concerned," he said, "have all acted in good faith and performed their duties with due diligence" (*SCMP* 28 January 1999 and Economic Services Bureau et al. 1999). According to Lee, Hong Kong's system of rule by generalists was a source of the problems. The relevant bodies "were dominated by AOs who were generalists by training … As amateurs to information technology they could only defer to the experts … They were also not sensitive to the technical implications of certain actions" (Lee 2000). As a result, they were unable to exercise their duty to supervise the technical work.

In 1998 and 1999 as the economy deteriorated and many people lost their jobs, the media and the Director of Audit revealed that government workers, especially cleaners and other blue collar workers were failing to do their jobs properly, a situation civil service managers appeared to tolerate. According to one account, night-shift drain cleaners regularly pumped tap water into their tanks to make up their daily quota and spent the rest of the time playing cards or sleeping, returning to the office the following morning to sign the log book (*SCMP* 5 May 1999). Workers drove the trucks around the streets to "make up the mileage" and actually cleaned drains only once a week rather than nightly as required, a practice that had become the norm (*SCMP* 5 May 1999). Many other cases of government workers shirking their duties were revealed by the Director of Audit or reported in the media (see *Wenhui bao* 19 November and 4 December 1998).

In 1999 and 2000 public housing scandals further tarnished the government's reputation. In 1999 the Housing Department revealed that it had discovered that nearly completed public housing blocks in Shatin had been built on short piles that rendered them unsafe. As a result the government was forced to demolish two new 31-story blocks of Home Ownership Scheme flats at a cost of $258 million (*SCMP* 17 March 2000). Short piles in other sites were also revealed. On 9 January 2000 the ICAC charged with corruption three government officials and five employees of construction companies who had tried to cover up the scandals, and at least one very large contractor (Zen Pacific) was banned from participating in public housing projects (*SCMP* 10 January 2000). After an inquiry set up by the Housing Department cleared the heads of the Housing Authority and the Housing Department of blame in the incident, Legco members demanded that they resign (*SCMP* 26 May 2000). Thousands of people protested in public demonstrations in late June over the public housing scandal and unpopular government policies (*SCMP* 26 June 2000). In an unprecedented vote on 28 June 2000 Legco censured both officials (*SCMP* 29 June 2000). In the event the Chair of the Housing Authority, Rosanna Wong Yick-ming (an Executive Councillor) resigned just before the censure vote (*SCMP* 25 June 2000). Amid much criticism the Head of the Housing Department, Tony Miller, a career civil servant, refused to resign, a decision strongly supported by the Chief Executive (*SCMP* 29 June 2000). The entire episode promoted renewed calls to strengthen the mechanisms to make the government more accountable. A month later, the Chief Executive revealed in newspaper interviews that his much-publicized policy goal of providing 85,000 housing units per year, announced in 1997, had been abandoned in 1998 (*SCMP* 1 July 2000). Housing officials apparently knew nothing of the change. Housing policy in 1999–2000 appeared to be in complete disarray.

The government's reputation received a further blow when on 24 August 2000 immigration officers at the Lo Wu border crossing with Shenzhen permitted a 15-year old autistic Hong Kong boy with a mental age of two to run through the border control point without stopping him. When he was returned to Hong Kong by Shenzhen immigration officials a short time later, HKSAR immigration officials held him for several hours and then returned him to Shenzhen as an illegal immigrant before his identity could be correctly established. A massive manhunt in Shenzhen has failed to find him (See Immigration Department 2000).

An Immigration Department official inquiry criticized staff for "failing to perform their duty" and "failing to follow the rules." Those who sent Yu Man-hon back to Shenzhen, the inquiry concluded, should be "held responsible for that decision." The report criticized the immigration officers concerned for their lack of "common sense, awareness, sensitivity and alertness" (Immigration Department 2000: 24, 25, 30, 31; *SCMP* 22 September 2000). As a result three immigration staff faced punishment for unprofessional behavior and negligence. An inquiry by the Ombudsman also concluded that the officers mishandled the case (*SCMP* 18 July 2001). To the disbelief of many in Hong Kong, however, Civil Service Bureau findings directly contradicted the department's report. The CSB concluded that the charges of unprofessional behavior and negligence "could not be substantiated" and the officers escaped punishment (*SCMP* 18 and 28 July 2001).

These incidents, coupled with the declining economy, put pressure on the government. The government responded in part with further reform of the civil service. Like governments overseas, the Hong Kong government initiated civil service reform during periods of economic decline. During the 1990s, the growth of gross domestic product fell in 1988–90, 1993–96, and 1998–99 and during these periods government attempted to reform the civil service.

The Reforms

During the 1990s civil service reform in Hong Kong included improving accountability, decentralization, centralization, simplification, downsizing, and managerialism. We will examine each of these areas in turn.

Improving Accountability

In his 2000 Policy Address, the Chief Executive acknowledged that Hong Kong's system of "executive accountability" needed to be improved (Tung 2000). The proposed reforms, outlined in brief a year later, have not, however, addressed the core problem which is the disarticulation of Hong Kong's political system.

The Basic Law requires the Chief Executive to be accountable to the central government and to the HKSAR (Article 19). The Basic Law does not say to whom the Chief Executive should be accountable in the HKSAR, but rather that he/she should be accountable to the HKSAR *as a whole*, a vagueness that seriously undermines accountability. Article 64 requires the HKSAR government to be accountable to Legco. From the Basic Law we are led to believe that accountability includes but is not necessarily limited to implementing the laws passed by Legco, presenting regular policy addresses to Legco, answering questions raised by members of Legco, and obtaining approval from Legco for taxation and public expenditure measures (Article 64).

During the first months of the new HKSAR's existence conservative members of the then Provisional Legislative Council fought to limit Legco's role to hold the government accountable. In July 1997 Provisional Legco member Leung Chun-ying sought to limit the role of Legco panels to question government officials. Leung argued: "Many panels and regular meetings are unnecessary. Panels should not question government officials or seek data or clarifications. Government should brief panels and solicit Legco's support…." Denying panels the right to question government officials would have stripped them of one of their few levers to hold the civil service accountable. Fellow panel member Selina Chow replied for other members that "We must effectively carry out our monitoring duties. Panels are not "rubber stamps" (Minutes of a Meeting of the Provisional Legco Joint Panel on Housing and Planning, Lands and Works, 24 July 1997). In the event she was supported by most other Legco members and a more activist role for Legco won the day.

Still, Legco's ability to hold the government accountable and to represent the people's interests is severely restricted, first, by the constitutional requirement that a majority of functional constituency representatives must approve all legislation; second, by draconian restrictions placed on the introduction of private members' bills;[3] and third, by the disarticulation of the political system that fails to provide a role for Legco or the citizens of Hong Kong in the formation of the government (Scott 2000).

Dissatisfaction with the mechanisms for holding the government politically accountable has grown in Hong Kong (See *SCMP* 13 January 2000). Examples such as the chaotic airport opening, discussed above, convinced many that in the absence of a democratic system where top officials are held politically accountable by institutional mechanisms such as elections, officials can escape responsibility especially where lines of responsibility are diffused and ambiguous, a common enough situation (Lee 2000: 70–71). Politicians, academics, and the media have suggested remedies, such as the introduction of a "ministerial system" or other new systems of accountability (*SCMP* 8 August 1998; 30 June and 23 October 2000). After several years of denying that there was a problem,[4] the Chief Executive in his October 2000 Policy Address changed tack and announced that the government would study ways to improve the system of "executive accountability" (Tung 2000: 37). In April 2002 the government announced that from July 2002 most principal officials would be appointed on new contract terms different from the civil service (Tung 2002). The new posts would cover the three top secretaries (Chief Secretary for Administration, Financial Secretary, and Secretary for Justice) and the directors of eleven bureaus, downsized through mergers from 16 bureaus as part of the reforms. According to the plans, the Chief Executive would nominate candidates for these positions from either inside or outside the civil service for appointment by the central government. The appointments would be made on non-civil service contracts different from those in the civil service and would not exceed the term of office of the Chief Executive who appointed them (Constitutional Affairs Bureau 2002). At least theoretically, the new politically appointed principal officials could more easily be removed from office than civil servants to take responsibility for policy blunders.

The new changes do not provide for any popular or Legco participation in the formation of the government, nor do they address the issue of the direct election of the Chief Executive. They may strengthen the hand of the Chief Executive, however, to manage the civil service. The reform builds on current and past practice which provides for non-civil servants to hold the top jobs. In 2001 two of the three top Secretaries were non-civil servants brought into government by the Chief Executive. The Secretary for Health and Welfare, a former Chair of the Hospital Authority, was also a non-civil service appointee. Whether these modest changes will have any impact at all on the political accountability of the HKSAR government is doubtful (Burns, forthcoming).

Decentralization

The government adopted policies to decentralize financial management and the management of the civil service in the mid-1990s. The government hoped that these policies would provide more flexibility to improve efficiency.

The policies included the establishment of trading funds in five government departments under the 1993 Trading Funds Ordinance (Companies Registry, Lands Registry, Office of Telecommunications Authority, Post Office, and the Electrical and Mechanical Services Department [EMSD]) (http://www.info.gov.hk/eu/psrhk/tfn_com.htm).[5] The trading funds provided financial decentralization and re-focused the missions of the departments on serving their customers, but they called for no fundamental changes. The trading fund departments continued to operate as government departments employing most staff on traditional civil service (permanent and pensionable) terms of service. Initial suggestions that they could adopt some private sector practices such as performance-based pay were not realized (See CSB 1995a: 5). With the exception of EMSD, all of the trading fund departments are government monopolies which do not allow them to realize the benefits of competition. From 1994 to 1999, three of the five trading funds increased their staff (Companies Registry, Office of the Telecommunications Authority, and Hong Kong Posts) (See Table 1 and Figure 3). During the same period the Lands Registry and the

Table 1. Strength of Trading Fund Departments, 1993 and 2000

Department	1993	2000
Companies Registry	318	391
Lands Registry	620	586
OFTA	230	279
Hong Kong Posts	5275	5821
EMSD	5236	4764

Source: Civil Service Branch/Bureau *Civil Service Personnel Statistics* (various years) (Hong Kong: Government Printer/Printing Department).

Figure 3. Strength of Trading Fund Departments, 1993–2000

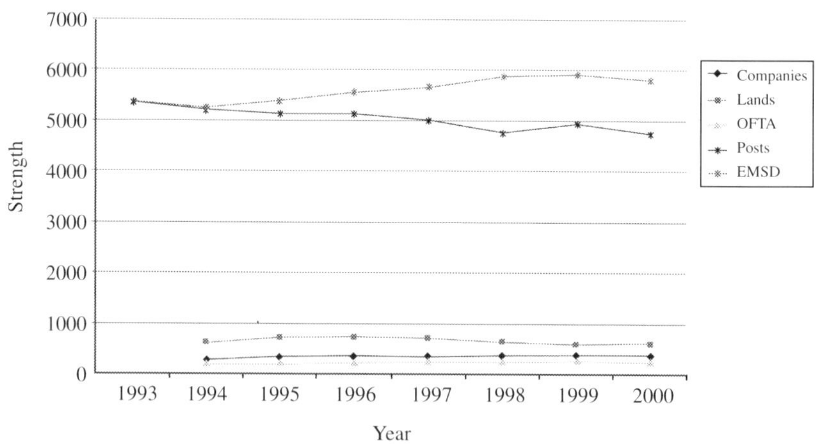

Source: Civil Service Branch/Bureau *Civil Service Personnel Statistics* (various years) (Hong Kong: Government Printer/Printing Department).

EMSD actually cut staff (by 5.5 per cent and nine per cent respectively). In the case of EMSD, the need to compete in the market may have pushed the department to make the comparatively larger cuts.

By the year 2000 none of the trading fund departments had taken advantage of their new flexibility to hire significantly more civil servants on non-permanent terms of service.[6] In each case except EMSD the number of civil servants on other than "permanent and pensionable" (p&p) terms was less than five per cent of total strength (often considerably less) and declining (See Table 2). In EMSD the government transferred nearly 2000 employees from "agreement" terms to "permanent and pensionable" terms in 1993–94, perhaps in anticipation of staff opposition to the proposed move of the department to trading fund status. Thus, from 1993 to 1994 the number of EMSD employees on terms other than p&p fell from 55 per cent to 17 per cent. By 2000 the number of non-p&p staff continued to fall to about 13 per cent. Moreover, none of the trading fund departments used their new found flexibility to substantially cut the number of employees on traditional civil service terms of service.

Decentralization of hiring authority to departments has probably been more successful. From 1995 heads of departments were permitted to lower entry qualifications to facilitate hiring and to employ staff on non-civil service terms mostly short-term contracts. Indeed, the use of non-civil service contract employees expanded especially during the civil service hiring freeze imposed from January 2000–April 2001 (CSB 2001b: 3). The freeze prohibited departments from hiring new staff on civil service terms of service. Even during the freeze, however, departments were

Table 2. Percentage of Civil Servants on Non-permanent and Pensionable Terms of Service in Trading Fund Departments, 1994–2000

Year	Companies	Lands	OFTA	Posts	EMSD
1994	5	3	3	1	17
1995	4	3	3	1	14
1996	2	3	2	1	13
1997	1	2	2	1	13
1998	2	2	2	1	13
1999	1	1	2	1	15
2000	1	2	2	<1	13

Note: The figures do not include non-civil service contract staff.

Source: Civil Service Branch/Bureau *Civil Service Personnel Statistics* (Various years) (Hong Kong: Government Printer/Printing Department).

permitted to fill 1,700 civil service posts "on an exceptional basis" for the years 2000–02. By July 2000, government departments had hired 7,600 non-civil service contract staff, 1,300 of whom were part-time employees.[7] Of these 2,400 worked in the newly established Leisure and Cultural Services Department and 1,200 in the Post Office. From 10 January 2001 to 30 April 2001, 4,477 non-civil service contracts were offered to new appointees, 3,351 of whom were full-time employees leading observers to speculate that perhaps 75 per cent of the new hires were doing jobs previously performed by civil servants (Wong 2001). According to Wong, in the Social Welfare Department from 1999–2000, 324 non-civil service contract staff took up jobs previously performed by civil servants (Social Security Assistants/Officers, Assistant Social Work Officers/ Social Work Assistants). To overcome problems of high-turnover among contract staff, in January 2001 the CSB promulgated revised guidelines that gave heads of departments "greater flexibility to offer better terms and conditions based on market conditions where justified" (CSB 2001a: 3; CSB 2001b). As the government has pointed out, departments have had the authority to hire part-time and seasonal staff for many years.

Decentralization of financial authority in trading fund departments was, then, not enough to move the civil service away from filling most posts on traditional p&p terms of service. Only when the government introduced changes service-wide in 2000 did departments (including presumably trading fund departments) avail themselves of the flexibility to hire non-civil service contract staff in significant numbers.

Centralization

Although the general trend of civil service reform abroad and in Hong Kong has been to decentralize, in some areas, such as in the handling of poor performers, the government, after first decentralizing authority to heads of departments, has recently re-centralized authority. The new arrangements, however, have lengthened the process and may be based on dubious assumptions.

As part of its earlier reforms, in 1993 the CSB decentralized authority to discipline lower-ranking civil servants (those on MPS 14 and below) to heads of government departments. As a result, certain inequities arose. The handling of disciplinary cases lacked consistency as civil servants committing the same offense were punished differently by different departments. Without access to a central database on offenses and punishments, departments failed to exercise their discretionary power to punish offenders equitably. Moreover, because disciplinary procedures were cumbersome, investigating officials (who were mostly Executive Officers [EOs]) lacked expertise, supervisors lacked commitment and institutions such as Medical Boards rendered inconsistent findings, departments tolerated substantial delays in the handling of discipline cases (Chan 2000). Disciplinary regulations lacked clarity and the consequences of violating them were not publicized within the service.

Abuses of discipline were uncovered that brought into question the ability of heads of departments to handle disciplinary cases. In one of the worst cases authorities discovered that from 1992 to 1993 many employees of the Housing Department were making short trips to Macau and/or China while "on duty" or had claimed paid overtime for work they did not do. After investigation, 1,171 cases were substantiated. Among these, 1,036 civil servants were found guilty of unauthorized absence, 29 were involved in fraudulent claims of overtime, while 106 were involved in both types of misconduct. As a result, the Housing Department issued 769 verbal or written warnings; 365 reprimands or severe reprimands; and removed 37 officials from the service (Chan 2000: 6). Cases such as these and data from the Independent Commission Against Corruption (ICAC) which indicated that many civil servants had committed disciplinary offenses (for example, in 1998 the ICAC recommended that 186 civil servants be considered for disciplinary action) led officials to conclude that reforms of the process were necessary (Chan 2000: 6 and Appendix I).

In April 2000 the government established a new Secretariat, staffed by a Senior Principal Executive Officer to supervise an office of ten EOs to process centrally all formal disciplinary cases. Two Chief EOs were deployed on a full-time basis to conduct disciplinary hearings. Government appointed a dedicated corps of 300 departmental and general grades officers (again, mostly EOs) in departments for a three-year period beginning in April 2000 to deal with disciplinary offenses. They are to be provided with training and regular briefings on disciplinary matters. The reform is designed to ensure that uniform standards are used to investigate and punish disciplinary infractions. In addition to these institutional arrangements, government has streamlined the disciplinary process, by, for example, cutting the length of time taken to dismiss a civil servant from 21 to 14 days (Chan 2000). By July 2000, three months after its inception the new Secretariat had been "inundated" with 150 cases during which time it resolved less than ten per cent (*SCMP* 31 July 2000).

Critics charge that these changes are unlikely to solve the problem. First, the new procedures have probably lengthened the time needed for processing disciplinary cases. Rather than departments handing cases directly to the Department of Justice to consider whether a *prima face* case of misconduct has occurred, cases now go first to the Secretariat and then to the Department of Justice. Because the Secretariat has no knowledge of the case, it has to study the case before forwarding it to the Department of Justice. If the Secretariat disagrees with the department on the type of disciplinary action to be taken, more time is required to clarify the matter with the department. According to Chan, officials in the Departments of Housing and Education believe that setting up the Secretariat has complicated the process, rather than streamlining it (Chan 2000: Chap 5; 8). If the Department of Justice concurs that there is a *prima facie* case of misconduct, the Secretariat then has to seek the approval of the department to institute formal disciplinary action. In other words, the Secretariat has been inserted into the process thereby creating further delays.

Second, the role of the Secretariat in maintaining a database on precedent cases and providing punishment standards overlaps with the role of the Public Service Commission. Moreover, because the Secretariat only provides precedent cases for the department's consideration, the Secretariat's role in determining punishments is perhaps unduly limited (Chan 2000).

Third, because the two dedicated Chief EOs who handle disciplinary hearings (the adjudicators) also supervise their subordinates within the Secretariat who act as investigators, there is potential role conflict which could jeopardize the independence of the hearings. Finally, the new procedures continue to rely heavily on EOs who often lack the expertise to make them work satisfactorily. EOs are subject to frequent postings and may not have the expertise needed to do the job satisfactorily (Chan, 2000). The new procedures should result in more equity, however, with like infractions being punished with uniform penalties.

Simplification

Reformers have also sought to simplify the complexity of the civil service. First, the government set out to rationalize and simplify civil service rules and regulations (CSB 1993: 10). Little progress has been made in this area, however. Reform of the civil service first with the introduction of common and then "new" terms of employment; new provisions to improve performance management (such as provisions for probation, termination, trials, further appointment, conduct and discipline), and attempts to tighten up the provision of housing benefits, leave, and allowances have all added extra rules to the CSRs. Indeed new regulations to accommodate civil service reform have been added at such a rate that from 1997 to 2001 the width of the *Civil Service Regulations* has grown from 2.5 inches to 4.25 inches!

Second, attempts to reduce the number of grades within the civil service have largely failed. The 1993 call to departmentalize the clerical and secretarial grades (CSB 1993: 9) met fierce opposition from staff associations and was not implemented. More recently, staff have opposed attempts to merge the amenities officers and recreation and sports officers grades in the Leisure and Cultural Services Department (*SCMP* 9 April 2000).

Third, government has been more successful at simplifying, or abolishing, allowances and encashing benefits. Education allowances, for example, have been abolished while housing benefits have increasingly been encashed (See CSB 1999).

Downsizing

In spite of more than a decade of public sector reform and reforms specifically targeted at the civil service, relatively little progress has been made at downsizing the public sector. The most significant steps have probably been the introduction of various retirement schemes since 1999.

In the 1980s the total size of the civil service grew until 1991 when the Hospital Authority was established and many left the service to join the Authority (See Figure 4). Beginning again in 1996, however, government began growing again reaching nearly 1990 levels. Beginning in 2000, however, government shed about 5,000 positions. In some departments such as Housing the change has been substantial, prompted by the decision to sell public housing to tenants. The Housing Department has cut 2000 posts since 1998. Service-wide many reductions have been accomplished through contracting out, outsourcing, and privatization.

In the 2000–01 Budget Speech the Financial Secretary announced the goal of cutting the civil service by 10,000 posts by 2003 (*SCMP* 15 July 2000). The government's Voluntary Retirement Scheme, initiated in the year 2000, sought to put the goal into practice. The government identified 59 grades with staff surpluses and invited staff to apply for voluntary

Figure 4. Strength of Selected Hong Kong Government Departments, 1989–2001

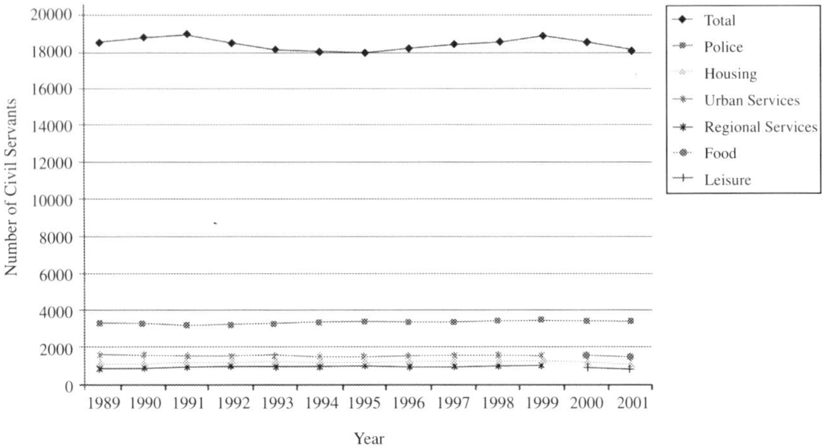

Source: Civil Service Branch/Bureau (various years) *Civil Service Personnel Statistics* (Hong Kong: Government Printer/Printing Department).

retirement with pension benefits and compensation. By October 2000, 11,000 civil servants applied to retire under the scheme, and the government eventually accepted 9,300 applications. Some applications were not accepted for operational reasons.[8] The government concluded that "the staff surplus problem in the majority of Voluntary Retirement grades in the civil service has largely been reduced or become manageable" (http://www.csb.gov.hk). Many of the grades employed lower-level blue-collar workers.[9]

Pressure to cut the size of the civil service has come mainly from the business community (See *SCMP* 19 February, 9 October, and 23 November 2001), which claims that the civil service is too big and that government has "over-hired" public sector workers in the past. There is some justification for these arguments. Indeed, government policy papers point out that government intends only to "... *contain* the civil service establishment" (CSB 2001a). Thorough reviews of the functions of government to achieve substantial downsizing is apparently not part of the plan. Rather heads of departments are urged to re-engineer work processes, streamline existing operations, make greater use of IT, and provide services through alternative delivery modes (such as contracting out). However, government does not contemplate a thorough review of its own functions that focuses on the appropriate role of government in the economy and society. Should government own and operate museums, provide and manage cultural venues, provide tennis coaches, and so forth? Are current staffing levels in large public organizations such as the Police Force justified?[10] Why does a government department provide printing services to departments and agencies? A thorough and comprehensive review of the role of government in the economy and society is, thus, long overdue.

Managerialism

Civil service reform has also sought to increase managerial flexibility to improve performance. Perhaps the greatest effort has been devoted to this area, especially since 1999 (See CSB 1999). Several reforms are significant. First, since June 2000 new recruits for many civil service positions are now put on an initial three-year contract followed by a second three-year contract before they are considered for a permanent position in the civil service. Previously most civil servants joined the permanent establishment after a probationary appointment of up to three years. The policy provides a longer period to evaluate the suitability of an employee for permanent service and thus perhaps more managerial flexibility. At the same time, the CSB has encouraged government departments to make more use of non-civil service contract employees, as we have seen above (See CSB 1999). Second, to increase flexibility, government is also proposing to abolish the pension system for all new employees replacing pensions with a portable provident fund. This will enable government workers to more easily leave public employment, taking their accumulated benefits with them (See CSB 2001e). Third, government has now proposed that people be recruited from outside the civil service directly into middle-level and higher-level positions in the civil service that traditionally have usually been held by those within the grade. In 2001 the CSB announced that it hoped to recruit up to ten Senior Administrative Officers from outside the AO grade, a competition that was opened up to the general public (See the advertisement in *SCMP* 29 September 2001). Fourth, government announced a new initiative to force permanently employed directorate-level officers to retire if their continued employment "would hinder organizational improvement" in a department or grade or if their retirement was "considered to be in the best interest of the grade" (CSB 2000b). The Scheme came into operation in September 2001 and details of the numbers of senior officials removed are not yet publicly available (See

CSB 2001d). Fifth, after conducting a starting salary pay level review, government cut starting salaries for many civil service positions by from six to 31 per cent and in the disciplined services from three to 17 per cent (See Standing Commission on Civil Service Salaries and Conditions of Service 1999 and http://www.csb.gov.hk/hkgcsb). This brought starting salaries more into line with those paid in the private sector but created new inequities within government departments. Finally, in 2001 government began to experiment with team-based performance rewards in six government departments (See http://www.csb.gov.hk/hkgcsb).[11] As of writing, the results of the experiments were not available. The 1999 reforms also included attempts to tighten up the granting of annual increments, suggestions that departments should use committees to moderate performance appraisals (a practice now fairly widespread in the government), and expanded training opportunities especially for those civil servants whose colleagues had taken voluntary retirement (See CSB 1999).

The reforms were designed for a contracting economy and labor surpluses. Whether the flexibilities built into the new policies will be used during periods of economic growth and labor scarcity remains to be seen.

Although they were consulted on the reforms, civil service unions opposed many of them especially those designed to downsize government or to cut benefits. Staff associations have expressed strong opposition to contracting out, outsourcing, and privatization because of concern over lost jobs (*SCMP* 24 May 1999). They also strongly opposed management-initiated retirement which they claimed could be open to abuse (See CSB 2000c and Hong Kong Chinese Civil Servants' Association 1999). Some unions have also argued in favor of retaining the current pension system. In May 1999, an estimated 10,000 civil servants marched on Central Government Offices from Victoria Park to express their strong dissatisfaction with the reform proposals (*SCMP* and *Wenhui bao* 24 May 1999). Opposition in the disciplined services, especially the Police Force, to introducing two three-year fixed-term contracts for all new recruits was so strong that the government has permitted the Police to continue with its current practice of offering probationary contracts leading to permanent positions. Still, as we have seen government was able to impose entry-level pay cuts even on new recruits to the disciplined services.

Conclusion

Our review of civil service reform in the 1990s indicates, first, that problems within the service pre-date the establishment of the HKSAR. Second, attempts to reform the civil service have mostly followed periods of economic decline. When the economy grew pressure for reform was less intense. Third, outside pressure for reform has come largely from the business community interested in balanced budgets and low taxation. Fourth, reform has been piecemeal and has left the traditional civil service largely intact.

The reforms have had some success, however, especially at providing managers with more flexibility to improve performance in a system that was and continues to be overly rigid. Much less success has been achieved in other areas such as downsizing or managing poor performers. The government's trading funds, although they have probably refocused agency culture on the customer, have failed to realize other reforms. Trading fund departments continued to employ civil servants on traditional (p&p) contracts and have yet to introduce performance-based rewards.

In many respects, civil service reform in Hong Kong lags behind reforms overseas. Although there is pressure from the business community for reform, the pressure is at best intermittent. Politicians in Hong Kong do not campaign on platforms of civil service reform as they do in other countries. Civil service reform will likely remain the result of a contest between the business community and the bureaucracy fraught by the needs of each to protect vested interests. In this situation the sorts of thorough reviews of the functions and operations of government that have characterized New Zealand and the UK will likely remain quite beyond our reach.

Notes

1. The 27 principal officials are nominated by the Chief Executive (Basic Law, Article 48 (5)).
2. The Basic Law calls for an 800-member Election Committee to "elect" the Chief Executive. The composition of the Election Committee, however, is tightly controlled by the central and local governments. See the Basic Law, Annex I.
3. The Basic Law prohibits private members' bills that relate to public expenditure or political structure or the operation of government. The Chief Executive must give written consent before any private members' bill may be introduced "relating to government policies" (Article 74).
4. See Anson Chan's comments on 29 June 1999 (*SCMP* 30 June 1999) and the Chief Executive's comments reported in *SCMP* 9 January 2000 and *Wenhui*

bao 9 January 2000.

5. An additional sewage trading fund was also established, but has since been wound up.
6. Undoubtedly the trading fund departments like other government departments have hired some short-term and part-time employees on non-civil service contracts.
7. Communication from Ms Anissa Wong, Deputy Secretary for the Civil Service to the author, 1 December 2000.
8. A further 600 applications were held in abeyance pending a review of staffing levels in the Food and Environmental Hygiene Department.
9. See the list of grades at http://www.csb.gov.hk/hkgcsb.
10. Large police forces were a characteristic of British colonies. With the change of sovereignty are the same levels of staffing warranted? Reference could be taken from other cities in the developed world with more or less the same population.
11. The departments are Buildings, Electrical and Mechanical Services (a trading fund department), Government Flying Service, Home Affairs, Judiciary Administration of the Judiciary, and Rating and Valuation.

References

The Basic Law of the Hong Kong Special Administrative Region of the People's Republic of China (1992) Hong Kong: One Country Two Systems Economic Research Institute, Ltd.

Burns, John P. "Accountability and the Senior Civil Service in Hong Kong," paper prepared for the Asian Forum on Public Management — Civil Service in Four Asian Developed Economies: Strategies, Problems and Paradoxes, City University of Hong Kong, 17–18 December 2001.

Chan Yin-ling, Linda (2000). "A Study of the Disciplinary Policy in the Hong Kong Civil Service," unpublished MPA dissertation, the University of Hong Kong.

Civil Service Branch (1993). *Consultation Document on Human Resource Management Review* (Hong Kong: CSB mimeo).

Civil Service Branch (1995). *Human Resource Management* (Hong Kong: Government Printer).

Civil Service Bureau (1998). "1968 Agreement Between the Hong Kong Government (Now Known as the Government of the HKSAR) and the Main Staff Associations (1998 Adapted Version)," September (Hong Kong: mimeo).

Civil Service Bureau (1999). *Civil Service into the 21st Century: Civil Service Reform Consultation Document* (Hong Kong: Printing Department).

Civil Service Bureau (2000a). *Civil Service Personnel Statistics 2000* (Hong Kong: Printing Department).

Civil Service Bureau (2000b). "Management-Initiated Retirement Scheme," paper prepared for the Legislative Council Panel on Public Service Meeting of 15 May.

Civil Service Bureau (2000c). "Management-Initiated Retirement Scheme" Legislative Council Brief (CSBCR/AP/5-090-005/11 Pt.4/99), 9 June.

Civil Service Bureau (2001a). "Containing the Size of the Civil Service," paper prepared for the Legislative Council Panel on Public Service Meeting of 19 March.

Civil Service Bureau (2001b). Circular No. 2/2001 "Employment of Non-Civil Service Contract Staff," Ref: AP/P350/163 Pt.10, 9 January.

Civil Service Bureau (2001c). *Civil Service Personnel Statistics 2001* (Hong Kong: Printing Department).

Civil Service Bureau (2001d). "Management-Initiated Retirement Scheme," paper prepared for the Legislative Council Panel on Public Service Meeting of 21 May.

Civil Service Bureau (2001e). *Proposal on Civil Service Provident Fund Scheme Consultation Document* (Hong Kong: Printing Department).

Constitutional Affairs Bureau (2002). "Accountability System for Principal Officials," paper prepared for the Legislative Council, April 17.

Economic Services Bureau et al. (1999). "Follow-up Action Taken or to be Taken in Respect of the Recommendations in the Three Inquiry Reports on the Opening of the New Airport," paper prepared for the Legislative Council Panels on Economic Services, Home Affairs, Planning, Lands and Works, and Public Service, 8 April.

Ghai, Yash (1999). *Hong Kong's New Constitutional Order: the Resumption of Chinese Sovereignty and the Basic Law*, 2nd ed. (Hong Kong: Hong Kong University Press.

Haque, A. S., Lee, Grace O. M., and Cheung, Anthony B. L. (1998). *The Civil Service in Hong Kong: Continuity and Change* (Hong Kong: Hong Kong University Press).

Hong Kong Chinese Civil Servants' Association (1999). *Recommendations on Civil Service System Reform* (*gongwuyuan tizhi gaige jianyishu*) (in Chinese) 26 May, (Hong Kong: mimeo).

Immigration Department (2000). *Investigation Report on the Incident of Master YU Man-hon* (Hong Kong: Immigration Department, mimeo), 14 September.

Lane, Jan-Erik (ed.) (1997). *Public Sector Reform: Rationale, Trends and Problems* (London: Sage).

Lee, Eliza (2000). "The New Hong Kong International Airport Fiasco: Accountability Failure and the Limits of the New Managerialism," *International Review of Administrative Science,* pp. 57–72.

Lee, Jane C. Y., and Cheung, Anthony B. L. (eds.) (1995). *Public Sector Reform in Hong Kong: Key Concepts, Progress-to-Date, Future Directions* (Hong Kong: The Chinese University Press).

Report of the Legislative Council Select Committee to Inquire into the Circumstances Leading to the Problems Surrounding the Commencement of the Operation of the New Hong Kong International Airport at Chek Lap Kok Since 6 July 1998 and Related Issues (1999) [Cited as Report] (Hong Kong: Printing Department).

SCMP [*South China Morning Post*], Hong Kong, various issues.

Scott, Ian (2000). "The Disarticulation of Hong Kong's Post-Handover Political System," *The China Journal*, pp. 29–53.

Standing Commission on Civil Service Salaries and Conditions of Service (1999). *Civil Service Starting Salaries Review 1999* Report No. 36 (Hong Kong: Printing Department).

Tung, Chee-hwa (2000). *Serving the Community Sharing Common Goals* (Policy Address to the Legislative Council October 11) Hong Kong: Printing Department.

Tung, Chee-hwa (2001). *Building on our Strengths Investing in the Future* (Policy Address to the Legislative Council 10 October) (Hong Kong: Printing Department).

Tung, Chee-hwa (2002). "Address to the Legislative Council on the Introduction of the Principal Officials Accountability System" (17 April) http://www.info.gov.hk/gia /general/200204/17 April 25.

Wenhui bao, Hong Kong, various issues.

Wong Ngok-ching, Samantha (2001). "The Effectiveness of Employing Non-civil Service Contract Staff in the Social Welfare Department," unpublished paper prepared for MPA Scope and Issues, the University of Hong Kong, 27 October.

12

The Chief Executive and the Business: A Marxist Class Perspective

Lo Shiu-hing

Associate Professor, Department of Politics and Public Administration
The University of Hong Kong

Introduction

The Hong Kong Special Administrative Region (HKSAR) of the People's Republic of China (PRC) is characterized by a special relationship between the ruling class (including the Chief Executive) and the capitalist class (including Barrington Moore's "landed upper class"). This unique relationship, as this chapter will argue, is not simply a hallmark of the capitalist city-state. It is partly a legacy of the colonial era when Britain possessed Hong Kong's sovereignty before 1 July 1997, and partly a product of the HKSAR government's pro-business policy. In a classic study of the social origins of dictatorship and democracy, Moore adopted a class perspective to explore the factors contributing to bourgeois democracy.[1] He observed that, in the case of England, the conditions for democracy included a relatively strong and independent Parliament; an autonomous bourgeoisie; an internally split landed upper class; and "a revolutionary break with the past."[2] In the case of India, which was a former British colony as with Hong Kong before 1 July 1997, colonial rule "prevented the formation of the characteristic reactionary coalition of landed elites with a weak bourgeoisie and thereby, along with British cultural influences, made an important contribution toward political democracy."[3]

This chapter will borrow some of the analytical concepts used by Moore, such as the bourgeoisie and the landed upper class, to explore the role of different classes and class fractions in Hong Kong under British and Chinese sovereignty. Unlike the historical development of England, Hong Kong lacks an independent legislature and a unified as well as an autonomous bourgeoisie. Instead, the HKSAR's bourgeoisie is divided and some of its elements have cultivated a seemingly symbiotic relationship with the post-colonial state. The coalition between the conservative fraction of the bourgeoisie and the post-colonial state is obstructing any attempt at introducing political reform in the HKSAR. Unlike India, Hong Kong under British and Chinese rule has been characterized by, to use the words of Moore, a reactionary coalition of landed upper class and the ruling class. Again, this coalition or alliance becomes an obstacle to the development of political democracy in the HKSAR.

Even worse, the ruling class governing the HKSAR's polity has failed to project an image of being an impartial referee, who is expected to balance the competing interests between the capitalist/landed classes and the petty bourgeoisie, and between the capitalist/landed classes and the lower working classes. Largely because of the failure of the post-colonial state to maintain at least an appearance of a relatively neutral arbitrator between the increasingly antagonistic upper and lower classes, the HKSAR's state apparatus is now seen as a captive of the capitalist class. Unless the HKSAR's ruling class senses the urgency of projecting a more impartial image, the on-going economic downturn in the HKSAR is bound to aggravate the contradictions between the capitalist class and their class enemy, namely the working class, thus plunging Hong Kong into an unprecedented crisis of class contradictions and class struggle. The manifestation of the increasingly prominent class struggle includes protests, demonstrations, threats issued by individual citizens to government officials and even the Chief Executive, and even violence initiated by the subordinated classes.[4]

Miliband's View of Capitalism and the Dominant Class

Very few scholars studying Hong Kong's political development have adopted a Marxist perspective.[5] However, using the Marxist class perspective, as this chapter will show, can contribute much to our deeper understanding of the complex relationships between the post-colonial government and the business people.[6] According to Ralph Miliband, capitalism is a mode of production shaping the social structure of societies. He wrote:

> It perpetuates a division of society between a relatively small dominant class on the one hand, and subordinate classes which constitute the vast majority of the population on the other. This division was common to most previous mode of production, but capitalism, far from obliterating it, perpetuates it in its own particular ways. Nor is this rendered any less true by the degree of social mobility, which distinguishes capitalism from earlier modes of production … [A]ccess to positions of power by members of subordinate classes does not change the fact of domination: it only changes the personnel.[7]

Miliband offered his insights of capitalism, whose features can also be applied to the case of Hong Kong. He emphasized that the dominant class is composed of not only the "power elite" as mentioned by C. Wright Mills but also the "business and professional bourgeoisie." He continued:

> At the upper levels of the social pyramid is to be found that part of the dominant class which, to use C. Wright Mill's term, constitutes its power elite. These are the people who own or control the 'strategic heights' of the economy; who control the central state apparatus; and who own and control the main means of communication which are in the public sector. The power elite is, so to speak, the 'vanguard' of the dominant class: it is largely recruited from that class, and members of the power elite return to it as a result of resignation or retirement. The (much larger) part of the dominant class which is not the power elite makes up a business and professional bourgeoisie which, although less powerful than the power elite, does nevertheless possess a great deal of power and influence … The point … is that the power elite in capitalist societies is to a very remarkable degree free from effective democratic control and thus constitutes something of an oligarchy only partially tempered by democratic reforms.[8]

In an earlier work, Miliband identified how the "business bourgeoisie" can penetrate the capitalist state apparatus and how it becomes the dominant class. As Miliband observed,

> [E]ven in the epoch of advanced capitalism …, businessmen have themselves assumed the major share of government. On the other hand, they have generally been well represented in the political executives and in other parts of the state system as well; and this has particularly true in the recent history of advanced capitalism.[9]

In the case of Hong Kong under British rule, businessmen had long been coopted to the state apparatus through appointments to various advisory bodies and political institutions such as the top policy-making

Executive Council (Exco) and the law-making Legislative Council (Legco).

Miliband delineated the characteristics of the "business bourgeoisie," which constitutes the dominant class in advanced capitalism. These features can also be applied to the HKSAR. He said:

> Businessmen themselves have often tended to stress their remoteness from, even their distaste for, 'politics'; and they have also tended to have a poor view of politicians as men who, in the hallowed phrase, have never had to meet a payroll and who therefore knew very little of the real world — yet who seek to interfere with the affairs of the hard-headed and practical men whose business it is to meet a payroll, and who therefore do know what the world is about. What this means is that businessmen, like administrators, wish to 'depoliticize' highly contentious issues and to have these issues judged according to the criteria favoured by business. This may look like an avoidance of politics and ideology: it is in fact their clandestine importation into public affairs ... But the government itself is by no means the only part of the state system in which businessmen have had a direct say. Indeed, one of the most notable features of advanced capitalism is precisely what might be called without much exaggeration their growing colonization of the upper riches of the administrative part of that system.[10]

In the case of the HKSAR, the business bourgeoisie always shows its "distaste" from politics and its desire to "depoliticize" highly contentious issues. Its "distaste" from politics can be seen in the development of the pro-business Liberal Party (LP), which was formed in 1992 and which was evolved from a loosely organized grouping of Legco's businessmen who wanted to curb the influence of the pro-democracy and pro-welfare legislators as early as 1991.[11] Despite the determination of the LP leadership to encourage their party members to participate in electoral politics, their performance has remained relatively unsatisfactory in Legco's direct elections.[12] Meanwhile, the businessmen's attempt at "depoliticising" contentious issues according to business criteria can be seen in their recent opposition to the HKSAR government's proposal of imposing a ban on smoking in restaurants.[13] Businessmen in the catering, hotel and entertainment industry mobilized their workers to protest against the ban, saying that the ban would break their "rice bowls."[14] Apparently, there was a commonality of interest, that is, preserving their jobs, between the businessmen and their workers. From the Marxist perspective, however, workers who participated in the protests were mouse-trapped by the capitalist class, which claimed that the government's proposed ban would not only lead to a drastic reduction in business but also cost the jobs of the proletariat. If the business bourgeoisie in capitalist societies has "false consciousness," meaning it proclaims that "partial and class interests have a universal and classless character,"[15] such "false consciousness" existed in the minds of the working-class people who participated in the protests and who believed that the protection of employment was the common interest. In short, the minority of workers participating in the protests against the ban on smoking in restaurants lacked "proletarian class-consciousness."[16]

Definitions of Analytical Concepts

If Miliband's observations on the features of capitalism can enlighten our understanding of the HKSAR's political dynamics, this chapter is going to define and employ the following concepts for the sake of exploring the relationships between the HKSAR government and the business people on the one hand, and between the Chief Executive and the business elites on the other. First, the ruling class is defined here as the power elite ruling the state apparatuses, such as the Exco, Legco and the bureaucracy. Specifically, the ruling class is composed of the Chief Executive, members of his think-tank in Exco and the Central Policy Unit (CPU), and all the principal officials in the civil service. My concept of the ruling class is similar to the notion of power elite articulated by Mills. Yet, in the context of the ruling class in Hong Kong, it does not include those legislators and District Councillors, because they are relatively less powerful and influential than their counterparts in Western democracy.[17] Second, the capitalist class or the bourgeoisie refers to the capitalists who own the means of production, such as land, capital and labour. The capitalist class, however, is by no means homogeneous. As Miliband argues, "the capitalist class or bourgeoisie is in functional, sociological and in most other terms an heterogeneous class, with many different elements or 'fractions'; and while the development of capitalism has fostered an ever-greater inter-relationship between different forms of capital, it has by no means obliterated their differences."[18]

This chapter will use Miliband's concepts of the "business" and "professional" bourgeoisie to analyze the HKSAR. The capitalist class has two major fractions, namely the business bourgeoisie and professional bourgeoisie. The business bourgeoisie refers to the big businessmen, land developers (or what Moore refers to as the "landed upper class"), bankers and entrepreneurs. The professional bourgeoisie refers to those professionals such as barristers, solicitors, accountants, engineers and medical doctors. Third, this chapter will use the concept of petty bourgeoisie to refer to the "medium and small businessmen, shopkeepers, self-employed craftsmen and artisans, small and medium farmers; in other words, that vast and diverse array of people who have not been 'proletarianized,' in the sense that they have not become wage and salary earners, and are not therefore part of the 'collective labourer,' even though they do of course fulfil definite economic tasks."[19] Fourth, the working class is referred here to "the 'collective labourer' which produces surplus value, from a position of subordination, at the lower ends of the income scale, and also at the lower ends of what might be called the 'scale of regard.'"[20] Both the working class and the petty bourgeoisie can be seen as the "subordinate classes" in capitalist societies. As Miliband maintains,

> The subordinate classes in capitalist societies are constituted by two different elements: a working or wage-earning class which makes up the great majority of the population of capitalist countries; and a lower middle class or petty bourgeoisie, itself divided between a small business and self-employed artisan stratum and a sub-professional, sub-managerial, supervisory stratum, comprising school teachers, social workers, civil servants and local government officers at the lower levels of the administrative structure, and many other people in a variety of occupations. These are the people who have some fairly small degree of power and responsibility in the operation of the mechanisms which help to ensure the daily reproduction of the social order.[21]

Using the concepts of (1) the ruling class, (2) the capitalist class (which divides into the business bourgeoisie and professional bourgeoisie), (3) petty bourgeoisie and (4) the working class (or the proletariat), this chapter is turning to a detailed analysis of their political interactions and interrelationships.

Class Politics in Colonial Hong Kong and the HKSAR

The Ruling Class

Under the British rule, the ruling class was composed of the governor, his Executive Council and the British expatriate senior civil servants who basically determined the political direction and policies in Hong Kong. All the members of the Exco appointed by the governor were usually supportive of his policy decisions, although there were cases in which a minority of Exco members openly spoke out against the governor's policy.[22] Prior to 1985, according to a former Exco member Sir S.Y. Chung, since "the governor and his mandarins did not really know who were suitable for the sensitive office [in Exco and Legco], they introduced a system for testing the candidates, a sort of probation."[23] This system of "probation" could ensure that political appointees would be politically loyal or reliable to the governor and the British senior expatriate bureaucrats. The ruling class in pre-1985 Hong Kong was composed mainly of the British governors and the British expatriate senior civil servants, while some members of the Chinese business and professional bourgeoisie were coopted into the colonial institutions. Ng Choy (alias Wu Ting-fang) was appointed to the colonial Legco in 1880 so as to "promote greater involvements and representation of the 'responsible' Chinese population in local affairs."[24] In general, the political absorption of the Chinese bourgeoisie was a hallmark of the ruling class in colonial Hong Kong.

In colonial Hong Kong, the governor played a critical role in shaping the way in which the territory was governed. Although the colonial constitutions — Letters Patent and Royal Instructions — conferred upon the governor tremendous powers, by convention he did not exercise such powers. Moreover, he relied on some Cantonese-speaking British expatriates to bridge the communication gap between the rulers and the ruled. The governor usually came from the British Foreign Office's establishment, utilizing his diplomatic skills and finesse to forge a generally harmonious relationship with the people of Hong Kong, especially the business and professional bourgeoisie. He also sensed the need to make himself appear to stand above political struggle and business interest. The relatively neutral image of the governor, however, changed in mid-1992 when Christopher Patten was appointed as the last governor of Hong Kong. Patten's background as a politician and his conviction of democratising Hong Kong brought about a rocky relationship with the business bourgeoisie, including some British taipans (except a few taipans such as the former managing director of Hutchison Whampoa Simon Murray) and the Chinese business magnets.[25] Governor Patten's pro-democracy, principled and confrontational style of political leadership alienated many members of the business and professional bourgeoisie, whose business interests in the PRC were increasingly bringing about their political pragmatism and conservatism.

In the HKSAR, the ruling class has remained relatively divided, unorganised and conflict-ridden, leading to a weak image of the post-colonial leadership. Chief Executive Tung Chee-hwa had a rocky relationship with the former Secretary for Administration, Anson Chan Fang On-sang. Their differed on many policy issues, ranging from the mother-tongue education policy to the fate of Tung's assistant, Andrew Lo, in the Robert Chung incident.[26] While Tung favoured the implementation of the mother-tongue education policy, Chan was reportedly adopting a more cautious attitude. Andrew Lo, a special assistant of Tung in the Chief Executive Office (CEO), reportedly played a crucial role in intervening the public opinion polls on the popularity of Tung conducted by an academic at the University of Hong Kong, Robert Chung. Chan demanded that Lo should leave the CEO, whereas Tung reportedly protected Lo's position. Tung's rocky relationship with Chan undermined the solidarity of the ruling class and directly generated the image of a chaotic leadership from 1998 to April 2001, when Chan departed the HKSAR government.

Even worse, the CEO itself showed signs of poor leadership and coordination. Andrew Lo had apparently not informed the CEO's Information Coordinator Stephen Lam of his contact with the former Vice-Chancellor of the University of Hong Kong, Patrick Cheng Yiu-chung. Prior to the revelation that Lo was involved in the Robert Chung saga, Lam had openly challenged Chung to reveal the identity of the third person who exerted pressure on the academic in his polling work. Obviously, Lam had not known about Lo's liaison activities — a testimony to the CEO's relatively weak internal coordination. Lam also publicly criticized the Housing Society for its plan to build apartments in mainland China for Hong Kong buyers. Since the Housing Society has been led by Exco member Chung Sui-ming, Lam's open disagreement with the Housing Society's plan was seen as another indication of poor coordination. Most importantly, sometimes the CEO's activities and remarks showed the lack of leadership at the top echelon of the HKSAR government. If the ruling class itself cannot close its rank and fails to present a united image, the post-colonial state leadership is bound to be relatively weak.

Another devastating blow to the solidarity of the ruling class is the complexities surrounding the senior civil servants and Exco members who are supposed to provide competent advice and effective support to Chief Executive Tung. Lacking charisma and political skills, Tung is bound to be a relatively weak political leader. Compounding his fragile leadership, although he is a sincere and honest leader without any integrity problem, is the complete failure of senior civil servants and Exco members who could promote the HKSAR government's policies and reforms in public. Many senior civil servants, who are supposed to be the elite in the HKSAR's ruling class, appear to lack the determination to provide sound policy advice to Tung; some seem to be yesmen and yeswomen pleasing the Chief Executive. The mentality of the senior civil servants is that they look to Tung for policy decisions and that they should better act as uncritical policy implementators, rather than imaginative policy formulators. Furthermore, Exco members are political appointees without policy-making powers. A minority of Exco members, such as C.Y. Leung, were reportedly far more interested in their own business interest than the affairs of the HKSAR government. A few Exco members appeared to have policy portfolios, such as Tam Yiu-chung who was supposed to deal with elderly affairs, but in reality they made very little contribution to the better formulation of various policies, which were implemented by the unimaginative and uncritical senior civil servants. As a result, Chief Executive Tung has been encircled by a clique of incompetent, unimaginative and uncritical supporters, who totally failed to provide sound policy advice to the top leader. The top ruling elite has become a relatively closed circle of political appointees and senior bureaucrats, who have little political vision but to please the politically inexperienced Chief Executive. If the "one country, two systems" is supposed to be an imaginative concept allowing Hongkongers much autonomy, it has degenerated into an unimaginative idea used by the ruling class to enrich itself without having any critical mind, not to mention a political acumen to appreciate public criticisms.

Some senior bureaucrats have adopted a distrustful attitude toward Tung and his political appointees (mostly members of the landed upper class) in the Exco, thus straining the previously harmonious relationship between the bureaucrats and the landed elites in colonial Hong Kong. That Tung himself had been a shipping tycoon before a 400-member Selection Committee "elected" him as the Chief Executive in late 1996 sowed the seeds of distrust between the senior bureaucrats and him. To some senior officials, Tung remained an inexperienced political leader using business strategies inappropriately to manage the HKSAR government. In the minds of Tung, however, the bureaucrats represented a colonial legacy with questionable political loyalty to him at least in the short run. Similarly, the bureaucrats regard the landed elites in Exco as merely the beneficiaries of Tung's political patronage without sufficient knowledge of governmental administration. They are also jealous of the Exco's landed elites who have acted like cabinet ministers responsible for some government policies.[27]

But in the eyes of the landed elites, the senior bureaucrats do not fully understand the complexities of the private sector and their arrogance was a product of colonial rule. Overall, the mistrust between the senior bureaucrats and the landed upper class has jeopardized the solidarity of the ruling class in the HKSAR.

Even worse, Tung's policy advisers and senior bureaucrats increasingly link their action and remarks to political correctness. In Hong Kong under British rule, political correctness existed but it did not at least appear to be a lethal blow to the colonial rulers, who often tolerated dissenting views and who monitored the behaviour of political dissidents. In the HKSAR, the idea of political correctness has been unduly elevated to a level that public criticisms of the Chief Executive could be easily interpreted as "anti-Tung" or having conspiratorial motive. The mouthpiece of the HKSAR government, namely *Ta Kung Pao* and *Wen Wei Pao*, not only fully support the HKSAR government policies — an understandable phenomenon — but also at one time regarded the Radio Television Hong Kong (RTHK) as broadcasting programmes that are deemed to be politically "incorrect," such as the Headline News and a leadership programme that interviewed political dissent and democrat Emily Lau. While the pro-government media have the legitimate right to question the role of the RTHK, sometimes such criticisms appear to exceed to traditional bottom line of political tolerance in Hong Kong. Traditionally, Hong Kong was characterized by having freedom of speech and freedom of press. But in the HKSAR, the unintended consequence of emphasizing political "correctness" is to limit the space for such freedom of expression. Sometimes the ruling class in the HKSAR does not know how to deal with the political assertiveness of the patriotic elites and pro-Beijing media, which often regard pro-democracy voice as the enemy of the post-colonial state. If the ruling class maintains a certain distance from such political pressure from the patriotic elites, its relative autonomy vis-à-vis them could be maintained. Yet, afraid of alienating the patriotic forces, the HKSAR's ruling class usually adopts a subservient and passive attitude toward their pressure. The outcome is a much weaker post-colonial state than conventional wisdom assumed. The ruling class composed of the Chief Executive, the senior civil servants and his political appointees in Exco is actually undermined by the tide of political correctness propagated by the patriotic elites and media.

Last but not the least, the ruling class in the Tung administration has been shadowed by the dominance of the business elites in Exco, leading to an inevitable public image that the post-colonial state is collaborating with the capitalist class. Tam, a working-class representative in Exco, was outnumbered by other business elites in the top advisory body. From the Marxist perspective, Tam himself appeared to become a labour aristocrat, who was increasingly co-opted into the bourgeois ideology, and who appeared to lose his political determination and power to constantly fight for the interests of the poor and the needy and that of the unemployed workers.[28] Overall, the chaotic leadership, poor coordination and domination of the business voice characterized the ruling class in the HKSAR.

It is urgent for the HKSAR's ruling class to demonstrate its administrative incompetence and political leadership. The relative slowness of the civil service's response to the bird flu crisis (newly discovered and lethal H5N1 virus), which transmitted from birds to chickens and which caused the deaths of several citizens in the HKSAR in December 1997, showed that the ruling class failed to handle crises.[29] The chaos surrounding the opening of the new Chek Lap Kok airport and the piling scandal in public housing construction leading to the resignation of Housing Authority chairperson Rosanna Wong all raised questions concerning the performance of senior civil servants either in monitoring public bodies or executing housing policies. Arguably, the British rulers in colonial Hong Kong spoiled many senior Chinese civil servants. They needed not make bold decisions in response to sudden crises. Whenever crises erupted in Hong Kong's colonial history, the colonial officials usually made bold decisions in response to them. Yet, in the HKSAR, the failure of senior local Chinese bureaucrats to adapt to the swiftly changing circumstances was revealed. It can be argued that with the passage of time they can learn the skills of governance and the confidence of reacting to crises. This may be true. However, as long as some senior civil servants adopt a subservient attitude towards their political bosses, and so long as they refrain from giving bold advice, the ruling class will likely continue to be marked by the lack of leadership and the triumph of political correctness.

Although the Tung administration in April 2002 introduced "the accountability system for senior officials," it is doubtful whether the politically appointed senior officials will shoulder the political responsibility of making policy blunders by voluntary resignation. While democracies have developed a constitutional convention of ministerial resignation in case of serious policy blunders or personal scandals, whether the HKSAR case envisages such development will hinge on (1) the willingness of the "ministers" or politically appointed officials to take the bold step of resignation, (2) the boldness on the part of the Chief Executive to accept such ministerial resignation without worrying about the pressure from the public and opposition, and (3) whether the HKSAR's ruling class as a whole will develop a democratic spirit of accepting the responsibility of making policy or personal blunders and thus opting for resignation. In the event that cronyism becomes a hallmark of "the accountability system," it can be anticipated that the politically appointed officials or ministers will be the faithful supporters of the Chief Executive. If close personal relationships and patron-client networks develop between the Chief Executive and his or her "ministers," it is doubtful whether ministerial resignation will be commonplace in the HKSAR. In other words, the so-called "accountability system" may degenerate into a spoils system in which the Chief Executive rewards his or her political friends and supporters by appointing them as the "ministers" or politically appointed officials. Cronyism and patron-client politics not only can sabotage the development of "the accountability system for senior officials," but they also have a dangerous potential of corrupting the ruling class. Personal factors will emerge as the most prominent factor shaping the development of "the accountability system" within the ruling class.

From a radical perspective, the "accountability system for senior officials" will exclude those senior civil servants who disagree with the policies and political views of the Chief Executive and his "ministers." The "system" will reinforce the entrenchment of a batch of political loyalists supportive of the Chief Executive. Indeed, as some pro-government commentators accurately point out, the "system" will likely improve the HKSAR government's policy-making in that the policy priorities will be better formulated. But from the class perspective, the "system" is going to perpetuate the governance of the HKSAR by the capitalist class, which will co-opt any member of the working class in the entire state apparatus. The crux of the problem is whether the rule by capitalists will be more benign (or less exploitative) and whether it will take into consideration other class interests in its policy formulation and implementation.

The Capitalist Class

From the perspective of ethnic politics, the capitalist class in colonial Hong Kong evolved from a dominant British bourgeoisie to a gradually emergent Chinese bourgeoisie. As early as 1845, the British merchants in Hong

Kong objected to being assessed by the colonial government for the payment of rates, to the Crown's monopoly over land and to shouldering the cost of government.[30] Ian Scott has observed that despite the occasionally rocky relationship between the governor and the British bourgeoisie, the colonial state enjoyed some degree of "relative autonomy" from the pressure of the capitalist class.

> [T]he government had a certain amount of relative autonomy. It had to rule primarily with the interests of the merchants in mind and it had to ensure that government expenditure was prudent and that taxation was kept as low as possible. But beyond this it had considerable leverage, particularly in serving as a buffer and arbiter between the merchants and the Chinese community. The merchants and the leaders of the Chinese community were generally at odds ... and this gave the colonial bureaucracy considerable discretionary decision-making authority.[31]

True, the emergence of the indigenous Chinese bourgeoisie served as a check against the power and influence of the British merchants. It had the unintended consequence of enhancing the "relative autonomy" of the colonial state.[32]

An indispensable element of the capitalist class is Moore's "landed upper class." The landed upper class in colonial Hong Kong was split into old and the new elements. The old landed class was composed of not only the British expatriates who came to Hong Kong long before the Second World War, but also the Chinese capitalists who fled to Hong Kong from Shanghai before the Chinese Communist Party came to power in the mainland in 1949. While the British merchant houses like Jardine Matheson and the Hong Kong and Shanghai Banking Corporation established Hong Kong's economic foundation, the Shanghai capitalists provided the necessary capital for the colony's industrialization in the 1950s and 1960s.[33] The British "fraction" of the landed upper class diversified into various economic sectors, including shipping, shipbuilding, property, public utilities and construction.[34] The British landed upper class enjoyed its business dominance in Hong Kong until the rapid emergence of a new generation of the Chinese landed upper class in the 1970s and the early 1980s.[35] With the rise of the new members of the Chinese landed upper class, like Li Ka-shing, the shares of such British companies as Wheelock, Kowloon Dockyard, Hutchison Whampoa and Hong Kong Electricity were bought off.[36] The declining influence of the British landed upper class was partly due to its fear of Hong Kong's future after 30 June

1997, and partly because of the success of the Chinese landed upper class to penetrate and expand the property market at a time when Hong Kong envisaged a rapid population growth.[37] Some British *hongs* began to relocate their headquarters from Hong Kong to elsewhere, such as Jardine Matheson's decision in 1984 to move its corporate operations to Bermuda.[38] Moreover, the non-interventionist economic philosophy of the colonial government indirectly contributed to the decline of the British landed upper class, which could not outperform the Chinese landed elites in the highly competitive market economy and whose fate did not lead to any rescue by the British rulers. Ironically, the "relative autonomy" of the British colonial state vis-à-vis the British merchants sounded the latter's inevitable decline.

Above all, a special relationship between the ruling class and the landed upper class was established firmly in the colonial era. By adopting a *laissez-faire* economic policy, the colonial state often acted like an impartial referee without interfering with the competition between the Chinese and British landed upper classes, thus maintaining an appearance of "relative autonomy."[39] The "relative autonomy" of the colonial state in Hong Kong was mainly due to divergent interests amongst the landed upper class, which had competing interests internally and which did not organize itself politically to oppose the government. The landed upper class included landowners and land developers, who themselves did not have homogeneous views on government policies, such as land prices and housing development. Collectively, the landed upper class shared the common interest of maximizing its economic profits and accelerating the process of capital accumulation. As long as the colonial state provided a favourable business environment, including the rule of law, for the landed upper class to achieve economic profits, it did not sense the need to participate in politics, to advocate bourgeois democracy, and to call for any political reform.

Meanwhile, the landed upper class enjoyed political influence through co-optation into the Exco, Legco and other advisory committees.[40] In 1985, functional constituencies were established to legitimize the political representation of the landed upper class in the colonial legislature.[41] Functional constituencies were composed of business, commerce, education, social work, labour, legal sector, industry, finance and engineering. Although some sectors were made up of representatives from the petty bourgeoisie and the working class, such as social workers and labour unionists respectively, the capitalist class dominated the majority of functional constituencies in Legco. Overall, the composition of the legislature was biased in favour of the capitalist class.

The relationship between the ruling class, including the governor and his senior bureaucrats, and the capitalist class was special. The ruling class was neither politically subservient to the landed upper class nor captured by the bourgeoisie. To put it in another way, there was a degree of "relative autonomy" enjoyed by the colonial state whose key elements comprised the governor and his senior civil servants, who understood the operation of the bureaucracy much better than any social class. Both the governor and senior civil servants believed that in order to maintain political stability and to avoid the occurrence of riots and massive protests, the colonial state had to appear to stand above all class interests, especially the interest of the landed upper class.

Another factor explaining the "relative autonomy" of the colonial state was the disinterest of the landed upper class in politics. Land developers/owners were dedicated to achieving profit maximization and capital accumulation. They believed political participation was time-consuming, yet without realizing that the existing political framework led to their over-representation and dominance. Political survival was never a problem to the traditionally over-protected capitalist class. The increased electoral participation of the capitalist class in the 1990s was partly forced by the changing political circumstances in which the pro-welfare and pro-democracy liberals constituted a menace to business interests. It was also a result of the PRC's encouragement and united front efforts.[42] The PRC, the capitalist class and the ruling class even formed an alliance during the governorship of David Wilson to postpone the introduction of direct election to Legco in 1988.[43] In spite of this temporary alliance, both the colonial state and the ruling class appeared to have some degree of relative autonomy vis-à-vis the capitalist class.[44]

Unlike the colonial state that appeared to have certain degree of autonomy from the landed upper class, since the handover the HKSAR government has increasingly appeared to be captured by the landed class. The governmental decision to develop the Cyberport without open tender aroused a widespread suspicion that the HKSAR government had cultivated an unholy alliance with the landed upper class. On the other hand, the senior civil servants and the Chief Executive have been under tremendous and constant pressure from the landed upper class on various government policies, such as the need to import skilled labourers from the PRC, the necessity of shelving the housing policy target of building 85,000 units per year, the demand for 24-hour border crossing at Shenzhen so as to facilitate trade flows and human traffic across the mainland border, the urgent need for university graduates to demonstrate competence in the English language, and the undesirability of increasing profit tax that would affect business interests. During the Asian financial crisis, the Financial Secretary, Donald Tsang Yam-kuen, met with the leaders of the landed upper class, trying to calm the latter's panic over a possible collapse of the property market in the HKSAR. Chief Executive Tung Chee-hwa said publicly that he did not want to envisage a collapse of the property market. Clearly, the post-colonial state is not only highly sensitive to the interests of the landed upper class, but it is also deeply concerned about the negative impact of any rapidly declining property market on public confidence, especially the confidence of the landed classes and the bourgeoisie. Arguably, the intervention of the HKSAR government in the stock market during the Asian financial crisis aimed at propping up the property market, satisfying and fully taking care of the interests of the landed upper class.

While the capitalist class in Hong Kong under British rule was split into the British and Chinese fractions, the Chinese capitalists have since the 1980s developed their personal connections with the PRC government. The mentality of many Chinese capitalists is that politics should be separated from economic development, and that the PRC's modernization can provide a golden opportunity for them to maximize capital accumulation. To the Chinese capitalists and the HKSAR's ruling class, the PRC's entry into the World Trade Organization provides a golden opportunity for the HKSAR to revive its economy. The HKSAR ruling class has gone so far as to believe that the HKSAR must benefit from the PRC's global emergence and capitalistic development, although critics warn that the its absorption into the globalized capitalist world might have negative consequences on mainland China.[45] To the Chinese capitalists, Western-style democracy can undermine Hong Kong's economic competitiveness. Under an environment in which economic pragmatism prevails over political ideals, the capitalist class in both colonial and post-colonial Hong Kong has developed its anti-democratic and highly conservative instincts. In short, the capitalist class, especially the land owners/developers, are viewing both the post-colonial state and the PRC government as indispensable and cooperative partners in achieving profit maximization and expanding the productive forces in capitalism.

The Chinese capitalists can be seen not only as the business fraction of the bourgeoisie but also as politically reactionary. On the other hand, the professional fraction tends to be more liberal-minded and pro-Western democracy. Professionals such as barristers, lawyers and educators have been traditionally supportive of political reform in Hong Kong. Led by barrister Martin Lee and educator Szeto Wah, the more liberal professional bourgeoisie elements in Hong Kong since the 1980s have advocated a faster pace of democratic development. Yet, the professional bourgeoisie remains less influential than the business bourgeoisie. The latter dominates the top policy-making Executive Council (Exco), the post-colonial legislature and all the advisory bodies. As a result, the professional bourgeoisie is forced to form a coalition with members of the petty bourgeoisie and some working-class representatives, such as Lau Chin-shek and Li Cheuk-yan, to advocate political and welfare reforms in the HKSAR.[46] Yet, by allying with the middle-lower classes, the professional bourgeoisie is seen by the business fraction as utilizing class tensions to achieve sinister political motives, namely grasping political power and implementing pro-welfare but anti-business policies. In short, the political struggle for Western-style democracy on the part of the liberal professional bourgeoisie exacerbated its class contradictions with the big business people.

Apart from the indigenous bourgeoisie, the mainland Chinese bourgeoisie working in Hong Kong has emerged rapidly since the open door policy of the PRC was implemented in the late 1970s. Members of this mainland Chinese bourgeoisie have invested heavily in Hong Kong, and they have their companies listed in the HKSAR's stock market in order to accumulate capital. Some members of the mainland Chinese bourgeoisie, like Larry Yung of the China International Trust and Investment Corporation (CITIC), have long been assimilated into Hong Kong's capitalist system and they have re-invested their profits back to the mainland.[47] The mainland Chinese bourgeoisie in the HKSAR is now providing a powerful capitalist force that can accelerate the process of making the PRC economically more similar to Hong Kong than ever before.[48] In cooperation with the Chinese landed upper class, the mainland Chinese bourgeoisie has already replaced the British taipans to become a politically and an economically dominant class coalition vis-à-vis the petty/professional bourgeoisie in the HKSAR.

Basically, the political views of the local Chinese landed upper class have much in common with that of the mainland Chinese bourgeoisie. Both regard capital accumulation as of primary importance and bourgeois democracy as of low priority. They view bourgeois democracy as a dangerous threat to their political influence and economic interests, particularly if democracy can generate more social conflicts, more demands for social welfare, more political uncertainties and perhaps less economic stability than before. However, they firmly believe in the protection of private property rights and the preservation of the rule of law. The mainland Chinese bourgeoisie in Hong Kong slowly appreciates the fact that the common law system as established by the British can safeguard an impartial and attractive business environment — a view that will perhaps contribute to the PRC's legal modernization. In other words, the mainland Chinese bourgeoisie in Hong Kong gradually develops the view that, for the PRC to achieve its capitalist modernization, the rule of law rather than the rule by men will sooner or later have to prevail in the mainland.[49]

From the perspective of ordinary citizens, the HKSAR government is too heavily influenced by the capitalist class — a phenomenon perhaps more prominent than the dominant role of business in colonial Hong Kong. A survey conducted by the Hong Kong Transition Project in November 2001 found that 39 per cent of the 759 respondents believed that the local big business leaders had "too much" influence on the government; 31 per cent said there was a "reasonable amount" of big business influence; 19 per cent said there was a "small amount" of influence; four per cent said none; and eight per cent replied that they did not know.[50] As a matter of fact, the big business people, particularly the landed upper class led by the indigenous Chinese, have been shaping the HKSAR government's land and housing policies. Immediately after the handover of Hong Kong, the Tung administration had the sincere intention of building 85,000 flats per year so that the target of 70 per cent of the Hong Kong people who would own their homes could be fulfilled.[51] When the HKSAR's economy was affected by the Asian financial and monetary crisis in late 1997, the Exco decided to import workers from mainland China to back up the government's decision of building 85,000 flats per year.[52] Later in 1999 and 2000, when the landed upper class complained about the "negative" impact of Tung's policy of building 85,000 housing units per year on the property market, the HKSAR government backed down and silently shelved the policy proposal without announcing it until the summer of 2000. In 2001, the Home Ownership Scheme was temporarily frozen for fear of lowering the property prices further. All the measures adopted by the HKSAR government gave rise to an impression that it has been yielding to the pressure from the big capitalist and landed class. If colonial

Hong Kong was ruled by Jardine Matheson together with the British administrators, the HKSAR appears to be governed by both the ruling class and the landed upper class.

In practice, the ruling class has traditionally developed close ties with the landed upper class. Under British rule, the bureaucratic element in Hong Kong's ruling class was composed of the British expatriates and senior local Chinese officials. Localization of the colonial bureaucracy was adopted as an official policy in 1947 and its pace was accelerated from September 1984 to June 1997, when the colony entered the final phase of British rule immediately after the Sino-British Joint Declaration on Hong Kong's future had been initialled.[53] Although the colonial bureaucracy was gradually localized by promoting more Hong Kong Chinese to the upper echelons of the civil service, the expatriate civil servants were recruited mainly from Britain (some from New Zealand and Australia). They enjoyed relatively high salaries and other benefits. This situation not only perpetuated an ethnic and artificial distinction between the locals and the expatriates, but it also triggered a campaign launched by some middle-level Chinese civil servants to abolish such distinction.[54]

There were two outstanding features associated with the bureaucratic fraction of the ruling class in colonial Hong Kong. First and foremost, the British expatriates dominated the key positions of the bureaucracy until the final years of colonial governance, when more Chinese permanent residents in Hong Kong were promoted to the top-level positions, such as Anson Chan Fang On-sang who became the Chief Secretary and Donald Tsang Yam-kuen who was promoted to Financial Secretary during the governorship of Christopher Patten. Prior to the Patten era, these key positions had been monopolized by the British expatriates who, in the eyes of the governors, were politically more reliable or loyal than the local Chinese. With the onset of the transition period in September 1984, however, the colonial rulers needed to decolonize the top-level of the bureaucracy for the sake of giving some substance to the assertion of preparing " the process of "Hong Kong people ruling Hong Kong" after 1 July 1997.

After the handover, the bureaucratic fraction of the ruling class is composed of not only the Chinese but also increasingly those people politically loyal to the Chief Executive. By implementing the "accountability system" for senior officials, Chief Executive Tung hopes to promote his political friends and supporters as the "ministers" or politically appointed top officials, who to him are far more reliable than the career civil servants nurtured by the British. Despite these changes in the profile of politically appointed officials, career civil servants still maintain harmonious relationships with the landed upper class. Career civil servants have to consult the views of the landed upper class on the government's housing and land policies, and on its tax reform measures. Due to the fact that those politically influential elites surrounding Tung are mostly business people, the career civil servants actually have no choice but to institutionalize and regularize their consultation with the landed upper class.

Second, the Chinese bureaucratic fraction of the ruling class enjoyed relatively high salaries and attractive fringe benefits, which were the means by which the colonial government secured its political loyalty. From the traditional Chinese perspective, being an official is tantamount to having an elite status.[55] This traditional Chinese view of officialdom in Hong Kong was reinforced by the British style of maintaining a merit-based, well-paid and efficient bureaucracy. Naturally, the majority of the Chinese civil servants viewed themselves as members of the societal elites and did not want to lose their "iron rice bowls."

Since the handover, this mentality of protecting the "iron rice bowl" on the part of the Chinese civil servants persists. However, as mentioned below, some members of the capitalist class dislike the rigidity within the civil service and they regard many middle-level and lower-level civil servants as enjoying salaries incommensurate with their counterparts in the private sector, such as secretaries, typists and workmen. While the "iron rice bowl" of civil servants was largely retained intact in Hong Kong under British rule, it is destined to confront challenges and transformations in the HKSAR mainly because of the political preponderance of the capitalists, who cherish managerial values such as efficiency, effectiveness and economy.[56] In March 2002, the HKSAR government proposed a pay cut of 4.75 per cent of the salary of civil servants. Some civil service unions reacted negatively, but some have adopted a low profile. Since the civil service unions represent different class interests, including petty bourgeoisie and working class, their varying reaction means that the HKSAR government will perhaps push forward its pay cut without great difficulties and severe opposition.

In the final analysis, a crucial continuity in the relationship between the senior bureaucrats and the capitalist class before and after the handover is that they share common bourgeois values (societal freedom, rule of law, property rights), lifestyle and even taste.[57] It is commonplace that senior bureaucrats, who can be seen as the ruling class, attend lavish banquets together with the affluent members of the capitalist class. Traditionally, the senior bureaucrats in Hong Kong have maintained a favourable business environment for the landed upper classes, mainly through relatively low taxation and pro-business policies, to maximize the capitalists' profits.[58] In a sense, the capitalists and the senior bureaucrats have cultivated a mutually beneficial relationship. Senior bureaucrats also seek the support of the capitalist class on various government policies and measures, thus providing the HKSAR government with an indispensable ingredient of legitimacy. From the Marxist perspective, the HKSAR remains a typical example of a capitalist regime where the ruling class shares the values and lifestyle of the capitalist class.

The Petty Bourgeoisie and the Proletariat: Subordinate Classes in Colonial and Post-Colonial Hong Kong

While the ruling class is governing the HKSAR with insufficient autonomy from the big capitalists, the petty bourgeoisie and the proletariats remain the two subordinate classes. Members of the petty bourgeoisie include social workers, teachers and middle-level civil servants. Their higher educational background and their participation in Hong Kong's social movement in the 1970s laid the groundwork for the pro-democracy movement in the 1980s and 1990s.[59] The class alliance between the professional bourgeoisie and the petty bourgeoisie was gradually forged in the mid-1980s and it grew after the Tiananmen Incident in June 1989. They formed political discussion groups and political parties, such as the United Democrats of Hong Kong and later the Democratic Party, to participate in local elections. Their source of voters' support was derived mainly from the members of the professional bourgeoisie and petty bourgeoisie.

However, the PRC government views the coalition between the professional bourgeoisie and the petty bourgeoisie as politically destabilizing and dangerous to the HKSAR government. PRC officials still regard this class alliance as a political threat because it advocates democratization and accountability in both Hong Kong and the mainland, a legacy of the Tiananmen Incident in 1989. From 1993 to 1997, the PRC government was deeply concerned about the common goals between governor Patten and the pro-democracy petty bourgeoisie/professional bourgeoisie. After Patten's confrontation with the PRC government over Hong Kong's political reform, Beijing was keen to prevent the professional/petty bourgeoisie from gaining political power in the HKSAR. As a result, the PRC government was determined to replace the last Legco under British rule with a Provisional Legislature, which excluded the participation of pro-democracy legislators. This exclusionary tactic is still seen in the PRC government's treatment of the mainstream democrats in the HKSAR, such as Emily Lau, Martin Lee and Szeto Wah.

Moore observed that a society that depended on a centralized bureaucracy for extracting surplus from the peasantry was vulnerable to peasant rebellion;[60] nevertheless, he did not explicitly regard civil servants as petty bourgeoisie. In the case of Hong Kong under British rule, civil servants generally became an instrument of the British to maintain law and order, to collect taxes from the people, to deliver good and services to citizens, and to stabilize as well as legitimize colonial rule. From the class perspective, middle-level civil servants were mostly petty bourgeoisie reluctant to envisage democratization of the colonial polity. Democratization would enhance public accountability and thus increasing the workload and political pressure upon civil servants in general, especially those middle-level and lower-level bureaucrats who had to interact with citizens daily. Throughout the colonial era, civil servants generally did not openly support democratic reforms, perhaps except for the final years of British rule when governor Patten decided to push forward his political reforms and demanded the bureaucracy's wholehearted support from mid-1992 to June 1997.[61] Under the Patten administration, a few local Chinese bureaucrats who opposed his reform proposals had opted for early retirement — an indication that his reforms did not gain the full support of civil servants.[62]

In the HKSAR, middle-ranking civil servants, who can be categorized as the petty bourgeoisie, have been opposed to some reforms such as corporatization and privatization that would destroy their "iron rice bowls." In a sense, they have become a reactionary force resisting civil service reforms initiated by the Tung administration. Such reforms were implemented with the full support of the business elites in Tung's Exco. His Exco members, especially the business people, favour civil service reforms, because they all believe that while many bureaucrats were sinecure, their efficiency should be improved and also the salaries of lower-level civil servants are much higher than similar occupations in the private sector. That the chairman of the Liberal Party, James Tien, has openly advocated a series of civil service reforms indicates the mentality of the business class. From the class perspective, civil service reform is a product of the class struggle between the big capitalist class and the working class (lower-level civil servants). After all, the Liberal Party had one of its members, Henry Tang, served as Tung's close adviser in the Exco, which also comprises other business people. In summer 2000, the confrontational tactics used by the petty bourgeoisie to oppose civil service reforms, such as the use of street demonstrations and rallies, shocked the Tung administration. Senior PRC officials had to come to the rescue of Tung by appealing to the civil servants to support him and the Basic Law. The desperate way in which the HKSAR and the PRC leaders reacted to the protests initiated by the civil servants proved the failure of their united front strategy of winning the hearts and minds of the public servants. From a critical perspective, Tung's reforms were a testimony of poor planning, an incompetent think tank and the fiasco of treating the middle-level and lower-level civil servants not as a tool of the post-colonial state, but as a potential political enemy. From a critical angle, civil service reforms have become the outcome of not only the triumph of the ruling class over the working class, but also the class struggle between the dominant capitalist class and the subordinate proletariat. Without much support from trade unions, which are relatively leaderless and disorganized, the lower-level civil servants have become powerless proletariat whose fate has been sealed by civil service reforms.

It must be noted that civil servants in both Hong Kong under British rule and the HKSAR have been internally divided into various class fractions. The upper-level civil servants can be viewed as the ruling class; the middle-level ones are the petty bourgeoisie; and the lower-level counterparts can be categorized as the proletariat. Unlike the Western proletariat whose political behaviour is confraontational vis-à-vis the ruling class, the HKSAR proletariat is relatively mild in its activities, such as protests and petitions.[63] Regardless of their class background, most members of the colonial bureaucracy shared the common interest of maintaining the political status quo and opposing any challenge to the British rule. The 1966–67 riots, which were the spill-over effects of the PRC's Cultural Revolution and which were also stimulated by a communication gap between the colonial government and the populace, were suppressed by the police force. Prior to the arrival of governor Patten, the colonial bureaucracy was politically united behind the British. "Political neutrality" was often a "myth" in colonial Hong Kong because civil servants fully supported the policies formulated by the government until the controversial democratizing reforms introduced by Patten.[64] The "political neutrality" of colonial bureaucrats was challenged by the Sino-British confrontation over Hong Kong's political reforms, for some civil servants who supported Patten's reform blueprint were openly criticized by PRC officials.[65] Regardless of opinion differences amongst the colonial bureaucrats about the desirability of Patten's political reforms, they all shared the interest of maintaining the stability and continuity of the civil service. As one former civil servant wrote:

> No matter whether civil servants are at the directorate-level, middle-level or lower-level, they all encounter the pressure from Sino-British dispute and from "democratic tide." [The Sino-British dispute] represents the struggle between the present "employer" and the future "employer," whereas the "democratic tide" represents some power-hungry politicians who use "public opinion," citizens ... and the media to ... exert pressure on civil servants at the directorate, middle and lower levels. They often talk about "fairness" ... and "fighting for the interest" of citizens. But their behaviour does not necessarily represent "fairness." They use the media and the citizens' lack of time to understand matters, exerting a lot of absolutely unfair pressure upon civil servants.[66]

Even now many bureaucrats at the directorate, middle and lower levels are distrusting and disliking politicians, for the former view political reforms toward the direction of bourgeois democracy as a menace to the status, power and job security of civil servants. In general, many civil servants in both colonial and post-colonial Hong Kong have nurtured a strong anti-democratic sentiment.

However, the income disparity in the bureaucracy between top-level officials and street-level workers at the grassroots level has remained very serious, thus producing class contradictions within the bureaucracy. Occasionally, the proletarian fraction of the bureaucracy complained about its low salaries and resorted to petitions or strike.[67] Nonetheless, the colonial and the post-colonial government have skilfully divided the proletarian fraction by co-opting civil servants from different government departments into different "consultative" bodies that discussed the pay and benefits of bureaucrats.[68] By using the colonial tactic of divide and rule, the HKSAR rulers have succeeded in neutralizing any political opposition from the proletarian fraction of the bureaucracy. The proletarian fraction within the civil service is no match for the ruling class, mainly because the former is internally divided by the latter's manipulative tactics.

In general, the proletariat in Hong Kong under British rule was loosely organized and failed to constitute a political force challenging the policies of the colonial administration. During the 1960s and the 1970s, the colonial state in Hong Kong expanded the productive forces by squeezing the surplus from labour.[69] Labour legislation was underdeveloped until the 1967 riots, when the colonial state realized that some reforms would be necessary to appease the anger of the working class.[70] In the 1980s, the proletariat became more conscious of exploitation and alienation than before, partly because of its failure to persuade the government to set up a Central Provident Fund, and partly because the issue of whether Hong Kong should import labourers from mainland China stimulated the consciousness to protect the interests of the local working class. However, proletarian solidarity in Hong Kong was and is seriously undermined by the ideological fragmentation into right-wing, independent and left-wing lines.[71] They failed to reach any consensus on the issue of political reform in Hong Kong during the entire transition period. Nor did they agree on how to push the colonial state to establish the Central Provident Fund for the working class. With only a few seats in the colonial legislature, the proletariat was politically under-represented and marginalized.

Yet, there were two major factors mitigating the grievances of the proletariat in colonial Hong Kong. First, as Hong Kong's economy continued to prosper in the 1970s, the 1980s and the early half of the 1990s, some members of the proletariat could move up the social ladder to become the bourgeoisie, thus creating an image that there was class mobility and thus minimizing proletariat discontent. Second, the proletariat tended to devote its time in work instead of political participation. Without a tradition of political activism, the proletariat was Chinese in the sense that its members expected the colonial state to be a benevolent one providing some social welfare benefits. Since the colonial state spent considerable public expenditure on social welfare after the 1966–67 riots, this dampened the demands of the proletariat and suppressed the working-class grievances at least in the short run.

Hong Kong under British rule was by and large politically stable, although the 1966–67 riots showed that some workers were dissatisfied with the colonial rule. Although the PRC and Britain argued over political reform in Hong Kong during the transition period, there was no riot parallel to the crises in 1966–67. Strictly speaking, Hong Kong during the transition period was full of political debate and controversies, instead of really having political "turbulence" or instability.[72] The stability of pre-July 1997 Hong Kong was characterized by the political dominance of the ruling class, the lack of any interest in bourgeois democracy on the part of the landed upper class, the deeply divided nature of the bourgeoisie, and the absence of proletarian solidarity. Political changes along the line of bourgeois democracy were more a top-down reform introduced by the British colonial rulers in the transition period than a bottom-up pressure exerted by any autonomous bourgeoisie. There was limited progress toward bourgeois democracy, for the coalition between the landed upper class and the ruling class treasured political stability and preferred colonial authoritarianism. The landed upper class viewed bourgeois democracy as a zero-sum game that would benefit the professional/petty bourgeoisie and the proletariat at the expense of its economic and political interests. This overall condition of class and politics in colonial Hong Kong, however, has gradually been transformed in the HKSAR since 1 July 1997.

Intensified Class Contradictions in the HKSAR

In the wake of the formation of the HKSAR, there are signs that, on the one hand, the professional/petty bourgeoisie and the proletariat have to resort to confrontational tactics and that, on the other hand, political instability will probably increase the intensity of the debate over bourgeois democracy in the long run. Moreover, social classes in the HKSAR are undergoing gradual transformations that would probably constitute a break from the past.

Most importantly, with the economic downturn of many capitalist states in Asia, the Hong Kong proletariat is facing with a danger of "pauperization."[73] Because the income disparity between the rich and the poor in the HKSAR is increasingly serious, more proletarians are complaining that they live from hands to mouth.[74] Although the HKSAR government encourages lower-class citizens to buy their flats in public housing estates in relatively cheap prices, it remains to be seen whether this policy will succeed in mitigating the grievances of the proletariat. Some proletarians were strongly opposed to the HKSAR government's decision of importing workers from mainland China, for they viewed it as a menace to their job opportunities locally. What is more, in the minds of some proletarians, working-class leaders such as Tam Yiu-chung of the pro-China Federation of Trade Unions have not only been co-opted into Exco but also politically neutralized. From a critical perspective, a minority of working-class unionists have become "labour aristocrat," to borrow from Lenin, because they appear to lose the will to fight for proletarian interest once they are co-opted into the post-colonial state apparatus.[75] In the event that more proletarians perceive their leaders as becoming part of the state apparatus without the determination to fight for their interests, they will become more critical of both the post-colonial state and their unionist leaders than ever before, thus precipitating a possible split within the pro-Beijing proletariat. In April 2002, the HKSAR's unemployment rate reached an unprecedented seven per cent, whether the government will tackle unemployment effectively determines the extent to which the proletariat will increasingly be "revolutionized" or radicalized. Radicalization of the proletariat will likely take the forms of more frequent violent confrontations and clashes with the police on the streets of Hong Kong.

Given the fact that the pro-Beijing or "patriotic" fraction of the proletariat is facing the dilemma of supporting the post-colonial state on the one hand and protecting the proletarian interest on the other, the independent fraction of the proletariat will likely be politically supported by more workers than before. Independent unions in Hong Kong, such as the Confederation of Trade Unions (CTU), have expanded rapidly since the military crackdown of student demonstrators in the PRC in June 1989.[76] Traditionally, independent unions have adopted a critical stance on both the government and the PRC's policies toward Hong Kong. Their emergence has already replaced the pro-Kuomintang Trade Union Council, which is plagued by the lack of leadership, the decline of membership and the dominance of old Chinese supportive of the Nationalist Party in Taiwan.[77] Nonetheless, the PRC and the post-colonial state attempted to co-opt a leader of the independent CTU, Lee Kai-ming, into political institutions, such as the Privisional Legislative Council.[78] Although PRC officials and the senior Hong Kong bureaucrats have used co-optation strategy to deal with the independent fraction of the proletariat, it is unlikely that the majority of its leaders will abandon a critical attitude to oppose the political establishment.

Given the increase in proletarian consciousness since the late 1980s and given the serious income gap between the haves and the have-nots in the HKSAR, it is likely that the proletariat will become more economically alienated and politically militant than the colonial era. Since the post-colonial state apparatus is increasingly dominated by the members of the landed upper class, their class contradictions with the proletariat are gradually becoming more prominent and acute than before. The frequent proletarian complaints about (1) a collusion between the HKSAR government and big business and (2) the failure of the government to reduce unemployment illustrate the rising discontent on the part of the proletariat. Such discontent, if not tackled by the HKSAR's ruling class urgently and effectively, will surely trigger violent confrontation between the proletariat and the police on the HKSAR streets in the long run.[79]

More alarmingly, the various fractions of bourgeoisie are increasingly dissatisfied with the post-colonial state. Except for the mainland Chinese bourgeoisie which fully supports the HKSAR government, the independent/professional bourgeoisie wants to envisage a faster pace of bourgeois democracy because its members were politically ignored and alienated from the chaotic governance of the HKSAR.[80] The independent/professional bourgeoisie was also antagonized by the Sino-British dispute over Hong Kong's political reforms in the final years of the British rule. The democrats such as Martin Lee were forced to leave the legislature on 1 July 1997 when the PRC used the provisional legislature to replace the former Legco elected in the Patten era. Although the independent bourgeoisie has returned to the first Legco of the HKSAR after the May 1998 elections, the reality is that it remains a political minority in the legislature where representation is constantly distorted in favour of the capitalist class. With only one-third of the 60-seat Legco directly elected by citizens, the independent/professional fraction of the bourgeoisie is bound to be an opposition in the law-making body. The crux of the problem is that there may be an internal split within the independent fraction of the bourgeoisie, for some Democratic Party (DP) members have formed a political discussion group named New Momentum in December 2001. In April 2002, some disgruntled DP members eventually left the party for another democratic flagship, the Frontier, that is led by Emily Lau. It is likely that the independent fraction of the bourgeoisie will continue to be split into various factions: one advocating reforms within the existing political institutions (Democratic Party), the moderates emphasizing dialogue with the ruling class and the PRC (the New Momentum led by Anthony Cheung), and the others opposing the ruling class through street protests and confrontation (political groups such as the Frontier and the now defunct Social Democratic Forum).

Even worse, the dependent (or the relatively less politically active and economically more pragmatic) fraction of the bourgeoisie is also increasingly dissatisfied with the post-colonial state. Some members of the dependent bourgeoisie belong to the propertied class, which has become the victim of the Asian economic crisis and the declining property market since October 1997. Some members of the dependent bourgeoisie, especially those landlords, were alienated by the refusal of the post-colonial state to lend a helping hand to those middle-class members with "negative equity." The dependent bourgeoisie also hated the government policy of building 85,000 flats per year because it regarded any increase in the number of flats as a further blow to the already debilitated property market. Moreover, some members of the dependent bourgeoisie belong to the population that shoulders the heaviest burden of taxation in Hong Kong. They are disappointed that the HKSAR administration decided to sell the flats of public housing estates in cheap price to the lower classes, for they believe that the post-colonial state does not really care about their well-being. In the event that the dependent sector of the bourgeoisie is continuing to be economically alienated and politically distrustful of the authorities, its members will probably be forced to support the independent bourgeoisie to call for more political reforms in the HKSAR. According to the Basic Law — a mini-constitution for the HKSAR — the year 2007 will envisage a review of the progress of political reform in the territory. It can be anticipated that the independent/professional bourgeoisie must push for more bourgeois democracy. If so, the alienated and dependent fraction of the bourgeoisie may support the political demands of the independent/professional/petty bourgeoisie. Subsequently, the HKSAR government dominated by the landed upper class and the senior bureaucrats will sooner or later encounter a more forceful, united, and perhaps more militant opposition from the bourgeoisie than ever before. If the economic downturn cannot be arrested by 2007, the alienated proletariat will probably seek to forge a temporary alliance with the pro-democracy bourgeoisie. At that juncture, the central government in Beijing may be forced to intervene in the HKSAR's politics in a bid to achieve political stability and to maintain the political preponderance of the conservative-minded ruling class.

Conclusion

Colonial Hong Kong was characterized by the collaboration between the ruling class and the capitalist class. However, the ruling class appeared to be relatively autonomous from the influence of the landed upper class. The loose coalition of the senior bureaucrats and the landed upper class blocked any drastic attempt to reform the colonial polity. While the landed upper class was opposed to bourgeois democracy, the senior bureaucrats reluctantly accepted some political reforms initiated by governor Patten in the final years of British rule in Hong Kong. The landed upper class was ethnically split into Chinese and British, who were competing amongst themselves, uninterested in politics, and were most concerned about capital accumulation and profit maximization.

The bourgeoisie was also divided into three fractions: (1) the dependent/professional bourgeoisie which was relatively politically less active; (2) the independent/liberal/professional bourgeoisie which was supportive of bourgeois democracy; and (3) the mainland Chinese bourgeoisie which was economically, culturally and politically assimilated by Hong Kong's capitalist values and lifestyle. Like the bourgeoisie, the proletariat remained ideologically divided. Some of the proletarian leaders were co-opted into the colonial polity, relegating to a political minority that failed to articulate working-class interests effectively.

With the establishment of the HKSAR, class contradictions have become much sharper and more acute than ever before. The landed upper class is trying to dominate the post-colonial apparatus, while at the same time exerting pressure on the ruling class to ensure that its business interests in the property market are fully protected. The proletariat, however, increasingly sees the landed upper class as the exploiter who squeezes its surplus labour. The proletariat is also undergoing an internal transformation, with the pro-Beijing or "patriotic" unionists facing the political dilemma of supporting the post-colonial state on the one hand and fighting for working-class interests on the other. Simultaneously, there is a gradual increase in the popular support of the independent fraction of the proletariat, whose critical attitude toward the post-colonial state in Hong Kong can win the hearts and minds of many members of the proletariat. Although the HKSAR proletariat is not as militant and revolutionary as its counterpart in the West, it is increasingly radicalized and pauperized because of the worsening unemployment and the income gap between the rich and the poor. Sooner or later, the proletariat will loom as a more powerful force that will have to be tackled by the capitalist-dominated HKSAR government.

Last but not the least, the bourgeoisie is increasingly alienated in the HKSAR both economically and politically. Some members of the bourgeoisie are increasingly proletarianized because of the Asian economic crisis, the global economic downturn after the September 11th incident in 2001, and the persistent unemployment in the HKSAR. The independent/liberal/professional fraction of the bourgeoisie will eventually try its best to push the post-colonial state to become more responsive to its demands. As a result, it will probably form a coalition with the independent proletariat to push for bourgeois democracy in the HKSAR in the long run. It can be anticipated that if the economic downturn cannot be improved in the short and medium terms, the HKSAR government will definitely encounter a serious and an unprecedented crisis of legitimacy in the years approaching 2007 when the public are encouraged to review the progress of political development.

However, one crucial determinant shaping whether the HKSAR will move forward along the path of bourgeois democracy remains the PRC's political stance. So long as the PRC is undergoing a capitalist modernization while at the same time maintaining its political authoritarianism, the development of bourgeois democracy in the HKSAR is bound to be piecemeal, limited, controversial and painful. Although the PRC is experiencing economic liberalization and globalization of capitalism, it is unclear whether such processes will definitely propel China along the road of bourgeois democratic revolution. The PRC's political development will undoubtedly determine the extent to which the HKSAR will move gradually toward bourgeois democracy. Yet, regardless of the unpredictable path of the PRC's democratization, it appears that the HKSAR's internal metamorphosis is pointing towards an inevitable class struggle that has traditionally been swept under the carpet by many political observers.

In the final analysis, the political conservatism of the ruling class, including the senior bureaucrats, and of the landed upper class in the HKSAR will constrain any movement toward bourgeois democracy. The ruling class and the landed upper class stick to the political bottom line of the central government in Beijing, maintaining the view that bourgeois democracy would constitute a national security threat. Moreover, bourgeois democracy would directly threaten the political power of the ruling class and the economic interest of the dominant capitalist class, especially the landed upper class. If so, the subordinate classes in support of bourgeois democracy will become politically frustrated and alienated. This alienation will, however, probably lead to inevitably violent confrontation, political instability and ironically an opportunity for the further development toward bourgeois democracy in the HKSAR in the distant future.

In order to maintain political stability in the HKSAR, the ruling class will be hard-pressed to maintain a certain distance from the dominant capitalist class. Any prolonged image of maintaining the unholy alliance between the ruling class and the dominant capitalist class will merely infuriate the independent/liberal/professional bourgeoisie and the independent proletariat. Unlike the colonial regime that sometimes attempted to maintain some degree of relative autonomy from the dominant capitalist class, the ruling class in the HKSAR has failed to do so. Various pro-business policies have been formulated without sufficient consultation with the public, let alone explanation or justification of such policies. As such, there is a deep-rooted impression amongst the ordinary citizens that the HKSAR government is ruling the territory in collusion with the capitalist class. Unless this impression is diluted and altered, the HKSAR's political instability will continue to be endangered, especially if economic problems such as unemployment and serious income disparity between the rich and the poor are not sufficiently addressed. If political stability in colonial Hong Kong was partly attributable to a precarious balance between the power of the ruling class and that of the capitalist class, political instability in the HKSAR will likely be a product of the failure of the ruling class to retain such precarious balance. Political development in the HKSAR will definitely be shaped by class politics and class struggle in the years to come.

Notes

1. Barrington Moore, Jr., *Social Origins of Dictatorship and Democracy: Lord and Peasant in the Making of the Modern World* (Boston: Beacon, 1966).
2. Ibid., p. 39 and pp. 430–31.
3. Ibid., p. 316.
4. In October 2001, a Hong Kong couple threatened to poison the Chief Executive and some of the pro-Beijing politicians, like legislators Chan Yuen-han and Tsang Yok-sing, for their failure to tackle the economic downturn of the HKSAR. See *Ming Pao*, 4 October 2001, p. A1.
5. There were some exceptions. See, for example, Joe England, *Hong Kong: Britain's Responsibility* (London: Fabian Society, 1976). Also see Lo Shiu Hing, "Hong Kong: Post-colonialism and political conflict," in Richard Robison and David S. G. Goodman, *The New Rich in Asia: Mobile Phones, McDonalds and Middle-class Revolution* (London: Routledge, 1996), pp. 163–81.
6. For a good review of Marx's discussion of class and the state, see Martin Carnoy, *The State and Political Theory* (New Jersey: Princeton University Press, 1984), Chapter Two, pp. 44–64. Also see P. H. Vigor, "Marx and Modern Capitalism," in David Thomson (ed.), *Political Ideas* (New York: Basic Books, 1966), pp. 176–88. For a critique of Marx, see Peter Saunders,

Social Class and Stratification (London: Routledge, 1990), pp. 10–19. Regardless of the criticisms of Marx, this chapter treats class as "a historical category: that is, it is derived from the observation of social process over time. We know about class because people have repeatedly behaved in class ways; these historical events disclose regularities of response to analogous situations, and at a certain stage (the 'mature' formations of class0 we observe the creation of institutions, and of culture with class notations, which admits of trans-national comparisons." For this excellent treatment of class, see E. P. Thompson, "Class and Class Struggle," in Patrick Joyce (ed.), *Class* (Oxford: Oxford University Press, 1995), p. 133.

7. Ralph Miliband, *Socialism for a Sceptical Age* (New York: Verso, 1995), p. 16.
8. Ibid., p. 16.
9. Ralph Miliband, *The State in Capitalist Society: The Analysis of the Western System of Power* (London: Quartet Books, 1976), p. 52.
10. Ibid., pp. 52–53.
11. The Cooperative Resources Centre was formed by some pro-business Legco members, like Allen Lee Peng-fei, after the resounding success of the pro-democracy United Democrats of Hong Kong. See Lo Shiu-hing, "Legislative Cliques, Political Parties, Political Groupings and Electoral System," in Joseph Y. S. Cheng and Sonny S. H. Lo (eds.), *From Colony to SAR: Hong Kong's Challenges Ahead* (Hong Kong: The Chinese University Press, 1995), pp. 53–54.
12. For the recent performance of the LP in Legco's elections, see Lo Shiu-hing, Yu Wing-yat and Wan Kwok-fai, "Introduction," in *Chinese Law & Government: The 2000 Legislative Council Elections in the Hong Kong Special Administrative Region*, Vol. 34, No. 2 (March/April 2001), pp. 3–27; and Lo Shiu-hing, "An Analysis of the Election Results," in *Chinese Law & Government: The First Hong Kong Special Administrative Region Legislative Council Elections*, Vol. 32, No. 2 (March/April 1999), pp. 12–27.
13. *Hong Kong iMail*, October 3, 2001, p. A6.
14. Ibid.
15. Ralph Miliband, *Marxism and Politics* (London: Oxford University Press, 1978), p. 32.
16. Miliband said: "In the Marxist perspective, proletarian class-consciousness may be taken to mean the achievement of an understanding that the emancipation of the proletariat and the liberation of the society require the overthrow of capitalism; and this understanding may also be taken to entail the will to overthrow it. It is in this sense that proletarian class-consciousness is also revolutionary consciousness." Ibid., p. 33.
17. For a critical discussion of the powerlessness of Hong Kong's legislators and District Councillors, see Lo Shiu-hing, *Governing Hong Kong: Legitimacy,*

Communication and Political Decay (New York: Nova Science, 2001), pp. 250–60.

18. Miliband, *Marxism and Politics*, p. 26.
19. Ibid., p. 25.
20. Ibid., p. 24.
21. Miliband, *Socialism for a Sceptical Age*, p. 18.
22. For example, Tung Chee-hwa, an Exco member appointed by governor Patten, disagreed with Patten's stance on the Provisional Legislative Council — a body established by the PRC to replace the last colonial legislature. Patten's Exco members like Raymond Chien and Felice Liehmak also spoke against his political reform blueprint in public. See Lo, *Governing Hong Kong*, Chapter 4; and Lo Shiu-hing, "Changing Dimensions of Executive–Legislative Relations: The Case of Hong Kong," *Public Policy and Administration*, Vol. 7, No. 2 (September 1998), pp. 73–103.
23. Sir Sze-yuen Chung, *Hong Kong's Journel to Reunification: Memoirs of Sze-yuen Chung* (Hong Kong: The Chinese University Press, 2001), p. 23.
24. See Steve Tsang (ed.), *A Documentary History of Hong Kong Government and Politics* (Hong Kong: Hong Kong University Press, 1995), p. 67.
25. For details, see Chris Patten, *East and West* (London: Macmillan, 1998), Chapter 2, pp. 38–83; Jonathan Dimbleby, *The Last Governor: Chris Patten & the Handover of Hong Kong* (London: Little, Brown and Company, 1997), pp. 211–32; and John Flowerdew, *The Final Years of British Hong Kong: The Discourse of Colonial Withdrawal* (London: Macmillan, 1998), pp. 124–25.
26. For details, see Lo Shiu-hing, *Governing Hong Kong: Legitimacy, Communication and Political Decay*.
27. Originally, Tung appointed land surveyor Leung Chun-ying as the Exco member responsible for land policy and businessman Anthony Leung Kam-chung as another Exco member dealing with education. Later, this design did not really work. With the exception of Anthony Leung who was active in the formulation of education policies before he became the Financial Secretary in April 2001, Leung Chun-ying and even Tam Yiu-chung, who were appointed by Tung to be responsible for housing and elderly policies, did not have any performance. Although policy-making powers remained in the hands of the senior bureaucrats, not Exco members, the former initially viewed the latter as politicians whose interest and working style are different from civil servants. Thus, mutual distrust and jealousy are inevitable.
28. In April 2002, a pro-Beijing elite openly criticized Tam as being co-opted by the HKSAR government without any determination to fight for the interest of the working class. This was actually a valid criticism because Tam appeared to act like a labour aristocrat.
29. Tung and his Exco also failed to act immediately, see Lo Shiu-hing,

"Leadership found wanting over bird flu," Letter to the editor, *South China Morning Post*, 30 December 1997, p. 14.

30. Ian Scott, *Political Change and the Crisis of Legitimacy in Hong Kong* (Hong Kong: Oxford University Press, 1989), p. 56.
31. Ibid., pp. 58–59.
32. For the concept of "relative autonomy," see Miliband, *Marxism and Politics*, pp. 74–90.
33. The Shanghai capitalists could also be seen as the "first generation of Hong Kong's bourgeoisie." See Lo, "Hong Kong: Post-colonialism and Political Conflict," p. 164.
34. C. K. Lau, *Hong Kong's Colonial Legacy* (Hong Kong: The Chinese University Press, 1997), p. 85.
35. Fung Pong-yin, *Hong Kong's British Capital and Financial Conglomerates* (in Chinese) (Hong Kong: Commercial Press, 1996), pp. 277–83.
36. Ibid., pp. 385–91.
37. Ibid., p. 387.
38. See Joseph Cheng (ed.), *Hong Kong In Search of a Future* (Hong Kong: Oxford University Press, 1984), p. 241.
39. Scott argues that the Hong Kong "bureaucracy's relative autonomy vis-à-vis economic interests remained, but those interests … had their representatives in the decision-making process." See Scott, *Political Change and the Crisis of Legitimacy*, p. 60.
40. Ambrose Yeo-chi King, "Administrative Absorption of Politics in Hong Kong: Emphasis on the Grass Roots Level," *Asian Survey*, Vol. 15, No. 5 (May 1975).
41. Joan Y. H. Leung, "Functional Representation in Hong Kong: Institutionalization and Legitimization of the Business and Professional Elites," *Asian Journal of Public Administration*, Vol. 12, No. 2 (December 1990).
42. The former director of the New China News Agency, Xu Jiatun, encouraged some businessmen to form the Hong Kong Progressive Alliance as another pro-business political force apart from the Liberal Party. For China's united front work in Hong Kong, see Benson Wong, "Can Co-optation Win Over the Hong Kong People? China's United Front Work in Hong Kong Since 1984," *Issues & Studies*, Vol. 33, No. 5 (May 1997).
43. Lo Shiu-hing, "Colonial Policy-Makers, Capitalist Class and China: Determinants of Electoral Reform in Hong Kong's and Macau's Legislatures," *Pacific Affairs*, Vol. 62, No. 2 (Summer 1989).
44. One interesting interpretation of how the colonial state operated in Hong Kong under British rule was offered by Ngo Tak-wing. He wrote: "'[T]he strategies of rule' used by the colonial state … aimed at maintaining governance, can hardly be conceived as 'indirect rule.' Quite the opposite, the colonial state had painstakingly tried to assert itself in the social fabrics of an alien populace.

This was necessary because, the conventional view to the contrary notwithstanding, Hong Kong society was not an apathetic, atomistic entity without political grievances and social conflicts so that the ruler faced little difficulty in governance. In reality, conflicts and social cleavages in turn provided the basis for the colonial state to serercise leverage and manoeuvre events into the desired directions — in other words, to advance its strategies of rule. In return, state manipulation allowed different social actors to make use of state sanctions to advance their own interests. The result is the unfolding of complex social relationships that formed the backbone of Hong Kong's history." See Ngo Tak-wing, "Colonialism in Hong Kong Revisited," in Ngo Tak-wing (ed.), *Hong Kong's History: State and Society under Colonial Rule* (London: Routledge, 1998), p. 5.

45. For the views of critics, see Luk Tak-chuen, "China and Hong Kong Free Trade Zone will expel the tiger but welcome the wolf," *Apple Daily*, 19 December 2001, p. E13.
46. For an insightful study of working-class politics in Hong Kong, see Ming Chan, "Hong Kong Workers toward 1997: Unionization, Labour Activism and Political Participation under the China Factor," *Australian Journal of Politics and History*, Vol. 47, No. 1 (2001).
47. Yung is now a member of the Board of Directors in the Hong Kong Jockey Club. In the past, the Royal Hong Kong Jockey Club was exclusively managed and dominated by the British expatriates. The fact that Yung is a Board member fully testifies the transformation of "socialists" in the mainland to capitalists in Hong Kong.
48. In 1992, the PRC's State Council granted CITIC autonomy to borrow and invest in the mainland without having to get official approval provided that the projects would not exceed *Renminbi* 200 million for domestic activities or US$30 million for foreign undertakings. See Cheung Tai Ming, "The Power of CITIC," in Frank Ching (ed.), *China in Transition* (Hong Kong: Review Publishing Company Limited, 1995), p. 66.
49. For a discussion of China's legal modernization, see Carlos Wing-hung Lo, *China's Legal Awakening: Legal Theory and Criminal Justice in Deng's Era* (Hong Kong: Hong Kong University Press, 1995).
50. Michael DeGolyer, "Winter of Despair: confidence and legitimacy in crisis in the Hong Kong SAR," a report of the Hong Kong Transition Project publicly released in December 2001, p. 46.
51. For Tung's target of achieving 70 per cent ownership rate in ten years, see *Building Hong Kong For A New Era: Address by the Chief Executive The Honourable Tung Chee-hwa at the Provisional Legislative Council Meeting on 8 October 1997* (Hong Kong: Government Printer, 1997).
52. See *Building Hong Kong For A New Era: Address by the Chief Executive The Honourable Tung Chee-hwa at the Provisional Legislative Council*

Meeting on 8 October 1997 (Hong Kong: Government Printer, 1997), pp. 19–20.

53. See John P. Burns, "Succession Planning and Localization," in Ian Scott and John P. Burns (eds.), *The Hong Kong Civil Service and Its Future* (Hong Kong: Oxford University Press, 1988), pp. 96–105.
54. Lo Shiu-hing, "The Politics of Localization of the Civil Service in Hong Kong and Macau," *Journal of Commonwealth & Comparative Politics*, Vol. 33, No. 1 (March 1995), pp. 103–36.
55. In traditional China, there was an examination-oriented civil service system and those intellectuals who passed the civil service examination became "the elite elements" that "mediated the sharply confrontational relationship between the monarchical power and ordinary citizens." See Chang Pao-min, *The Dilemmas of China's Modernization* (in Chinese) (Hong Kong: Ming Pao, 1992), p. 173.
56. For these managerial values, see David H. Rosenblaum, *Public Administration: Understanding Management, Politics, and Law in the Public Sector* (New York: McGraw-Hill Book Company, 1989), p. 17.
57. For the situation in the colonial era, see S. N. G. Davies, "One Brand of Politics Rekindled," *Hong Kong Law Journal*, Vol. 7 (1977).
58. Property tax and business profit tax are traditionally maintained at 15 per cent, thus providing "little or no disincentive effect on work effort, investment and enterprise." See Y. C. Jao, "The Financial Structure," in David Lethbridge (ed.), *The Business Environment in Hong Kong* (Hong Kong: Oxford University Press, 1987), p. 164.
59. Alvin Y. So, *Hong Kong's Embattled Democracy* (Baltimore: The Johns Hopkins University Press, 1999), pp. 28–51.
60. Moore, *Social Origins of Dictatorship and Democracy*, p. 459.
61. For Patten's reform blueprint, see Jonathan Dimbleby, *The Last Governor: Chris Patten & The Handover of Hong Kong* (London: Little, Brown and Company, 1997), pp. 114–24.
62. The Chinese bureaucrats who disagreed with Patten's political reform policy and opted for early retirement included the former Secretary for Transport, Yeung Kai-yin, and the former Secretary for Education and Manpower, John Chan Cho-chak. Even Anson Chan, the Chief Secretary, felt that there was no rush for Patten's reform blueprint to be passed by the law-making Legislative Council. If this was true, Chan hoped for successful Sino-British negotiations over Patten's reform package rather than encountering a breakdown in negotiations. For Chan's response to reforms, see ibid., pp. 207–8.
63. I totally disagree with the reviewer's argument that proletariat is "a well-established Euro-centric terms [that is imposed by me] on the contemporary Hong Kong socio-economic landscape." It is a useful analytical category that can be comfortably applied to the HKSAR setting. Although the HKSAR

proletariat does not necessarily have the "revolutionary" potential as its counterpart in Europe, the increasing income disparity in the HKSAR is arguably revolutionizing the local proletariat silently. What is interesting is that in the HKSAR where some mainland Chinese are struggling to have the right of abode in the territory, they are increasingly using protests and petitions to make their demands heard. Arguably, they belong to a new fraction of the proletariat in the HKSAR. Their plight is understood by some local trade unionists, who fight for their collective interest of struggling for the welfare of the proletariat. Thereby, a loose alliance between the mainland Chinese workers and the local Hong Kong Chinese unionists has emerged, albeit the local Chinese civil servants are spectators without participation in their cause. Anyway, the author thanks the reviewer for his or her sharp observations and arguments, 22 February 2002.

64. Political neutrality is a concept that entails several dimensions, including the civil servants' behavior of not participating in political activities, of being loyal to the government, and of maintaining impartiality in policy advice and administration. See Ian Scott, "Civil Service Neutrality in Hong Kong," in Haile K. Asmeron and Elisa P. Reis (eds.), *Democratization and Bureaucratic Neutrality* (London: Macmillan, 1996), pp. 277–312.
65. The former Secretary for Education and manpower, John Chan, pointed out this problem. He said: "On the one hand, it would make sense to establish good working relations with the future sovereign power, in order to gain its confidence and trust in their ability to exercise the autonomy that has been promised in the Joint Declaration to the future HKSAR. On the other hand, their professional ethics require them to work within the boundaries of the 'corporate objectives' of the existing Hong Kong government." See John C.C. Chan, "The Civil Service: Continuity and Change," in Wang Gungwu and Wong Siu-lun (eds.), *Hong Kong's Transition: A Decade After the Deal* (Hong Kong: Oxford University Press, 1995), pp. 30–31.
66. Tsin Sai-nin, *1997: A Review and Prospects of the Hong Kong Civil Service Structure* (in Chinese) (Hong Kong: The Civil Service Pensioner's Association Limited, December 1996), pp. 18–19.
67. The year 1989–1990 saw numerous industrial disputes involving government doctors, court interpreters, land and surveying officers and firemen. See Anthony B. L. Cheung, "The Civil Service," in Richard Y. C. Wong and Joseph Y. S. Cheng (eds.), *The Other Hong Kong Report 1990* (Hong Kong: The Chinese University Press, 1990), pp. 100–4.
68. These bodies include the Standing Commission on Civil Service Salaries and Conditions of Service, the Standing Committee on Disciplined Services Salaries and Conditions of Service, the Standing Committee on Directorate Salaries and Conditions and Service, and the Standing Committee on Judicial Salaries and Conditions and Services. See Anthony B. L. Cheung, "The Civil

Service Pay System in Hong Kong: Implications for Efficiency and Equity," in John P. Burns (ed.), *Asian Civil Service Systems: Improving Efficiency and Productivity* (Singapore: Times Academic Press, 1994), p. 273.

69. Lau Chin-shek, an independent trade union leader in Hong Kong, said: "There were some girls who were clearly below the legal employment age, but, since they were desperate to work, they brought their mother's or their sister's identity cards when they applied for a job. They were really exploited, and were paid a lot less than I was earning. It was quite common in those days during the 1960s for children to work seven days a week, twelve hours a day, in a factory." Interview with Lau, "Lau Chin-shek: From Refugee to Trade Union Leader," in Sally Blyth and Ian Wotherspoon (eds.), *Hong Kong Remembers* (Hong Kong: Oxford University Press, 1996), p. 71.
70. One reform was the reduction of working hours of women and young person (those aged 14 to 17 years) from 60 hours a week to 48 hours a week. See Joe England, *Industrial Relations and Law in Hong Kong* (Hong Kong: Oxford University Press, 1989), p. 180.
71. Ibid., pp. 128–30.
72. For the argument that Hong Kong during the transition period envisaged political "turbulence," see Ian Scott, "Policy-making in a Turbulent Environment: The Case of Hong Kong," *International Review of Administrative Sciences*, Vol. 52, No. 4 (December 1986).
73. Anthony Giddens, *Capitalism and Modern Social Theory* (Cambridge: Cambridge University Press, 1987), pp. 56–57.
74. Members of the proletariat are increasing as more immigrants from the PRC arrive the HKSAR. They are struggling to find jobs and to feed their family members. As a matter of fact, Hong Kong has a "lumpenproletariat," to use Marx's term, such as beggars and the "cagemen." The "cagemen" are "pensioners without a family, whose home is a bed space surrounded by wire mesh to keep their few belongings safe, with a one-twentieth share of a lavatory and bathroom." See Frank Welsh, *A History of Hong Kong* (London: Harper Collins, 1997), p. 483.
75. For Lenin, the "labour aristocrat" represented trade unionism, which was "the ideological enslavement of the workers to the bourgeoisie." See R. N. Carew Hunt, *The Theory and Practice of Communism* (Middlesex: Penguin, 1978), p. 168.
76. Lau Chin-shek said: "The June 4th protests in Beijing had a profound effect on the labour movement, and resulted in a change in our policies. Tiananmen brought home the fact that there was a need for a truly independent trade union in Hong Kong before 1997 ... The CTU was therefore inaugurated in 1990, comprising thirty-nine trade unions. In 1996, it had more than 120,000 members." See "Lau Chin-shek: From Refugee to Trade Union Leader," in Blyth and Wotherspoon (eds.), *Hong Kong Remembers*, p. 74.

77. The decline of membership in the Trade Union Council took place as early as the late 1970s. See England, *Industrial Relations and Law in Hong Kong*, p. 139.
78. Lee participated in the 400-member Election Committee selecting the Chief Executive and he was later elected to the provisional legislature. For a good discussion of how PRC officials co-opted various classes into a network of political institutions, see Owen H. H. Wong, *China and Britain: Diplomatic Controversies and Hong Kong Policies* (Hong Kong: Chong Kin Academic Society, 1994), pp. 189–206.
79. See Lo Shiu-hing, "Hidden Frustrations Threaten Hong Kong's Stability," *Asian Wall Street Journal*, 8 October 1997. In fact, 67 per cent of the 759 respondents in the Hong Kong Transition Project's survey in November 2001 were worried about the likelihood of social unrest in the HKSAR. See DeGolyer, "Winter of Despair," p. 64.
80. For misgovernance in the HKSAR, see Lo, *Governing Hong Kong: Legitimacy, Communication and Political Decay*.

13

The Politics of Health Reform

P. C. Leung

Professor of Orthopaedics and Traumatology
The Chinese University of Hong Kong
and
Chairman, Ethics Committee, Medical Council, Hong Kong

Synopsis

Health Reform became a sensitive and urgent issue ever since the Harvard Report which analysed the Hong Kong health delivery system and proposed changes. Health Reform became more urgent when Hong Kong faced a desperate need for budget cut and when medical graduates became unemployed. The need for reform was made more complicated by the recognition of Chinese medicine and the outcry for the provision of such service.

In the two past decades, there has been a lot of official effort to reform the health delivery system in Hong Kong such as the Halnan Report, the formation of the Hospital Authority, the Harvard Report and the current reform green paper. In spite of the many papers, studies and discussions, the major targets viz., improving the service and limiting costs, have not been reached. Leadership and effective implementation have been particularly worrying after 1997.

Introduction

It would not be an over statement to say that the past ten years, with the year of change of sovereignty in the middle, was a decade of change. Changes occurred in all fields and affected every walk of life. Apart from the drastic changes in the political system, there were equivalent changes in all branches of the civil service. Of all the changes, the most dramatic can be seen in the medical and health sectors. Before this decade of change, no one in the field would have imagined that things could be totally changed within a short period, and changes are still continuing month by month and week by week. The changes that occurred were replaced by new changes before any proper assessment of results.

Slow change allows for simultaneous evaluation; rapid, multiple, complex alternations do not allow for proper assessment, and can bring with it uncertainties and frustration. Such changes not only took the existing system in new directions, they introduced basic issues like peoples' expectations of a profession and the requirements of a professional's response to those expectations.

In this chapter, I will discuss the changes in the different aspects of health services in the hospitals and clinics, experts' recommendations, the changing policy, and the situation in training arrangements. This approach is a macroscopic one, including historical considerations. Events and issues are used to illustrate development trends. They will not be analysed or evaluated in detail.

Towards 1997

In the late 1980s, although Hong Kong was enjoying the long period of prosperity, and civil services were reasonably funded, the Medical and Health Service took a prophetic look at health care finance and realized that the rising costs of medical care would not be met solely by taxpayers' revenue (Medical and Health Department 1987).

In an effort to bring in a new system of health care service, Halnan, a consultant from the United Kingdom was brought in. A drastic reform was considered necessary to replace the old charity system. Under the charity system that had been in place since Hong Kong's colonial days, hospital and clinic fees were minimal gestures of payment. All disease management necessities, expensive or ordinary, were paid by taxpayers' contributions. Nearly every item in government hospitals was given free to the patients (Leung 1998). During those years, medical and health expenses constituted about five per cent of income tax revenue. The problems facing the health care system during those years were as follows:

- Overcrowding of the hospitals;
- rapidly rising health expenses;
- rigid civil service regulations limiting flexibilities of positive reforms;

- work of the health deliverers not accountable to the cost;
- lack of transparency of policy making and administrative implementation; and
- lack of incentives for working professionals.

Obviously, the problems of those years were not confined to costs and expenses alone. Halnan's report was the result of an outcry from the profession and the public for improvement of services, of administrative efficiency and professional standards. Therefore the purpose of the Halnan review was to propose ways to change the charity system so that reasonable reforms could be started, by separating hospital service from civil service, so that the quality of hospital services could be improved and so that the hospitals would be more accountable to the users (Halnan 1988). The report might have downplayed problems other than the rising costs and overcrowded hospitals.

The direct result of the Halnan Report was the establishment of the Hospital Authority in 1990. This administrative body got direct funding from the government yet workers serving the hospitals did not belong to the civil service. The concept was that civil services were under too much bureaucracy which prevented advances and undermined accountability. Separating the hospitals from the civil service would allow for better management and allocation of resources, would make workers more responsible and disciplined, and the whole service would be more accountable to the community.

The Hospital Authority did not work directly under the civil service. Therefore it had more independence in establishing its staff, salary structure, planning, and responsibilities. One remarkable difference of the new authority was the political orientation it adopted compared with the old system. The fact that local politicians of different levels were invited to serve as advisers brought on a conversion towards more accountability and transparency. It also meant that the authority could now mobilize political forces to achieve its goals related to funding and welfare.

The Board Chairman was the most powerful executive councilor in the government and had no difficulty getting a five to ten-fold increase of management personnel, extra millions to build new hospitals, new annexes, and new wings, and personnel were happy because their income was increased tow to three fold (Hospital Authority 1993–95).

The doubling to tripling of the work force, the sudden appearance of managerial strength at both upper and middle ranks and above all the rising income for all, gave the hospitals a remarkable new appearance. Canvas beds for temporary accommodation became history. On the other hand, the majestic, marble laden entry halls to the big public hospitals were eye-pleasing show windows. The early outcome of the establishment of the Hospital Authority was certainly more expenses, which ran counter to the Halnan Report. Nevertheless, Hong Kong was enjoying the most prosperous years, and apparently, the government was not concerned.

This was the situation before and after the change of political sovereignty. The hospital services possessed great new buildings, ran effective teams of working personnel and were equipped with state-of-the-art equipment.

These achievements were attained by pumping in extra resources. Before the establishment of the Hospital Authority, public medical expenses were kept below five to seven per cent of the annual budget. With the new initiative, the budget was markedly increased to an annual rate of 1–1.5 per cent, and if the trend continued it would double. The attempt the charge the users more so as to better balance the budget remained stagnant. There was a short period of exploration in 1994 to see how people reacted to paying more at government hospitals. The proposal was to increase hospital fees so that an overall five per cent of total expenses would be paid by users. The result had been most disappointing. Politicians took up the issue and the attempt was terminated almost immediately.

With the increased resources, new hospitals with marbled reception halls, teams of staff, and a variety new services catering to the growing need of the general population, were established. Waiting lists were effectively shortened. Citizens were impressed and praised the tremendous improvements. Within hospital circles, workers enjoyed the improved environment and hastened to attribute the improvements to modern management skills. Even more new positions on administration were created.

Actually during the prosperous years, the Hospital Authority involved itself in areas which, historically, and in other countries, did not belong to the Hospital Administration such as training and research as well as primary health care.

Normally academic institutions and professional groups took care of the training of the young professionals. However, during the early years of the Hospital Authority, it had the ambition of getting involved in training and research by getting its own funding sources. It spent millions of dollars every year running international conferences and many smaller training courses on managerial subjects. Instead of giving more support to the universities on training and research, it built up its own separate network which intentionally ignored what was happening in the local academic circles.

One of the much criticized principles during the formation of the Hospital Authority was the failure of linking primary care with hospital service. Health service given to the citizens should start with primary care, going to hospital service, after which the hospital group shares its role with the primary care clinic. The hospital care in Hong Kong became so expensive because there was no "interface," i.e. connection and co-ordination between the hospital and family practice clinics. General practitioners (GPs), either in civil service or in private practice, were not aware of the need to maintain a holistic care for their clients. Never in the history of Hong Kong, had the government attempted to organize their own GPs to attend their patients, from mild ailment to hospitalization. Neither had the government engaged itself on trying to convince the GPs in private practice to start holistic, comprehensive practice.

Since its establishment, the Hospital Authority must have recorded such criticism and was aware of the need. Instead of moving in the direction of getting the Department of Health (which runs primary care clinics and controls GP registrations) involved in the establishment of primary health care/hospital care interface, it unilaterally took up the challenge. The brave authority started to take new graduates into the hospital system for "GP training."

The result of the comprehensive involvement of the Hospital Authority was ever-rising costs. In solid figures even before taking over GP training the Hong Kong hospital expenditure has increased within the first seven years of establishment of the Hospital Authority from its original below ten to 14 per cent.

In 1998 the stock market plummeted and the resulting financial crisis dealt a big blow to Hong Kong. Resources had to be cut and restricted. The reduced resources immediately dimmed the glamour of the hospital system.

For a long time people did not realize that the impressive improvements in hospital service were very much the result of budget increase. Staff already took it for granted that with good resources, they gave quality service. With the reduction of the budget, they assumed that there would be an automatic decline. An ethical insistence to maintain performance of the best quality in spite of adverse conditions was not built up during the prosperous days.

Changes came rapidly. Administration and professional staff were cut, resources for drugs and equipment were reduced, some new services collapsed and training programs were held up. Under such adverse circumstances, the government was preparing to bring about more drastic changes.

Before the 1997 change of sovereignty, the colonial government took a conservative attitude towards changes. Very often, changes were initiated after careful in-circle consultation with experts from the United Kingdom and search for local opinion among academics and experts. In the years that followed 1997, the simple interpretation of "executive directed" government and civil service had been fervently adopted, so that more drastic changes decided by a few top officials were frequently observed. Opinion and advice from the local academic and experienced professionals were considered unnecessary.

The Harvard Report (1999) was produced under such atmosphere when health economists were called in to study the local health problems with the aim of producing a report to guide future changes.

The Health Problems

The post-1997 health service problems can be summarized as follows:

- The ever-increasing demand for funding would not be met by the Hong Kong government;
- the downward economic trend brought special attention to unmet demand;
- budget tightening led to immediate deterioration of service quality;
- professional hazardous events occurred one after the other during this period of disillusion; and
- The demand from other sections of welfare for adding resources further intensified the awareness of the need to limit medical and hospital expenses.

With the Halnan Report only a few years previous and the consequent setting up of the Hospital Authority, the government missed the chance of making use of the Hospital Authority and the copious resources during the prosperous years to achieve a comprehensive solution to the complex problem. It did not consider the coupling of Health Services with Hospital Service. It did not mobilize the private sector, nor did it attempt to build up an ethical team of workers who would give the same good service in prosperous as well as adverse times. The successes were superficial and were dependent on extra resources which, when challenged, led to another collapse of confidence at which point the Harvard health economists were called in.

The Harvard Report

The Harvard Report, entitled "Why should there be changes and for whom are the changes?" was produced by health economists who came to Hong Kong for a special study, made an attempt to see different groups of medical people and utilize principles of health finance. Although the small team claimed that they had a wide coverage of people involved in the hospital services, it had been criticized for ignoring essential groups and individuals like the academic and professionals of influential ranks.

Since the public had enjoyed free medical services which got better and better since the establishment of the Hospital Authority, they might not support any change at all. The changes were mainly prepared for the government which foresaw already that it could no longer afford the ever-rising hospital costs. Actually, the Hong Kong government was so proud of the vital statistics in Hong Kong which was comparable to any affluent country in the world (Harvard Report 1999) and yet, people did not need to pay for health insurance or social security. They had needed only to wait a little longer in cue for hospital management. The Harvard experts tried to help by finding a way which would be able to maintain the better service (less waiting for quality care) and yet keeping the cost within everybody's ability.

The extensive commitment of the Hospital Authority, and the rising standards of hospital facilities being provided without a parallel demand on the users' responsibilities, created a culture among the users, i.e. the citizens in Hong Kong, to demand and continue to do so, to have better and even better free facilities. This logic might support the observation that increasing complaints and alleged grievances were basically the results of the increasing expectations and demands.

There exists a real dilemma. On the one hand, praises were widely heard on the great improvement of hospital facilities and services. On the other, complaints and grievances mounted. The Harvard experts were called in to solve the short-term need of bringing more harmony to the hospital and related services while in the long term to help introducing a practical system of raising health resources and controlling costs.

Essence of the Harvard Report

The health economists came to Hong Kong at the end of 1997 to start their survey and study. It took them eighteen months to complete the study and the reports were completed towards the end of 1999.

The study depended largely on published data, government information and limited consultations and discussions with professional groups and individuals. The economists were very happy with the information they collected, but the local medical profession at large was skeptical about the narrowness of the scale of consultation.

The foci of the study were on the following:

- Strengths and weaknesses of the Hong Kong system of financing health care delivery;
- sustainability of the present system;
- causes of weakness of the present system;
- the strategic options for improving the Hong Kong system; and
- institutions required for a particular option.

The Harvard study emphasized health finance and of course, the experts were health economists. The problems raised by Halnan in his report of 1988, which did not find adequate solution with the Hospital Authority were not specifically attended.

The methodology used for the study, apart from document studies, included household telephone surveys to explore service users' attitude, providers' (medical practitioners) survey on private practice, one more patient survey and then many explorations on finance models. Efforts to explore workers within the Hospital Authority and universities were scant or nil. Had they done so, they might have gained more insight into other issues apart from the finance problems like professional training, work ethic, and better division of labour with the academic institutes. Presumably, these issues were considered to be unimportant.

The economic strength of Hong Kong is well known to the experts who would be using the experience and insight of the United States, another nation with a genuinely strong economy, to evaluate our present system of health provision. The experts might not be able to realize that in spite of the obvious economic strength, Hong Kong has its own unique features. Hong Kong people used to enjoy the charity system which did not impose on users' responsibility. Hong Kong did not have a social security system although the discrepancy between the rich and poor has been increasing all the time, particularly after the financial crisis.

Any recommendation, based purely on financial re-arrangement alone, would therefore be deficient.

The recommendations of the Harvard Report contain mainly five suggestions, three of which address what should not be done while two others are genuine proposals. The report advised not to keep the present status, not to set an upper limit on medical expenses above which a patient would pay, and discouraged full privatization. The report did encourage health insurance and compulsory health savings.

Why are the first three proposals unadvisable? Firstly, the present system worked on a charity for all people. The projection, based on the rising trend in the last ten years, indicated that the annual revenue spent on health would reach 20 per cent of the total income of Hong Kong. This is too much to be acceptable. Therefore the present system must change. Secondly, can we impose a ceiling to individual patient's utilization of public facilities? Expensive equipment and procedures are so plentiful in the hospitals. Doesn't it mean that most patients have to buy their own service? It would be particularly difficult to impose this rule at this stage when the past ten years of extravagance have given so much free services as presents to the users. Thirdly, privatization does not require any special study to realize that shifting from a total charity to a totally unsupported system would not be tolerated. What remains, therefore, would be some form of health insurance or compulsory health saving.

One should actually be optimistic about the introduction of a new system, and there should be no hurry. Health insurance should go hand in hand with a social security arrangement. Now that Hong Kong is just starting to introduce its Mandatory Provident Fund, it will take at least a few years before more wisdom could be collected to take a further step to health coverage.

Worries about the Harvard Report

The Harvard experts proposed that we need three years' discussion. Maybe we need a longer period, given the present political atmosphere of political disharmony and bizarre motivation. We could afford to wait because just repairing some of the wrong done in the past could already bring about an effective slowdown the present rise in expenditure.

The Hospital Authority relied on the use of government resources for solving problems. Its great successes laid on the adding of infrastructures and manpower. It also polished its system of management.

There are still a lot of commitments from the formation of the authority left unfulfilled, therefore, if a retrospective fulfillment of the unaccomplished commitments (which does not require additional resources) could be achieved one would expect appreciation from the politicians, even before a major revolutionary proposal or medical insurance and compulsory saving scheme is worked out. The unfulfilled commitments are:

- The lack of interface between family practice and hospital practice;
- the uniform treatment given to staff workers without considering their performances;
- the saving of resources by putting equipments and expertise in clustering network;
- a better division of labour between the academics and service settings;
- the introduction of more middle class beds; and
- the removal of weak administration.

Taking up these challenges require great determination and managerial skill, not resources. The Harvard proposal deals with health finances, assuming that requesting the users to contribute more would solve all problems.

Actually, with the rising costs, medical investigation and treatment are affordable by only the well-off people. As affluent as the US is, experience had been bad. Health Management Organizations appeared and controlled the service market. They managed their service business by setting ceilings to different customers. Therefore controlling medical costs is more important than finding means to make the users pay more. Shifting the payment responsibility to the patients relieves budget tension but does not help the patients.

On the social side, the recommendations on finance arrangements did not take into consideration social stability, which owe a lot to a free, charity health care. Before a system for the retiring, elderly and disabled is proven effective in Hong Kong, the charity system can only be modified and not be removed or replaced.

On the financial estimation, it is optimistically assumed that a two per cent salary contribution by the worker, coupled with an equivalent of two per cent from the employer, would take care of anybody's hospital fees. Moreover, the savings would also support the retired person for a two years' care. Up to now, no one understands how the two per cent is worked out. If the requirements are higher, what are the alternatives? If the Harvard experts understood our hospitals and social conditions better, it might come out with more suggestions on changes in the managerial side, as well as the ethical side.

The disturbing facts of the report are that all problems can be solved by getting more resources which were spent in more provision of space and equipment, employing more experts and paying them better. Very little effort has been spent on the establishment of a fair charging system on the private sector, the establishment of a system of comprehensive family practice and elevating the ethical standard among all workers.

What Happened after the Harvard Report?

The Harvard experts were called in when the Hong Kong economy was in recession and when more and more critical comments were made against the medical practitioners. Therefore it was expected that changes related to a deteriorating economy would continue and likewise practitioners' reputation would further deteriorate. The report was able to attract sympathy because it tried to address the rising cost. However, with increasing unemployment and a stagnant economy, politicians and concerned people alike would be skeptical against any arrangement that involves the increase of fees. The Harvard Report was issued for general consultation while government bodies made use of various occasions to indicate that changing the financing structure of medical care in a time of economical downturn would be unfavourable.

Two years then passed while people in Hong Kong urgently looked for some official announcement in response to the report, and they remained disappointed. There was no indication of implementation of any one of the options recommended by the Harvard experts. The post-colonial government chose health care as a priority for international advice. Nevertheless, after receiving the advice it was unable to decide on an implementation. In the meantime, unusual problems in health chose this odd time to bother Hong Kong. The attack of Avian Influenzia put Hong Kong to the world map of crisis. The massive killing of poultry won world approval although some might suspect that the intervention was over drastic. A little later, medical graduates failed to find sufficient placements and triggered another sentimental social issue.

New Issues

Freezing of Resources

Widely observed were the freezing of new positions, and a new development, the elimination of overlapping jobs and the temporary halting of building new premises. The unofficial response to the Harvard's report was a negative rejection while every gesture was obvious that the essential philosophy of having patients paying more fees would be followed.

The official stand of the resource allocation was one of non-expansion and "value-adding" management. Therefore in absolute terms, resources remained the same. However, a system that enjoyed additional resources for years would experience a hard time through a frozen budget. Thus, in every hospital, staff-establishment was seldom maintained after retirement, transferal or lay-offs. New drugs were not allowed and much tighter budget control was widely insisted on.

A Collapsing Training System for Medical Doctors

One of the direct results of budget reduction was the failure to create sufficient jobs for the new medical graduates after their internship because of the manpower shrinkage. Hong Kong has the tradition of taking care of all medical graduates by absorbing them into the hospital or health service. In this era of deterioration, the government insisted on the continuation of the same policy. It took up the Canadian model of placing the new graduates into the hospital service as trainees for general practice. As private practice opportunities were not good, Hong Kong government paid hospital practitioners who enjoyed their job stability, contentedly stayed in their job positions, thus leaving no space for recruitment or training. Some clinical units did not receive new officers for training for two years. The loss of active, healthy, in-and out-flow of trainees in the different specialties is particularly worrying. Brilliant graduates fail to find training positions while unwanted individuals might be assigned to specialties for "training in family practice" (Leung 2000).

The Declining Reputation of the Medical Profession

While it is not possible to differentiate whether the critical attitude of some patients against their practitioners is due to a genuine decline in ethical practice or is the result of much greater awareness of patients' rights, the image of the medical practitioner is suffering a genuine deterioration. The profession, on the other hand, remains rigid, respectable, but insensitive. When angry and concerned people called for tight controls or even taking over the disciplinary mechanism, they did not realize that they certainly went too far because nowhere in the world should a highly specific profession lose its autonomy. At this point, the government seriously considered the establishment of a government-based organization to take over the Hong Kong Medical Council's role in the investigation and disciplinary activities.

The New Department for Environmental and Food Hygiene

With the removal of the old Urban Council and Urban Services Department, which were controlled by the Department of Health in matters related to environmental and food hygiene, instead of keeping the old supervision, a new department was created. The assumption was more capable leadership and management would eliminate disasters like the bird flu incident and would make Hong Kong a better city.

At the time of this writing, this dream was already disappearing because of the second bird flu in May 2001, many urban cases of cholera and persistent sanitation problems. If the situation does not improve, the creation of the new department would be a solid demonstration of the fallacy of changing management structure without sufficient objective analysis and consultation.

New Chinese Medicine Service

After several years of waiting, the government's position on the service of Chinese medicine at last became clear. The assumption that Chinese medicine could do whatever modern medicine could was at last given up. The code of practice for Chinese medicine practitioners clearly spells out that they confine their work on traditional methods and materials. It therefore becomes a specialty and not a comprehensive stream of service that challenges the modern system (Hong Kong Medical Council 2000). However, the struggle between the advocates and antagonists goes on. There is no clear policy from the central administration on:

- What sort of service will be supported?
- What sort of clinic will be established?

- What sort of wards will be established?
- Where do the Chinese medicine practitioners come from?
- How would they cooperate with the modern practitioners?

The struggle is likely to continue.

The government was proactive initially to call in experts to help solving health problems. However, the experts were only sensitive on financing options and the administration decided not to respond to the experts' report during the economic downturn.

Other health tissues unkindly appeared. Instead of local consultations and discussions, the Hospital Authority took up the relevant issue and offered solution, e.g. in the case of interns not finding placement, the hospitals offered training positions for GP's. In the case of Chinese medicine, the hospitals are going to offer clinics. It is therefore difficult to understand how the Hospital Authority, in the midst of a frozen budget, could continue its policy of expansion.

Green Paper on the Reform of Medical Services

The Green Paper was released in April 2001. It was the direct result of the Harvard Report. It aimed at a rearrangement of emphasis on the delivery of medical services while at the same time, tried to take care of the constraints on the health budget (Consultation Document on Health Care Reform 2001).

The philosophy adopted for the easing of hospital load is two-fold: (1) work on prevention so as to reduce hospital need, (2) work on primary health care which, expectedly, would take over hospital load. Actually, both prevention and primary health care had been discussed in the past reform proposals which were supported but not implemented. By what means could we be optimistic about the present proposal? Preventive work takes time to accomplish. It requires adjuvant establishments and welfare arrangements. The merits of preventive work intensified today will be demonstrated in the hospital practice of a decade later.

While 90 per cent of primary health care in Hong Kong is contributed by the general practitioner, one is perplexed to realize that the Green Paper does not contain a proposed procedure to start dialogue with general practitioners.

The only obvious change today is that the Hospital Authority takes over the role of the Department of Health. Is there solid ground to support the assumption that a change of guards, without a dialogue with the practitioners involved, would make a difference?

The second emphasis of the Green Paper is on the means to assure the quality of medical practice. Quality of practice is reflected in mortality, morbidity and complaints from patients. While mortality and morbidity are objective reflections which could be expressed through proper auditing, complaints could be subjective and are also under other influences like misunderstanding, poor public relations and media attitude. The Green Paper suggests that "an effective complaint system" be established. This might mean the overriding of the present hospital complaint system and the overriding of the Medical Council. While the government today is confident to initiate reforms by taking up more responsibilities, one wonders why the ombudsman has to work outside civil service influence. There may be better ways to improve the relationship between medical personnel and patients. There are easier ways to improve the transparency of any committee or council maintaining the discipline of its own profession.

Of course the most important component of the Green Paper relates to future financial arrangements. There are three main areas: (1) reducing costs, (2) increasing income, and (3) compulsory health saving.

Reducing Costs

There could be a lot of theoretical ways to reduce costs in the public hospitals like sharing of technology, sharing of manpower and equipment. As discussed in the previous paragraphs, unless a genuine networking system is implemented, sharing is not easy. Sharing is not easy particularly because in the past ten years the public hospitals have been encouraged to complete and surpass other setups in terms of modern equipment and state-of-the-art practice. The comprehensive computerization of medical records is a good example of the need to spend money, rather than saving.

Increasing Income

On the fees increase issue, maybe the administrators could identify areas that legitimately require fees and explain it to the public. There are plenty of such examples, only that the administrators are reluctant to explain. Abuses of the accident-emergency department are frequent and obvious, directly causing overcrowding and long waiting. Why not charge? Surgical implants and drugs of astronomical costs: why not charge? The top income group making use of charity service: why not charge?

Compulsory Health Savings

This might be a practical, clever move because it aims at the elderly (over 65) and those above 40. However, it takes a long time for the savings to work, because at this moment, already over 15 per cent of the population are over 65, and they are enjoying free services. Moreover two and a half times the number of elderly, i.e. those aged 40 to 65 years should be saving and yet they are not required to do so. When they reach 65, they will get free subsidy automatically. If they fall sick before 65 and start requiring health care and hospitalization, will they enjoy free service as before? When one considers the vast administrative expenses managing the savings, one has additional worries, particularly facing the rough surges of the finance market.

The administrators might yet have to consult the experts in the insurance business, whether health insurance, e.g. starting minimally in the very young age, gradually increasing on the addition of rising age, is feasible and practical.

Introduction of Chinese Medicine Service

First of all, we have to ask a few fundamental questions: Is the introduction of Chinese medicine a political decision? Is it going to be a comprehensive service or limited to selective areas according to the need of modern practitioners? Do we possess qualified practitioners of Chinese medicine in Hong Kong? Who would competently run hospital services?

Now that we are running short of hospital funds, to add the service of Chinese medicine would not be popular to the hospitals, the departments and servicing units that are hit by fund restrictions. Moreover, the intake of medical students has been reduced by about ten percent. To introduce a new batch of workers specialized in Chinese medicine well within an atmosphere of staff reduction is going to be more unpopular.

The policyholders have learned to be very careful and uncommitted when they introduce new systems. Major questions are just not addressed.

Once the new service of Chinese medicine is established inside the hospitals, it needs to be offered as a free service like the current hospital services. The result of this offer would attract all those who have a preference for Chinese medicine. The livelihood of the practicing Chinese practitioners scattered over Hong Kong would therefore be worrying.

If quality service is the aim, the skill and ability of attending physicians must be of special caliber in comparison with Chinese medicine practitioners in town. When patients under treatment confirm the superiority of the hospital, one wonders how many of them will still stay with those who used to attend them, and charge fees. The decision to introduce a service of Chinese medicine therefore cannot be just a political one, the social implications involved need to be addressed at the same time.

Conclusion

Observers of health policy and health finance have been using Hong Kong and Singapore as examples of successes because these two cities enjoy health indicators of high international standard; the total medical expenses with reference to GDP in these two cities are amongst the lowest; both governments comfortably provide the financial needs for health deliveries; medical services are basically free; and health expenses by households remains low (Mok and Sze 1999).

Based on such arguments, what Hong Kong needs to do is to maintain what has been successful, contain the rising costs and maintain the reputation of the medical profession.

The ever-rising medical costs and patients' demands make it impossible for any government to maintain a free, non-charging health delivery system. Singapore successfully overcame this by a comprehensive social security scheme. Hong Kong has never tried this before and is only starting to bring forward a limited-scale employer–employee responsible system of security. The outcome of this new venture will have a lot of influence on any health finance initiative. Obviously Hong Kong is yet not ready to take any drastic measures in health reform.

Canada is one of the most successful health providers based on a comprehensive national health system, and has persisted in it for 17 years. But recent data shows that although the Canadian government has insisted on the maintenance of the system, about 30 per cent of the expenses have already been channeled to private providers (Editorial, *National Post* 3 July 2001). How could our government successfully shift its medical budget in a period of economic downturn and general uncertainty?

Whoever tries to predict Hong Kong's health needs and expenses may not possibly claim reasonable accuracy for the obvious reasons that data records are hopelessly deficient. There are no data about different diseases, their treatment expenses and outcome. Nor is there data about gender differences (Mok and Sze 1999). Prediction indices would therefore turn out to be desperately inaccurate. It is therefore understood, that reform architects could only propose simple initiatives like increasing fees and forcing people to save money for their later use (Health Protection Account).

By nature, health finance involves long-term government policy on social welfare and involves complicated professional considerations, not only politics. Facing the present tendency of lawmakers who argue more or less purely according to political motivations, how could Mr. Tung initiate any solid practice by which fees would be increased? How could Mr. Tung ask certain ages to start compulsory saving? Both measures are equivalent to tax increases.

What makes the initiation of such a policy more difficult is that the government, at no stage before or after 1997, has ever clearly spelled out what exactly its health policy is. Is it a totally socialistic approach so that no one will be deprived of any treatment that is needed? Is it, as not infrequently expressed, going to accept the participation of a private sector based on need and market forces? Is it going to advocate a real mixture? (Consultation Document on Health Care Reform 2001).

Mr. Tung needs to clearly explain what policy is to be adopted in the next ten years. He might have to look at health care in China today with 10 per cent insured, 40 per cent partially covered as part of the terms of employment and the rest, i.e. 60 per cent, receiving no special benefits. Hong Kong remains a much more attractive city, not insignificantly, because of these obvious welfare differences (Wang 2001).

We all know that the fee increases will result in immediate pain while the Health Protection Account will not show any effect for at least ten years. What is required today is intensive political skills to gain the support of lawmakers who are concerned with peoples' health, as much as their votes. Nevertheless, even if health care revenue could be increased, the neglected areas left by the past colonial government needed to be corrected.

Two major policy areas needed to be addressed and yet, since Mr. Tung took over, was never discussed or acknowledged as important. Firstly there was no policy concerning the role of the private sector and, secondly, how hospital and family practice should interface was not systemically looked at. Private practitioners had a good time in prosperous economic environments. On the contrary when economy was not good, they had a hard time. In the past few years, there had been an outcry among the general practitioners for more chances to provide services, since patients were attracted to the inexpensive government hospitals that offered excellent facilities. The government should no longer ignore them.

Again, the overemphasis of hospital service resulted in expensive set ups and provisions. Had family practices, either private or government-based, been created to exist as interfaces between hospital care and the subsequent rehabilitation, the budget situation could swing to a significantly better balance even without additional resources. We therefore look forward to genuine leadership to reform the health policies and to bring about its effective implementation. It would be a great blessing if the following practical issues could be attended to:

- Improving medical resources by introducing a practical system of hospital charges for special expensive items;
- Liasing with the private sector to gain more support and initiate more co-operation;
- Consolidating family practice so as to build up a proper interface between hospital practice and primary care;
- Starting hospital programs on the ethical commitment of staff workers;
- Developing better sharing of responsibilities with the academic institutions and fully recognizing their educational and research roles; and
- Revitalizing the training programs for young graduates in different specialties.

Health Financing is undoubtedly important, but there are other outstanding issues to be addressed, and practical initiatives to be started

References

Consultation Document on Health Care Reform (2001). *Lifelong Investment in Health* (Hong Kong Government Publication).

Leung, P. C. (1998). "Health and Medical Services," in *The Other Hong Kong Report* (Hong Kong: The Chinese University Press).

Leung, P. C. (2000). "Collapse of the Training System," (Chinese), *Hong Kong Economic Journal*, 6 April.

Halnan, S. (1988). *Report after Consultancy Given to the Government of Hong Kong* (Hong Kong: Hong Kong Government Publication).

Harvard Report (1999). "Hong Kong Health Care Reform: Why Change? For Whom to Change?" Consultancy Report, Hong Kong SAR Government.

Hong Kong Medical Council (2000). *Code of Practice for Medical Practitioners in Hong Kong* (Hong Kong Government Publication).

Hospital Authority (1993–1995). *Annual Report of the Hospital Authority* (Hong Kong: Hong Kong Government Publications).

Medical and Health Department (1987). *Annual Report* (Hong Kong: Hong Kong Government Publication).

Mok, T. K., and Sze, Y. H. (1999). "Health Care Policies in Singapore and Hong Kong — Medical Financing and Beyond," paper presented at the Seminar on Health Care Policy, Social Policy Institute, Chinese Academy of Social Sciences, Beijing, December 1999.

Wang, Yu (2001). "Matching Health Care Personnel to Health Needs in China," Proceeding on "Health Care East and West, Moving into 21st Century," Harvard.

14

Executive–Legislative Relations: Assessing Legislative Influence in an Executive-Dominant System

Ma Ngok

Assistant Professor, Division of Social Science
Hong Kong University of Science and Technology

Introduction

It is generally believed that the relationship between the SAR administration and the Legislative Council (Legco) has impaired after 1997. The executive branch accused the legislature of being over-critical of the government, while the legislators claimed that the government had not given them due respect. In 2000, several experienced legislators retired from Legco, some of which citing disrespect from the executive branch as a major reason.[1] In the 2000 Policy Address, Chief Executive Tung Chee-hwa acknowledged that "tension exists between the two institutions" (HKSAR Government 2000: 38).

The view that these two institutions are in a state of tension, however, fails to capture the full pattern of interaction between the executive and legislature after 1997. This paper will have a more systematic review of the executive–legislative relationship after the handover, in particular the changing influences and functions of the Legco after 1997. The paper will start by reviewing the evolution of executive–legislative relations in Hong Kong and the nature of the "executive-dominant" constitutional framework. By comparing various indicators of legislative influence, I will compare the performance and influence of the post-1997 Legco with that of the 1995–97 Legco. The comparison shows that the general image of a hapless Legco is largely inaccurate. The policy-making power of the Legco is no doubt curtailed after 1997, but the Legco plays a more active role in oversight and bill deliberation after 1997. The Legco also has a critical role in providing legitimacy and popular mandate for SAR governance. The Legco's financial control power also posed a major constraint to the SAR's public finance policy. All these translate into mild forms of policy influence for the legislators after 1997.

Evolution of Executive–Legislative Relations in Hong Kong before 1997

In the early colonial regime, both the Legislative Council (Legco) and the Executive Council (Exco) were channels of co-option through which the colonial government absorbed business and professional leaders to build a synarchy of colonial bureaucrats and local elites (King 1975; Scott 1989). With all Legco members appointed by the Governor before 1985, bills and financial proposals had little difficulty in passing through the Legco. The Legco before 1985 had been described as "submissive" or "minimal," having negligible policy influence on the colonial administration (Lam and Lee 1993; Cheek-Milby 1995).

After elected members were introduced in 1985, the Legco became more active in examining government proposals. A handful of members elected from functional constituencies, such as Martin Lee and Szeto Wah, voiced dissent from time to time. Government bills could still cruise through the Legco without significant amendments (Miners 1994: 230), as appointed seats were still in the majority before 1991. The executive–legislative relations underwent a drastic change after directly elected seats were introduced into the Legco in 1991. In 1991–92, the colonial government largely counted on the support of the Cooperative Resource Center (CRC), a group of appointed members plus pro-business conservatives, to fend off the challenge of the democrats. Leaders of the CRC such as Allen Lee and Selina Chow were also Exco members who, bounded by the Exco collective responsibility rule, had to support government policy in the Legco.

The executive branch no longer had the CRC as a "loyal partner" (Choy and Lau 1996) after Chris Patten arrived as the last Governor in 1992. Patten first de-linked Exco and Legco, making it impossible for members to serve simultaneously as both Exco and Legco members. Patten's political reform package also irritated the Chinese government.

Many conservative or pro-business Legco members were then loath to lend Patten unconditional support after 1992. The forthcoming abolition of all appointed seats in 1995 also means that some appointed members had to prepare for future elections and would not support unpopular government policies if future electoral fortunes were at stake (Choy and Lau 1996).

After 1992, the executive branch in Hong Kong has largely lost control of the majority in the Legco. Choy and Lau (1996) detailed how the Legco exerted pressure on the government and affected government policy by various means: motion debates, questions, panels, resolutions, financial control, private members' bills, and bill amendments or vetoing legislations. The government managed to secure majorities in Legco in 1992–97 by entering into ad hoc alliances with different parties on different policy issues. The Legco changed from a "minimal legislature" to a "marginal legislature" (Cheek-Milby 1995; Mezey 1979 and 1990) or from a "policy-questioning" legislature to a "policy-influencing" legislature (Choy and Lau 1996).

The Constitutional Structure and Constraints after 1997

The Executive-Dominant System

The political system of the HKSAR is commonly described as "executive-dominant" or "executive-led" (*Xingzheng Zhudao*). "Executive-dominant," however, is neither a widely used and well-defined term in political science, nor a constitutional principle clearly stated in the Basic Law. Lau (2000) and Li (2001) have tried to summarize the main features of this "executive-dominant" system:

(1) The SAR Chief Executive (CE) and the bureau secretaries control most of the policy-making power. Most government policies do not need the approval of the legislature unless they entail changing of laws and appropriations.

(2) The Chief Executive has a superior constitutional status to other branches of the government. The CE is elected by an Election Committee, thus elected independent of the Legco.

(3) The executive holds the initiative to legislations. Government bills have a priority to get onto the Legco agenda (Article 72(2)). All bills passed by the Legco need the signature and promulgation of the CE to become effective laws.

(4) The CE has a wide range of appointment powers. He can appoint and remove major government officials and almost all other public office holders. Approval from the legislature or the courts is not required.
(5) If the CE considers a bill passed by the Legco "not compatible with the overall interests" of Hong Kong, he can return it to the Legco for reconsideration. The CE can dissolve the Legco if he does not want to sign a bill passed the second time by the Legco, or if the Legco refuses to pass the annual budget or any important government bills (Article 50).

The other side of the executive-dominant coin is the constraints to the power of the Legco. The Basic Law imposes two constraints on the Legco: the voting-by-group system (Annex II) and the constraint to private members' bills (Article 74). While all government proposals need only a simple majority to pass in the Legco, motions, bills or amendments moved by individual Legco members require majority support from two groups of members. One group is the members returned by functional constituencies, and the other includes those returned by direct election and the Election Committee. Secondly, Article 74 of the Basic Law stipulates that Legco members can introduce private members' bills to the Legco only if the bills are not related to public expenditure, political structure or operation of the government. Bills related to government policy need written approval by the CE before it can be tabled to the Legco. These two constraints make it difficult for the Legco to introduce alternative policies, which weakens the policy influence of the legislature.

"Executive-Dominance" in Comparative Perspective

How "dominant" is the Hong Kong executive branch vis-à-vis the legislature? We can assess the degree of dominance of the Hong Kong executive branch in two ways. One is to compare it with the constitutional arrangements before 1997. The other is to compare it with executive branches all over the world. Compared with colonial times, the SAR Legco in fact has more constraining power on the executive. First of all, the CE is not the Legco chair, as the colonial governor was before 1994, thus he cannot directly control the agenda or proceedings of the Legco. Secondly, the Legco has the power of impeachment if the CE has a "serious breach of law or dereliction of duty" (Article 73 (9)), although the power of dismissal lies with the Central Government. Thirdly, unlike the Governor who had unrestrained power to veto legislations and dissolve the Legco, there are constraints to the power of the CE of the HKSAR in both aspects. After a CE veto, if the Legco passes the bill again by a two-third majority, the CE has to sign the bill or dissolve the Legco. The power to dissolve the Legco, however, is a double-edged sword. If the re-elected Legco refuses to pass the bill again, the CE has to resign (Article 52). If the policy or budget voted down by the Legco is unpopular, the CE may well face a Legco that is more opposed to the policy after the election, thus running the risk of resignation or a bigger political crisis when he dissolves the Legco (Lau 2000). All these show that constitutionally the SAR Legco in fact has more constraining power on the executive than before 1997.

How powerful is the Hong Kong executive vis-à-vis the legislature, compared to other executives of the world? Constitutionally, the Hong Kong system resembles a presidential system, as the Chief Executive and the Legco have separate survival (Shugart and Carey 1992). The Chief Executive and the Legco are elected independently, and the formation of the cabinet (Exco and/or bureau secretaries) is totally autonomous from the confidence of the legislature. Appendix 1 shows a schema by Shugart and Carey (1992: 150) for a comparative measurement of presidential power. Totting up the scores for the Hong Kong Chief Executive, the SAR CE has a total score of 8 in legislative powers and 15 in non-legislative powers. Compared with other presidents of the world (see Appendix 2), the HKSAR Chief Executive has extraordinary non-legislative powers and is also considerably powerful in terms of legislative powers.[2] All over the world, only the 1989 Chilean presidency and the Paraguayan presidency can be considered more powerful than the Hong Kong CE.

The puzzle is: constitutionally the colonial governor was even more powerful than the SAR CE, yet people commonly believe that the 1995–97 Legco was better able to influence government policy. There are two possible explanations. One is that the influence of the Legco much depends on the ability for the government to engineer a majority in Legco. The Legco had more influence in 1995–97 because the government lost control of the majority in the Legco. After 1997, the SAR government could usually count on the support of the pro-Beijing parties such as the Hong Kong Progressive Alliance (HKPA), the Democratic Alliance for the Betterment of Hong Kong (DAB), the Liberal Party (LP), and other pro-Beijing legislators, who usually outnumbered the democrats who played the role of the opposition. This is similar to a powerful presidency with control of congressional majority. The opposition or minority parties in this system naturally have very little influence.

The second possibility is that the powerlessness of the post-1997 Legco has been exaggerated. Most scholars have focused on the Legco's policy-making power (Li 1997 and 2000; Kuan 1999; Ma and Choy 1999; Lo 1998; Ma 2001), and as this power is constrained by the Basic Law, their natural conclusion is that the Legco has become ineffectual after the handover. But after all, all over the world the legislature is not the chief policy-making organ, and the "decline of legislatures" has been underway in western democracies for many years (Lord Bryce 1921; Blondel 1973; Olsen and Mezey 1991; Beer 1966). It is the exception rather than the rule for a legislature to have a lot of policy-making power vis-à-vis the government. The constraints under the Basic Law mostly delimit Legco's power to raise alternative policies and amend government legislations. The assembly has other functions such as representation, oversight, and financial control that should not be affected by the Basic Law.

The emphasis on Legco's powerlessness drives analysts to focus on the "disharmony" aspect of the executive–legislative relations. Li (1997 2001) claimed that there is an inherent "mis-matching of the operational logic of popular elections with the new HKSAR constitutional arrangements." Li maintained that as the Legco remains the most representative political institution, but its power is constrained under the Basic Law, the Legco members would be increasingly hostile to the non-elected executive branch. Media reports usually describe the relation between the executive and legislature as in a state of "disharmony," "tension," "confrontation," if not outright hostile to each other. Some Exco members saw all Legco members as opposition members (HKEJ 26 July 1998: 6), while the Legco slammed the SAR government of being "non-cooperative and disrespect" (*Apple Daily* 31 December 1998).

These academic and journalistic accounts for the post-1997 executive–legislative relations may be too simplistic. A "harmonious" executive–legislative relation is not the norm in the world's democracies. In parliamentary democracies, the government is invariably heavily criticized by the opposition in the parliament. Divided governments under the presidential system can bring about "gridlocks" between the President and the Congress. Executive–legislative relations are most "harmonious" in places where the executive can largely control the legislature, as in one-party dictatorships and oligarchies in Africa or Middle East. Thus the degree of "harmony" is not an adequate indicator to qualify executive–legislative relations of a polity.

To obtain a more objective picture of the executive–legislative relations in Hong Kong after 1997, I compare figures of various legislative activities of the 1998–2000 Legco with those of the 1995–97 Legco.[3] The comparison will allow us to have a more objective and comprehensive assessment of the influence of the Legco in its various functions including policy-making, oversight, and financial control. It will also more effectively assess how the influence of Legco changed before and after the handover.

The SAR Legco: Various Channels of Influence

Policy Influence

(A) Legislation

A large part of a legislature's policy-making power lies in its power of legislation. Before 1997, the private members' bills was the most effective weapon of the legislators to put alternative policies on the policy agenda, posing a major challenge to the "executive-dominant" system (Chow 1995; Choy and Lau 1996). In the years 1995–97, 53 private members' bills were tabled, and 26 of them were passed. The 53 private bills made up 23.2 per cent of all the bills tabled in the Legco (228) in 1995–97. The private bills enjoyed a passage rate of 49.1 per cent, a stunning rate if compared with the about 10% passage rate in the British House of Commons (Chow 1995, pp. 169–170).

Private members' bills no longer served as a major policy-making tool after 1997. Under Article 74 of the Basic Law, members' bills cannot involve public expenditure, political structure or operation of government. Bills that are related to government policy need the written approval of the Chief Executive. This essentially kills off the private members' bills as a powerful policy-influencing weapon of the Legco.

After 1997, the Legco president (Rita Fan since 1997) will rule on all proposed members' bills and decide if they can be tabled or if they need the CE's approval. She will first ask for the opinion from the administration, and then the response from the member(s) who propose the bill, and makes the ruling after seeking advice from the Legco legal adviser. From July 1998 to July 2001, Legco members proposed a total of 22 members' bills.

The President only allowed four of them to be tabled. Eight were ruled out of order and four needed the consent of the CE. For the other six, the members who initiated the bill decided not to pursue after the administration claimed that the bill involved public expenditure or public policy, thus the bills were effectively killed when the 1998–2000 Legco session ended although the President had not made a ruling.[4] Two bills got approval from the CE and were tabled and passed. In the end, a total of six members' bills were tabled from 1998 to July 2001, which was only about 2 per cent of the total bills (298) tabled in 1998–2001, an insignificant figure. It is noteworthy that five of these members' bills were private bills that only govern the operation of private corporations and organizations and do not involve government policy.[5] Only the Smoking (Public Health) (Amendment) Bill could be said to have a substantive policy effect. Private members' bills have ceased to be a policy tool of the Legco after 1997.

The power of the Legco in amending legislation also diminished after 1997. The first hurdle is the president: she will first rule if an amendment entails public expenses or is relevant to the main purpose of the bill. In 1998–2001, there were 47 committee-stage amendments that required the president's ruling, and the president ruled 20 of them out of order.[6] Compared to her predecessors before the handover, Rita Fan is generally more stringent in her definition of what will entail public expenses or what is considered a relevant amendment. The second hurdle, of course, is for the tabled private amendment to pass both groups of legislators present, as stipulated by Annex II of the Basic Law.

Table 1 compares the success rate of government bills and of amendments of government and members before and after 1997.[7] The success rate of government bills was almost identical before and after 1997. The success rate was 92.9 per cent (170 out of 183) in 1995–97 and 91.9 per cent (159 out of 173) in 1998–2000. The difference is, in 1995–97 most of the failed government bills were actually voted down in the Legco second reading. After 1998, most of the non-passed bills were bogged down in the bill committee stage, and the government did not rush to table for second reading. The bill was then "killed" when the session expired in July 2000, but the government of course can revise the bill and go through the legislative process again in the 2000–04 Legco.

The difference in success rate of members' amendments was striking. In 1995–97 the members' amendments had a success rate of 71 per cent (98 out of 138)! After 1997, while government amendments still enjoy a very

Table 1. The Success Rate of Government and Members' Amendments, 1995–2000

	1995–96	1996–97	1998–99	1999–2000
Government bills proposed	99	84	122	51
Government bills passed	89	81	117	42
Government amendments	47	147	104	227
Government amendments passed	44	142	104	224
Members' Amendments	17	121	53	49
Members' Amendments passed	14	84	5	10
Total bills tabled	112	116	123	51

high success rate (99.1 per cent, 338 out of 341), only 14.7 per cent (15 out of 102) of the members' amendments were passed. Only 15 members' amendments were passed in 1998–2000, a much smaller number than the 98 amendments in 1995–97. The number of amendments proposed by members was also reduced by 26 per cent (138 to 102). The difficulty in passing amendments may also have discouraged some members from raising amendments. Among the 87 members' amendments vetoed in 1998–2000, 17 of them in fact received simple majority support but were vetoed because of the voting-by-group rule.

(B) Legislative Viscosity

The above figures show that the bill initiation and amendment power of the Legco has been much restricted after 1997. The inability of Legco members to initiate, veto or amend bills, however, does not necessarily mean that the Legco has become a rubber stamp. Blondel (1970) pointed out that even in liberal democracies, most of the bills are passed by the legislatures, and amendments against the wishes of the government are not that often. In comparing influences of legislatures, other milder forms of influence need to be taken into account. He thus suggested the concept of "viscosity" in measuring legislative influence (Blondel 1970, 1973). There is a qualitative difference between legislatures that passes government bills in one day, and those who spent months in bill committees trying to force governments into amendments. When the legislature is very compliant, bills are passed and passed very easily, with little time spent on debates or deliberation. The number of amendments and time spent on legislative deliberation thus serve as measurements of the "viscosity" of a legislature in the policy-making process.

Table 2. Indicators of Legislative Viscosity, HKSAR Legco, 1995–2000

	1995–96	1996–97	1998–99	1999–2000
Number of bill committees	38	55	42	45
Average time Spent on bills (days)	83.2	114.4	177	91.8
Number of government amendments	47	147	104	227
Number of Members' amendments	17	121	53	49
Number of Members' amendments passed	14	84	5	10
Total bills tabled	112	116	123	51

Did the HKSAR Legco turn less "viscous" after 1997? In Table 2, I compare several indicators of legislative viscosity of the Hong Kong Legco before and after 1997. The indicators include: (a) the number of bill committees formed; (b) time spent on bill deliberation (defined by the time between first reading and third reading of a bill); (c) the number of government amendments; (d) the number of proposed non-government amendments; (e) the number of non-government amendments passed.

The comparison shows that the post-1997 Legco in fact scored higher than the 1995–97 Legco on several viscosity indicators. The 1998–2000 Legco formed 87 bill committees for 174 bills (50 per cent), a higher proportion than the 1995–97 Legco (40.8 per cent). On average the 1998–2000 Legco spent 152 days on a bill, 50 per cent more than the 99 days in 1995–97. The Legco also forced the government to make more amendments itself. The government made 331 amendments for the 174 bills in 1998–2000, or 1.9 amendments per bill, compared to 194 amendments for 228 bills in 1995–97 (0.85 amendments per bill).

Judging from the above figures on bill amendments, the bill committees in fact did a remarkable job in forcing the government to make its own amendments. Without the pressure or scrutiny from the bill committees, it was unlikely for the government to put in the amendments of their own accord. For example, the bill committee on the Chief Executive Election Bill met for 14 times between March and June 2001, forcing the government to put in several amendments. The amendments included changing the election date, setting a ceiling for the campaign expenses, and making persons convicted of treason ineligible, all of which are non-trivial amendments. Even for the much-contested provision on the power of the Central Government to dismiss the CE, criticisms from bill committee members drove the government to change the wording from "under any circumstances" to "according to the Basic Law," which is much less ambiguous and should be regarded as an improvement over the previous version. In face of committee pressure, the administration sometimes chooses to withhold problematic legislation, or revise and then re-submit later. The general attitude of the administration after the handover is that they would rather make their own amendments or delay tabling, rather than allowing members to amend or veto government legislations.

(C) Committee Work

Committee work is usually a more effective means for opposition parties to exert influence on governments (Strom 1990). Other than the bill committees, the panels pose a source of mild policy influence. The Legco currently has 18 panels that roughly correspond to the policy bureaus of the SAR government. The panels do not have the power to block government policy, but they serve both policy and oversight functions (see also the section on *oversight*). It gives members a venue to question face-to-face the officials in charge of the respective policies, and push for policy changes. After 1997, the members are more adept in picking up issues of public concern and put them onto panel agendas to press for government action. It has also become more common for the panels to pass motions, demanding the government to provide information or take certain action or expressing members' attitude on a certain issue. The motions have no binding power on the government, but they undoubtedly pose a source of pressure for government to take policy action.

In 1996, the Legco House Committee passed a resolution that demanded the government to put all policy changes that entail appropriation or change of legislation to the corresponding panel(s) for discussion. It has since been normal practice for the administration to discuss the policies in the panels. The panels still do not have power to veto the policies, but the Legco's power of appropriation and legislation gives the panels' opinions more weight. After 2000, it has also become more common for the bureaus to table new policy proposals in the panels before they are tabled to the Exco. The panels thus become an arena from which the officials can get a sense of the possible response from the Legislative Councilors about their newly proposed policies, before they are seriously considered by top decision-makers.

(D) Motion Debates

Motion debates in the Legco have no binding force on the government. It is a venue for Legco members to express their views, create public opinion pressure, and show their differences with their party rivals (Lau 1995). Shortly after direct election was introduced into the Legco in 1991, motion debates received widespread coverage in the media and had considerable political impact. The media attention gradually waned as the media realized the powerlessness of the motion debates and turned their attention to channels of more substantial influence. This served to weaken the public opinion impact of the motion debates as a policy-influencing tool.

After the handover, the motion debates were further constrained by the voting-by-group rule. In 1998–2001, the Legco had 175 motion debates, and 117 motions were passed. Of all the 58 motions negated, there were 19 motions that in fact received simple majority support, but were vetoed because of the voting-by-group rule. Sometimes the members have to make the motion rather un-controversial to give it a chance to pass. The increased difficulty in passing substantial and controversial motions in turn made the media less likely to focus on motion debates as political events. All these make the motion debates a much less effective means in pressuring the government. Yet the mechanism of motion debates poses an opportunity for members to put something to vote, which at times can cause grave embarrassment for the administration. (See the section on "no-confidence motions.")

Oversight

If the Legco was no longer able to initiate policy after 1997, to what extent could it control and supervise the government? Rockman (1985) defined the function of oversight as: (a) check dishonesty and waste; (b) guard against harsh and callous administration; (c) evaluate implementation; (d) ensure administrative compliance with statutory intent. There are several mechanisms of the Legco that are related to the function of oversight: the Redress Information System, investigation committees, the panels, and the question session in the Wednesday meeting.

(A) The Redress Information System

The Redress Information System (RIS) is often overlooked by scholars and

Table 3. Cases Handled by the Legco Redress Information System, 1995–2000

Type of cases	1995–96	1996–97	1998–99	1999–2000
Complaints	343	270	429	308
Appeal	20	12	7	4
Request for Assistance	367	252	506	516
Proposal /View	371	374	418	328
Enquiry	66	27	53	39
Private/Subjudice	58	39	47	28
Civil Service Matters	4	2	17	25
Total	1229	976	1477	1248

Source: Annual Reports of the Legislative Council, various years.

journalists. Its predecessor, the Office of Members of Executive and Legislative Councilors (OMELCO), has played a major role in handling complaints, addressing grievances and channeling public opinion before directly elected members were introduced to the Legco (Miners 1998: 150–52). Table 3 shows the figures for the cases handled by the RIS from 1995 to 2000. It shows that the 1998–2000 Legco handled 23.6 per cent more cases than the 1995–97 Legco. From the distribution of the cases we can see that the major functions of the system include channeling of public opinion (views/proposals made up about 27 per cent), solving citizens' problems (assistance cases 37.5 per cent), and certainly oversight of the administration (complaints made up another 27 per cent).

The RIS can also refer the cases to the Ombudsman for further investigation. More importantly, some of these cases were picked up by members and then discussed in the panels, which would press the government officials to pay attention to the policy matter. In the 1998–2000 Legco, 68 issues were picked up from the RIS and then subsequently discussed in Legco panels.[8] The RIS thus is a channel where public grievances and administrative complaints can, through the members and the panels, get the attention of the government officials.

(B) Questions and Panels

Similarly, the Question time in the Wednesday session and the panel meetings have oversight and policy functions. Questions usually play a more important role of oversight in Commonwealth legislatures (Blondel 1973). The members can use the Questions to ask for information, make suggestions, press for action, and criticize government decisions or failures (Miners 1998: 149). Since the 1980s, the number of Questions asked on Wednesday kept rising (Cheek-Milby 1995: 155). The trend was continued after the handover. In 1998–2000, the Legco members asked 1,394 questions (both oral and written), a 17 per cent increase if compared with the 1,191 questions of the 1995–97 Legco. Moreover, members often follow up their questions by putting the issues of concern in panel agendas, which brings face-to-face pressure on the officials.

After 1997, it was common for members to pick up incidents that had policy implications or involved alleged administrative misdeeds, and forced explanations from officials in the panels. In doing so, the panels are quite successful in arousing public attention and forcing the government to disclose information. In the case of Su Zhiyi, which the Security Panel picked up in January 2001, the panel forced the government to conduct an investigation that confirmed mainland security police had come to Hong Kong.[9] Hearings of the Security Panel in May 2001 on how police handled protests during the Global Fortune Forum pushed the administration to admit that they had a "black list" of people that they would deny entry to Hong Kong (HKEJ, May 23, 2001: 6). Similarly, in response to the public criticisms against granting the Grand Bauhinia Medal to Yeung Kwong, former President of Hong Kong Federation of Trade Union, the Home Affairs Panel forced the government to reveal the previously undisclosed decision-making process of granting of these medals.

The above cases show that while the panels do not have the institutional power to change or veto policy, they have been relatively successful in forcing the non-elected administration to become more transparent and responsive in its operations. As panel meetings will be covered by the press and sometimes broadcast live on cable television, extensive hearings on administrative or policy mistakes is a definite source of embarrassment for officials. By bringing the event into the media spotlight, the panels keep the pressure on the government and play a considerable role in oversight.

(C) No-confidence Motions and Investigation Powers

Constitutionally the Legco does not have censure power against the Chief Executive, the Exco or individual senior officials. In case of serious government blunders or scandals, the Legco can set up an investigation committee that, under the Power and Privileges Bill, has the power to summon government officials to give evidence. After the handover, the Legco only set up two such committees, one on the confusion over the opening of the new airport, and the second concerning the problem of substandard public housing problem. Both committees created a lot of pressure for the administration, as officials faced lengthy interrogations from the members and had to disclose confidential documents. The report of the Airport Investigation Committee criticized Chief Secretary Anson Chan and other officials, which forced Anson Chan to apologize publicly in the Legco meeting of 3 February 1999.

Members' attempts to use motion debates as no-confidence votes also created much pressure for the government. There had been three no-confidence motions moved (as motion debates) against government officials after 1997: against Secretary of Justice Elsie Leung on 10 March 2000, against Housing Authority Chair Rosanna Wong and Director of Housing Tony Miller on 26 June 2000, and against Andrew Lo, aide to the CE on 8 November 2000. The motion against Rosanna Wong and Tony Miller created immense public pressure that subsequently led to the resignation of Wong. The civil servant Tony Miller remained unscathed although the motion was passed.

Both the no-confidence motions and the investigative committees did not have the constitutional power to remove officials. Yet it gave all public officials a clear signal that the Legco members are waiting in the wings. Serious mistakes can bring no-confidence motions and/or investigations, both bringing huge embarrassment. It can be expected that under the forthcoming "accountability system for principal officials," when political appointees replace civil servants as bureau secretaries, the political pressure brought by no-confidence motions will be even greater. The prerequisite, however, is for the scandal or mistakes to arouse enough public outrage, to the extent that the usually pro-government parties (mostly the LP and the DAB) hesitate to act against public opinion. The motion against Andrew Lo brought no pressure to the government, as the LP and the DAB had made it clear very early that they would not support the motion. But the government fought tooth and nail to lobby against the motions against Leung and Wong/Miller, as both had realistic chances to pass. This also means that if the power balance in the Legco changes in the future following introduction of more directly elected seats, these quasi-censuring means may be more effective in providing oversight.

Financial Control

Traditionally the Hong Kong Legco enjoyed greater power in the realm of financial control, as an overriding principle of the colonial policy was financial self-sufficiency, to avoid laying a financial burden on the British government (Ngo 1999: 133). The Legco thus has more constitutional power to control government expenditure and revenue raising. The annual budget and all government appropriations exceeding ten million dollars must get the approval of the Finance Committee of the Legco.

With the majority of members pro-government, most appropriations got the approval of the Finance Committee after 1997. The most salient cases over which the government stumbled included the appropriations for Home Starter Loan in July 1998, and the compensation and loans to poultry operators affected by the bird flu in May 2001. The two cases, however, had different results. In the Home Starter Loan case, the vetoing of the original proposal caused a public opinion backlash against the Democratic Party (DP) and the Liberal Party (LP) who voted against the proposal. The administration re-submitted the proposal two weeks later without amendments. The appropriation was approved, with both LP and DP changing their positions. In the case of the bird flu compensation, a majority of the Legco members opposed to the government proposal on the grounds that it did not include compensations to poultry shop employees. Knowing that they could not get majority support, the government withdrew the application and resubmitted days later, with an extra appropriation of 80 million for more loans for operators and rent-break incentives for operators who gave compensation to employees (HKEJ, 26 and 30 May 2001). The difference in the outcomes of these two cases was largely due to the difference in public opinion response. However, the bird flu case shows that with the backing of public opinion, a unified opposition from the Legco parties can effectively force policy concessions out of the administration.

If the Legco was not very successful in stopping the government from spending money, it certainly was effective in stopping it from raising it. After the economic recession set in, nearly all new tax proposals or fee-hikes of government services met harsh scrutiny from the Legco. With budget deficits looming, it had been reported since 1998 that the government was contemplating levying a land departure tax and a sales tax (HKET, 11 October 1999; *Apple Daily*, 6 January 2000). Parties that were opposed to these new levies quickly moved motion debates to make their positions clear. The motion that opposed sales tax was passed by an overwhelming majority of 36 to two, with the four major parties opposing the measure. The motion against land departure tax was narrowly defeated by one vote, but the abstaining LP declared that they might not support the measure in the future. Both motions largely killed off government initiatives to raise new taxes.

Government fee-hikes met similar fate. As some fee-hikes entailed amendment of subsidiary legislations, the Legco could block government initiatives. Since 1999, the government had put in hundreds of fee-hike items that had mixed results in the Legco. Government officials tried very hard to convince the Legco that the fee-hikes would not affect the living conditions of citizens. However, more than 100 items of fee-hikes were still blocked by the Legco in 1999–2001. Fee-hike items in the annual budget did not fare any better. The Legco's opposition to fee-hikes and tax-raising posed a major constraint to the government's public finance policy, which was in fact consequential in driving the government to economize on public expenditure and adopt more drastic civil service reforms.

Popular Mandate and Legitimacy

Last but not least, the Legco occupies a central position in providing popular mandate and legitimacy for government policy. The no-confidence motions discussed above was a case in point. Constitutionally the Legco did not have power to remove officials, and the no-confidence motions were no more than gestures that the government could have dismissed with a shrug. However, as the Chief Executive and the executive branch are not popularly elected, the SAR government suffers from an inherent legitimacy problem. As the most representative political institution, the majority view of Legco commands a certain authority that the government cannot ignore. The government just hates to lose any vote or motion in the Legco, even if the motions have no legal implications. Support from the fully elected Legco for government proposals and policies also accord the government better legitimacy.

Because of this the government took the initiative to move two Resolutions in the Legco in 1998–2000, in an attempt to seek popular mandate via the Legco. The first urged the Legco to support the SAR government inviting the National People's Congress to reinterpret the Basic Law over the right of abode issue in July 1999. The second one was in December 2000, asking the Legco to support the current Public Order Ordinance. Both Resolutions were carried in favor of the government. From 1999 onwards, the administration was also more intent on whipping up "public opinion" support in Legco's hearings. On controversial issues such as the reinterpretation of the Basic Law, the Public Order Ordinance, and the appointment system in the District Councils, the government tried to mobilize support from pro-government community organizations to present in Legco hearings. This created a "majority" of opinion in support of the government's position, in the "public opinion" collected by the Legco.

These events show that the government is still very concerned about the majority opinion of the Legco and the apparent public mandate it can get from the support of the Legco. As a less representative institution, the executive branch of Hong Kong still have to pay due regard to the legislature, although constitutionally it is in a much more powerful position. This in fact brings more influence to the Legco than is constitutionally allowed, in exercising legislative oversight and exerting more subtle forms of policy pressure in panels and other channels.

Conclusion

The above comparison shows that the post-1997 Legco has been deprived of its policy initiation power and bill amendment prowess. The motion debates cease to be an effective political tool (with the exception of the no-confidence motions). With pro-government members in the majority, the Legco seldom vetoed government bills and appropriations. However, the Legco spent more time on bill deliberation, and had more success in driving the government to reconsider legislation or make amendments. A comparison of various indicators shows that the legislature is in fact more "viscous" after 1997. Compared to 1995–97, the post-97 Legco members were more adept in using a combination of panels, questions and the RIS to demand information, provide oversight and push for policy action. The investigation, no-confidence motions and financial control powers remain major means of controlling the government.

The weak policy influence of the Legco, however, has a lot to do with the presence of a pro-government majority. Unable to veto government bills and appropriations to force policy changes, the minority opposition (mostly the democrats) is reduced to an oversight role. Yet the design in the Basic Law cannot guarantee that there will be a pro-government majority in the Legco. If the government loses control of the Legco majority, they can well face more vetoing of bills and appropriations, more investigations, more motions passed demanding policy action, etc. This is entirely possible especially with the gradual increase of directly elected members in the future.

All these point to the conclusion that the constitutional weakness of the post-1997 Legco has been exaggerated. The post-1997 Legco is relatively more successful (even more so than before 1997) in increasing the transparency and responsiveness of the non-elected SAR government. The popular mandate commanded by the Legco also accords with it more symbolic power. The colonial tradition of consultative democracy, years of democratization and the slogan of "Hong Kong people ruling Hong Kong" mean the government has to seek policy legitimation through answering to the Legco and strive for popular mandate through Legco approval. The administration's desire to win every vote brings it into conflict with the Legco, but it also means symbolic moves such as no-confidence motions can have much greater political impact than is constitutionally implied.

Good administration is not newsworthy, nor is effective monitoring (Rockman 1985: 553). The more active role played by the Legco in oversight was easily overlooked by the media and academics. The 1995–97 Legco experience also distorted the perspectives of many, including probably of some Legco members, who thought that the legislature should have a lot of policy-making power, which is seldom the case all over the world. In an attempt to demonstrate executive dominance, the administration is also determined not to let the Legco score moral victories. The officials always pose an uncompromising gesture; and even if compromises are necessary, they prefer to delay legislation or make amendments themselves rather than letting the Legco amend or veto government proposals. All these add to the impression that the Legco is toothless. Yet this perception can create a self-fulfilling prophecy. The perception of Legco incapacity will bring less public support to the institution and stifle public participation to elections and parties. Experienced legislators retire because they think they do not have enough influence. The media shies away from reporting Legco events, considering them unimportant. This creates a vicious circle. Reduced public attention and confidence in the Legco means less prowess in controlling the government, influencing policy and representing public interests. The problem is: a weak legislature does not necessarily bring a strong executive. If the SAR government cannot show a convincing capacity to solve policy problems, the reduced confidence in the elected Legco can only aggravate the confidence crisis and governmentality problems of SAR governance. A weak executive facing a weak legislature can be the worst nightmare for the future SAR governance.

Notes

1. For example, Ronald Arculli accused the government officials of being reluctant to make changes in face of criticisms by Legco members in bill committees (*Sing Tao Daily News*, 21 June 2000, p. A12); C.H. Leong lamented that the executive-dominant system constrained the Legco members too much (*Apple Daily*, 29 June 2000, p. A18; HKET, 29 June 2000, p. A38).
2. The CE has almost unrestricted power in naming and changing of his/her cabinet (4 + 4 points), and the Legco does not have any censure powers (4 points). The only restriction to CE's non-legislative power is that the CE can only dissolve the Legco once during his/her term (3 points). As far as legislative powers are concerned, the Legco only has restricted budgetary and amendment powers (3 + 2 points). The CE has limited decree powers (1 point), and no power to call a referendum (zero). The CE cannot have a partial veto (cannot veto only part of a bill) (zero), and the CE veto can be overridden only by a two-third majority (2 points).
3. The 1995–97 period was chosen because it was commonly seen as the period when the Legco had the greatest policy influence. It was also, like the 1998–2000 one, fully elected. The 1991–95 Legco was partly appointed, and the Provisional Legco was elected by an appointed Selection Committee. Both will not serve as good cases for comparison with the first SAR Legco. The figures of the Legco activities are obtained from the *Hansard*, Legco annual reports and the Legco homepage: www.legco.gov.hk. Some figures are provided by the Legco Secretariat, and some calculations are made by the author. The author thanks Carmen Yu and Royce Chau for their invaluable help in collecting and analyzing the data.
4. Information provided by the Legco Secretariat.
5. These private bills included the Bank of East Asia Limited Bill (2001), Bank of China (Hong Kong) Limited (Merger) Bill (2001), Alice Ho Miu Ling Nethersole Incorporation (Amendment) Bill 1999, Order of Friar Minors in Hong Kong Incorporation Bill, and the Prior of the Order of Cistercians of the Strict Observance Incorporation (Amendment) Bill 2000.
6. Source of data: Legco's homepage: www.legco.gov.hk/general/english/presdet/pre_rul.htm
7. The method of "counting" amendments warrants some explanation here. The author tracked down all the committee stage amendments in each Legco

plenary meeting from 1995–97 and 1998–2000 from the Hansard. The difficulty is that sometimes one tabled amendment pre-empted another and the latter was never put to vote, and sometimes an "amendment" was divided into several parts that was voted separately. In all the cases the author counted each vote as an "amendment." That is, an "amendment" moved by the government may take three votings in the Legco to pass, and it would be counted as three amendments here.

8. For a list of these issues, see the Legco homepage: www.legco.gov.hk/yr99 00/english/sec/mem_red.htm
9. Su Zhiyi was a Hong Kong businessman who was convicted of economic crimes in mainland China. His daughter revealed to the press in 2000 that mainland security police had come to their residence in Hong Kong and ransacked their home for documents in 1995.

References

Beer, Samuel (1966). "The British Legislature and the Problem of Mobilizing Consent," in E. Frank (ed.), *Lawmakers in a Changing World* (Englewood Cliffs, New Jersey: Prentice-Hall), pp. 30–48.

Blondel, Jean, et al. (1970). "Legislative Behavior: Some Steps towards a Cross-National Measurement," *Government and Opposition* 5, 1, pp. 67–85.

Blondel, Jean (1973). *Comparative Legislatures* (Englewood Cliffs, New Jersey: Prentice Hall).

Bryce, Lord (1921). *Modern Democracies I* (London: MacMillan), pp. 367–77.

Cheek-Milby, Kathleen (1995). *A Legislature Comes of Age: Hong Kong's Search for Influence and Identity* (Hong Kong: Oxford University Press).

Chow, Pak-kwan (1996). "Feiguanfang yiyuan tiaoli cao'an dui xingzheng zhudao zhengfu zuochudi kaoyan" (The Challenge of Non-Official Members' Bills to the Executive-Dominant Government), in Choy Chi-keung, Lau Sai-leung and Chow Pak-kwan (eds.), *Xuanju yu Yihui Zhengzhi* (Elections and Parliamentary Politics: The New Political Face of Hong Kong after the Rise of Party Politics) (Hong Kong: Hong Kong Humanities Press), pp. 159–73.

Choy Chi-keung and Lau Sai-leung (1996). "Jiuqi Huiguiqianxidi Xianggang Xingzheng yu Lifa guanxi" (The Executive–Legislative Relations in Hong Kong Before 1997). *Hong Kong Journal of Social Sciences* 8 (Autumn), pp. 237–66.

Choy Chi-keung and Tsoi, Richard (1998). *Xianggang lifaju zhongyao toupiaojilu huibian* (Selected Vote Counts of the Legislative Council of Hong Kong, 1995–1997) (Hong Kong: Hong Kong Humanities Press).

Hong Kong Special Administrative Region Government (HKSAR Government). 2000. *The 2000 Policy Address: Serving the Community, Sharing Common Goals* (Hong Kong: Printing Department, HKSAR Government).

King, Ambrose (1975). "Administrative Absorption of Politics in Hong Kong: Emphasis on the Grassroots Level." *Asian Survey* 15, 5, pp. 422–39.

Kuan, Hsin-chi (1999). "Elections without Political Clout," in Kuan Hsin-chi et al. (eds.), *Power Transfer and Electoral Politics: The First Legislative Election in the Hong Kong Special Administrative Region* (Hong Kong: The Chinese University Press), pp. 277–301.

Lam, Jermain, and Lee, Jane (1993). *The Dynamic Political Actors in Hong Kong's Transition* (Hong Kong: Writers' and Publishers' Cooperative).

Lau, Sai-leung (1995). "Dungyi bianlun: yihuide zhengzhixiu?" (Motion Debates: the Political "Show" in the Legco?), in Choy Chi-keung, Lau Sai-leung and Chow Pak-kwan (eds.), *Xuanju yuyihui zhengzhi* (Elections and Parliamentary Politics: The New Political Face of Hong Kong after the Rise of Party Politics) (Hong Kong: Hong Kong Humanities Press), pp. 175–80.

Lau Siu-kai (2000). "*Xingzheng zhudaode zhengzhi tizhi: xieshang yuxiansi*," (The Executive-Dominant System: Design and Reality), in Lau Siu-kai (ed.), *Xianggang ershiyi shiji lantu* (The Twenty-First Century Blueprint for Hong Kong) (Hong Kong: The Chinese University Press), pp. 3–36.

Li, Pang-kwong (1997). "Executive and Legislature: Institutional Design, Electoral Dynamics and the Management of Conflicts in the Hong Kong Transition," in Li Pang-kwong (ed.), *Political Order and Power Transition in Hong Kong* (Hong Kong: The Chinese University Press), pp. 53–78.

Li, Pang-kwong (2001). "The Executive–Legislature Relationship in Hong Kong: Evolution and Development," in Joseph Cheng (ed.), *Political Development in the HKSAR* (Hong Kong: City University Press), pp. 85–100.

Lo, Shiu-hing (1998). "The Changing Dimensions of Executive–Legislative Relations: The Case of Hong Kong," *Public Administration and Policy* 7, 2, pp. 73–103.

Ma, Ngok, and Choy, Chi-keung (1999). "The Evolution of the Electoral System and Party Politics in Hong Kong," *Issues and Studies* 35, 1 (January/February), pp. 167–94.

Ma, Ngok (2001). "The Decline of the Democratic Party in Hong Kong: The Second Legislative Election in HKSAR," *Asian Survey* (July/August), pp. 564–83.

Mezey, Michael (1979). *Comparative Legislatures* (Durham: Duke University Press).

Mezey, Michael (1990). "Classifying Legislatures," in Philip Norton (ed.) *Legislatures* (New York: Oxford University Press), pp.149–76.

Miners, Norman (1994). "The Transformation of the Hong Kong Legislative Council 1970–1994: From Consensus to Confrontation," *Asian Journal of Public Administration* (December), pp. 224–48.

Miners, Norman (1998). *The Government and Politics of Hong Kong* (5th ed.) (Hong Kong: Oxford University Press).

Ngo, Tak-Wing (ed.) (1999). *Hong Kong's History: State and Society under Colonial Rule* (London: Routledge).

Olsen, David, and Mezey, Michael (1991). *Legislatures in the Policy Process: The Dilemmas of Economic Policy* (New York: Cambridge University Press).

Rockman, Bert (1985). "Legislative–Executive Relations and Legislative Oversight," in Gerhard Loewenberg, Samuel Patterson and Malcolm Jewell (eds.), *Handbook of Legislative Research* (Cambridge, Massachusetts: Harvard University Press) pp. 519–72.

Scott, Ian (1989). *Political Change and The Crisis of Legitimacy in Hong Kong* (Hong Kong: Oxford University Press).

Shugart, Matthew S., and Carey, John (1992). *Presidents and Assemblies: Constitutional Design and Electoral Dynamics* (Cambridge, UK: Cambridge University Press).

Strom, Kaare (1990). *Minority Government and Majority Rule* (Cambridge: Cambridge University Press).

Appendix 1 Indicators for Powers of Presidents

LEGISLATIVE POWERS

	Package Veto / Override		**Partial Veto / Override**
4	Veto with no override	4	No override
3	Veto with override requiring majority greater than 2/3 (of quorum)	3	Override by extraordinary majority
2	Veto with override requiring 2/3	2	Override by absolute majority of whole membership
1	Veto with override requiring absolute majority of assembly or extraordinary majority less than 2/3	1	Override by simple majority of quorum
0	No veto; or veto requires only simple majority override	0	No partial veto
	Decree		**Exclusive Introduction of Legislation (Reserved Policy Areas)**
4	Reserved powers, no rescission	4	No amendment by assembly
2	President has temporary decree authority with few restrictions	2	Restricted amendment by assembly
1	Authority to enact decrees limited	1	Unrestricted amendment by assembly
0	No decree powers; or only as delegated by assembly	0	No exclusive powers
	Budgetary Powers		**Proposal of Referenda**
4	President prepares budget; no amendment permitted	4	Unrestricted
3	Assembly may reduce but not increase amount of budgetary items		
2	President sets upper limit on total spending, within which assembly may amend	2	Restricted
1	Assembly may increase expenditures only if it designated new revenues		
0	Unrestricted authority of assembly to prepare of amend budget	0	No presidential authority to propose referenda

NONLEGISLATIVE POWERS

	Cabinet Formation		**Cabinet Dismissal**
4	President names cabinet without need for confirmation or investiture	4	President dismisses cabinet ministers at will
3	President names cabinet ministers subject to confirmation or investiture by assembly	2	Restricted powers of dismissal
1	President names premier, subject to investiture, who then names other ministers	1	President may dismiss only upon acceptance by assembly of alternative minister or cabinet
0	President cannot name ministers except upon recommendation of assembly	0	Cabinet or ministers may be censured and removed by assembly
	Censure		**Dissolution of Assembly**
4	Assembly may not ensure and remove cabinet or ministers	4	Unrestricted
3	Restricted by frequency or point within term		
2	Assembly may censure, but president may respond by dissolving assembly	2	Requires new presidential election
1	"Constructive" vote of no confidence (assembly majority must present alternative cabinet)	1	Restricted: only as response to censures
0	Unrestricted censure	0	No provision

Source: Shugart and Carey (1992: 150).

Appendix 2 Powers of Popularly Elected Presidents by Country

Country	Legislative Power Score	Non-Legislative Power Score	Country	Legislative Power Score	Non-Legislative Power Score
Argentina			Guatemala	4	12
Current	2	12	Haiti	0	0
Proposal	2	7	Honduras	2	12
Austria	0	5	Iceland	3	8
Bolivia	2	12	Ireland	0	0
Brazil			Korea		
1946	7	12	1948	2	8
1988	9	12	1962	6	12
Bulgaria	0	0	1987	6	9
Chile			Mexico	5	12
1891	8	8	Namibia	2	10
1925	8	12	Nicaragua	3	12
1969	12	12	Nigeria	2	11
1989	5	15	Panama	5	12
Colombia			Paraguay	6	16
Pre-1991	8	12	Peru	0	9
1991	5	8	Philippines	5	11
Costa Rica	1	12	Portugal		
Cuba 1940	2	11	1976	4	9
Dominican Republic	2	12	1982	1.5	6
Ecuador	6	8	Romania	2	2
El Salvador	3	12	Sri Lanka	4	12
Finland	0	8	USA	2	11
France	1	4	Uruguay	6	11
Germany (Weimar)	4	12	Venezuela	0	12

Source: Shugart and Carey (1992: 155).

15

The Changing Public Perception of the Chief Executive

Timothy Ka-ying Wong

Research Officer, Hong Kong Institute of Asia-Pacific Studies
The Chinese University of Hong Kong

Introduction

Four years have passed since the transition on 1 July 1997 of Hong Kong from a British colony to a Special Administrative Region (SAR) under Chinese sovereignty. The period has witnessed a sharp plump in attitudes of the Hong Kong public toward the new SAR government, particularly Chief Executive Tung Chee-hwa. Various opinion surveys show that the public support for Mr. Tung remained low throughout the period except for the initial months of his rule before the outbreak of the Asian financial crisis in the fall of 1997. Many have thus raised questions concerning his governance and legitimacy. Some have even felt that Mr. Tung and his government are facing a serious legitimacy crisis.[1] This chapter attempts to depict the changing public perception of Mr. Tung and his rule after he took office, discuss the current condition of his ruling legitimacy, analyze the socio-demographic differences of his public support, and examine the major causes for the decline of his legitimacy. Unless otherwise noted, the data used here are from a continuing telephone survey research project conducted by the Hong Kong Institute of Asia-Pacific Studies of the Chinese University of Hong Kong at the end of every month beginning July 1997.[2]

Legitimacy and Popularity of the Chief Executive

The concept of legitimacy can be defined as "the extent to which citizens regard the state, its institutions, personnel, or policies as morally right or acceptable."[3] The sources of legitimacy may include legitimacy by results, by habits, by historical, religious or ethnic identity, and by procedures.[4] Scott has analyzed the question of legitimacy in the case of colonial Hong Kong by using three criteria proposed by Beetham: legal validity, moral justiciability and expressed consent, pointing out that the colonial government acquired its legitimacy by output and that the future regime would likely attempt to construct its rule on a similar basis.[5] Thus, the evaluation of the legitimacy of the Hong Kong SAR government should turn to the concept of "performance legitimacy," which is based upon the expressed consent from the local community regarding government performance.

According to the mini-constitution of the Hong Kong SAR, the Basic Law, the Chief Executive holds a pivotal position in the local political system. He is both the head of the Hong Kong SAR government and the head of the SAR in general. He is vested with great constitutional powers similar to those previously enjoyed by the colonial governor. He has the power to sign bills, nominate major officials, appoint judges of the courts at all levels, and dissolve the Legislative Council. Such constitutional powers allow him to play a leading role, albeit in varying degrees, in the administrative, judiciary and legislative arms of the government. This leading role of the Chief Executive is further strengthened by the special constitutional arrangement that before 2007 only up to one half of the Legislative Council members are returned by direct elections of geographical constituencies, with the rest of them returned by elections of functional constituencies mainly composed of professional and business elites who are also largely pro-Beijing in political orientation.[6] The partial democracy of the Legislative Council has also kept the newly emerged popularly oriented political parties to a marginal position in the political system.[7]

Thus public opinion about the performance of the Chief Executive can be seen as an evaluation of the performance of the SAR government. Furthermore, if legitimacy means citizen support for key value systems, a consensus on the validity of system structures and identification with system leadership,[8] the measurement of the popularity of the Chief Executive is undoubtedly an important indicator of legitimacy.

Some may argue that since the Chief Executive is not directly elected but picked up by a selection committee of 400 pro-Beijing members in Hong Kong and then formally appointed by the Chinese government in

Beijing, theoretically he should not have to worry about public evaluation of his performance. In reality, however, as low popular support for the Chief Executive may strain Hong Kong's "one country, two systems" practice, it is not unnatural that Beijing would consider popularity as one of the major conditions for its continued endorsement of support for the Chief Executive. Hence, in order to win Beijing's continued blessing, the Chief Executive has to ensure that his policies are generally acceptable to the local population. In addition, it is commonly believed that the chief executive is an indispensable ingredient in the mix of attributes that constitute the ability of the incumbent to get things done. Other things being equal, a chief executive with higher approval rating should have more room to maneuver.[9]

Public Perception of the Chief Executive

Our measurement of the public support for the Chief Executive consists of eleven indicators, ten on his performance in various specific areas and one on his overall performance. The ten specific indicators are: trustworthy, clean and just, competence, care for people, balance between mainland and Hong Kong interests, tolerate different political forces, balance various social and political interests, protect human rights and freedom, promote democracy, and improve Hong Kong's economy. The first four indicators measure Tung's personal quality and integrity; the fifth measures his ability to manage Hong Kong-mainland relations; the sixth and the seventh measure his ability to maintain social and political harmony; the eighth and the ninth measure his commitment to freedom and democracy; and the tenth measures his ability to manage the economy. Respondents were asked to give a score on each indicator, from 0 to 100 with 50 for a pass. Table 1 summarizes the findings.

Several observations can be made from the findings. First, public ratings of all the indicators were quite positive and reached their apex in the first three months after Mr. Tung assumed office as Chief Executive. This means that though Mr. Tung was not popularly elected, he was basically well received by the people of Hong Kong by the time he took office.

Second, Mr. Tung's popularity started to deteriorate rapidly after October 1997 when Hong Kong was hit hard by the spreading Asian financial turmoil, reflecting the importance of economic development to his legitimacy.

Third, all the eleven public ratings experienced a similar declining

Table 1. Public Evaluation on Mr. Tung Chee-hwa

Date of survey conducted	Trust-worthy	Clean & just	Compet-ence	Care for people	Balance between Mainland and HK interests	Tolerate different political forces	Balance various social and political interests	Protect human rights and freedom	Promote democracy	Improve HK's economy	Overall perform-ance	(N)
July 1997	61.8	64.4	62.7	65.0	64.0	58.5	60.4	56.9	55.6	64.3	63.7	(585)
Aug 1997	65.0	68.2	65.8	**68.5**	**67.6**	59.8	63.4	58.6	57.0	**66.4**	67.2	(530)
Sept 1997	**66.0**	**70.2**	**66.7**	68.3	67.1	**60.7**	**64.8**	**59.8**	**58.0**	66.2	**68.0**	(544)
Oct 1997	62.3	63.1	62.8	62.7	63.3	57.1	59.3	55.2	52.0	61.5	63.2	(516)
Nov 1997	61.6	64.9	61.5	62.4	62.0	58.3	59.1	55.9	54.2	59.5	63.7	(512)
Dec 1997	62.4	66.4	61.9	63.7	62.2	56.8	59.6	56.0	53.9	59.2	63.3	(573)
Jan 1998	58.1	63.7	57.1	60.9	60.9	54.8	54.0	54.1	50.8	51.3	59.1	(554)
Feb 1998	61.3	66.0	59.9	65.1	63.5	57.4	59.1	56.0	53.6	58.1	63.3	(565)
March 1998	60.9	64.6	59.7	64.6	63.3	57.6	58.0	57.2	55.0	56.3	62.4	(548)
April 1998	58.4	63.2	57.9	61.5	61.5	55.1	54.5	54.8	51.6	51.7	60.1	(588)
May 1998	54.1	63.9	53.2	60.0	58.6	53.9	51.2	51.1	47.7	45.8	56.2	(576)
June 1998	60.0	66.8	57.2	65.4	62.5	59.0	56.7	58.7	56.3	53.1	60.9	(559)
July 1998	55.8	64.3	53.5	61.5	60.6	55.2	54.3	55.7	52.3	47.6	56.5	(575)
Aug 1998	55.1	63.2	52.7	61.6	59.8	54.9	53.1	55.3	52.4	48.0	56.9	(591)
Sept 1998	52.9	62.8	51.8	60.0	59.4	53.1	50.6	52.7	49.2	45.2	55.5	(560)
Oct 1998	58.4	65.9	56.2	60.2	60.8	55.6	54.5	56.0	52.6	51.7	58.1	(589)
Nov 1998	61.9	67.2	59.1	63.0	61.6	57.8	56.9	57.6	54.0	53.8	60.6	(569)
Dec 1998	58.4	66.7	55.7	61.2	57.7	55.7	54.6	55.5	52.3	50.7	59.2	(535)
Jan 1999	56.4	63.5	55.2	61.0	60.8	55.4	55.1	54.3	50.8	50.2	58.6	(547)
Feb 1999	57.3	66.0	54.2	62.2	60.0	56.4	54.4	55.8	53.0	50.2	57.7	(567)
March 1999	61.5	69.1	58.9	63.9	62.9	58.6	59.0	58.6	54.0	56.3	61.4	(542)
April 1999	58.6	66.2	55.9	61.0	60.0	55.1	56.3	55.9	52.0	54.7	59.1	(550)
May 1999	56.7	65.2	54.8	58.5	58.2	54.3	54.7	55.9	50.6	52.5	58.1	(543)
June 1999	60.6	67.2	60.6	61.2	61.9	56.4	58.3	59.1	54.6	55.7	59.8	(527)
July 1999	56.6	65.1	56.5	58.8	59.8	54.1	54.8	55.8	51.3	54.9	58.4	(585)

Aug 1999	55.4	63.4	54.6	59.2	58.2	52.0	54.2	54.0	48.9	50.7	57.1	(548)
Sept 1999	54.1	62.5	53.1	57.9	55.2	50.8	51.3	49.8	48.1	49.5	55.5	(503)
Oct 1999	52.3	60.9	51.8	55.0	55.1	48.7	50.6	**47.4**	44.7	48.0	54.1	(574)
Nov 1999	54.6	63.2	53.8	57.1	58.9	52.6	53.0	50.2	49.0	52.1	55.8	(622)
Dec 1999	54.7	61.9	53.9	56.1	58.2	52.1	53.0	49.9	47.1	51.7	55.6	(566)
Jan 2000	52.9	61.5	52.3	57.6	57.3	51.5	51.0	51.8	48.9	50.5	55.9	(538)
Feb 2000	56.5	63.6	55.0	57.6	57.1	52.6	53.3	52.9	49.3	52.1	57.2	(520)
March 2000	57.1	63.3	55.5	57.6	58.6	52.9	54.0	53.0	50.9	52.9	59.1	(537)
May 2000	50.4	59.8	48.7	53.2	55.1	50.1	48.2	47.8	**44.6**	46.3	52.9	(546)
June 2000	50.9	59.4	50.4	53.1	55.6	51.4	48.5	49.6	47.1	46.1	53.0	(538)
July 2000	47.5	56.5	46.4	48.3	**52.6**	47.8	47.6	49.5	**44.6**	46.9	49.7	(946)
Aug 2000	47.6	57.1	46.0	49.4	52.8	47.2	47.0	47.8	**44.6**	47.2	49.9	(913)
Sept 2000	**47.0**	**55.1**	45.4	**47.7**	53.0	**46.6**	46.3	49.0	44.7	46.3	49.4	(828)
Oct 2000	49.9	57.0	47.7	50.2	54.2	49.6	47.8	48.6	45.3	46.7	50.7	(801)
Nov 2000	50.5	59.1	49.3	51.5	55.0	50.6	49.8	51.1	47.4	48.7	52.3	(884)
Dec 2000	51.1	58.8	49.9	52.9	54.6	50.9	50.6	51.1	46.9	49.0	53.9	(831)
Jan 2001	51.3	58.5	50.1	52.1	55.1	50.6	50.6	50.3	47.1	48.7	53.3	(766)
Feb 2001	52.9	60.5	52.6	53.5	55.6	52.2	52.2	51.9	48.7	50.8	54.5	(731)
March 2001	52.6	60.2	51.4	52.6	55.6	52.3	51.7	52.8	49.3	48.8	54.8	(785)
April 2001	51.4	60.1	50.1	53.9	55.0	51.7	50.9	52.3	49.2	48.2	53.3	(760)
May 2001	52.4	61.9	52.0	54.9	56.2	51.7	50.3	50.8	47.6	46.7	53.6	(893)
June 2001	52.9	61.0	52.1	54.6	56.8	51.8	50.7	48.6	46.5	46.8	53.8	(842)
July 2001	50.6	60.1	49.4	51.9	55.3	50.0	49.7	49.1	45.9	45.1	52.1	(712)
Aug 2001	48.8	59.2	47.1	51.3	53.3	48.9	48.3	49.9	45.5	43.2	50.9	(850)
Sept 2001	47.9	59.0	44.6	48.3	53.3	49.3	46.6	49.4	44.9	**40.9**	**49.0**	(732)
Oct 2001	47.2	58.5	**44.0**	48.3	53.0	48.9	**45.7**	50.7	45.3	41.6	**49.0**	(893)
Mean	55.3	62.7	54.1	57.8	58.4	53.5	53.3	53.2	49.9	51.2	56.8	
Range of fluctuation	19.0	15.1	22.7	20.8	15.0	14.1	19.1	12.4	13.4	25.5	19.0	

trend over the period, albeit with different extent of fluctuation. That is, they rapidly climbed to their historical peak in August or September 1997 and then started to fall sharply. The ratings reached their first lows in September 1998 and from there slowly bottomed out. But they fell again after March 1999 and hit another wave of new lows in October that year. Since then the ratings had fluctuated at a low level for a number of months and then dropped further to new historical lows in July–September 2000. They then climbed back a little bit but fell again after July 2001. As of October 2001, 8 of the 11 ratings stayed below the passing level and almost all ratings recorded new lows or were close to their July-September lows of 2000.

Fourth, we can see from the ten specific ratings that initially people were most positive about Mr. Tung's "clean and just" (its highest rating is 70.2 recorded in September 1997), followed by "care for people" (68.5 in August 1997), "balance between mainland and Hong Kong interests" (67.6 in August 1997), "competence" (66.7 in September 1997), "improve Hong Kong's economy" (66.4 in August in 1997), "trustworthy" (66 in September 1997), "balance various social and political interests" (64.8 in September 1997), "tolerate different political forces" (60.7 in September 1997), "protect human rights and freedom" (59.8 in September 1997), and "promote democracy" (58 in September 1997). Apparently, the scores of the last three ratings in the ordering are all near or below 60, which are significantly lower than those of the rest of the ratings, and they are all directly connected to Mr. Tung's commitment to political harmony, freedom and democracy. It is thus sufficient to conclude that relatively speaking, people had least expectation from their Chief Executive politically even at the beginning of his term of office.

Fifth, the ranges of fluctuation of the ten specific ratings take the following descending order: "improve Hong Kong's economy"(25.5), "competence" (22.7), "care for the people" (20.8), "balance various social and political forces" (19.1), "trustworthy" (19), "clean and just" (15.1), "balance between mainland and Hong Kong interests" (15), "tolerate different political forces" (14.1), "promote democracy" (13.4), and "protect human rights and freedom" (12.4). Compared with the overall performance's 19, the first four ratings' ranges of fluctuation are greater, meaning that people have experienced greater loss of confidence over Mr. Tung on these four areas. This is especially true in regard to "improve Hong Kong's economy" and "competence." Their occupation of the first and second greatest ranges of fluctuation not only reconfirms our earlier observation about the importance of economic development to Mr. Tung's popularity, it also reflects that people's increasing dissatisfaction with the Chief Executive's economic performance has seriously eroded their confidence over his ability to lead the city. That the two ratings almost concurrently marked their new lows in September and October 2001 should further show their close relationship. On the other hand, "tolerate different political forces," "promote democracy," and "protect human rights and freedom" have the smallest ranges of fluctuation, implying that these three areas have had less effect on the deterioration of Mr. Tung's popularity. This is understandable because as pointed out earlier, politically people did not have much expectation from the Chief Executive when he assumed office. When people's expectation was low, it is simply not surprising that their disappointment would be less dramatic.

Sixth, as mentioned above, in October 2001, eight of the 11 ratings, including "overall performance," stayed below the passing level and almost all ratings recorded new lows or were close to their July-September lows of 2000. The low ratings indicate that Mr. Tung's legitimacy is currently under heavy pressure, if not in crisis. In fact, as the scores of "trustworthy" (47.2,) "competence" (44), and "care for people" (48.3) were not only below the passing level but also lower than that of "overall performance" (49), and as these ratings are mainly indicators of Mr. Tung's personal quality and integrity, it is not difficult to see that people's dissatisfaction with the Chief Executive has gone beyond the functional level of policy performance to a more psychological level of questioning his personal quality and integrity. As the latter aspect is more deep-seated and more enduring, this trend of development will believably create more difficulty for Mr. Tung to improve his popular support in the future.

The seriousness of Mr. Tung's legitimacy problem can be further illustrated by the poor public support for him to have a second term of office. According to Table 2, in June 2001 when the second economic recession after the handover was still not fully in place, public support for Mr. Tung to have another term of office was already very weak. Only 31.5 per cent of respondents expressed their support while more than half opposed. The situation deteriorated further after August. As of October, only 22.7 per cent of respondents indicated their support, a drop of almost ten per cent in four months, while more than 60 per cent opposed, an increase of more than ten per cent compared to June. The rapid deterioration again is closely linked to the emerging fact that Hong Kong is really heading toward a new recession.

Table 2. Public Support for Mr. Tung to Have a Second Term of Office (%)

Date of survey conducted	Not support	Support	Don't know	(N)
June 2001	52.7	31.5	15.8	(854)
Aug 2001	60.7	22.4	17.0	(859)
Sept 2001	67.3	19.2	13.4	(738)
Oct 2001	62.5	22.7	14.8	(907)

In sum, the above observations show clearly that while the Chief Executive was rather well received by the public at the beginning of his term of office, his popularity soon dropped rapidly and continued to record new low in the past four years. By October 2001, public perception of him was quite negative. People not only doubted his ability to revive the local economy and to a lesser degree, his commitment to democracy and freedom, but also questioned his overall competence as Chief Executive. The only areas that he has so far all along received positive evaluations are his being "clean and just" and his ability to "balance between mainland and Hong Kong interests," but the weight of them is obviously far from enough for the public to support him to have a second term of office.

Social and Demographic Differences in the Chief Executive's Public Support

Do the respondents' different social and demographic backgrounds have an impact on their support for the Chief Executive? If yes, has there been any change over the period under study? We selected gender, age, education, working status and personal income and for simplicity, correlated them only with the July 1997 and October 2001 ratings of Mr. Tung's overall performance by means of analysis of variance (ANOVA). The results are presented in Table 3.

Both gender and income have no significant effect on the public rating of Mr. Tung's overall performance, be it the July 1997 survey or October 2001 survey. The influence of age, education and working status is significant in both surveys. Specifically, respondents who are 51 or above of age, with primary or less education, or not working are more likely to give a higher rating for Mr. Tung's overall performance. Since older and less educated people are conventionally more pro-Beijing,[10] their expressed higher support for the Chief Executive should not be surprising given his close association with Beijing. What is somewhat unexpected is

Table 3. Mr. Tung's Overall Performance by Various Demographic Variables

	Mean (July 1997)	Mean (October 2001)
Gender		
Male	64.48	48.16
Female	63.00	49.81
Total	63.73	48.97
F value	1.148	1.462
Age		
30 or below	62.79	47.29
31–50	62.96	47.04
51 or above	70.77	58.30
Total	63.82	48.96
F value	7.001**	18.870**
Education		
Primary or below	68.25	56.65
Secondary	64.28	47.78
Post-secondary	58.83	47.07
Total	63.71	48.95
F value	9.692**	11.626**
Working status		
Not working	66.32	53.81
Working	62.40	46.11
Total	63.73	48.95
F value	7.350**	30.254**
Personal Income		
Less than $10,000	65.04	49.43
$10,000 to less than $20,000	62.83	44.31
$20,000 or above	59.99	46.57
Total	62.55	46.56
F value	2.577	3.184

* $p > 0.05$; ** $p > 0.01$.

that people who are not working also express a more favorable tendency toward Mr. Tung. However, if we learn that the category of "not working" includes not only the unemployed people but also a relatively large number of retirees, our puzzle will likely disappear. These retirees are all older in age and their reason for being more supportive of the Chief Executive should therefore be very similar to that of the older people.

Besides, it is noteworthy that comparatively all the F values of the three significant variables of the October 2001 survey are larger than those of the July 1997 one, especially on age and working status. Behind the phenomenon should be that while public support for Mr. Tung has declined steadily over time, older, less educated and retired people still constitute the Chief Executive's major core supporters. In fact, in the October 2001 survey, these groups of people's average ratings of Mr. Tung's overall performance are 58.3, 56.65 and 53.81, respectively, which are not only much higher than the passing level, but also significantly higher than the average score of the general population.

Causes for the Decline of the Chief Executive's Popularity

What are the major factors that have contributed to the continuing decline of the Chief Executive's popularity? A close examination of the period reveals three major factors: economic deterioration, administrative mismanagement, and political conservatism.

Economic development is always an important basis of political legitimacy, especially for undemocratic regimes.[11] Hong Kong is no exception. As pointed out earlier, the drastic downturn in public opinion regarding the Chief Executive occurred right after Hong Kong was first hit hard by the Asian financial crisis in October 1997. The crisis erupted in Thailand shortly after Hong Kong's handover to mainland China and continued to spread to other Asian economies, including Hong Kong. Indeed, the four waves of the lowest ratings on the Chief Executive between July 1997 and December 1998 (i.e., October 1997, January, May, and July–September 1998) our survey recorded were all directly connected to the continuing spread of the Asian financial crisis.

In October 1997, the Asian financial crisis finally spread to Hong Kong and the Hong Kong dollar fell under fierce attacks. At that time, the inter-bank interest rates increased to 280 per cent. In January 1998, the Hong Kong dollar suffered a new round of attacks, with the interest rate rising another 30 per cent in a battered economy. In May 1998, the government announced a negative economic growth rate — a situation rarely seen in recent years. From July through September 1998, the Hong Kong stock and financial markets were under a third round of voracious attacks by international speculators and the SAR was forced to defend itself by pouring HK$120 billion into the stock market. With the worsening of the Asian financial crisis, many Asian countries devalued their currency, a move that led international speculators to launch several attacks on the Hong Kong dollar. The Hong Kong Monetary Authority (HKMA), in an effort to keep the peg of the Hong Kong dollar to the U.S. dollar, raised interest rates sharply. With this sudden jump in interest rates, the Hang Seng Index of the local stock market plummeted from a peak of some 16, 000 points in September 1997 to about 6,500 points in August 1998, a more than 50 per cent drop in less than one year's time.[12]

Meanwhile, the property prices in Hong Kong, which were immediately affected by the financial market, also shrank by about 50 per cent from a peak in 1997 to a low in August 1998. Furthermore, under the weight of high interest rates and a "meltdown" in the stock and property markets, industries and services had to cast off employees and streamline business, which sent the unemployment rate soaring from 2.2 per cent at time of the handover to 5 per cent in September 1998, with over 180,000 workers losing their jobs. The GDP growth rate fell from 5.8 per cent in the third quarter of 1997 to minus 7.1 per cent one year later.[13]

The financial sector, which is a stabilizing factor in Hong Kong's economy, was also faced with a grave challenge unseen since the early 1980s, when Hong Kong was hit by the political uncertainty unleashed by the Sino-British negotiations over the island's future. The panic withdrawal of savings by account holders from the International Bank of Asia in early November 1997 and the subsequent collapse of the Peregrine Investments Holdings and the CA Pacific Securities in January 1998 are cases in point. Although the International Bank of Asia survived thanks to the intervention of the HKMA,[14] the eventual closedown of the Peregrine Investments Holdings and the CA Pacific Securities both led to great losses for thousands of their customers and dampened hopes among the Hong Kong public of a rapid economic upturn. At the time, the two companies were ranked as the first and third largest local securities companies in Hong Kong, with a combined total asset value of tens of billions Hong Kong dollars.[15] With the worsening of the Hong Kong dollar-denominated assets, pressure on the banking sector mounted.[16] The SAR government, doing little other than raising the interest rate, aroused discontent in the community.

The economy gradually improved after the second quarter of 1999, so were the Chief Executive's popular ratings. In 2000, the GDP growth rate reached a record high of 10.5 per cent. The unemployment rate also moderated from its peak of 6.3 per cent in the fall of 1999 to below 5 per cent in mid-2000, but it was unable to return to the pre-handover's 2-per cent level.[17] Unfortunately, the economic recovery did not last long as signs of economic downturn appeared again since the second quarter of

2001 as a result of the rapidly slowing down of the global economy, along with a new wave of decline in Mr. Tung's popularity. According to government statistics, the GDP growth rate of the second quarter of 2001 already fell to 0.5 per cent, significantly lower than the government's original forecast of 4 per cent at the beginning of the year. Almost at the same time, the unemployment rate deteriorated rapidly again, jumping from July's 4.5 per cent to September's 5.3 per cent in the same year.[18]

Table 4 shows that changes in public confidence in Hong Kong's economic future proceeded almost in parallel with changes in the public support for the Chief Executive, indicating the close relationship between the two. In addition, as shown in Table 1, one of the items that have declined most closely with the rating of the SAR Chief Executive's overall performance is "improve the economy,"[19] giving proof that changes in the economic situation have a major influence on public opinion regarding Mr. Tung's performance.

Table 4. Public Attitude toward Hong Kong's Economic Future (%)

Date of survey conducted	Worse	Same	Better	Don't know/ unclear	(N)
July 1997	16.8	36.6	37.1	9.6	(585)
Aug 1997	16.4	30.6	43.9	9.1	(602)
Sept 1997	14.9	35.9	41.4	7.8	(616)
Oct 1997	31.7	29.9	29.6	8.7	(561)
Nov 1997	40.0	28.8	23.4	7.8	(580)
Dec 1997	49.9	29.5	12.4	8.3	(688)
Jan 1998	54.8	24.5	12.8	7.9	(609)
Feb 1998	39.8	38.8	17.1	4.3	(580)
March 1998	38.9	32.4	23.0	5.8	(553)
April 1998	52.3	14.5	25.8	7.4	(553)
May 1998	56.6	9.9	17.7	15.8	(615)
June 1998	39.7	33.7	14.7	11.9	(591)
July 1998	46.8	33.5	14.3	5.3	(600)
Aug 1998	45.6	35.2	12.9	6.3	(603)
Sept 1998	43.1	37.1	12.8	7.0	(603)
Oct 1998	30.8	38.1	24.4	6.6	(603)
Nov 1998	26.4	41.3	23.5	8.8	(588)
Dec 1998	31.7	38.6	22.2	7.4	(567)
Jan 1999	37.6	39.5	17.2	5.7	(575)
Feb 1999	32.4	40.8	21.7	5.2	(581)
March 1999	21.9	39.6	34.2	4.2	(565)

Table 4. (Cont'd)

Date of survey conducted	Worse	Same	Better	Don't know/ unclear	(N)
April 1999	22.5	40.3	32.6	4.6	(568)
May 1999	21.2	44.3	30.9	3.6	(557)
June 1999	18.6	40.7	31.3	9.4	(553)
July 1999	64.9	22.9	11.4	0.8	(590)
Aug 1999	66.7	21.7	10.0	1.6	(562)
Sept 1999	60.2	25.5	12.1	2.3	(522)
Oct 1999	68.3	17.7	12.2	1.8	(599)
Nov 1999	60.4	25.7	12.1	1.9	(647)
Dec 1999	51.6	32.0	13.6	2.8	(579)
Jan 2000	58.1	27.8	10.0	4.1	(561)
Feb 2000	44.2	38.7	14.7	2.4	(545)
March 2000	43.5	40.3	14.7	1.4	(556)
May 2000	58.5	29.2	9.7	2.7	(566)
June 2000	59.8	30.0	8.1	2.2	(557)
July 2000	58.5	28.2	11.7	1.6	(954)
Aug 2000	52.7	35.5	10.9	1.0	(921)
Sept 2000	55.4	33.3	10.5	0.8	(848)
Oct 2000	59.1	28.1	11.7	1.1	(812)
Nov 2000	56.2	34.3	8.0	1.5	(895)
Dec 2000	49.8	38.6	10.7	0.9	(843)
Jan 2001	51.7	38.5	8.4	1.4	(784)
Feb 2001	46.6	40.8	11.2	1.5	(743)
March 2001	52.5	38.2	8.2	1.1	(802)
April 2001	56.6	34.3	8.4	0.6	(775)
May 2001	53.4	38.2	7.4	1.0	(905)
June 2001	61.8	31.7	5.5	0.8	(854)
July 2001	60.7	31.7	6.8	0.8	(732)
Aug 2001	73.5	22.1	3.8	0.6	(865)
Sept 2001	73.4	22.3	3.4	0.9	(743)
Oct 2001	72.2	23.0	3.6	1.2	(909)

Along with the deteriorating economy, Hong Kong was hit by a host of disasters after the handover, from which the serious administrative mismanagement problem of the SAR government under the leadership of Mr. Tung Chee-hwa was exposed. In November 1997, a medical officer at a hospital inadvertently treated several hundred sick children with toxic mouthwash rather than anti-fever medicine, which caused panic among the parents of the young victims. Earlier on, several residents were affected by the H5N1 bird flu virus, resulting in one death. The bird flu then spread via human contacts with chickens, and because the government failed to respond quickly, the disease spread rapidly, often with deadly results. In December the same year, faced with a boisterous public, the government ordered to destroy all chickens in the territory and suspend the chicken business temporarily. In the same month, a number of residents were poisoned by pesticide residues in green vegetables and were hospitalized. The incident caused the price of green vegetables to fall sharply. In January 1998, a dozen people were hospitalized after eating poisonous fish, with the price of fish plunging in its wake. In March and April of 1998, Hong Kong waters were invaded by so-called "red tides," killing off large quantities of fish in the vicinity and incurring an immediate loss of HK$800 million to the fishing industry. In July the same year, the newly opened Hong Kong International Airport was in serious chaos when the major air cargo terminal was paralyzed due to an overall computer breakdown and the lack of a corresponding emergency management system for nearly two months, with an estimated loss of over HK$20 billion.[20] In January 2000, a Home Ownership Scheme project at Yuen Chau Kok in Shatin was detected of faulty foundation piles connected to corruption. The housing Authority later ordered to demolish the project, resulting a serious loss of public money and causing public outcry spearing at the government's problematic supervision and management of public housing construction.

The above incidents, among others, seriously damaged the public confidence in the Tung administration. The government's supervision and handling of these incidents were under heavy criticisms, particularly in the cases of the misplaced medicine, the chicken flu, the airport chaos, and the Yuen Chau Kok event. For instance, in the cases of the chaos associated with the new international airport and the corruption with the Home Ownership Scheme project at Yuen Chau Kok, the government was clearly in charge of implementing and supervising the entire construction. The unmatched chaos and massive corruption involved in the two incidents manifested clearly the rapidly worsening problems in regard to government administration during the transitional period. The government's handling of the incidents only made things worse. The public was particularly upset when the government failed to punish the respective senior officials or more radically to reshuffle the government leadership even, for example, after a non-confidence vote for Housing Authority chairwoman Rosanna Wong and Director of Hosing Tony Miller was passed in the Legislative Council in the case of the Yuen Chau Kok event. The failure was partly due to the rigid civil service system which made the removal of incompetent officials extremely difficult (in the case of Tony Miller) and partly due to Mr. Tung's personal character (in the case of Rosanna Wong). In any case, the insensitivity of the government to public dissatisfaction only added fuel to people's fury and made the credibility of the SAR government and the Chief Executive nose-dived. No wonder the SAR government and Mr. Tung's popularity recorded historical lows in the third quarter of 1998 and in the summer of 2000 when the development of the two incidents gathered momentum (see Tables 5 and 1). The close relationship was simply not a coincidence.

Table 5. Public Satisfaction with the SAR Government's Performance (%)

Date of survey conducted	Not satisfied	So so	Satisfied	Don't know/ unclear	(N)
July 1997	12.0	31.8	35.6	20.5	(584)
Aug 1997	10.9	35.8	40.5	12.9	(598)
Sept 1997	9.0	30.8	54.3	5.9	(613)
Oct 1997	21.2	30.1	42.1	6.6	(561)
Nov 1997	18.7	36.3	40.4	4.7	(579)
Jan 1998	36.9	35.1	22.0	6.0	(579)
Feb 1998	24.0	41.9	30.9	3.3	(580)
March 1998	28.6	35.3	31.7	4.3	(555)
April 1998	31.1	34.6	31.9	2.3	(598)
May 1998	46.4	31.6	14.7	7.3	(586)
June 1998	35.7	34.7	25.3	4.3	(582)
July 1998	53.4	27.5	15.2	3.8	(599)
Aug 1998	52.0	30.1	15.4	2.5	(602)
Sept 1998	48.2	32.0	16.1	3.7	(566)
Oct 1998	39.3	35.1	22.3	3.3	(601)
Nov 1998	41.8	30.8	25.0	2.4	(588)
Dec 1998	37.6	33.2	26.0	3.2	(566)
Jan 1999	46.5	32.9	16.9	3.7	(574)
Feb 1999	49.7	29.3	19.1	1.9	(580)
March 1999	34.5	35.9	27.8	1.8	(565)
April 1999	40.9	34.4	22.8	1.9	(567)
May 1999	41.3	31.2	25.9	1.6	(557)
June 1999	46.3	24.9	25.6	3.3	(551)
July 1999	45.4	30.0	23.7	0.8	(590)
Aug 1999	44.9	31.9	21.4	1.8	(561)

Table 5. (Cont'd)

Date of survey conducted	Not satisfied	So so	Satisfied	Don't know/ unclear	(N)
Sept 1999	41.5	34.5	19.8	4.2	(525)
Oct 1999	46.8	33.3	17.9	2.0	(598)
Nov 1999	43.9	32.6	21.6	1.9	(644)
Dec 1999	37.2	39.3	20.1	3.3	(572)
Jan 2000	44.6	33.3	18.7	3.4	(561)
Feb 2000	41.3	35.0	20.2	3.5	(545)
March 2000	38.1	40.3	20.1	1.4	(556)
May 2000	49.3	35.0	13.1	2.7	(566)
June 2000	53.3	33.8	10.6	2.3	(557)
July 2000	52.2	33.7	12.1	2.0	(952)
Aug 2000	52.5	30.8	14.8	2.0	(920)
Sept 2000	51.8	31.3	15.3	1.7	(848)
Oct 2000	46.2	33.4	18.7	1.7	(812)
Nov 2000	47.4	34.1	17.1	1.5	(895)
Dec 2000	44.4	33.7	20.0	1.9	(843)
Jan 2001	44.3	37.1	16.1	2.6	(784)
Feb 2001	40.2	39.2	18.4	2.2	(743)
March 2001	40.3	39.8	18.7	1.2	(802)
April 2001	41.9	41.0	15.6	1.6	(774)
May 2001	40.7	40.3	18.0	1.0	(904)
June 2001	32.7	52.5	13.7	1.2	(854)
July 2001	42.3	40.0	16.3	1.4	(732)
Aug 2001	47.9	33.1	17.0	2.0	(864)
Sept 2001	49.1	38.5	11.2	1.2	(743)
Oct 2001	50.9	34.3	13.6	1.1	(909)

Finally, Mr. Tung's unsecretive political conservatism also served to constrain his popularity and, at times, cost him dearly in terms of his public image. Mr. Tung became the Chief Executive of the SAR government with the support of the Chinese government. To minimize any possible confrontation or friction with the central government and to seek the continuing trust from Beijing, he took an overt pro-Beijing stand on many political issues, including his commitment to the democratic gradualism stipulated in the Basic Law by turning away local calls for faster democratic reforms. This is perhaps why he continuously received positive ratings in the area "balance between mainland and HK interests" (see Table 1). To compensate such political conservatism, he attempted to win public support by presenting a grand scheme of constructing a future Hong Kong.[21] The sudden economic downturn in Hong Kong, however, caught Mr. Tung by surprise, seriously challenging his grand blueprint as well as his ruling strategy of political conservatism. When mobilization by popularly oriented political parties against his problematic leadership and his government's mismanagement intensified, Hong Kong society became ever more politicized than before the handover. This politicization was surely detrimental to his ruling legitimacy.[22]

What is more, in the past four years under the rule of Mr. Tung, politically controversial incidents occurred in Hong Kong one after the other, and every time his role was seriously questioned, especially by pro-democracy forces. In January 1999, for example, the Court of Final Appeal declared some provisions in an immigration ordinance unconstitutional and ruled that children born out of Hong Kong permanent residents in the mainland were entitled the right of abode in Hong Kong regardless of whether their parents were permanent residents or not at the time of their birth. The ruling also asserted that the Court of Final Appeal had the right to review the constitutionality of laws passed by the Chinese National People's Congress Standing Committee, the highest organ of power in the Chinese Constitution. However, the SAR government argued that the ruling not only violated the legislative intent in the provisions but also would result in an influx of 1.67 million mainland people to Hong Kong. The Chief Executive thus requested the Chinese National People's Congress Standing Committee to reinterpret two relevant sections of the Basic Law. The Chinese National People's Congress Standing Committee accepted the request and subsequently overturned the Court of Final Appeal's ruling by stating that only those children one or both of whose parents were permanent residents of Hong Kong at the time of their birth had the right of abode. After the reinterpretation, the government estimated that the number of potential immigrants was dramatically reduced from the original 1.7 million to only 170,000. The incident deeply divided the local community. While some were frightened by the possible massive influx of 1.67 million people to Hong Kong and supported the government's move, many were troubled by the government's active invitation of the Chinese central government to interfere with Hong Kong's domestic affairs. The mainstream legal community and pro-democracy forces even condemned the government for undermining the judicial independence of Hong Kong.

Another example is the Cheung Man-yee incident. In July 1999, Cheng An-kuo, the de facto Taiwan official representative in Hong Kong defended the "two state" theory in a radio programme of the Radio Television of Hong Kong put forward earlier by Taiwanese president Lee Teng-hui. The theory claimed that cross-strait relations should be treated as a state-to-state instead of central-to-local relationship. Cheng's speech was later strongly attacked by pro-Beijing forces in Hong Kong as spreading the idea of Taiwan independence. The Radio Television of Hong Kong was also heavily criticized for its active role in inviting and allowing Cheng to deliver the speech. In October, Director of Broadcasting Cheung Man-yee was mysteriously transferred to the post of the Principal Representative of Trade and Economic Affairs in Tokyo. Two months later, Cheng was also transferred back to Taiwan after a prolonged waiting for the renewal of his working visa. The incident drew wide suspicion in the city that Cheung's removal and Cheng's working visa renewal problem were all connected to political considerations. Many people thought that the incident was an attempt of the Chief Executive to please Beijing at the expense of the freedom of press in Hong Kong.

A further example is the Robert Chung incident. In July 2000, Robert Chung, a prominent pollster at the Hong Kong University, wrote an article in two local newspapers alleging that the Chief Executive had pressured him via a third channel to stop conducting polls on his popularity. According to Chung's polls, Mr. Tung's popularity experienced a continued declined since 1998. It was later revealed that Mr. Tung's senior special assistant Andrew Lo raised some concern over Chung's polling activities at a meeting with the University's Vice-Chancellor Cheng Yiu-chung. The Chief Executive, Lo and Cheng all denied the allegations. Capturing both local and international attention surrounding the role of the Chief Executive in the incident, the scandal was seen as a threat to the academic freedom in Hong Kong. Under enormous pressure, an independent commission was set up to investigate the allegations. Contrary to the respective parties' denial, the commission finally concluded that Chung's allegations were credible whereas Lo and Cheng were not truthful in their testimonies. Faced with the commission's unfavorable conclusion, Cheng reluctantly resigned from the Vice-Chancellor post, but Lo, defended by the Chief Executive for being fully reliable and trustworthy, did not follow suit. The commission's conclusion, together with the Chief Executive's defense and insistence to retain Lo, only deepened the negative public perception of Mr. Tung's political conservatism.

The last, but not the least, example is the Falun Gong incident. In 2000, Beijing intensified its nationwide campaign against the Falun Gong in the mainland, a spiritual movement outlawed and subsequently defined as cult and subversive by the Chinese government in recent years. In Hong Kong, however, the group was registered under the Societies Ordinance and therefore its existence was lawful. In January 2001, the group held an international conference at a government venue, with some 1,000 practitioners from around the world staging a march protesting Beijing's suppression of the movement in the mainland. The incident triggered strong reactions from both local pro-Beijing forces and mainland officials. The latter also warned that Hong Kong should not be used as a base for subversive activities. Under pressure, the Chief Executive and his senior aides began to criticize the group for creating social unrest in the mainland. On one occasion in the Legislative Council, Mr. Tung even echoed Beijing's tone by labeling the Hong Kong Falun Gong as a cult. In May 2001, the SAR government further indicated that they were studying a new law on the handling of cults, a move widely interpreted as targeted at the group. The series of developments provoked concerns over freedoms of speech and association in Hong Kong. Many people saw the developments as attempts by Mr. Tung to appease Beijing. They particularly feared that Beijing might gradually limit, through the SAR government, its tolerance of activities in Hong Kong that were in conflict with Beijing's political values.

The above incidents, among others, inevitably dealt severe blows to Mr. Tung's popularity. As we can see in Table 1, the public ratings of Mr. Tung's performance, particularly in "protect human rights and freedom" and "promote democracy," dropped significantly in May and October 1999, September 2000, and June 2001, and the timings coincided almost exactly with the development of the above incidents. Such close association thus forcefully demonstrates the important impact of Mr. Tung's political conservatism on his popularity.

Conclusion

Based on the findings of an ongoing telephone survey, this chapter has depicted the changing public perception of Chief Executive Tung Chee-hwa after he took office in July 1997 and discussed the current condition of his ruling legitimacy. While Mr. Tung was basically well received by the public at the beginning of his term of office, his popularity soon experienced a rapid and continued decline in the past four years. By October 2001, public perception of him was quite negative. People not only doubted his ability to revive the local economy and his commitment to democracy and freedom. They also displayed reservations regarding his overall competence as Chief Executive. The only areas that he all along received positive evaluations are his being "clean and just" and his ability to "balance between mainland and Hong Kong interests." However, these two areas are far from balancing the public's negative evaluations in his other areas of performance, as the majority of people still do not support him for a second term of office. Cross-tabulation analysis also indicates that his support is mainly narrowly limited to the less educated, older generation, and this support is also on the decline. It is thus clear that the Chief Executive is now more or less experiencing a legitimacy crisis. In this regard, in order to rule with stability, he must try his best to resolve or contain this legitimacy crisis, especially if he is determined to stay for a second term. Otherwise, he may find Hong Kong increasingly ungovernable even with Beijing's continued support.

To solve or contain the legitimacy crisis, Mr. Tung must first identify its causes. For this purpose, three major factors have been accounted: economic deterioration, administrative mismanagement, and political conservatism. Hong Kong's economic deterioration is mainly triggered off internally by the bursting of the bubble economy and subsequent economic restructuring and externally by the Asian financial crisis and recently the rapidly slowing down of the global economy. As the internal restructuring takes time to improve and the external factors are beyond the government's control, Mr. Tung and his government cannot do much even if they fully realize the enormous adverse impact of economic deterioration on legitimacy.

What Mr. Tung can do more therefore lies in administrative mismanagement or political conservatism, and it appears that he has been well aware of the problem of the former. In his 2001 Policy Address, he devoted a section outlining his plan to improve the quality of administration, including in particular the introduction of a new system of appointing principal officials. These new officials, appointed on terms different to those in the civil service, would be responsible for formulating and explaining policies, defending policies, canvassing support from the Legislative Council and the public, and being answerable to the Chief Executive for the success or failure of their policies. [23] The introduction of the new system, if properly implemented, should correct some of the rigidity problem of the civil service, enhance the accountability of the government and eventually improve the legitimacy of the Chief Executive.

Yet, without fundamentally changing his political conservatism, the effect of the administrative reforms Mr. Tung intends to achieve on boosting his legitimacy is nevertheless very limited. The reason is that the introduction of the new appointing system does not guarantee the future administration will shift its orientation from pro-Beijing to pro-Hong Kong. As demonstrated earlier, the two orientations are often in conflict. If a principal official walks a pro-Beijing line and is opposed by the public, what should Mr. Tung choose? To remove this official or keep him despite public dissatisfaction? However, one should be mindful that even if Mr. Tung shifts his orientation from pro-Beijing to pro-Hong Kong, he may first risk losing support from Beijing. This is certainly the most difficult dilemma he faces. It also reveals the major political predicament of Hong Kong under "one country, two systems."

Notes

1. See Li-kung Sung, "The Social Consequences of Government Intervention in the Market: A State Theory Perspective," *Hong Kong Economic Journal Monthly*, Vol. 22, 7 (1998), pp. 4–5; Ching-shi Chan, "Tung Chee-hwa and the Ruling Crisis of the SAR Government," *Ming Pao*, 5 August 1998, p. B4.
2. The project is in charge by the author of this paper and is sponsored by *Apple Daily*. It is an on-going project attempting to chart the condition and change of Hong Kong's public attitude toward the "one country, two systems" practice in Hong Kong after the 1997 handover. The sampling for every monthly survey takes two steps. First, a fixed set of telephone numbers is randomly selected from the latest *Hong Kong Residential Telephone Directory*. In order to include those numbers unpublished in the *Directory*, the last two numbers of the selected telephone numbers are replaced with two new, random numbers by computer. Second, after successfully reaching the selected resident, a family member aged 18 or above is selected for an interview in accordance with the last birthday rule. For every valid phone number, a maximum of three contacts at different times is made before it is classified as "unanswered." The survey is conducted at the end of each month. Some of the survey findings are published in *Apple Daily* every month, and a full report of every monthly survey is kept in the Institute's Documentation Unit for record.
3. Carlton Rodee, Totton J. Anderson, Carl Q. Christol and Thomas H. Greene, *Introduction to Political Science* (New York: McGraw-Hill, 1983), p. 21.
4. Phillip W. Shively, *Power and Choice: An Introduction to Political Science* (New York: Newbery Award Records, 1987), pp. 102–5.
5. Ian Scott, " Legitimacy and Its Discontents: Hong Kong and the Reversion to

Chinese Sovereignty," *Asian Journal of Political Science*, Vol. 1, No. 1 (1993), p. 75.

6. One Country Two Systems Economic Research Institute, *The Basic Law of the Hong Kong Special Administrative Region of the People's Republic of China* (Hong Kong: One Country Two Systems Economic Research Institute, 1992), pp. 19–24.
7. Timothy Ka-ying Wong, "Constraints on Tung Chee-hwa's Power and His Governance of Hong Kong," *Issues & Studies,* Vol. 33, No. 8 (1997), p. 15.
8. David Conradt, "Changing German Political Culture," in Gabriel A. Almond and Sidney Verba (eds.), The Civic Culture Revisited (Boston: Little, Brown and Company, 1980), p. 222.
9. Milan Tung-wen Sun and Peng Lian, "Gone with the Wind: Legitimacy and Governor Patten's Popularity in the Transitional Period," *The Chinese Public Administration Review*, Vol. 4, No. 3 (1995), pp. 77–81.
10. Timothy Ka-ying Wong, "Issue Voting," in Kuan Hsin-chi et al. (eds.), *Power Transfer and Electoral Politics: The First Legislative Election in the Hong Kong Special Administrative Region* (Hong Kong: The Chinese University Press, 1999), pp. 105–30.
11. Robert Wade, *Governing the Market* (Princeton: Princeton University Press, 1990).
12. Timothy Ka-ying Wong, "The Legitimacy Problem of the Hong Kong SAR Government: Challenge and Response," *Issues & Studies,* Vol. 35, No. 4 (1999), pp. 67–71.
13. See http://www.info.gov.hk/censtatd/eng/hkstat/fas/nat_account/gdp/gdp1.htm.
14. For details of the intervention, see *South China Morning Post*, 11 November 1997, p. B1.
15. For details of the two securities companies, see *Hong Kong Standard*, 11 January 1998, p. A3.
16. Shu-ki Tsang, "An Unfinished Story: A Reappraisal of the Defense of the Hong Kong Peg and the Lowering of the Interest Rates in the Economic Crisis," *Ming Pao*, 19 June 1998, p. E12.
17. See http://www.info.gov.hk/censtatd/eng/hkstat/fas/labour/ghs/labour1_index.html.
18. See http://www.info.gov.hk/censtatd/eng/hkstat/fas/nat_account/gdp/gdp1.htm.
19. The correlation coefficient between the rating of "improve the economy" and the rating of "overall performance" is high as 0.906.
20. Timothy Ka-ying Wong, "The Legitimacy Problem of the Hong Kong SAR Government," pp. 69–70.
21. Tung Chee-hwa, *Building Hong Kong for a New Era: Address by the Chief Executive the Honourable Tung Chee-hwa at the Provisional Legislature on 8 October 1997* (Hong Kong: The Hong Kong SAR Government Printing Department, 1997).

22. Siu-kai Lau, "Ministers in the Making," *South China Morning Post*, 3 April 1998, p. A25.
23. Tung Chee-hwa, *Building on our Strengths Investing in our Future: Address by the Chief Executive the Honourable Tung Chee-hwa at the Legislature Council Meeting on 10 October 2001* (Hong Kong: The Hong Kong SAR Government Printing Department, 2001), pp. 35–39

16

Social Protests, Legitimacy Crisis, and the Impetus Toward Soft Authoritarianism in the Hong Kong SAR

Alvin Y. So*

Professor, Division of Social Science

Hong Kong University of Science and Technology

Introduction

On 20 April 2000, about 50 students from nine tertiary education institutions marched from the Southern Center in Wan Chai to the Hong Kong government's headquarters in Central at around 3.30 p.m. to protest against a plan to increase tuition fees. The Hong Kong government had suggested the fee system be changed so students are charged according to the costs of their course. Medical students, for instance, would have to pay more tuition than those studying English or history. Students, however, believed that the government should enable everybody to have equal rights to choose what they want to study without worrying about the financial status of their families. When the protesting students tried to break through a police cordon in order to see Joseph Wing-ping Wong, Secretary for Education and Manpower at the Central Government Offices, scuffles broke out with police. After the students failed to force their way into Wong's office, they posted a protest letter signed by about 3,600 students

* The author would like to thank an anonymous reviewer for his critical comments and careful editing of this chapter.

outside the government headquarters and ended the rally. Later, four students were trailed and stopped by four plainclothes officers wearing earpieces in Lan Kwai Fong. They were asked to show Hong Kong ID cards, as was a fifth student at the Central MTR station. Wan Chai Police Commander Pang Moon-kwan said an investigation had been launched into why the students had not notified police of the demonstration as required by law. He also said that a report would be sent to the Department of Justice and did not rule out prosecutions (*SCMP* 21 April 2000).

On 25 June 2000, about 1,200 people demonstrated over the right-of-abode issue, criticizing the SAR government for seeking the mainland's interpretation of the Basic Law a year ago. A hardcore group of students and mainland protesters stayed overnight outside the Court of Final Appeal before holding a candlelight vigil in Chater Garden at Central. At around 3 a.m. the next day, the protesters took shelter from the rain by moving from the Court of Final Appeal to the nearby Chief Executive's Office. The police allowed only 20 protesters in, while another 70 stayed outside the Office's main gate. Police dispersed those inside the Office at 6.45 a.m. after failing to persuade them to leave. The protesters then squatted outside the Office's main gate and refused to leave. Since the Chief Executive Tung Chee-hwa and other top officials would soon arrive for work in early morning, police wanted to clear the protesters from outside the Chief Executive's Office. Violent clashes then broke out. Television news footage showed police pushing and shoving the protesters, with one officer using pepper spray and another waving his fist. Four protestors said they were pepper-sprayed in the face. Another injured protester, Chan King-chi, a former Hong Kong University Students Union president, said he was carried and hurled out of the gate by several police officers, and Aas I was still lying on the ground, scores of officers walked across me and stepped on me." Chan suffered injuries on the leg, chest, and arm. A total of six abode-seekers and six Hong Kong Federation of Student's members were injured during scuffles with dozens of police officers. Secretary for Security Regina Ip said the police action was necessary and justified, and she criticized the protesters for failing to inform the police in advance about their demonstration as required by law (*SCMP* 27 June 2000).

On 15 August 2000, five students involved in the above 26 June 2000 incidence were arrested. They were accused of taking part in an unlawful assembly, assisting in the organization of an unauthorized assembly, and obstructing police in the execution of their duties. All were members of the Hong Kong Federation of Students (HKFS). They were released on police bail of $500 each, pending further inquiries. On 28 September 2000, police further arrested five students leaders who took part in the 20 April 2000 protest against government plans to alter tuition fees. They were arrested on the same ground of taking part in and assisting in the organization of an unauthorized assembly and obstructing police duties.

These incidences are landmark cases because it is the first time that protesters were arrested on the ground of taking part in or organizing an unauthorized assembly since Hong Kong became a SAR of the PRC in mid 1997. The aim of this chapter is to study in what ways social protests have provided the impetus toward the formation of a "soft authoritarian" state in Hong Kong. It will argue that despite the Basic Law and the Public Order Ordinance have laid the foundation of an authoritarian state in Hong Kong, the Tung government had initially tried hard to strive for a liberal state in Hong Kong. It was only when the Tung government faced a serious legitimacy crisis and after an explosion of social protests in summer 2000 that it resolved to soft authoritarian measures in order to regain political control of the SAR. In the following discussion, therefore, it will examine the origins and the formation process of the soft authoritarian state in the Hong Kong SAR.

Laying the Foundation of an Authoritarian State

The Basic Law has provided the foundation for an authoritarian state in Hong Kong. In the light of the unanticipated upsurge of public support by Hong Kong people for the Chinese democracy movement in mid 1989, the mainland government became alarmed at the prospect that Hong Kong could become a base of subversion against the Chinese Communist Party after the 1997 handover. As such, the mainland government insisted in inserting a new provision (Article 23) into the Basic Law. Suzanne Pepper (forthcoming) points out that Article 23 mandated special local legislation to prohibit subversion against the PRC Central Government, the theft of state secrets, and political activities by foreign organizations, as well as ties between them and counterparts in the SAR. If the Basic Law Article 23 were to be implemented as stated, and to be interpreted as similar legal concepts as elsewhere in the PRC, the implications would be grave indeed for Hong Kong's political life. The result would be either prison terms, or an underground existence, or at least drastically curtailed freedoms of speech and association for Hong Kong's most popular political leaders.

In addition, the new Public Order Ordinance and the Societies

Ordinance, which were passed by the Provisional Legislative Council (Legco) right after the mid-1997 handover, further consolidated the foundation for authoritarian rule in the HKSAR. Sing Ming (2001) laments that under the Public Order Ordinance of 1995, the Hong Kong police could legally interfere with public gathering or procession only to prevent an imminent threat to public safety or public order. This 1995 version largely reduces the abuses of power by the government by requiring the presence of a "public observable" threat to "public safety or public order." However, the 1997 version passed by the Provisional Legco incorporates the new concept of "national security," defined as the "safeguarding of the territorial integrity and independence of the People's Republic of China." Under this 1997 version, the police can lawfully interfere and forbid any public procession and social gathering from being held, whenever the vaguely defined notion of "national security" is perceived to be under threat, even in the absence of any threat of violence on the part of demonstrators. Furthermore, while the 1995 version only requires the protesters to notify the police in advance, the 1997 version says that protesters must apply for "letters of no objection" from police at least seven days before a sit-down meeting of more than 50 people or any procession of more than 30 people. The maximum penalty for breaching the ordinance is a fine of HK$5,000 and a three-year jail term.

With regard to freedom of association, the Societies Ordinance passed in 1992 stipulated that societies are granted the freedom of association unless they are prejudicial to the security of Hong Kong, to public safety, or to public order. Organizers of different associations needed only to inform the police about their formation and did not need to undergo compulsory registration with the police. But Sing Ming (2001) points out that in the latest version passed by the Provisional Legco in mid 1997, all organizations (except those with solely religious, charitable, social, or recreational purposes) have to apply for registration from the local police. The latter can refuse registration for new societies or revoke the registration of existing ones if they are deemed to be a threat to "national security" or defined as political bodies with "links" to foreign political organizations.

Also, there are worries that mainland policies could spill over to the HKSAR and threaten its freedom of the press. For example, in March 2000 the Wharf Cable Television news channel interview of Anne Lu Hsiu-lien, then the Taipei regime's vice president-elect, provoked strong criticism by Wang Fengchao (Deputy Director, Central Government Liaison Office in

Hong Kong). Wang charged that Hong Kong's mass media should fulfill their duty and responsibility of safeguarding Chinese national unity and territorial integrity by refraining from reporting the views for Taiwan independence. In October 2000, the criticisms of Hong Kong's mass media by PRC President Jiang Zemin, who labeled Hong Kong's journalists as "too simple and naïve," sent shock waves to the mass media community in Hong Kong (Lau and To forthcoming).

The Basic Law, the Public Order Ordinance, the Societies Ordinance, and mainland's possible intrusion of Hong Kong's affairs then laid the foundation for an authoritarian rule in the SAR. If the Hong Kong government wants to curb public demonstrations, ban unfriendly associations, and censor publications critical to the mainland government, it could find ample ground from the mini-constitution and the legal order as well as from mainland officials. Nevertheless, up to mid 2000, the SAR government had been trying very hard to act as a liberal state.

The Striving Toward a Liberal State

Studies which are skeptical of the "One Country, Two Systems" arrangement have generally overlooked the fact that the Hong Kong government has been blessed by the following factors. The first blessing is the positive China factor. During the 1997 transition era, the PRC had a stable leadership, a cordial relationship with the U.S., and a strong growth economy. A stable PRC regime enabled its leaders to speak with one voice and to actualize the HKSAR's promised high degree of autonomy without being labeled as betraying Chinese national interests. Friendly ties with the U.S. and glaring attention from the global media induced the Beijing leaders to be more cautious toward any attempt at overt interference in Hong Kong. The second blessing is the inverted Taiwan factor. The Taipei regime's "state to state" concept and the election of Progressive Democratic Party's Chen Shui-bian as president worsened cross-strait relations. As Hong Kong has been the prime "One country, Two systems" showcase in the PRC's drive for reunification with Taiwan, it might seem that the more intense the hostility between Beijing and Taipei, the greater efforts would be exerted by Beijing to ensure the effective functioning of the HKSAR system with its high degree of autonomy in internal affairs. Finally, Hong Kong had already built up a basically sound economic foundation with very substantial fiscal and foreign exchanges reserves before the 1997 handover. Such resources have greatly increased the state capacity of the HKSAR.

With a high degree of state autonomy and a strong state capacity, the Tung government had strived hard toward building up a liberal state in the first three years of its administration. Due to the pacified civil society and the decline of the Democratic Party in Hong Kong, the Tung government needed no authoritarian policy to consolidate its power and to maintain political order. After all, the Democratic Party had agreed to a democratic compromise with the Tung government; it not only accepted its fate of being a minority party in the Legco for a long time to come, but it also tolerated all the new electoral rules (such as the proportional representative system) and legislative procedure (such as it requires a simple majority vote of each functional constituencies and geographical/election constituencies to pass a bill) that could marginalize democratic forces in the HKSAR legislature (So 1999; Chan forthcoming).

On the other hand, a liberal state image is a valuable asset to the Tung government's effort to develop Hong Kong into a global city on the scale of New York and London. The government was proud that Hong Kong has been rated as the world's freest economy for the sixth year in a row in 1999. If Hong Kong intends to become a world financial center and a global high-tech hub, it is required to possess such modern traits as freedom of the press, freedom of association, and freedom of public demonstration in order to attract foreign transnational corporations and middle class professionals to invest and work and Hong Kong. Hong Kong's image as a global city would be greatly tarnished if it is reported that the SAR government has resorted to press censorship and political repression.

In striving toward a liberal state, the Tung government put off the enactment of laws that would lead to an erosion of rights and freedom. Frank Ching (2001) points out that under Article 23 of the Basic Law, Hong Kong is obliged to enact laws relating to subversion, secession, sedition, and treason. But the Tung government let it be known in 1997 that it preferred to wait for an elected legislature to pass such legislation. Even after the first SAR legislature was elected in 1998, the Tung government did not propose such legislation to be passed, saying that there was no urgency.

Another indicator of the striving toward a liberal state was the tolerance of social protests in Hong Kong by the Tung government. Despite the Public Order Ordinance stipulates that protesters need to obtain "letters of no objection" from police at least seven days before their demonstrations, the Tung government took no action against the protesters even their demonstrations were supposedly illegal. *Sing Tao Daily News* (4 October 2000) reported that the organizers of 126 protests in 1998 and the organizers of 183 protests in 1999 did not apply for the required "letters of no objection" from police, but the Tung government took no action against them. On the other hand, the Tung government had approved 1,388 protests in 1998 and 1,283 protests in 1999. As such, Joseph Cheng (2001) remarks that although the Public Order Ordinance is aimed to reintroduce licensing for demonstrations, the ordinance in practice worked only like a notification procedure.

What, then, explains the reversal of the liberal state policy by the Tung government in mid 2000? Why did the Tung government decide to arrest the student protesters on 15 August 2000 and 28 September 2000 on the ground that they took part in and assisting in the organization of an unauthorized assembly? Is the Tung government moving toward the path of an authoritarian state? As the following section shows, the reversal of the liberal policy was a product of the legitimacy crisis that the Tung government was facing in the hot summer of 2000.

The Legitimacy Crisis

Knowing its narrow basis of legitimacy (because the Chief Executive was elected only by a 400-member pro-Beijing and pro-big business Selection Committee), the Tung government formulated the following policies and values to broaden its social support. First, the Tung government moved closer to the path of a developmental state, setting up a high-powered Commission of Innovation and Technology to propel Hong Kong into a high-tech global city, actively intervening in the financial markets in August 1988, and proposing all sorts of reform and privatization packages to enhance the performance of government workers and of the education, social welfare, housing, and medical sectors. Second, the Tung government wanted to gain social support through improvements in social welfare and livelihood. Thus, Tung promised to resolve the housing problem by increasing the overall housing supply at a target of no less than 85,000 flats a year, pledged to develop a comprehensive policy to take care of the various needs of senior citizens, vowed to improve Hong Kong's education, etc. Finally, the Tung government wanted to present itself as a caring paternalistic regime, and Tung stressed such Chinese traditional values as collectivism, the family, filial piety, respect to the elderly, obligation to the community, benevolence, etc. (Lau 2000).

Although the above policies and values helped to boost the legitimacy of the Tung government for a brief period in mid 1997, they became ineffective by the end of 1997. First, the Tung government suffered from crisis of mismanagement and public scandals. In December 1997, the confusions and ineptness in which government departments handled the outbreak of the bird flu epidemic with the subsequent slaughter of more than 1.2 million chickens and fowls put the public image of the new SAR government in jeopardy. The chaos during the July 1998 opening of the new and very expensive Chek Lap Kok international airport resulted in huge economic losses in addition to adverse international publicity. In July 2000 Legco passed a non-confidence motion in Housing Authority chair Rosanna Wong and Director of Housing Tony Miller over the widespread "short piling" scandals in public housing construction. As Agnes Ku (forthcoming) remarks, the myth of administrative capacity of the Hong Kong government has become so badly shaken since the handover that the civil service is now re-characterized as incompetent, arrogant, inefficient, unresponsive to public sentiments, and lacking real public accountability.

Second, there was the unexpected Asian financial crisis. In just one year after the handover, stock prices plummeted by as much as 60 per cent from the peak in July 1997 to the bottom in August 1998. The sharp decline in real estate value also reached the 50 per cent mark in many instances, effectively causing investors to revert their long-held belief that the property value in Hong Kong could only appreciate upward. On the income side, the real-term GDP per capita went down by 7.8 per cent in 1998, a negative growth phenomenon almost unknown to Hong Kong, which had never experienced a year of declining GDP in its recent history. This was followed by an all-time high unemployment rate (6.5 per cent), resulting in massive layoffs and retrenchment (Lui forthcoming). Since the Tung government relied upon economic growth and raising living standards for its basis of support, the recession during the Asian financial crisis has greatly undermined its claims to popular legitimacy.

Third, SAR Chief Executive C. H. Tung, as Hong Kong's first home-groomed leader, has to take personal blame for the poor performance of his administration. While personally sincere and honest, Tung suffered from his apolitical leadership style. Lau Siu-Kai explains that Tung was very reluctant to reach out to the public because of his anti-political bent, his lack of charisma, his elitist instinct, and his lack of political decisiveness and populist skills. Government policies were not adequately explained to the public, and the public was only minimally consulted before major policy decisions were made. As a result, in the opinion polls, the proportion of people who were satisfied with the overall performance of the SAR government dropped from 53 per cent in September 1997 to 25 per cent in July 1998 (Lau 2000).

Finally, the Tung government did not gain much legitimacy even though it has developed a cordial relationship with the mainland government. Frank Ching (2001) remarks that in the first three years of the HKSA, the Tung government's handling of sensitive political and legal issues (like the right of abode case) was marked largely by ambivalence, hesitation, and prevarication. On no occasion was it willing to stand up for the rights of Hong Kong people when those rights were threatened by the mainland authorities. Instead, the inclination of the Tung government was always to leap to the defense of the mainland government.

Government's crisis of mismanagement and public scandals, rising rates of unemployment and bankruptcies, falling popularity of the Tung government, unwilling to assert the rights of Hong Kong people in handling sensitive political and legal issues — together with Tung's over-extended reform packages in the civil service, housing, education, social welfare, and medical sectors — had triggered a serious legitimacy crisis and massive social protests against the HKSAR government in the hot summer of 2000.

Social Protests and Impetus Toward Authoritarianism

The five protests took place on 25 June 2000 epitomize the explosion of social protests against the Tung government (*SCMP* 26 June 2000). The first protest involved more than 1,000 doctors, who staged the biggest protest of its kind in a decade against the government's reform to revamp the medical profession's grading structure. Under the reforms, the current three grades of doctors will be cut to consultants and residents, who will have to be supervised in most medical tasks. The protesters said the reform would waste resources and undermine morale and quality of service provided to patients. The group staged an hour-long silent protest at the headquarters of the Hospital Authority in Argyle Street, Kowloon City.

The second protest was waged by about 1,300 frontline social welfare workers, who marched from Wan Chai to government headquarters in Central to protest at the new lump-sum financing system for non-government organizations. The third protest was waged by 300 residents, who marched along Nathan Road in Yau Ma Tei against the soon-to-be-established Urban Renewal Authority, saying its land resumption power would be too great and its compensation unfair.

In the fourth protest, the pro-business Liberal Party led more than 2,000 people in the so-called "Save Our Assets" march in Central. The march was aimed to highlight the plight of flat owners and entrepreneurs in small and medium-sized companies whose assets had depreciated by up to a half since the financial crisis hit Hong Kong in late 1997. Some carried placards accusing Executive Council convener Leung Chun-ying, a vocal defender of Tung's policy of producing 85,000 new flats each year, of shattering the property market. This rally took an unexpected turn when a group of demonstrators chanted "Down with Tung" and demanded him to step down.

Finally, in the fifth protest, about 1,200 people, including many mainlanders and students, demonstrated over the right-of-abode issue. Their marches marked the first anniversary of a June 1999 ruling by the National People's Congress Standing Committee which effectively overturned a landmark immigration ruling by Hong Kong's Court of Appeal in late January 1999. The latter decision led the Tung government to seek a reinterpretation of Basic Law provisions to restrict abode rights for mainland children of HKSAR permanent residents. As reported at the beginning of this chapter, a hardcore group of the protesters stayed overnight outside the Court of Final Appeal. When they refused to move out of the government headquarters at 6.45 a.m., violence broke out and 12 protesters were hurt. About two months later, five student protesters were arrested on the ground of taking part in and assisting in the organization of an unauthorized assembly.

It is amazing that there could be as many as five large-scale protests on one day. Since the participants of these protests were from a variety of social backgrounds (doctors, social workers, community residents, property owners, small businesspeople, right-of-abode seekers, and students), it shows that there was widespread dissatisfaction with the Tung government in Hong Kong society. What is more, even the pro-government Liberal Party was compelled to organize a rally to express the grievances of its small business constituencies. Too many times, the protesters blamed the Chief Executive for their problems and they chanted "Down with Tung." This anti-Tung sentiment may explain why a comic-book portrait called *Old Idiot Tung* published in August 2000 became a local publishing sensation with over 30,000 copies sold in the first two weeks of issue.

Since Tung wished to seek reelection in early 2002, he must be deeply concerned by his losing support from the new middle class and small businesspeople, by the protests waged by the pro-government Liberal Party, and by the rising personal attack against him. He knows that even with the firm support from Beijing, the "leftists," and the big businesspeople, his chance of winning the 2002 election is not fully guaranteed if social protests and the legitimacy crisis continue unabated.

The above context explains why the Tung government turned to authoritarian measures in the summer of 2000. Since the liberal developmentalism package was not working, the Tung government wanted to try some doses of the authoritarian medicine in order to intimidate the protesters, to weaken the social movements, and to restore political order in Hong Kong society. But where to begin the battle of authoritarian rule in the light of an explosion of social protests in mid 2000?

It turns out that the Tung government picked the five student protesters in the right-of-abode rally on 25 June 2000 to try out its authoritarian measures. The Hong Kong Federation of Students (HKFS) is only a loosely organized student body with little mobilization power on its own. The right-of-abode movement has lost much of its credibility since the arson attack at Immigration Tower on 2 August 2000, which led to the death of an immigration officer and a right-of-abode seeker as well as the injuring of 46 other people. After all, the student protesters had violated the Public Order Ordinance, which requires protesters to apply for "letters of no objection" from police at least seven days before their demonstration. Since the student protesters did not apply for any letter of no objection, their protest was illegal. As the Secretary for Security, Regina Ip, explained: students should not put themselves above the law and expect to be exempted from prosecution; it is impossible for the government to condone such open and repeated flouting of the rule of law; and the students should have the courage to face up to the consequences of their actions (*SCMP* 24 August 2000).

On 16 August 2000, police arrested five student leaders for taking part in and assisting in the organization of an unauthorized assembly on June 26. A week before the arrest, however, the students claimed that their family members had received rude and threatening telephone calls from the police. Derek Chu, an HKFS staff member, reported that the police called his mother and then his father on August 5, warning them that their son was the "black hand" behind an illegal assembly and they should not let their son organize such activity anymore. Siu Yu-Kwan, an editor of the HKFS newspaper, also said his brother received a call from the police on 5 August saying that "You tell Siu Yu-Kwan that the police are investigating him. Tell him that there is no use to hide. We have to meet anyway. Otherwise, we will go to his home to arrest him" (*Tin Tin Daily* 9 August 2000; *SCMP* 16 August 2000).

Knowing that the students showed no remorse and planned to organize a series of unauthorized protests on and after the October National Day, the police on 28 September 2000 made further arrest of five student leaders who organized the demonstration against the change of tuition fees on 20 April 2000 (*SCMP* 29 September 2000). This is the second time that the Tung government invoked the Public Order Ordinance to make arrests, and it sent a stern message that even five months after protesters organized an illegal assembly, they could still be arrested and faced charges.

Anti-Authoritarian Protests

What the Tung administration failed to predict were the robust anti-authoritarian struggles waged by students and their supporters against the arrests. From the students' viewpoint, the 1997 version of Public Order Ordinance was an "evil law" illegitimately sneaked into the legal order during the mid-1997 handover through the Provisional Legco. The HKFS never recognized the legality of the Public Order Ordinance. Since the HKFS saw the ordinance as a breach of the International Covenant on Civil and Political Rights and the Basic Law, it has been organizing public demonstrations with only one-day notice to the police for many years.

The students were further angered by the perceived injustice about the arrest of their five leaders because they questioned the timing and the nature of the arrests. If organizing and participating in unauthorized assembly is illegal, why did the police not arrest the students right away or shortly after their protest? Why did the arrest of a 26 June offense take place on 15 August, and why did the arrest of a 20 April offense take place on 28 September? In addition, since there were more than a few dozen student protesters in both the 20 April and 26 June demonstrations, why did the police arrest only five in each protest? Why did the police pick on the leaders but not the other student protesters? Thus, the students felt justified to perceive the arrests as politically motivated prosecutions intended to break up the students' movement. They were also angry at police harassment of their family members.

In the beginning, the student leaders could only mobilize their fellow students and movement activists for support. On 20 August 2000, about 120 students and activists from such organizations as the Frontier and April 5th Action rallied outside the Central Government offices and condemned the arrests as political repression. At the front of the rally was a big banner with the words "Illegal Assembly in Process: Please Do Not Disturb." The rally was organized by an anonymous group called "Mr. Democracy." The protesters wore the masks marked with crosses to dramatize suppression of free speech. Since this was a silent peaceful protest without any chanting, it did not give any excuse to the police to make arrests even though its organizers did not possess a "letter of no objection" (*The Sun* 21 August 2000).

Later, the students had enlisted the supports of their professors. On 28 August 2000, 85 academics from the eight local tertiary education institutions issued a joint-statement of support for the five arrested students. They said prosecuting the students would deal a blow to social harmony and the credibility of the government. Stephen Sze Man-hung, who helped to draft the statement, said that "We're speaking out because the government is attacking the social conscience of the academic sector.... It would be very stupid for the government to [prosecute] as it would stir up more social resentment." Sze further charged that the students were the victims of violence by the police and he demanded the Security Bureau give a detailed account of alleged police abuse in the clash and apologize to the students (*SCMP* 29 August 2000).

Anti-authoritarian struggles were further intensified by the arrest of five more students on 28 September 2000. By early October, the protest has spread as its rank of supporters expanded to include legislative councilors, the Democratic Party, Professional Teachers' Union, religious and women's groups. Also, the protesters were more bolded than before, talking loudly about public defiance and civil disobedience instead of merely wearing symbolic masks. Therefore, on 2 October 2000, defying police warnings that they were acting illegally, about 30 students and activists started out at noon from Tai Koo Shing. By 3:30 p.m., more than 300 people had gathered at the rally in Chater Garden, Central, which then moved to the Central Government Offices. During the rally, legislator Szeto Wah challenged a policeman by saying that "Go ahead to register my Hong Kong ID! I am participating in an illegal assembly." Another legislator, Democratic Party chair Martin Lee, was more vocal, declaring that "I already washed my 'Pat Pat' [bottom] to be imprisoned!" And many protesters chanted "Arrest me! Arrest me!" Still, the police took no action. Police later tried to interrupt speeches from speakers to issue warnings, saying the demonstration was illegal under the Public Order Ordinance, but these warnings were simply drowned out by the chanting of the protesters (*Apply Daily* 3 October 2000; *SCMP* 3 October 2000).

Maybe influenced by this militant manifestation of public defiance on 2 October 2000, the Department of Justice decided on 5 October not to prosecute against those five student leaders arrested for unlawful assembly on 20 April due to "insufficient evidence." Nevertheless, the Department of Justice said that it was still investigating the June 26 incidence and had not decided whether to prosecute the students or not (*Hong Kong Globe* 6 October 2000). On 7 October, it was reported that Secretary for Security, Regina Ip, compared the local media with the "dictatorial leaders" portrayed in George Orwell's political satire *Animal Farm*. To Ip, SAR officials are on trial by the mass media while the mass media itself is above criticism. These attacks by senior officials have only worsened the official and media relationship, since these attacks are perceived as threats by the Tung government to intimidate the mass media and thus curtailing press freedom (Lau and To forthcoming).

On 8 October 2000, in another blatant challenge to police, about 1,200 protesters took to the streets in an unauthorized rally against the Public Order Ordinance. This rally was distinguished by its size (the largest so far) as well as by the participation of many well-known figures, including leading Democrats Szeto Wah, Yeung Sum, Cheung Man-Kwong, and Albert Ho, radio persons Raymond Wong Yuk-man and Sham Kin-fun, "Long Hair" Leung Kwok-hung, the "bull" Tsang Kin-shing, and many well-known former student movement leaders from the past three decades. The march was from Southern Playground in Wan Chai to the Central Government Offices. The protesters carried two banners with the words, "Down with Public Order Ordinance. Hand me back my civil rights." They chanted slogans such as "students are innocence, protests are right." At the Central Government Offices, a placard symbolizing the "draconian ordinance" was burnt (*SCMP* 9 October 2000).

By mid October, public endorsements in support of the arrested students from many different professional associations mushroomed. The Bar Association held a press conference to denounce the arrests. In another unprecedented move, about 300 government workers and union leaders on 15 October marched from Wan Chai to Central Government Offices to show their defiance of the Public Order Ordinance. The workers shouted "today they arrest students, tomorrow they arrest workers." Social worker unions and church groups mount a full-page advertisement in local newspapers to endorse the freedom of association. Through the internet, more than 250 academics signed another joint letter calling for the government to drop the charges against the students (*Ming Pao* 16 and 18 October 2000).

The Formation of Soft Authoritarianism

Realizing such arrest of students had little public support, the Tung government was finally forced to back down. Proceeding with the prosecution of students would risk even more serious protests from the community and more fierce condemnation from the mass media both locally and externally. Besides, it was not certain whether the generally liberal judges would be on the side of the Tung government in their ruling. It would be disastrous for the government if the court were to rule in favor of the students. On the other hand, the decision to drop the case could defuse any further criticism that the government was deliberately picking on the powerless students to show its authority. Dropping the case would also deny protesters a common cause to rally around, and the government hoped that public sentiment would die down after that.

Due to the above considerations, when the students reported back to police on 25 October 2000, they were given a letter saying that the Secretary for Justice had decided not to prosecute them. The Tung government provided only a vague explanation that in the light of all the public concern about this case, to have pushed ahead with charges would have undermined "confidence in the administration of justice" (*SCMP* 26 October 2000).

Nevertheless, the Tung government still hanged onto a policy which could be called "soft authoritarianism" despite this reluctant retreat. First, the Tung government insisted that Public Order Ordinance was still effective. In its letter to the students, it said that they were suspected to have violated a section of the Public Order Ordinance on governing the joining or organizing of an unlawful public rally or procession. The Tung government warned that the students could face a maximum fine of HK$5,000 and a three-year jail term if convicted. Secretary for Security Regina Ip further stressed that the non-prosecution of the students this time would not set a precedent: "No one is above the law. Just because some people are not prosecuted this time, it does not mean they would be exempted from prosecution forever." In fact, the letter to the students also carried a clear warning: "If you have similar behavior in future, the police will consider taking prosecution action against you" (*SCMP* 26 October 2000).

Second, Ip's stern warning and her threat to make arrests next time had worked to scare off students from joining protests. On 5 November 2000 the HKFS held an unauthorized public forum in Central to show their public defiance of the ordinance. The HKFS had expected 100 people, including at least 50 students, to take part in the forum. But fewer than 20 students turned up for the discussion, which attracted at most 40 people at its peak — fewer than the 50 required by the law to notify seven days in advance. As HKFS spokesman Lo Wai-ming explained, "Some students told us that it was not convenient for them as they said they had felt pressure from their families after the Secretary for Security issued a warning on Saturday" (*SCMP* 6 November 2000).

Third, the Tung government had tried hard to intimidate the protesters at unauthorized rallies. In the 5 November 2000 HKFS forum, for instance, even though the protest had attracted only 40 people at its peak, there were ten uniformed police officers monitoring the forum while another 40 police tactical unit officers were on standby. There were also two teams of seven police officers filming the forum proceedings. Thus, there were more policemen than protesters! The police said that the filming was needed in case the situation turned chaotic, but the students complained that since their forum was legal (because they unintentionally had less than 50 participants), the police should not video their protest to intimidate them. An on-looker was reported to make a remark that "Was it necessary to have so many policemen?" (*SCMP* 6 November 2000; *The Sun* 6 November 2000).

Finally, instead of heeding the calls from students, academics, lawyers, unionists, and social movement activists to revise the Public Order Ordinance, the Tung government took the unusual step of tabling a motion to support the existing ordinance in the Legco in an attempt to end the arguments. The 1997 version of the ordinance was frequently criticized because it was passed by the Provisional Legco immediately after the handover. Thus, a vote of confidence over the ordinance by the "popularly elected" Legco in 2000 would certainly lend the ordinance more legitimacy. After all, the Tung government was confident that it could muster enough votes in the Legco to pass the motion because the Liberal Party, the Democratic Alliance for Betterment of Hong Kong, and the

Hong Kong Progressive Alliance all supported the government in this case. It needed only a simple majority vote to pass the motion. In the end, in spite of the fact that the democratic camp had put up a fight at the Legco to debate the motion for eight hours over a two-day period, the motion supporting the Public Order Ordinance was passed by 36 to 21 (*SCMP* 22 December 2000).

In sum, despite the Tung government decided not to pursue the authoritarian policy to prosecute the students on the ground of their unlawful assembly, still it has adopted a set of "soft" authoritarian measures to enhance its control over the Hong Kong society. It insisted that the Public Order Ordinance remained in force; it issued warnings that participants in any unlawful assembly would be arrested; it used police surveillance, police warnings, and police videoing to intimidate the protesters; and it tried to enhance the legitimacy of the ordinance by pushing its motion of support through the Legco. By taking a strong position on the ordinance, the Tung government made it clear that it would continue to make threats, to conduct surveillance, and to intimidate protesters of unlawful assemblies.

Conclusion: The Future of "Soft Authoritarianism"

This chapter traces the origins and the formation process of soft authoritarianism in the Hong Kong SAR. It argues that Article 23 of the Basic Law, the Public Order Ordinance, the Societies Ordinance, and possible official mainland pressures have laid the foundation of authoritarian rule in Hong Kong. However, the Tung government did try hard to strive for a liberal state for the first three years of its administration, because its power was not threatened by the democratic forces, and because liberalism was a valuable asset for developing Hong Kong into a global financial and high-tech city.

It was the looming crisis of legitimacy that made the Tung government changed its policy of liberalism. The government's credibility was tarnished by crisis mismanagement and public scandals. Its promises of developmentalism, economic growth, and raising living standard were unfulfilled because of the drastic downfall of the stock market and the real estate market, the high rate of unemployment, and the bankruptcies of small businesses during the Asian financial crisis. In addition, the Tung government's over-extended reforms in the civil service, medical care, education, housing, and social welfare sectors led to all sorts of protests by civil servants, doctors, teachers, students, social workers, community residents, property owners, small businesspeople, etc. The Chief Executive himself became the target of attack by protesters, because he was blamed for the regime's inability to revive the troubled economy and the poor situation that the protesters were in. The mass discontents became so widespread and serious that they could threaten the chance for the Chief Executive to win reelection for another five-year term in spring 2002.

In mid 2000, the Tung government therefore adopted some measures of authoritarianism in order to curb the rising tide of protests and to regain political control over the civil society. It invoked the Public Order Ordinance, arrested the students on the ground of taking part in and assisting in organizing unlawful assembly, and planned to proceed with prosecution and imprisonment. However, the arrests had triggered a series of anti-authoritarian struggles. The size of demonstration grew from 120 people on August 20 to 300 people on 2 October, and further to 1,200 people on 8 October. Protesters challenged the police to arrest them, and they received support from academics, former student leaders, movement activists, legislators, unionists, church groups, the Bar Associations, etc. In the end, the Tung government was overwhelmed by such strong public support for the arrested students and decided not to proceed with their prosecution. Still, the Tung government refused to yield in its policy of "soft authoritarianism" by pushing a support motion for the Public Order Ordinance in the Legco and by using the ordinance and the police to make threats, to conduct surveillance, and to intimidate protesters of unlawful assembly.

In sum, this chapter shows that soft authoritarianism in the HKSAR was a product of two key factors: legitimacy crisis and social protests. It is the serious legitimacy crisis that induced Tung to try out some "hard" authoritarianism measures like political arrests and prosecution. And it is the robust anti-authoritarian protests that forced the Tung government to retreat into a milder "soft" authoritarian policy of intimidation and surveillance.

As such, the future of soft authoritarianism hinges on whether Hong Kong will experience any drastic changes in the legitimacy crisis and social protests. At one extreme, there could be a "hard authoritarian" scenario if the legitimacy crisis is growing worse. Hong Kong's economy will get worse, stock market and property market keep on falling, while unemployment and bankruptcies keep on rising. The Tung government's reforms are going nowhere, and people blame Tung for their dire plights.

Under such circumstance, every weekend there would be several protests from different groups over a variety of issues. As the protests became more violent, the Tung government would invoke the Public Order Ordinance to make arrests and prosecutions. It might even enact very stern laws of subversion, secession, sedition, and treason to strengthen political control. However, this "hard authoritarian" scenario is highly unlikely in the near future, because it seems that the legitimacy crisis would not worsen than that in mid 2000.

At the other extreme, there could be a liberalism scenario if anti-authoritarian protests are gaining strength. Seeing that they won a victory by forcing the Tung government to stop prosecuting the students, and seeing that their strategy of public defiance and civil disobedience has worked, civil society activists are determined to continue the movement not only to trim the Public Order Ordinance but also to democratize the Legco. After months of large-scale protests and public defiance, the civil society activists would finally succeed in changing election laws and tone down the Public Order Ordinance. However, this liberalism scenario is also highly unlikely in the near future, because the Democratic Party has been losing strength, and because there have been fragmentation and discontinuity among civil society organizations.

As a result, it seems that "soft authoritarianism" is likely to stay in the HKSAR in near future, unless there is a sudden worsening of the legitimacy crisis or a drastic strengthening of the anti-authoritarian protests.

References

Chan, Ming K. (Forthcoming). "Realpolitik Realignment of the Democratic Camp in the Hong Kong SAR," in Ming K. Chan and Alvin Y. So (eds.), *Crisis and Transformation in China's Hong Kong, 1997–2001* (Armonk: M.E. Sharpe).

Cheng, Joseph (2001). "The Constitution, Political, and Legal Order of the Hong Kong Special Administrative Region," in Joseph Cheng (ed.), *Political Development in the HKSAR* (Hong Kong: Contemporary China Research Project, City University of Hong Kong), pp. 13–40

Ching, Frank (2001). "The Handling of Sensitive Political and Legal Issues by the Hong Kong Government During the First Three Years of the HKSAR," in Joseph Cheng (ed.), *Political Development in the HKSAR* (Hong Kong: Contemporary China Research Project, City University of Hong Kong), pp. 119–38.

Ku, Agnes (Forthcoming). "Post-Colonial Cultural Trends in the Hong Kong SAR

— Imagining the Local, National, and Global," in Ming K. Chan and Alvin Y. So (eds.), *Crisis and Transformation in China's Hong Kong, 1997–2001* (Armonk: M.E. Sharpe).

Lau, Siu-Kai (2000). "Government and Political Change in the Hong Kong Special Administrative Region" in James C. Hsiung (ed.), *Hong Kong The Super Paradox Life after Return to China* (New York: St. Martin Press), pp. 35–58

Lau, Tuen-yu, and To, Yiu-ming (Forthcoming). "Walking on a Tight Rope: Hong Kong Media Facing Political and Economic Challenges Since Sovereignty Transfer, 1997–2001," in Ming K. Chan and Alvin Y. So (eds.), *Crisis and Transformation in China's Hong Kong, 1997–2001* (Armonk: M.E. Sharpe).

Lui, Francis T. (Forthcoming). "Hong Kong's Economy since 1997," in Ming K. Chan and Alvin Y. So (eds.), *Crisis and Transformation in China's Hong Kong, 1997–2001* (Armonk: M.E. Sharpe).

Pepper, Suzanne (Forthcoming). "Hong Kong and the Reconstruction of China's Political Order," in Ming K. Chan and Alvin Y. So (eds.), *Crisis and Transformation in China's Hong Kong, 1997–2001* (Armonk: M.E. Sharpe).

Sing Ming (2001). "The Handover of Hong Kong and the Retrogression of its Democratic Development," in Joseph Cheng (ed.), *Political Development in the HKSAR* (Hong Kong: Contemporary China Research Project, City University of Hong Kong), pp. 101–18.

SCMP [*South China Morning Post*].

So, Alvin Y. (1999). "1997 and Democratic Compromise in Hong Kong," *Bulletin of Concerned Asian Scholars* 31, pp. 59–65.

Contributors

John P. BURNS is Chair Professor of Politics and Public Administration at the University of Hong Kong, where he does research on civil service management, administrative reform, and party-state relations in China, including Hong Kong. His most recent book is *Civil Service Systems in Asia* (co-edited with B. Bowornwathana) (Cheltenham: Edward Elgar, 2001).

Johannes M. M. CHAN is currently the Dean of the Faculty of Law, The University of Hong Kong. Educated in Hong Kong and England, he specializes in human rights, constitutional law and administrative law. He also appears as a barrister in many leading Bill of Rights cases. He serves on many governmental/public and professional bodies, both locally and internationally. His latest books include: *On the Way to Justice* (2000); *Hong Kong's Constitutional Debate: Conflict over Interpretation* (with Fu Hualing and Y. Ghai, 2000), and *General Principles of Hong Kong Law* (with Albert Chen and others, 1999).

Kenneth L. CHAU, Ph.D., is Professor of Social Work and Dean of Social Science at the Chinese University of Hong Kong. Prior to 1994, he was on the faculty of the California State University and the University of Hong Kong. Professor Chau's research interests and publications are in the areas of needs, welfare choices and institutional arrangements; citizenship and identity; refugee and minority issues in mental health; cross-cultural practice and theory development in social work.

Albert H. Y. CHEN is a graduate of the University of Hong Kong (LLB 1980) and Harvard University (LLM 1982). He began his teaching career at the University of Hong Kong in 1984, and is currently a Professor in the Department of Law of that University. He has written 6 books and over 70 articles in English and Chinese. His latest books are *An Introduction to the Legal System of the People's Republic of China* (Singapore: Butterworths Asia, rev. ed. 1998) and *The Rule of Law, Enlightenment and the Spirit of Modern Law* (Beijing: China University of Politics and Law Press, 1998) (in Chinese).

Kai-ming CHENG is Chair Professor of Education and Pro-Vice-Chancellor at the University of Hong Kong. A Ph.D. from the London Institute of Education, his research interests include education in rural China, and recently, India. More recently, he studies workplace changes in knowledge societies, education reforms, cultural dimension of education and qualitative research methodology. He teaches as a Visiting Professor at the Harvard Graduate School of Education since 1996. Locally, he is a member of the Education Commission and Chairman of the Advisory Committee on Teacher Education and Qualification.

Anthony B. L. CHEUNG is Professor of the Department of Public and Social Administration, City University of Hong Kong, and Associate Director of the university's Governance in Asia Research Centre. An ex-civil servant and ex-legislator, he received his Ph.D. degree in Government from the London School of Economics and Political Science. He has written extensively on privatization, civil service and public sector reforms, and government and politics in Hong Kong. His recent books are: *The Civil Service in Hong Kong: Continuity and Change* (co-authored, Hong Kong University Press, 1998), *Public Sector Reform in Hong Kong: Into the 21st Century* (co-edited, The Chinese University Press, 2001) and *Governance and Public Sector Reform in Asia: Paradigm Shift or Business As Usual?* (co-edited, RoutledgeCurzon, 2002 forthcoming). Professor Cheung also sits on major civil service pay advisory bodies.

Lok Sang HO is currently Head of the Economics Department and Director of the Centre for Public Policy Studies at Lingnan University. A graduate of the University of Hong Kong, he holds a Ph.D. in economics from University of Toronto. His research interest covers a large range of public policy areas, including housing, labour, education, social security, health care, banking, and open economy macroeconomics. He authored *Principles of Public Policy Practice,* published by Kluwer Academic Publishers, and *Health Care Financing and Delivery: A Model for Reform,* published by the City University of HK Press, and co-authored with

Thomas Voon *Economic Impacts of Logistics Infrastructure Development: The Case of Hong Kong*, published by Nova Science Publishers. His latest research interest is international monetary system reform.

Y. C. JAO is Honorary Professor and Honorary University Fellow, School of Economics and Finance, University of Hong Kong, where he has taught for over three decades. His research interests are money, banking and finance, where he has published extensively in both English and Chinese. He was a member of the Hong Kong Government's Exchange Fund Advisory Committee in 1997–98, and in that capacity, he participated in the decision-making process for the defence of Hong Kong's currency and financial system during the Asian crisis. He is a Past President of the Hong Kong Economic Association, and a Guest Professor at several universities in China. Currently he is also serving as an independent director of Nanyang Commercial Bank in Hong Kong.

LAU Siu-kai graduated from the University of Hong Kong in 1971, and from the University of Minnesota in 1975 with a Ph.D. in Sociology. He joined the Chinese University of Hong Kong in 1975. Currently he is on leave from the Chinese University of Hong Kong as the newly-appointed Head of the Central Policy Unit, the official think-tank of the Hong Kong Special Administrative Region Government. He is Professor of Sociology at The Chinese University of Hong Kong where he has taught since 1975. He had also served as the Associate Director of the University's Hong Kong Institute of Asia-Pacific Studies. Professor Lau's research interests are: comparative political and social development, society and politics in Hong Kong, and political development in traditional and modern China. He studies both macroscopic issues such as institutional development and microscopic issues such as political culture and political behavior.

P. C. LEUNG is Chair Professor of Orthopaedics and Traumatology at the Chinese University of Hong Kong. He has published extensively in the fields of orthopaedics, traumatology, hand and microsurgery, including over 300 manuscripts and 25 books and book chapters. He has served the community in medical areas including medical ethics, Chinese medicine and public health. Professor Leung has been a leading figure in tertiary education, professional associations, professional editorial boards, Hong Kong Medical Council and other Government Advisory Committees, including Occupational Health and Safety, Rehabilitation, Hospital

Governing Committees, etc. He is currently Chairman of the Ethics Committee, Hong Kong Medical Council.

LO Shiu-hing is Associate Professor in the Department of Politics and Public Administration at the University of Hong Kong. His most recent book is *Governing Hong Kong: Legitimacy, Communication and Political Decay* (New York: Nova Science, 2001). His books include *The Politics of Democratization in Hong Kong* (London: Macmillan, 1997) and *Political Development in Macau* (Hong Kong: The Chinese University Press, 1995). Since 1993, he has been a co-investigator of the Baptist University-based Hong Kong Transition Project that is regularly surveying the political attitudes of the people of Hong Kong.

MA Ngok is currently Assistant Professor in the Division of Social Science, Hong Kong University of Science and Technology. His research areas include party politics and elections in Hong Kong, comparative politics, political economy and the post-communist transformation in East-Central Europe. He currently focuses on teaching and researching on a wide range of issues concerning post-1997 political development in Hong Kong.

Alvin Y. SO is Professor of Division of Social Science and Associate Dean of the School of Humanities and Social Science at the Hong Kong University of Science and Technology. His research interests are on social class and development of Hong Kong, China, and East Asia. His recent publications include *Crisis and Transformation of China's Hong Kong* (co-editor, M.E. Sharpe, 2002) and *Hong Kong's Embattled Democracy: A Societal Analysis* (Johns Hopkins University Press, 1999).

Yun-Wing SUNG is Chariman and Professor in the Department of Economics, The Chinese University of Hong Kong, Co-Director of the Hong Kong and Asia-Pacific Economies Research Programme, The Chinese University of Hong Kong, as well as Editor of *Asian Economic Journal*. Professor Sung received his Ph.D. in Economics from the University of Minnesota in 1979. His fields of expertise lie in international trade and economic development, Chinese economy, and Hong Kong economy. His current research interests are economic integration of Greater China (China, Taiwan, and Hong Kong), and economic development of Yangzi Delta and Pearl River Delta.

Chack-kie WONG is Professor in the Department of Social Work, The Chinese University of Hong Kong. His research interest and focus lie in social policy and comparative analysis, poverty, social welfare reform in China, public opinions of welfare, and social work and social change.

Timothy Ka-ying WONG received his Ph.D. in Sociology at the University of Manitoba. He is currently a Researcher Officer and Director of the Telephone Survey Research Laboratory of the Hong Kong Institute of Asia-Pacific Studies, the Chinese University of Hong Kong. Dr. Wong's major research interests include social and political development in Hong Kong and Taiwan and cross-Taiwan-Strait relations. He has published a number of books and has contributed to *Nations and Nationalism*, *Journal of Contemporary China*, *Democratization, Asian Perspective*, *Journal of East Asian Affairs*, *Social Development Issues*, *Social Policy and Society*, and *Issues and Studies*.

Chris YEUNG is currently an Associate Editor and the Political Editor of *South China Morning Post (SCMP).* He joined *SCMP* in 1984 after graduating from the Hong Kong Baptist College (now Hong Kong Baptist University) where he studied journalism. He left the newspaper between 1992 and 1993 to complete a Master of Arts (International Relations) in Australian National University. Between September 2000 and June 2001, Mr. Yeung was a visiting fellow at the Brookings Institution's Centre for Northeast Asian Policy Studies in Washington. At *SCMP,* Mr. Yeung oversees the political news coverage and is a regular writer on a wide range of political, social policy and mainland-Hong Kong issues. He is editor of *Red Dawn* published by Prentice-Hall in 1998 that outlines the first year of Hong Kong after the sovereignty changeover.

Index